NOT WORKING

NOT WORKING

Where Have All the Good Jobs Gone?

David G. Blanchflower

PRINCETON UNIVERSITY PRESS

PRINCETON AND OXFORD

Requests for permission to reproduce material from this work
should be sent to permissions@press.princeton.edu

Published by Princeton University Press
41 William Street, Princeton, New Jersey 08540
6 Oxford Street, Woodstock, Oxfordshire OX20 1TR

press.princeton.edu

Library of Congress Control Number 2018962709
ISBN 978-0-691-18124-0

British Library Cataloging-in-Publication Data is available

Editorial: Joe Jackson and Jacqueline Delaney
Production Editorial: Jill Harris
Text Design: Pamela Schnitter
Jacket Design: Will Brown
Production: Erin Suydam
Publicity: James Schneider and Caroline Priday

This book has been composed in Adobe Garamond Pro and Helvetica Lt Pro

Printed on acid-free paper. ∞

Printed in the United States of America

1 3 5 7 9 10 8 6 4 2

TO BERNARD CORRY AND MAURICE PESTON, WHO TAUGHT

ME TO DO ECONOMICS WITH A CONSCIENCE

CONTENTS

Chapter 1. What the Whole World Wants Is a Good Job   1

**Part I   The Problem: The Great Recession
Exposed Underlying Fractures**

Chapter 2. Unemployment and Its Consequences   15

Chapter 3. Wage Growth and the Lack of It   47

Chapter 4. The Semi-Slump and the Housing Market   78

Chapter 5. Underemployment   118

Part II   The Response to the Great Recession

Chapter 6. Something Horrible Happened   151

Chapter 7. Sniffing the Air and Spotting the Great Recession   181

Chapter 8. The People Have Lost Their Pep   212

Chapter 9. Somebody Has to Be Blamed   238

Chapter 10. Disastrous Cries for Help   264

Part III   What to Do?

Chapter 11. Full Employment   297

Chapter 12. Put the Pedal to the Metal   316

Appendix   349
Acknowledgments   353
Dedication   355
Notes   357
References   389
Index   423

NOT WORKING

CHAPTER 1

What the Whole World
Wants Is a Good Job

Gizza job. Gis a job, eh? Go on give's it. Give us a go. Go on. I can be funny. I can do
that. Do I have to walk funny? I can be funny. Go on give us a job. Go on give us a go.

—YOSSER HUGHES[1]

Founded by George Gallup in 1935, Gallup has become known for its public opinion polls, conducted worldwide. Gallup claims it "knows more about
the attitudes and behaviors of employees, customers, students and citizens
than any other organization in the world."[2]

On its website, Gallup says the following: "Here is one of Gallup's most
important discoveries since its founding in 1935: what the whole world
wants is a good job."[3] Gallup defines a "good job" as working thirty or more
hours per week for an employer that provides a regular paycheck. Good jobs,
Gallup claims, are essential to a thriving economy, a growing middle class,
a booming entrepreneurial sector, and, most important, human development. "Creating as many good jobs as possible should be the number one
priority for business and government leaders everywhere." It is hard to disagree with that.

One of the most important findings from the relatively new field of behavioral economics is that one of the main determinants of happiness is
having a job. That finding applies across countries and through time. Losing
a job decreases well-being, while finding a job improves it.

This book is about jobs, decent jobs that pay well and the lack of them. It is about looking at data and uncovering the deep underlying patterns.

How to Look at the Labor Market

It is up to labor economists like me to figure out exactly how events such as economic downturns impact real people and how to avoid them or, more realistically, lessen their impact in the future.

Just as there is a market for houses, fish, fast food, and works of art there is a market for people's labor. The economics of the labor market is what labor economists like me study—the field is known as labor economics. It studies work.[4] Just as with any good like shirts and haircuts, we are interested in looking at prices, which in this case are incomes, wages or earnings. We are also interested in quantities. Labor economists study the numbers of people who are working, measured in all sorts of ways including employment, unemployment, inactivity, and underemployment as well as hours worked. There is both a supply curve and a demand curve of labor, and the price of labor is the wage.

The labor market is continuously changing due to improvements in technology and changes in people's preferences. In the 1950s most men wore hats and smoked; today most do neither. Before the coming of the motor car millions of people were employed around horses, driving carriages, working in stables, making leather for bridles, and so forth. There were knacker's yards everywhere, which were slaughterhouses for horses; the carcasses were used for glue, but few exist nowadays. The motor car created jobs for mechanics and petrol pump attendants. Many workers, though, still come home from work feeling "knackered."[5]

The labor market in a capitalist economy is always in a state of flux. As new firms are born and old ones die, there will inevitably be shortages that take time to fill as technology advances. There are never enough people with the new skills required for the new products. The least educated and least skilled find it hardest to adapt to rapid economic changes. The Luddites at the start of the nineteenth century broke weaving machines because they were fearful they were job destroying. Just because there are shortages doesn't mean the labor market isn't working. It takes time for a captain to turn or to stop an oil tanker. The fix to a shortage would normally be to raise the wage.

A shortage may occur simply because the employer is offering to pay below the going rate.

The world of work, of course, is heavily impacted by the state of the macroeconomy. In good times jobs are plentiful and in bad times they go away. The two biggest events during peacetime in the last hundred years to impact the labor market were the Great Depression and the Great Recession. Both followed stock market collapses in the United States, caused by falls in the housing market, in 1929 and 2007, that spread around the world. As John Kenneth Galbraith noted, lessons were not learned from the 1929 Great Crash.[6] Indeed, in a new introduction to his book written in the 1990s, Galbraith argued that "all this is better now. But there could be a recession; that would be normal" (2009, xvi). Galbraith also noted that "the descent is always more sudden than the increase: a balloon that has been punctured does not deflate in an orderly way" (xiv). And so it was.

The Great Recession started in the Arizona, Florida, California, and Nevada housing markets and grew and grew as the subprime housing market collapsed. It spread around the world and took banks down with it. As Carmen Reinhart and Kenneth Rogoff (2009) have famously noted, financial crises take an inordinate amount of time for economies to recover from.

This book will be published a dozen years after the start of the Great Recession, which the National Bureau of Economic Research (NBER) estimates started in the United States in December 2007.[7] In most other advanced countries, including the UK, France, Japan, and Italy, it started a few months later. In 2008 and 2009, most of the major advanced countries' economies met the usual definition of recession, which is two successive quarters of negative growth.

All these big events had huge impacts on people's lives, not least because of their direct effect on living standards and an overall sense of security. In the UK, real wages in September 2018, more than a decade from the start of the Great Recession, are still 5.7 percent lower than they were in February 2008. Workers have been shaken to their very core. In 1931 John Maynard Keynes warned of the long, dragging conditions of what he called a "semi-slump," a period of subnormal prosperity. That is the state we are in.

As a result, the years after the recession hit full bore in 2008—the biggest economic shock to hit in a generation—are vastly different than those before. It may well be that the patterns that existed between 1945 and 2007 tell us little or nothing about what has happened in the years since. There has never been a situation in anyone's memory when central banks, including the European Central Bank, the Bank of Japan, and those in Sweden and Switzerland, continue to have negative interest rates. At the time of writing both the European Central Bank (ECB) and the Bank of Japan are still buying assets as part of an ongoing quantitative easing program.[8] This is unprecedented in our lifetime. It may be that we will have to look at what happened in the 1930s in the years after the Great Crash. Some of my economist friends continue to call this "the crisis that keeps on giving." It is likely to keep on giving for many years to come.

It is my job and that of my colleagues to figure out how to make the labor market work.

The most watched economic data release in the United States, and probably the world, given the importance of the U.S. economy, is the Employment Situation Report, which is published monthly by the Bureau of Labor Statistics (BLS) on a Friday. Labor market data are important politically. The May 2018 unemployment rate was released at 8:30 a.m. on June 1, 2018, as 3.8 percent. In a breach of protocol President Donald Trump, who receives early sight of the BLS data releases, tweeted out at 7:21 a.m., "Looking forward to seeing the employment numbers at 8:30 this morning." Trump wanted to celebrate the news of a solid jobs report, but there was a puzzle buried within it.

Normally, when the unemployment rate is below 4 percent, wages grow. For example, between February 1966 and January 1970 the unemployment rate averaged 3.6 percent, and in 47 of the 48 months it was below 4 percent. Hourly wage growth of production and non-supervisory workers, who make up around three-quarters of all workers, averaged 5.1 percent. Not this time. It is a continuing puzzle as to why wage growth continues to be benign. It seems that the unemployment rate may not be as useful a guide as it was in the past.

What's Going On with the Unemployment Rate?

Let's take a quick look at how the unemployment rate has traditionally worked. Figure 1.1 plots a long time series of the unemployment rate for the UK and the United States.

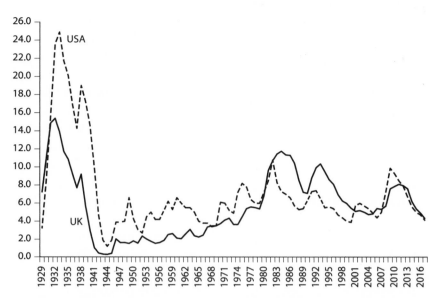

Figure 1.1. U.S. and UK unemployment rates, 1929–2017. The data source for the UK is the Bank of England, "A Millennium of Macroeconomic Data," https://www.bank ofengland.co.uk/statistics/research-datasets. The early U.S. data are taken from the OECD and for 1929–54 from Kimberley Amadeo, "Unemployment Rate by Year since 1929 Compared to Inflation and GDP," October 6, 2017, https://www.thebalance.com /unemployment-rate-by-year-3305506.

The first thing we see is the peak in the early 1930s that is the Great Depression. Unemployment rates in the United States went to 25 percent. There was a smaller rise in the unemployment rate in the UK, to around 15 percent. The rate fell quickly in both countries, in part in the United States because of the New Deal and in the UK because of military preparation and rearmament prior to World War II. Unemployment essentially disappeared during the war years as it was all hands to the pump, including large numbers of women who went to work to help the war effort. There was a second peak in 1984 of around 12 percent in the UK but a much lower one in the United States of around 10 percent in 1982.

The unemployment rate of both countries has now fallen dramatically, but as we will see, the published unemployment rate, these days, is much more unreliable than it used to be. For one thing, it understates the number

of people who want work that pays decently. Even though the unemployment rate is low, there are lots of people chasing high-paying jobs. In bad
times workers are pushed down the occupational pyramid and are forced
into lower-paying jobs. College graduates take jobs previously done by high
school graduates, who have to take jobs previously done by high school
dropouts, who struggle to find work.

There are very high levels of what economists call "underemployment"
prevailing around the world. That is, some workers want more hours but
don't get them and some are pushed into part-time jobs when they want
full-time jobs. Post-recession, considerable numbers of part-timers who are
content with part-time jobs want more hours. Underemployment is an example of what we call "labor market slack."

By labor market slack I mean how many potential hours of work are out
there that could be put to work. These hours could come from workers
simply increasing the hours they work or from hiring new workers. The more
labor market slack there is, the weaker the worker's bargaining power to push
up wages. The smaller the level of slack, the greater the worker's power. This
concept of labor market slack is the equivalent of Karl Marx's concept in *Das
Kapital* of the reserve army of the unemployed. I am especially interested in
how much labor market slack over time there is in the economy. In 2019 this
is largely a conscript, not a volunteer, army.

Underemployment has not returned to its pre-recession levels even
though unemployment rates have fallen in the United States and the UK
in particular. Before the Great Recession, when the unemployment rate
was high, wage growth was lower, and vice versa. Since 2008 wage growth is
lower for a given unemployment rate.

The high-paying union private-sector jobs for the less educated are long
gone. Real weekly wages in February 2019 in the United States were around
9 percent below their 1973 peak for private-sector production and non-
supervisory workers in constant 1982–84 dollars. In the UK real wages in
2018 are 6 percent below their 2008 level.

Because of the high levels of labor market slack around the world, wages
are the dog that hasn't barked. If there were no labor market slack, meaning
economies were at what's considered "full employment," wages would be
rising, as employers would have to attract workers from competitors, given
there are so few people without jobs looking for work. To do that they
would have to raise wages. The fact that they haven't suggests full employ-

ment is a faraway dream. Despite this reality the Federal Reserve Board, known as "the Fed," believes the United States is at full employment and wage growth is set to rise, and hence they are raising interest rates. This looks like a mistake.

Pain, Immigration, and Politics

Recessions, slow recoveries, and policy mistakes have consequences. Pain is up, depression and stress are up, binge drinking is up, obesity is up, and drug addiction is up. Hopelessness is up; anxiety is up. Deaths of despair—from alcohol and drug poisoning and suicide—are up. America now has a massive opioid crisis, with 72,000 dying of opioid drug overdoses in 2017, up nearly 7 percent from 2016.[9] The death toll is higher than the peak yearly death totals from HIV, car crashes, or firearms.[10]

Low earnings and the loss of high-paying jobs have led to feelings of instability, insecurity, and helplessness, especially for the less educated. Suicide rates in the United States are up 25 percent since 1999. The United States has a labor market crisis, one that has grown into a crisis of desperation. The loss of good, well-paying jobs has had severe consequences. The relatively high living standards of the least educated in America used to be a lot higher than the lot of the less educated in Europe, for example, in the 1960s and 1970s. Perhaps no longer, as with global competition we may see a great equalizing.

When people are hurting it is easy to find scapegoats. Immigrants are easy targets. Trump ran on an anti-immigrant platform. Brexit was much about keeping foreigners out after an influx of several million East Europeans, especially Poles, who came to work since 2004. Syrian refugees crossing the Mediterranean fleeing from war became a major problem.

In this book, I will show how the rise of right-wing populism has been driven by developments in labor markets and by the failure of the elites to get economic policy right. Those who were left behind voted for Trump in the United States, Brexit in the UK, the Front National in France, and the anti-establishment Five Star Movement and the hard-right League in Italy, to name but a few. The fundamental workings of labor markets appear to have altered significantly since the crash of 2007–8. And until we figure out what happened, and how to look at the labor market, social cohesion will continue to break down.

The Economics of Walking About

I will document in some detail what I call the "economics of walking about." There was a long tradition in labor economics to try to understand how the world worked and to reveal, what the great Harvard economist John Dunlop once told me, rules of thumb on how people make decisions. It involves listening to what people say and taking it seriously. Richard Thaler (2018) in his 2017 Nobel Prize lecture noted that "what economists often call estimates or forecasts, and heuristics is a fancy word for rules-of-thumb . . . faced with a complex prediction problem ('What is the chance this applicant will do well in graduate school?') people often rely on simple rules-of-thumb ('heuristics') to help them." Heuristics sounds better.

The economics of walking about involves looking at qualitative data from the representatives of firms on how the firm is doing and from individuals on their well-being. Happiness data, on the well-being of people and firms, contain useful information. Consumer and business confidence indices contain useful data. The qualitative data gave an early warning of the onset of recession in 2007–8 in a way that quantitative data didn't, and that was mostly missed by policymakers.

A good example of this type of qualitative data is publicly available for download and published monthly by the European Commission on the attitudes of firms in construction, industry, retail, and services, as well as from individuals. These data are combined to generate a monthly Economic Sentiment Index (ESI), which I follow closely. A collapse in these data across almost every EU country beginning in 2007 was, wrongly, largely ignored by economists.[11]

Some economists want to deny that it is relevant to look at feelings. This is destructive nihilism and has the broad implication that subjects like social psychology and psychiatry that study feelings shouldn't exist. Suggesting that there is nothing to be learned from other fields just makes us look arrogant and silly.

Journalist Pedro Nicolaci da Costa told me in private communications that he thinks the problem has been that central bankers, politicians, and policymakers around the world have been totally out of touch with what has been happening to ordinary people: "Because of the revolving door between the private sector and public industry, politicians and other policy makers are often wealthy themselves. They tend to mingle and identify with other rich individuals for whom the economy is doing just fine, thank you. Unless they make a concerted effort to reach outside their own circles, this leaves many of our most powerful leaders blind to the struggles of the vast majority."[12]

The elites didn't make it out of their big-city streets to see what was going on in Wakefield, Yorkshire, or Dreamland, Ohio. There may have been a commercial property boom in Boston, but there certainly wasn't one in New Hampshire or Charleston, West Virginia. Eventually disillusioned voters around the world, especially outside the big cities, spoke up and voted for Brexit, Le Pen, Trump, and Five Star and the League. The people turned against the experts. Where I live in New Hampshire, the housing market is slowing again, and the local store and gas station just closed. That is exactly what happened in 2007.

Understanding Reality and No Longer Walking on Water

This book is about trying to understand reality. It is about life experience and taking seriously what people say and do. My thinking is driven mostly by observing how the world works and attempting to uncover fundamental truths and patterns in the data. It inevitably involves trying to uncover the rules of thumb that are used in everyday life by firms and ordinary people. A surgeon doesn't need a fully specified multi-equation model of how the body works to remove an ingrown toenail or to lance a boil. It's the facts that matter. If policymakers had focused on the facts, we may well not have gotten into this mess in the first place. Facts trump ideology. Feelings matter.

The data from the real world often speak loudly. The question is, who is listening? My hope is that this book will throw some light on the real world. Ever onward, ever upward. Who could have known? Seek and you shall find.

In August 2008 the chief economist of the International Monetary Fund (IMF) claimed that the state of macroeconomics was "good" (Blanchard, 2009, 209). It wasn't. There was no mention of any real-world data, the housing market, or anything at all about the fact that just nine months earlier the United States had entered what turned out to be the worst recession in a generation. We economists missed the big one and have had a very bad decade; our models have failed to understand the post-recession world. I document that policymakers don't seem to have learned much from their mistakes of the past and are still relying on these same economic models that have been disastrous. Recoveries have been slow.

In the book, we'll see how the world has changed since 2008 and how economies are a long way from full employment. Workers have been scared by what they saw in the Great Recession. They know they have little bargaining power and care about security more than small wage increases. Their employers can move some or all of their production abroad or bring in migrant workers. Higher-paying options in the public sector have largely disappeared with the onset of austerity.

Learning from the Past

The most popular British movie until *Titanic* was *The Full Monty*. It charted the desperation of a group of unemployed men in the 1980s in Sheffield, Yorkshire, as the steel works closed and there was simply no work. They were desperate for work and resorted to striptease to make money. It wasn't the slightest bit flirtatious. At the Nugget Theater in Hanover, where I watched the movie, everyone else seemed to find it very funny. I cried. I knew what it meant and the others in the cinema didn't seem to. America hadn't experienced long-term unemployment until the Great Recession. During the 1980s, under Margaret Thatcher, a million male manual workers who were union members in the North became unemployed and never worked again. There is little evidence that the jobless are lazy bastards shunning work as they enjoy their indolence. *The Full Monty* suggests just the opposite. People will do almost anything to get a decent-paying job.

George Orwell noted the horrible effects of enforced joblessness in the Great Depression: "There is no doubt about the deadening, debilitating effect of unemployment upon everybody" (1937, 81). And later, "When I first saw unemployed men at close quarters, the thing that horrified me was to find that many of them were ashamed of being unemployed" (85).

I am writing just after the seventy-fifth anniversary of the Beveridge Report, first published in the UK in December 1942. Essentially promising a reward for the hard work done in the war, it was the basis for the establishment of the welfare state in the UK and working toward full employment and avoiding the unemployment of the Great Depression. Sir William Beveridge, its author, reported on the effects of unemployment in the Great

Depression and made recommendations on what should be done after the war to avoid a repetition. He noted that "misery generates hate." The Beveridge Report was about decent jobs and a nation fit for the troops to come home to. Misery once again seems to have generated hate. Too many people are hurting and hating and are in a fury.

This book is especially about well-paying jobs for the less educated and the failure of the elites to deliver them. Jobs make people happy. Unemployment lowers people's self-esteem and worsens well-being and both mental and physical health. Happy people live longer.

It seems to me we should learn from the lessons of the past. In the 1940s in the UK William Beveridge and John Maynard Keynes didn't think that the unemployment rate could go below 3 percent. Between 1948 and 1959 it averaged around 2 percent. Today it could probably go that low, without massive wage growth. The world has changed.

The puzzle for central bankers is that the models keep telling them that at this unemployment rate, lots of price and wage inflation is on the horizon. So the Fed and the Bank of England are currently trying to drive inflation down by raising interest rates. The problem is that inflation continues to surprise on the downside, and inflation expectations remain low as well. Central banks have wrongly concluded full employment is near at hand when it isn't.

Once economies reach full employment, workers are standing by, as in the past, waiting for decent job offers. Good. The elites have said this would be inflationary—but they have been wrong so many times, why believe them? The problem now, as we will see, is both price inflation and wage inflation are both too low, not too high. Past remedies have failed. Now is the time for a big rethink.

I see no reason why advanced economies need to continue to run on empty. The fix is to get the unemployment rate in advanced countries down to levels not seen since the 1940s and 1950s; this can plausibly be done. At full employment the country would not be running on empty. If we were anywhere close to full employment so many people wouldn't be hurting. It's time to put the pedal to the metal.

PART I

The Problem: The Great Recession
Exposed Underlying Fractures

CHAPTER 2

Unemployment and Its Consequences

At a rally in Des Moines, Iowa, on December 8, 2016, Donald Trump argued as follows: "The unemployment number, as you know, is totally fiction. If you look for a job for six months and then you give up, they consider you give up. You just give up. You go home. You say, 'Darling, I can't get a job.' They consider you statistically employed. It's not the way. But don't worry about it because it's going to take care of itself pretty quickly."[1]

In fact, Trump had earlier argued that *every* adult aged 16 and over who was not a member of the labor force—that is, neither employed nor unemployed—was "out of work." "We have 93 million people out of work. They look for jobs, they give up and, all of a sudden, statistically, they're considered employed."[2]

That is an obvious overstatement, but Trump actually has a point. Trump is right that there is much more labor market slack than the six million unemployed, but ninety-three million is many steps too far. The amount of labor market slack is probably closer to ten million than a hundred million individuals. Whatever it is, the unemployment rate clearly underestimates badly what is going on.

In a Public Policy poll taken on December 6–7, 2016, two-thirds (67%) of Donald Trump's supporters said they thought the unemployment rate had increased since Barack Obama became president versus 18 percent of Hillary Clinton supporters. The unemployment rate reported by the Bureau of Labor Statistics (BLS) was 7.8 percent in January 2009 and 4.6 percent in December 2016.[3]

Trump is wrongly assuming a huge chunk of those who are out of the labor force (OLF) would like jobs. Some would, some wouldn't. Trump is right that people will move in and out of the labor force over time, as economic conditions as well as their own circumstances change, but his 93 million number is way too high. It is true, as I will explain in detail later, the unemployment rate in the years since the Great Recession of 2008–9 understates labor market slack and how much Americans are hurting. The overreliance on the unemployment rate has consequences.

Alana Semuels noted in the *Atlantic* that "the idea that the government falsified unemployment numbers was a popular narrative among Republicans during the Obama administration, and was 'most notoriously trumpeted' by former General Electric CEO Jack Welch on Twitter."[4] Welch tweeted in October 2012: "unbelievable jobs numbers. . . . these Chicago guys will do anything. . . . can't debate so change numbers." In an interview later in the day he admitted he had no evidence whatsoever to support such a statement.[5] Liz Peek, on the Fox News website, on June 7, 2016, asked, "Did Team Obama fudge the job numbers to stave off a Fed rate hike?" She wrote 1,079 words in the article when one would have sufficed: "no"!

In May 2018 convicted felon Don Blankenship, who was standing as a candidate in the GOP primary for a Senate seat in West Virginia, continued the theme that unemployment was really sky-high. He said the "establishment" and the media lie about the true U.S. unemployment rate. He said that multinational corporations and those "beholden" to them are a "great risk to the American worker. That's the reason they lie to you about what the unemployment rate is. The unemployment rate is probably 10 percent, not under four percent," Blankenship said.[6]

In a post on the blog of the Economic Policy Institute (EPI), Larry Mishel, the institute's president, wrote, "There was nothing particularly strange about this month's jobs reports—and certainly nothing to spur accusations of outright fraud," and called the claim that the BLS manipulated the jobs report a "slanderous lie," which of course it was. University of Michigan economist Betsey Stevenson, an ex-member of President Obama's Council of Economic Advisers, rightly responded, "Anyone who thinks that political folks can manipulate the unemployment data are completely ignorant."[7] True.

The BLS doesn't fiddle the data, period. The unemployment rate is calculated in a consistent way across advanced countries using a definition established by the International Labour Organisation (ILO).[8] The unemployment rate is obtained from a survey of individuals that has been taken monthly for over half a century, and the microdata are downloadable for researchers like me to analyze within a few weeks. Anyone can get the data at www.nber.org/data/cps_basic.html. The data files and codebooks are available, so the numbers can be checked out and, trust me, they do check out. At the time of writing, the files up to September 2018 are available. You need some statistical training to analyze the data, but my Dartmouth undergraduates do so all the time. I even helped write some of the NBER software to read the data. Download the data and check it out if you dare.

However, over time we have seen non-response rates rising in surveys such as the Current Population Survey, which is used to collect the unemployment rate and other individual statistics about the labor market, including wages. Unfortunately, even if folks respond there are often very high refusal rates to particular questions. For example, in 2018 there was a 38 percent non-response rate to questions on wages from those who took the survey. This problem has been growing over time, with the non-response rate up from 30 percent in 2008 and 23 percent in 1995, which reduces the reliability of the surveys. We don't really know why. These are the best data we have so we are stuck with them.

The published unemployment rate hasn't been fiddled, but it is much more unreliable than it used to be. It understates the number of people who want work that pays decently. Even though the unemployment rate is low, there are lots of people chasing high-paying jobs. And even people who do have jobs might not be using their skills fully. In bad times workers are pushed down the occupational pyramid and are forced into lower-paying jobs.

People Want to Work

In 2017 Delta Air Lines had 1,200 flight attendant jobs available and received 150,000 applications. In 2018 it has so far had 1,000 jobs available and, CNN reports, it has already had 125,000 applications.[9] Entry-level flight attendants earn roughly $25,000 a year but can earn more depending upon their schedule, plus there are lots of benefits including free travel. Not anyone can be a flight attendant. They cannot have any tattoos that are visible while in the company's uniform. Visible body piercings and earlobe plugs are also not allowed. Flight attendants must be able to pass a background check and fingerprint and drug screening.

In August 2017, thousands went to a job fair in Baltimore in hopes of getting one of 1,200 Amazon jobs. Amazon was preparing to open a third Maryland center, a 1.15-million-square-foot facility in Cecil County, by the end of 2017 with 700 new jobs promised. Christopher Moyer, economic development director of Cecil County, said Amazon had posted 60 job openings and received more than 1,700 applications.[10] DC Walmart stores in 2013 got 11,000 applications in the first week for 1,800 jobs.[11] There aren't enough decent, high-paying jobs to go around. Hence so many applications. The whole world wants a decent job. But if so many people want jobs, how can the unemployment rate be so low?

The unemployment rate is calculated as the number of unemployed divided by the labor force, which is the sum of the unemployed and the employed. Another measure is the employment rate, which is just the number of employed divided by the population aged 16 and over. This is how these numbers are calculated in every advanced country in the European Union (EU) and the Organisation for Economic Co-operation and Development (OECD) using criteria set out by the ILO.

I need to present some simple arithmetic to get four main labor market concepts out of the way: (1) the labor force, (2) the unemployment rate, (3) the employment rate, and (4) the participation rate. Never fear, all you need is addition and division. For October 2018 in the United States the seasonally adjusted 16+ population in thousands was 258,514. There were 6,075 unemployed and 156,562 employed, in thousands, based on the estimates from the Current Population Survey.[12] The labor force is just employment plus unemployment, which in April 2018 was 162,637 (= 6,075 + 156,562). Hence the unemployment rate was 6,075 / (6,075 + 156,562) = 3.7%. The employment rate, sometimes called the employment-population ratio, was 156,562 / 258,514 = 60.6%. The participation rate is just the labor force divided by the population, which for March 2018 was 162,637 / 258,514 = 62.9%. Simple as that.

Figure 2.1 illustrates what is going on in the U.S. labor market. It plots the unemployment rate on the right-hand axis against the employment rate and the participation rate since 1948 on the left-hand axis. In the years up to 2008 when the unemployment rate troughed, the employment rate peaked and vice versa. For example, in May 1999, the unemployment rate

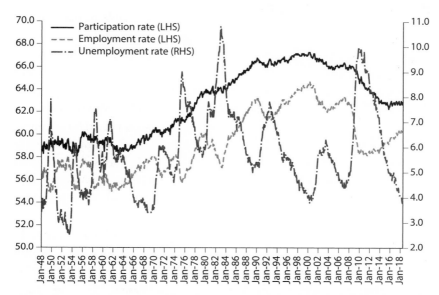

Figure 2.1. Labor market monthly rates, United States, January 1948–June 2018.
LHS = left-hand side; RHS = right-hand side.

was 4.2 percent and the employment rate was 64.3 percent; in October 2009, the unemployment rate was 10 percent and the employment rate 58.5 percent. Since then the connection has broken; an unemployment rate of 3.7 percent in November 2018, which is the latest figure available at the time of writing, is associated with an employment rate of 60.4 percent versus 63.3 percent in March 2007, as the labor market started to slow as the U.S. economy headed into recession.

The participation rate peaked at the end of the 1990s, fell through around 2001 and was flat for a few years before plummeting with the onset of recession. The unemployment rate and the employment rate used to be mirror images of each other, but they are not anymore. So much has changed. What happened pre-recession in the U.S. labor market isn't much help in explaining what has happened in subsequent years. To restore the employment rate to pre-recession levels would require over seven million additional jobs.

In a household, decisions to work tend to be made jointly. If one member of the household becomes unemployed the other may decide to find a job. In labor economics, we talk about added and discouraged workers. The former case is an example of a worker who joins the labor force as an endogenous response to another household member losing his or her job. Discouraged workers give up looking for jobs when unemployment is high. They withdraw from the labor force when the search for a job turns up empty. Also, people who had been considering joining the labor force are less likely to do so when unemployment is high. The discouraged worker effect explains why the labor force shrinks during times of high unemployment.

So which effect dominates? In practice, the size of the labor force tends to be negatively related to unemployment, which indicates the discouraged worker effect dominates. This should not be surprising because added workers can come only from the pool of households that are directly affected by unemployment.[13] Both the added and discouraged worker effects, though, will be going on at the same time.

An unemployed person does not have to be claiming benefits to be counted as unemployed in the BLS data file. Some countries such as the UK and the United States do report the numbers who are doing that. An example is the claimant count in the UK, which reports the (smaller) numbers claiming benefits. One way to enter the labor force is to move from OLF to unemployment. It should be noted that many job moves do not involve an intervening spell of unemployment. That would be the case, say, with a promotion. If Dartmouth hires a senior professor from another university, it is highly unlikely there would be an intervening unemployment spell. When we hire a graduate student who has just finished his or her PhD as an assistant professor, that person moves from OLF to employment also with no intervening unemployment spell. It is also possible that people could move from out of the labor force to unemployment as they start to search for work. So, employment and unemployment could both be going up together.

There are people who are OLF who would like a job. They could move, say, to unemployment first and then on to a job or, alternatively, move directly to a job from OLF. People can move from OLF to either employment or unemployment. So, the participation rate and the unemployment rate can go up together. Usually, though, as the participation rate rises, the employment rate rises and the unemployment rate falls.

I use the word "jobless" rather than "unemployed." The underemployed want to work more not less. I count the unemployed as jobless, but there are also individuals who are out of the labor force who would like a job but can't get one. They may have been unemployed in the past for a long time and became so discouraged they gave up looking for a job and left the labor force.

But if a good job came along they would take it. It is a common occurrence to see the long-term unemployed becoming disabled especially when unemployment benefits run out. Being unable to find a job when you want one tends to have harmful consequences, not least on your health and happiness.

In the 1980s the Thatcher government in its early years made a series of changes to the unemployment statistics that moved people from unemployment to OLF. All of these changes lowered unemployment. A commentator at the time noted that in previous years, Thatcher had been successful in lowering the unemployment statistics; the aim over the next few years was to actually get unemployment down. I went to a meeting in Downing Street in the mid-1980s with Sir David Metcalf to discuss why, as the UK economy was recovering, employment was rising but the unemployment rate was not falling. The reason was that the OLFs, rather than the unemployed, were moving back to jobs. What you gain on the roundabouts you lose on the swings. Politicians can't have it both ways.

As a young researcher, I wanted to find a fix for the plague of unemployment. It is a scourge. I still do. But now it is better to think more broadly to include those who work fewer hours than they would like as well as those who have left the labor force because of a lack of decent jobs. In *Hillbilly Elegy*, J. D. Vance noted that "many of us have dropped out of the labor force or have chosen not to relocate for better opportunities" (2016, 4).

Lazy Bastards (Not)

It turns out that the vast majority of the jobless are not lazy bastards. Unemployment does not raise well-being, it lowers it. During the Great Recession the U.S. Congress extended unemployment benefits because the rise in unemployment was largely involuntary. The evidence is that joblessness hurts, so why would anyone choose to hurt themselves? The fall in income hurts too. Work unequivocally raises well-being.

It makes sense to learn from the past. There was a good deal of controversy when I was a graduate student generated by an article by Benjamin and Kochin that argued that unemployment in the 1930s was largely voluntary:

Three largely independent sets of evidence indicate that the prolonged high unemployment was due to the operation of an unemployment insurance scheme that paid benefits that were high relative to wages and available subject to few restrictions. We estimate that the insurance system raised the unemployment rate by five to eight percentage points on average and that in the absence of the system unemployment would have been at normal levels through much of the period.

Many commentators disagreed. Indeed, there were four published critiques in April 1982, with a response from Benjamin and Kochin, in the *Journal of Political Economy*, who claimed in the original article that "the army of the unemployed standing watch in Britain at the publication of the General Theory was largely a volunteer army" (1979, 474).

The broad consensus from that debate, in my judgment, was that unemployment was mostly involuntary. Ormerod and Worswick (1982) criticized the econometric analysis while Collins argued that Benjamin and Kochin's results have "only limited application" and their model is "too narrowly based" (1982, 378). Rod Cross, for example, argued that Benjamin and Kochin's results were flawed by their almost complete failure to take account of the "genuinely seeking-work" and "means-test" clauses that were actively used in much of the 1921–38 period to disqualify many of the unemployed from receiving benefits and by what he called "their unconvincing dismissal of the reverse-causation argument that many of the increases in liberality of unemployment insurance provision resulted, directly and indirectly, from increases in unemployment rather than vice versa" (1982, 380). Metcalf, Nickell, and Floros argue that, contrary to the claims of Benjamin and Kochin, the prewar unemployment benefit system was less generous than that of the postwar period. Given the exceedingly low levels of unemployment in the latter period, "this fact alone is enough to invalidate the conclusion presented above" (1982, 387).[14]

There is little or no evidence that unemployment is a happiness-improving lifestyle choice for the lazy. We will never know what would have happened to unemployment if World War II hadn't happened. War resulted in full employment.

Marx's reserve army of the unemployed in the 1930s was a conscript army, not a volunteer army. It seems that is also true today. There is strong evidence from the happiness literature in support of the claim that unemployment is not something the majority choose in the modern era. In every one of the many hundreds of surveys of happiness, the unemployed are especially unhappy, and those with longer spells of unemployment are less happy than those with shorter spells. There is also evidence that not only does unemployment lower the happiness of the individual who is out of work, it lowers everyone else's happiness around that individual. Most people don't like walking past homeless people. In part that seems to be because people have friends, nephews, nieces, and even children who are unemployed and they don't like what they see. People are fearful it might happen to them. It turns out that a 1-percentage-point rise in the unemployment rate lowers well-being much more than an equivalent rise in the inflation rate.

A Low Unemployment Rate Does Not Mean People Are Happy

Even though the unemployment rate is low, it turns out that in the United States and elsewhere it doesn't currently give a full picture. You wouldn't get a sense of hurt by looking at the unemployment rate in several states in October 2018—4.6 percent in Ohio and 4.8 percent in Pennsylvania, for example, which are well below 2008 averages of 6.5 and 5.4 percent, respectively. There is something else going on not being picked up by the low unemployment rate.

The United States Conference of Mayors in their 2017 report, *U.S. Metro Economies: Past and Future Employment Levels*, noted that 121 metros (32 percent) entered 2017 with fewer jobs than they supported almost a decade ago. These metros are predominantly older midwestern communities suffering from the loss of heavy manufacturing jobs, an aging population, and crumbling infrastructure. These areas have yet to regain recession losses, have suffered a low rate of employment gain during this decade, and are forecast to continue to do so.

As manufacturing declined, it had impacts on towns that had provided decent-paying jobs for those with lower levels of education. The steel mill, the car plant, the paper mill, and the coal mine are disappearing. Sadly, there are no easy solutions. Getting out of Trans-Pacific Partnership (TPP), NAFTA, and the Paris climate deals won't create lots of well-paying jobs for the left-behinds. It just isn't that simple. Just as is the case nationally, the employment rate across states is lower today than pre-recession, despite some recent small recovery. That is true, for example, in states such as Michigan and Ohio that were crucial in Trump's election victory in 2016. In Michigan employment rates in 2017 were 58.6 versus 66.2 percent in 2000. In Ohio they were 59.8 percent in 2017 versus 64.4 percent in 2000. Jobs matter.

White, prime-age, less-educated people living outside the big cities, especially in what some have called flyover America, who have been hurting disproportionately voted for Trump. They had been left behind. This long drift where the less educated in particular were being excluded had been going on for years but was exacerbated by the Great Recession. Free trade benefited most people in the United States, for example, through lower prices, but the winners didn't adequately compensate the losers who spoke up. The good jobs went away to China and the Far East, but the big-city elites did just fine. Immigrants became the obvious targets of people's anger and frustration. Illegal immigrants lowered the price of food and gardening and childcare, for example, but workers at the low end felt they were taking their jobs away. Similarly, these folks voted for Brexit in the UK and Le Pen in France. Mexicans in the United States, the Poles in the UK, and North Africans in France.

People and places that voted for Trump in 2016 were hurting. Shannon Monnat plotted drug, alcohol, and suicide rates by the Trump-Romney difference by county and found a positive and significant relationship. She found that counties that voted more heavily for Trump than expected were positively correlated with counties that experienced high rates of death caused by drugs, alcohol, and suicide. Monnat commented, "People are literally dying. There was such a sense of hopelessness that it makes sense they would vote for massive change."[15]

Kathleen Frydl found that nearly every Ohio county with a high overdose death rate saw voting gains of 10 percent or more for Trump compared to Romney. Twenty-nine of thirty-three Pennsylvania counties with high overdose death rates, Frydl reported, flipped from Democrat to Republican.[16] All of the Pennsylvania counties that chose Obama in 2012 and Trump in 2016 have exceptionally high overdose rates, and in none of these counties did vote totals fall. Goodwin et al. (2018) analyzed a national sample of Medicare claims data and found that chronic use of prescription opioid drugs was correlated with support for the Republican candidate in the 2016 U.S. presidential election. Individual- and county-level socioeconomic measures explained much of the association between the presidential vote and opioid use.

Only 472 counties voted for Clinton on Election Day. Mark Muro and Sifan Liu of Brookings have found that they account for 64 percent of the nation's economic activity. The 2,584 counties where Trump won accounted for 36 percent.[17] In 2000, the 659 counties that Gore won accounted for 54 percent of GDP.

Nicholas Eberstadt has noted that for every unemployed American man between the ages of 25 and 55, there are another three who are neither working nor looking for work. He colorfully concludes that the unemployment rate "increasingly looks like an antique index devised from some earlier and increasingly distant war: the economic equivalent of a musket inventory or a cavalry count."[18] He and I are on the same page on this one. More on that later. In his book *Men without Work* (2016), Eberstadt complains about the lack of decent jobs for men in the United States; he is right, but there is also a lack of decent jobs for women. My two well-educated daughters, like many other working mothers, both struggle to pay the high costs of childcare.

So, something is clearly wrong with the unemployment rate as a measure of what is happening in the labor market. When it is around 4 percent, as it was in the spring of 2018, the labor market ought to be humming and decent-paying jobs should be aplenty, but they aren't. If there are so few people looking for jobs, as is suggested by a very low unemployment rate, firms should be having to attract workers from other firms by offering them higher wages. That also isn't happening, although there have been some signs of a small pickup in recent months. One possibility is that the employment rate is giving a better indication of labor market slack, and it is still 3 percentage points below its pre-recession levels.

The U.S. unemployment rate now says one thing—that there isn't much slack—while the employment rate says quite another—that there is. My advice is to go with the underemployment rate as the best indicator of slack, which suggests the United States is a long way from full employment. The unemployment rate is seriously flawed nowadays and no longer is your personal guide to the level of slack in the labor market. Many people have left the labor force, which is also why the participation rate has fallen, but would return to the labor force and take a decent-paying job if and when one was offered. There is a huge potential workforce out there that Trump cleverly tapped into. The underemployment rate post-2008 is also a very good indicator of slack and much more accurate than the unemployment rate.

Despite the low unemployment rate, the participation rate in the United States remains below pre-recession levels—66 percent at the start of recession in December 2007 versus 62.9 percent in November 2018—and it remains unclear why. Prime-age rates in particular, for both men and women, have picked up of late but remain stubbornly low.

This is not what has happened in other countries, which have mostly seen rises in the participation rates of older age groups. For example, in the UK the participation rates of those under the age of 25 have fallen, but for those 25 and over, all rates have risen. The overall 16+ rate is flat while the 16–64 rate is up. The participation rates for the UK are set out below for the most recent data in 2018 versus March–May 2008 at the start of the recession.

	July–September 2018	May–March 2008
16+	63.6	63.7
16–64	78.8	77.1
16–17	30.1	45.4
18–24	69.7	73.4
25–34	86.7	84.8
35–49	87.5	85.6
50–64	74.2	67.5
65+	10.7	7.4

There is a major concern about what prime-age men in the United States in particular who are neither employed nor unemployed are actually doing with their time. The biggest difference in how men in and out of the labor force spend their time, the Council of Economic Advisers (CEA) found (2016a), is in time spent on leisure activities, socializing, and relaxing, with non-participating men spending almost twice as much time on these activities than prime-age men overall and more than twice as much time watching television. They concluded that "these patterns suggest that men are, on average, not dropping out of the labor force to specialize in home production or to invest in skills to improve their future labor market opportunities" (2016a, 24). It appears that these men have simply given up because there are no decent jobs available. It is by no means obvious what they are doing.

Aguiar and Hurst (2007) found that between 1965 and 2005, weekly nonwork hours rose by about 8 hours a week for men without college degrees while it fell for men with a college degree or more. Eberstadt (2016) notes that, based on data from the Survey of Income and Program Participation, in 1996 2.6 percent of nonworking men aged 20–64 who did not work over the previous four consecutive months said they were caring for children. That number rose to 4.6 percent in 2013. Eberstadt also confirmed the CEA finding using American Time Use Survey data that prime-age men who were not in the labor force (NILF) spent disproportionate amounts of time socializing, relaxing, and engaging in leisure activities. He found that compared with unemployed men, on average NILF men spent a similar amount of time per day, in minutes, on personal care including sleeping; similar time on household care; less time caring for household members; similar time on eating and drinking; and much more time on socializing, relaxing, and leisure activities.

Eberstadt further documented that NILF men 25–54 spent more time than working men and women or unemployed men in gambling establishments, listening to the radio, using tobacco and drugs, and doing arts and crafts. They watch TV and movies 5.5 hours a day, which is two hours more than unemployed men. Eberstadt concludes, "To a distressing degree these men appear to have relinquished what we think of as adult responsibilities not only as breadwinners but as parents, family members, community members and citizens. Having largely freed themselves of such obligations, they fill their days in the pursuit of more immediate sources of gratification. . . . The data suggests that something like infantilization besets some un-working men" (2016, 93). Many less-educated, prime-age NILF men appear to be indolent. Eberstadt argues these men "have become essentially dispensable" (2016, 5).

There are a couple of quotes in J. D. Vance's *Hillbilly Elegy* that seem relevant here:

We talked about how things had changed. "Drugs have come in," Rick told me, "And nobody's interested in holding a job." (2016, 18)

And later,

We choose not to work when we should be looking for jobs. Sometimes we'll get a job, but it won't last. We'll get fired for tardiness, or for stealing merchandise and selling it on eBay, or for having a customer complain about the smell of alcohol on our breath, or for taking five thirty-minute restroom breaks per shift. (2016, 147)

Only five!

The Fear of Unemployment

Sir William Beveridge noted that when unemployment is high, over and above the unemployed themselves, there are "millions more in work at that moment but never knowing how long that work or any work for them may last" ([1944] 1960, 247). Workers fear unemployment.

It turns out that not only does unemployment decrease well-being but so does the prospect of becoming unemployed. Twenty-five years ago I published an article (1991) in which I showed that the fear of unemployment appears to depress pay substantially. Workers who expect to be made redundant earn 9 percent less, other things being equal. Also, workers in non-union workplaces who say they expect their plant to close earn 19 percent less than those who do not. No evidence could be found for such an effect in the union sector. There is some evidence of an asymmetry or "wage ratchet" in the UK. Workers in expanding plants receive a pay premium while those in contracting plants suffer no pay disadvantage, which is consistent with the claim that wages are more flexible upward than downward.

On the same theme, job insecurity lowers job satisfaction.[19] We know this from self-reports from workers on how satisfied they are with their jobs and how fearful they are of losing that job. Table 2.1 shows that in France, Italy, and the UK there was a rise in perceptions of job insecurity between 2005 and 2010 as the Great Recession hit. Job insecurity was higher in 2015 than it was in 2005 in these three countries but lower in Germany.

In the United States, since 1977 the General Social Surveys have asked workers relevant questions to allow us to establish whether job insecurity impacts happiness at work.

Q1. On the whole how satisfied are you with the work you do—would you say you are very satisfied, moderately satisfied, a little dissatisfied, or very dissatisfied? (variable = *jobsat*)

Q2. Thinking about the next twelve months, how likely do you think it is that you will lose your job or be laid off—very likely, fairly likely, not too likely, or not at all likely? (variable = *joblose*)

I simply coded the job satisfaction score from 1 to 4, with 4 = very satisfied. The score varied markedly from those who said job loss was not at all likely (3.42), not too likely (3.21), fairly likely (3.05), and very likely (3.04). Job satisfaction is thus higher if your job is secure. Conversely, job insecurity

Table 2.1. "I Might Lose My Job in the Next Six Months": Percentage Saying "Strongly Agree" or "Tend to Agree"

	Job loss %		
	2005	2010	2015
France	9	12	15
Germany	14	13	11
Italy	12	14	21
UK	7	13	14

Source: European Working Conditions Surveys, https://www.eurofound.europa.eu/surveys/european-working-conditions-surveys.

hurts as it lowers job satisfaction. The decline in income is not the only thing that hurts; having a job conveys higher self-esteem. Insecurity lowers job satisfaction. It is not just the unemployed in the United States who are hurting; prime-age men and women who are labor market non-participants are, too. They are the "left-behinds."

In an article I wrote with Chris Shadforth (2009), when we were both at the Bank of England, we found evidence that the fear of unemployment had risen in the UK. We argued this was likely to have contained wage pressure. The research on the fear of unemployment emerged from a firm visit I did in 2008 while I was on the Monetary Policy Committee (MPC). The firm shall remain nameless, but it was a large EU multinational. The plant subsequently closed. I was particularly interested to visit their factory as I was told by the bank's agent, who organized the visit, that the firm employed lots of East Europeans. The manager showed me that there were three production lines: two with local workers and a third line composed entirely of East Europeans. He explained to me that they had tried to introduce a new automated line, but it had failed so they hired lots of East Europeans for a few months to complete the work by hand. He said he was hugely impressed with them; they were never late and worked hard. When I subsequently asked him about the next pay round he told me there wasn't going to be one. When I asked why not he told me, "Because the workers over there know the East Europeans would like their jobs and would do them better, for less money."

We have some real-world qualitative data from individuals on what they think is going to happen to unemployment, and they are pretty accurate. The data are taken from a survey conducted by the European Commission in every EU country every month. It is a survey balance, calculated in re-

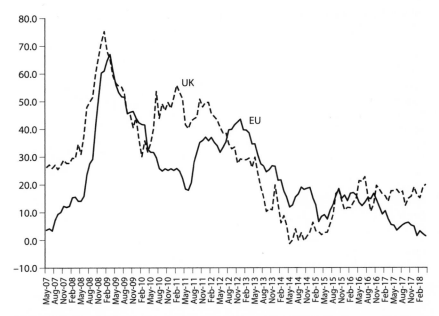

Figure 2.2. Monthly fear of unemployment, UK and EU, 2007–18. *Source:* EU Commission, https://ec.europa.eu/info/business-economy-euro/indicators-statistics/economic -databases/business-and-consumer-surveys_en.

sponse to the following question: How do you expect the number of people unemployed in this country to change over the next 12 months? Figure 2.2 plots the results for the EU and the UK separately. A higher number means more unemployment is coming; a lower number means less unemployment is coming. In February 2019, the fear of unemployment balance in the UK was 25, up from 10.3 in September 2016. In the EU as a whole, the balance is 9 against 14.8 in September 2016. So, the fear of unemployment in the UK is up recently despite the fact that the unemployment rate over this period fell from 5.2 to 4.1 percent. Of note is that in both the EU and the UK the fear of unemployment series was elevated at the start of 2008 in the months before recession. People seemed to know the economy was slowing even though policymakers in general and central bankers in particular seemed unaware of it. In August 2008 the fear index was 49.8 in the UK versus a series average from 1985 to 2007 of 25.3.

Table 2.2 reports the pre-recession score averages on what respondents in the UK and five other major EU countries thought would happen to unem-

Table 2.2. Fear of Unemployment Scores from EU Consumer Confidence Surveys

	Germany	Spain	France	Italy	Netherlands	UK
1985–2008	24	−17	29	28	10	20
Jan-07	−4	11	10	18	−19	33
Apr-08	−8	31	10	21	−2	35
Aug-08	15	46	26	26	6	50
Dec-08	48	71	68	52	64	71
Apr-09	71	51	69	45	71	59
Apr-10	25	27	43	42	33	32
Apr-12	6	43	39	52	47	43
Apr-14	3	−3	36	21	32	5
Apr-15	−3	−16	34	10	2	2
Apr-16	18	−3	31	10	11	15
Apr-18	−2	−11	3	7	−29	20
Oct-18	5	13	11	7	-20	17

Question: How do you expect the number of people unemployed in this country will change over the next 12 months? The number will: 1. Increase sharply; 2. Increase slightly; 3. Remain the same; 4. Fall slightly; 5. Fall sharply? These numbers are used to construct scores; see https://ec.europa.eu/info/files/user-guide-joint-harmonised-eu-programme-business-and-consumer-surveys_en.
Source: European Commission, https://ec.europa.eu/info/business-economy-euro/indicators-statistics/economic-databases/business-and-consumer-surveys/download-business-and-consumer-survey-data/time-series_en.

ployment. The table shows the increase in 2008 in the fear of unemployment and the steady decrease after that. The UK, however, saw a rise in the fear of unemployment from 2016 to 2018.

Of note is that accompanying the rise in the fear of unemployment in the UK there has been a rise in reported anxiety. The Office for National Statistics (ONS) in the UK has included this question in its Labour Force Survey since April 2011: "On a scale where nought is 'not at all anxious' and 10 is 'completely anxious,' overall, how anxious did you feel yesterday?" In a recent release the ONS provided time-series estimates of anxiety showing they had declined steadily from 2011 through 2015, but as with the fear of unemployment, they have increased since 2015.[20]

April 2011 to March 2012	3.13
January 2012 to December 2012	3.03
January 2013 to December 2013	2.95
January 2014 to December 2014	2.89
January 2015 to December 2015	2.85
January 2016 to December 2016	2.89
January 2017 to December 2017	2.91

Bell and Blanchflower (2018c) also reported a marked rise in the incidence of depression in the UK in the years since 2011 as austerity hit.

Workers in 2019 aren't demanding big pay increases as they are still fearful of losing their jobs. They saw the prices of their houses decline and the value of their pensions tumble in the Great Recession. Any job is better than no job. This is what the long, dragging conditions of semi-slump look like. My limo driver on the way to Logan International Airport on the day of the midterm elections in the United States told me that he doesn't think the economy is that good. Everyone he knows, he said, is underemployed. He told me that many are doing jobs that they are overqualified for—in part because they won't move.

Want, Disease, Ignorance, Squalor, and Idleness

On the front page of his 1944 report, *Full Employment in a Free Society*, Sir William Beveridge has three words under the title: "Misery generates hate." On page 248, paragraph 363, he elaborated further, arguing that "the greatest evil of unemployment is not the loss of additional material wealth which we might have with full employment. There are two greater evils. First that unemployment makes men 'seem useless, not wanted, without a country,' second that unemployment makes men live in fear and that from that fear springs hate." Beveridge continued with words that ring so true seventy-five years later.

> So long as chronic mass unemployment seems possible, each man appears as the enemy of his fellows in a scramble for jobs. So long as there is a scramble for jobs it is idle to deplore the inevitable growth of jealous restrictions, of demarcations, of organized or voluntary limitations of output, of resistance to technical advance. By this scramble are fostered many still uglier growths—hatred of foreigners, hatred of Jews, enmity between the sexes. Failure to use our productive power is the source of an interminable succession of evils. (para. 364)

The Beveridge Report identified five "giant" evils—want, disease, ignorance, squalor, and idleness—that are still relevant today.[21] As Stephen Armstrong has noted in an excellent op-ed and book, joblessness in the UK is as much an issue today as it was seventy-five years ago, despite the very low unemployment rate.[22] He looks at the five giant evils and finds bad stuff. Here is a summary of what he found for the UK.

WANT AND DESTITUTION

The Joseph Rowntree Foundation defines a destitute person as someone facing two or more of the following in a month: sleeping rough; having one or no meals a day for two or more days; being unable to heat or light your home for five or more days; going without weather-appropriate clothes; or going without basic toiletries. In a report by Fitzpatrick et al. (2018) titled "Destitution in the UK 2018," the Joseph Rowntree Foundation found that over 1.5 million people, including 365,000 children, faced destitution at some point in the year. UNICEF (2017) reported that nearly one in five UK children lacked sufficient safe and nutritious food. More than two-thirds of the children living in poverty in the UK are in families where at least one parent is working, according to official figures. There is poverty both in and out of work.

DISEASE

Babies born in the poorest areas of the UK weigh on average 200 grams less than those born in the richest areas. The average life expectancy for men in the richest borough of Kensington and Chelsea is 83; in Blackpool, in the north, it is 74. For the poorest residents in Kensington and Chelsea where the Grenfell Tower fire occurred, life expectancy is fourteen years shorter.

A report from the Royal College of Paediatrics and Child Health (2017) and Child Poverty Action Group paints a bleak picture of the well-being of children in low-income households. Among the problems cited in a survey of pediatricians in the report were poor growth in children whose parents cannot afford healthy food or to take them to medical appointments; respiratory illnesses caused or exacerbated by cold, damp housing; and mental health problems resulting from financial stress. Two in five of the surveyed doctors said they had experienced difficulty discharging a child in the previous six months because of concerns about housing or food insecurity.

IGNORANCE

England and Northern Ireland rank in the bottom four OECD countries for literacy and numeracy among those aged 16–24, with employers investing less in skills than in most other EU countries. Armstrong notes that this situation is unlikely to improve.[23] In September 2017, Armstrong noted that 4,000 head teachers across England wrote to parents to warn that budgets were facing a real-terms cut of 4.6 percent by 2020. Roughly 20 percent of UK adults—one-fifth of the country—don't have broadband access at home. Significantly, universal credit, which is gradually replacing the job seeker's allowance, is a digital-only service. Claimants are expected to make their applications and manage all relevant contact with the Department for Work and Pensions online. Mandatory job searches require claimants to use the government's online Universal Jobmatch for a minimum number of hours a week.

There has been much consternation at the time of writing that the UK government has provided helpline phone service for those with questions, billed at 55 pence (about 75 cents) a minute from a mobile phone. Claimants who haven't received their benefits have to call to say they have no money but haven't the money to pay for the call.[24]

Government minister Liz Truss, the second-in-command at the UK Treasury, defended these charges in a car-crash interview by saying, "Well, I'd encourage people to visit the Job Centre, go in and get the advice."[25] Loopstra and Lalor (2017) found that nearly 2 in 5 people who used food banks were awaiting a benefit payment, with most of these waiting up to six weeks, though a fifth were waiting seven weeks or more. Ignorance of government ministers seems an issue too. Let them eat cake.

SQUALOR

One-third of private rental homes in the UK, Armstrong reports in his op-ed, contain safety hazards or do not have acceptable kitchen and bathroom facilities or adequate heating. More than 795,000 homes in the UK harbor severe health threats from damp and mold, pests, improper electrical installations, excess cold, and dangerous levels of carbon monoxide, lead, and other chemicals, including asbestos. One in ten private renters were worried they would be kicked out if they made a fuss.

In November 2016, the maximum benefit for a room in shared accommodation in Manchester, for instance, was £291 per month. For a two-bedroom flat, it was £519 per month. According to numbers from the Valuation Office Agency, the lowest rent for shared accommodation in Manchester was £325 per month, and for two bedrooms it was £585 per month. The housing benefit, in other words, no longer covers people's rent.

IDLENESS

Real wages haven't grown for a decade in the UK and in 2018 are still 5 percent below their level in 2008. Unstable, precarious, low-paying, and temporary jobs have a huge part to play in this. Around 900,000 people were on "zero-hours contracts" in 2017, according to ONS data; since many of these people need two jobs to make ends meet, some 1.8 million zero-hours contracts are in place (5 percent of all employment agreements).[26] People on zero-hours contracts are more likely to be young, part-time, women, or in full-time education when compared with other employed people. On average, someone on a zero-hours contract usually works 25.2 hours a week. Just over one-quarter of people (25.3%) on a zero-hours contract want more hours, with most wanting them in their current job, as opposed to a different job that offers more hours. In comparison, 7.3 percent of other workers wanted more hours.

The United Nations Special Rapporteur on extreme poverty and human rights to the UK, Philip Alston, reported at the end of a twelve-day visit to the UK in 2018 that "the government's policies and drastic cuts to social support are entrenching high levels of poverty and inflicting unnecessary misery. . . . In the fifth richest country in the world, this is not just a disgrace, but a social calamity and an economic disaster, all rolled into one." He continued: "Government policies have inflicted great misery unnecessarily, especially on the working poor, on single mothers struggling against mighty odds, on people with disabilities who are already marginalised, and on millions of children who are locked into a cycle of poverty from which many will have great difficulty escaping."[27] That says it all.

It seems we have learned little in three-quarters of a century. So many are in need. A lack of well-paying jobs was always going to have consequences. Good, well-paying jobs make people happy and contented. They worry less. Joblessness worsens mental health. Over the last decade there has been a marked deterioration in mental health around the world. Depression is up; the use of antidepressants is up, as are suicides. Helplessness, homelessness, and stress are up. In the UK, the use of food banks is on the rise. In the United States, happiness is down for the least educated and there is a deepening opioid crisis. There has been an increase in the United States in deaths of despair from drug and alcohol poisoning. This seems unlikely to be unrelated to the worsening economic position of many, especially white, non-Hispanic, middle-aged, working-class men and women with low levels of education.

Carpenter, Chandler, McClellan, and Rees (2016) have found robust evidence that economic downturns lead to increases in the intensity of prescription pain reliever use as well as increases in clinically relevant substance-use disorders involving opioids. These effects are concentrated among working-age white men with low educational attainment. They also find that recent use of ecstasy and heroin is significantly countercyclical, while use of LSD, crack, and cocaine is significantly procyclical. They find clear evidence that substance-use disorders involving alcohol, marijuana, analgesics, and hallucinogens are strongly countercyclical. The findings for analgesics are robust to estimation method and are consistently larger, compared with other groups, for prime-age white men with low levels of education who were hardest hit by the Great Recession. The authors argue that as state budgets contract during economic downturns, drug-treatment funding is particularly vulnerable.

This worsening of mental health was likely not caused by the Great Recession; it simply exacerbated underlying problems and brought them to the forefront. Underlying weaknesses were exposed. Declining hope and a lack of prospects have had disastrous mental health repercussions. The culture war may well have been lost for many. Want, disease, ignorance, squalor, and idleness remain ever present in 2018. If countries are at full employment and doing so well, why are so many hurting?

The onset of austerity has made matters worse. A recent paper by Thiemo Fetzer (2018) concluded that the onset of austerity in the UK in 2010 directly contributed to the Brexit vote. His findings suggest that the EU referendum could well have resulted in a Remain victory had it not been for a range of austerity-induced welfare reforms. These reforms, Fetzer suggests, "activated existing economic grievances" (2018, 1). Further, he finds that the rise of popular support for the UK Independence Party (UKIP) is the single most important correlate of the subsequent Leave vote in the 2016 EU referendum; this along with broader measures of political dissatisfaction are strongly and causally associated with an individual's or an area's exposure to austerity since 2010.

The Young Are Not Striking Out on Their Own and There Is a Storm of Fury Building

Harry Leslie Smith, the famed anti-poverty activist who died recently at the age of ninety-five, had big concerns about young people. He was worried that there is little hope for a brighter tomorrow for them: "I think there is a gathering storm of fury building" (2017, 139). He was probably right.

A recent analysis of census data by real estate tracker Trulia in the United States found that almost 40 percent of young Americans were living with their parents, siblings, or other relatives in 2015, the largest percentage since 1940. Despite a rebounding economy and recent job growth, the share of those between the ages of 18 and 34 doubling up with parents or other family members has been rising since 2005. Back then, before the start of the last recession, roughly one-third were living with family. The share of young Americans living with parents hit a high of 41 percent in 1940, just a year after the official end of the Great Depression, and fell to a low of 24 percent in 1960. It hovered between about 31 and 33 percent from 1980 to the mid-2000s, when the rate started climbing steadily.[28]

Fry (2016) found that in 2014, for the first time in more than 130 years, adults ages 18 to 34 were slightly more likely to be living in their parents' home than they were to be living with a spouse or partner in their own household. Among young adults, living arrangements differ significantly by gender. For men ages 18 to 34, living at home with their parents has been the dominant living arrangement since 2009. In 2014, 28 percent of young men were living with a spouse or partner in their own home, while 35 percent were living in the home of their parent(s). For their part, young women are on the cusp of crossing over this threshold. They are still more likely to be living with a spouse or romantic partner (35%) than they are to be living with their parents (29%).

For young adults without a bachelor's degree, as of 2008, Fry also found that living at home with their parents was more prevalent than living with a romantic partner. By 2014, 36 percent of those ages 18 to 34 who had not completed a bachelor's degree were still living with their parents while 27 percent were living with a spouse or partner. Among college graduates, in 2014, 46 percent were married or living with a partner, and only 19 percent were living with their parent(s). Young adults with a college degree have fared much better in the labor market than their less-educated counterparts, which has in turn made it easier to establish their own households.

Vespa (2017), in a Census Bureau report, found that the percentage of young people 18 to 34 who lived with their parents rose from 26 percent in 2005 to 34.1 percent in 2015. The highest proportions by state were where house prices are high: New York, New Jersey, and Connecticut. Of the young adults who lived at home, 10 percent were unemployed versus 6 percent for those living independently and 8 percent if living with roommates. One in four young Americans living at home was neither in school nor working.

Vespa had several other important findings. Young people are delaying marriage. In the 1970s, eight in ten people were married by the time they turned 30. Today that doesn't happen until the age of 45. In 2005, the majority of young adults lived independently in their own household, which was the predominant living arrangement in thirty-five states. A decade later, by 2015, the number of states where the majority of young people lived independently fell to just six. The main highlights of Vespa's report are as follows.

- More young men are falling to the bottom of the income ladder. In 1975, only 25 percent of men ages 25 to 34 had incomes of less than $30,000 per year. By 2016, that share rose to 41 percent. (Incomes for both years are in 2015 dollars.)
- Between 1975 and 2016, the share of young women who were homemakers fell from 43 percent to 14 percent of all women 25 to 34. Of young people living in their parents' home, one-quarter are idle; that is, they neither go to school nor work. This figure represents about 2.2 million 25- to 34-year-olds.
- For Hispanics, blacks, and other race groups, a greater share of young people now reside at home than in any other arrangement. For whites, as many live in their parents' home as live with a spouse, while for Asians, living with a spouse is the most common arrangement for young people.

In 2014 three-quarters of 15- to 29-year-olds lived with their parents in Italy, Greece, Portugal, and Spain. The proportions rose between 2007 and

2014 in the United States (63% to 67%), in Germany (54% to 56%), and in France (41% to 54%) but fell in the UK (59% to 52%).

A Pew Research Center Study (Fry and Brown 2016) found that in the United States in 1982, 41 percent of heads of households who were younger than 35 were homeowners, compared with 35 percent in 2016. In the UK a study for the Local Government Association showed that the proportion of 25-year-olds who own their own home has slumped from almost half twenty years ago to just a fifth in 2016.[29]

The recession has made it harder for young people to strike out on their own. The transition from school to work has always been hard, especially for the least educated; now it is even more difficult for youngsters to live independently and form their own households. Having a decent job that pays good wages makes it possible for young people to move away from home. The phenomenon of young people remaining at home in the United States mirrors what is happening in countries like Spain where there are not fully functioning housing markets and people rarely move. A concern in the United States is that mobility has halved since World War II.

It is not good that young people are increasingly living in their parents' basements and unable or unwilling to strike out on their own. Youngsters living with their parents used to be a European and not an American phenomenon; it is now. Long-term unemployment used to be mostly a European but not an American phenomenon, but that has changed also. Breaking out on your own is good for a young person; it teaches needed life skills. Mobility matters.

The Impact of Long Spells of Joblessness

In recessions prior to the Great Recession, the United States did not experience long-term unemployment to anywhere near the same degree as other countries. I recall Lord Layard of the London School of Economics once telling me, colorfully, that the way to think about a European unemployment rate of 10 percent was that 90 percent of the people were employed all the time while 10 percent were unemployed all the time.

If spells of joblessness are long when an individual is young, it makes it hard for them to recover. Long spells of unemployment are especially bad for young people as this prevents them from gaining a solid foothold in the labor market. It seems that, in the United States, with the big decrease in the participation rate, it is appropriate to look at joblessness in particular, which

Table 2.3. OECD Long-Term Unemployment Rates and Harmonized Unemployment Rates

a) Long-term unemployment rate (% of unemployed with durations >1 year)

Location	1985	2010	2017
Canada	12	12	12
France	44	40	44
Germany	48	47	42
Italy	66	48	59
Japan	13	38	37
United Kingdom	50	33	26
United States	9	29	15

b) Harmonized unemployment rate (%)

Location	1985	2010	2016
Canada	10.7	8.1	6.3
France	10.4	9.3	9.4
Germany	n/a	7.0	3.8
Italy	8.1	8.4	11.2
Japan	2.6	5.1	2.8
United Kingdom	11.2	7.8	4.4
United States	7.2	9.6	4.3

Source: Eurostat, https://ec.europa.eu/eurostat/statistics-explained/index.php/Unemployment_statistics.

encompasses periods not in employment including unemployment and spells outside the labor force. But long-term unemployment came to the United States in 2008.

Table 2.3 reports the long-term unemployment (LTU) rates and harmonized unemployment rates, both from the OECD, for a number of countries in 1985, 2010, and 2017. The long-term unemployed are people who have been unemployed in a continuous spell for twelve months or more. The long-term unemployment rate is the proportion of these long-term unemployed among all unemployed. Unemployment is usually measured by national labor force surveys and refers to people reporting that they have worked in gainful employment for less than one hour in the previous week, who are available for work and who have sought employment in the previous four weeks.

European countries have experienced high levels of long-term unemployment for decades as measured by the proportion of the unemployed with durations of at least a year. The LTU rate was especially high in the 1980s and 1990s. In 1985, for example, it was 50 percent or more in Italy and the UK. In 2017, the LTU rate was still above 50 percent in Italy. Canada didn't have LTU in 1985 or in the Great Recession. Higher unemployment rates tend to be associated with higher long-term unemployment rates, which means that as unemployment rises it becomes increasingly hard to get the unemployed to move into jobs. Frequently the LTU leave unemployment by moving to disability and hence to OLF rather than to jobs. Of note in the table is that the United States did not have an LTU problem until the Great Recession, when it acquired one as unemployment rates hit double digits.

The Great Recession was a great equalizer, as almost everybody was affected by it, including the United States, although at a lower level than in Europe. But long-term unemployment still hasn't gone away, remaining well above levels in 2008, even in the United States. Given the widespread experience of LTU outside the United States, much of the recent work on its impact is just repeating lessons European labor economists knew from the 1980s. The findings are the same, that long-term unemployment is *not* an important part of the story of why wage growth is weak.

The most recent OECD annual estimate for 2017 shows that in seven OECD countries (Belgium, Bulgaria, Macedonia, Greece, Italy, the Slovak Republic, and Portugal) at least half of the unemployed were jobless for longer than a year. The rates in 2017 for France (44%), Germany (42%), the Netherlands (41%), Japan (38%), and the UK (26%) are still much higher than those of the United States (15%) and Canada (12%). The U.S. annual rate went as high as 31 percent in 2011 versus a high of only 14 percent that year in Canada.[30]

Long-term unemployment tends to cause significant mental and material stress for those affected and their families. It is also of concern for policymakers, as high rates of long-term unemployment indicate that labor markets are operating inefficiently.

Alan Krueger and coauthors (2014) found that after fifteen months, the long-term unemployed are more than twice as likely to have withdrawn from the labor force as to have settled into steady, full-time employment. And when they do exit the labor force, the unemployed tend to say that they no longer want a job, suggesting that many exits from the labor force could be enduring. The authors conclude that the main benefit of a stronger economy in relation to long-term unemployment may be that it reduces the likelihood that the short-term unemployed become long-term unemployed. Skills tend to deteriorate, or become out of date, the longer they are not used.

The number of people experiencing unemployment for more than twenty-six weeks in the United States rose from 1.4 million in January 2008 (18% of the unemployed) to a high of 6.8 million in April 2010 (44%) to 1.29 million (20%) in April 2018. Neither the proportion nor the level of long-term unemployed has returned to pre-recession levels, but the numbers have fallen fast. Indeed, the fall in long-term unemployment is twice as fast as that of overall unemployment. Since January 2016 unemployment has fallen from 7.8 million to 6.3 million, or to 81 percent of its starting level, whereas long-term unemployment has fallen from 2.1 million to 1.3 million, or to 63 percent of its starting level.

The gloomy predictions of some that the long-term unemployment numbers wouldn't come down as the economy recovered have turned out to be short of the mark.

Why Do We Care about Joblessness?

The major reasons cited in the literature for why we care about the fact that people can't find jobs when they want them are outlined in what follows. The longer a spell of unemployment is, the greater any impact tends to be. Involuntary joblessness brings bad stuff. These effects are especially strong for young people, but there are bad consequences for older adults too. My assumption is that long spells out of the labor force for prime-age adults in particular will generate similar bad effects as long spells of unemployment.

1) During a long period of unemployment, workers can lose their skills, causing a loss of human capital. So that's a double whammy— instantaneous loss of output but also a permanent loss of output due to skill depreciation.

2) Unemployment is a stressful life event that makes people unhappy.[31] In every happiness equation I have ever seen, no matter what the country, the measure or the time period examined, unemployment enters significantly and negatively. It also has a big effect. Unemployment does not appear to be voluntary; all the evidence shows it is involuntary as jobs make people happier and healthier. Unemployment hurts and it hurts a lot. Everyone loves a story

about scroungers, but an anecdote isn't the same as evidence. My data gather together lots of possible anecdotes. The unemployed are not a bunch of lazy bastards sunning themselves on the dole. In general, they are conscripted without a choice.

My ex–University of Stirling colleague Liam Delaney and coauthors (2017a) examined whether past unemployment has long-term repercussions for psychological well-being across Europe. They examined the effect of past unemployment on various aspects of contemporary well-being, namely, self-reported quality of life, psychological distress, and life satisfaction, across fourteen European countries. They found that the long-run negative well-being effect of past unemployment is a broad, cross-country phenomenon. The impact of prolonged time spent in unemployment on depression symptoms appears to be explained by individual demographic factors in the sampled countries.

3) Unemployment increases susceptibility to malnutrition, illness, mental stress, and loss of self-esteem, leading to depression.[32] There is evidence for the United States that being jobless injures self-esteem and fosters feelings of externality and helplessness among youths.[33] The psychological imprint of joblessness persists. Paul and Moser (2009) in a meta-analysis of 237 cross-sectional and 87 longitudinal studies concluded that the unemployed exhibit more distress than the employed. A significant difference was found for several indicator variables of mental health including symptoms of distress, depression, anxiety, psychosomatic symptoms, subjective well-being, and self-esteem. Meta-analyses of longitudinal studies and natural experiments endorsed the assumption, they argued, that unemployment not only is correlated to distress but also causes it.

4) Being unemployed can reduce the life expectancy of workers.[34] There is evidence that mortality for the previously unemployed was 2.5 times higher than for people not previously unemployed.[35] One study followed 20,632 twins in Sweden from 1973 to 1996 and found that unemployment increased mortality, with significant increases in suicide, injuries, and accidents.[36] Low levels of education, use of sleeping pills or tranquilizers, and serious or long-lasting

illness tended to strengthen the association between unemployment and early mortality.

5) Increases in the unemployment rate tend to be associated with increases in the suicide rate.[37] The unemployed appear to have a higher propensity to commit suicide.

6) Unemployment increases the probability of poor physical health outcomes such as heart attacks in later life.[38]

7) There is evidence of increases in smoking after unemployment.[39]

8) Many of the unemployed delay important life decisions, such as marriage and having children.[40] As noted above, unemployment makes it harder for young people to strike out on their own and they often end up living with their parents.

9) Teenage unemployment leaves scars rather than temporary blemishes.[41] Young people who suffer periods of unemployment have a 13–21 percent decrease in earnings by age 41.[42]

10) The long-term unemployed are at a disadvantage when they try to find work. The effects of unemployment appear to depend a lot on how long the person has been unemployed. Morale sinks as the duration of unemployment rises. Long-term unemployment, therefore, is especially harmful. The long-term unemployed "have largely given up hope," argues Layard (1986, 96).

11) As unemployment rates increase, crime rates tend to rise, especially the property crime rate.[43] Thornberry and Christensen (1984) find evidence that a cycle develops whereby involvement in crime reduces subsequent employment prospects, which then raises the likelihood of participating in crime. Increases in youth unemployment cause increases in burglaries, thefts, and drug offenses.[44]

Declines in unemployment rates reduce the crime rate, which seems to be highly responsive to employment opportunities for low-skilled men.[45] Wage rises significantly lower the crime rate. Higher wages for low-skilled workers reduce both property and violent crime, as well as crime among adolescents.[46] The impact of wages on crime is substantial; one study estimates that a 10 percent increase in wages for non-college-educated men results in approximately a 10 to 20 percent reduction in crime rates.

Hansen and Machin (2002) find a statistically significant negative relationship between the number of offenses reported by the police over a two-year period for property and vehicle crime and the proportion of workers paid beneath the minimum before the introduction of the minimum wage. Hence, in the UK, areas that initially had more low-wage workers saw more crime reduction once the minimum wage was introduced. Falk and Zweimüller (2005) find a significant positive relationship between unemployment and right-wing criminal activities.

In Great Britain youth unemployment and adult unemployment are both significantly and positively related to burglary, theft, fraud and forgery, and total crime rates. For each of these offense categories the relationship between youth unemployment and the specific crime was found to be somewhat stronger. Two studies have found that there is a systematic positive relationship between burglary rates and male unemployment, regardless of age.[47]

Interestingly, the U.S. Council of Economic Advisers (2016b) reported that increasing the minimum wage "reduces crime by 3 to 5 percent." The CEA found that:

- A $10 billion increase in incarceration spending would reduce crime by 1–4 percent (or 55,000–340,000 crimes) and have a net societal benefit of –$8–$1 billion dollars.
- A $10 billion investment in police hiring would decrease crime by 5–16 percent (440,000–1.5 million crimes) and have a net societal benefit of $4–38 billion.
- Drawing on literature that finds that higher wages for low-income individuals reduce crime by providing viable and sustainable employment, the CEA found that raising the minimum wage to $12 by 2020 would result in a 3–5 percent decrease in crime (250,000–510,000 crimes) and a societal benefit of $8–17 billion.

12) Increases in the unemployment rate decrease the happiness of everyone, not just the unemployed.

Joblessness matters as it clearly hurts. Long periods without work are harmful and especially so for the young. For young people, joblessness can cause permanent scars and prevent family formation including having children and getting married. Unemployment is stressful and hurts morale; it lowers self-esteem and increases susceptibility to malnutrition, illness, and mental stress. It raises the probability of smoking, lowers life expectancy, and raises the possibility of suicide. The unemployed commit more crime.

If everyone else is unemployed it isn't so bad because "we are all in it together." As George Orwell noted in his 1937 masterpiece *The Road to Wigan Pier*, "When people live on the dole for years at a time they grow used to it, and drawing the dole, though it remains unpleasant, ceases to be shameful. . . . It is not only Alf Smith who is out of work now; Bert Jones is out of work as well, and both of them have been 'out' for years. It makes a great deal of difference when things are the same for everybody" (48).

People want to work.

CHAPTER 3

Wage Growth and the Lack of It

"American businesses big and small increasingly have the same problem: they can't find workers."[1] I hear this all the time. It turns out it is mostly untrue. If it were true, wage growth would be accelerating and it is not.

In a dynamic capitalist economy, in which innovative firms are being born all the time and displacing old firms, there will always be a demand for workers with the new skills these new firms require. With the onset of the motor car there were too few people who knew about engines and too many working with horses who would soon be displaced. There is not much call for shorthand typists these days. In addition, any statement about shortages must have a price tag attached to be meaningful. If the going rate for a job is twenty bucks an hour and the firm is offering ten bucks an hour and can't get any applicants then that isn't a shortage. In addition, if there really were shortages at the going rate that would mean there is no available pool of labor to go to, so the only way to get workers is to hire them away from other firms at higher wages. Hence wage growth is an indicator that there really is a shortage. If wages aren't rising, there isn't a real shortage and employers are crying wolf.

A column in the *Wall Street Journal* in May 2018 reported on the "gushing labor market for plumbers." The author claimed that "drained from a labor shortage, the plumbing industry is throwing the kitchen sink at job candidates. . . . The annual median pay for plumbers, pipefitters and steamfitters was nearly $53,000 a year in 2017, according to federal data, but it isn't uncommon to see jobs advertised for far higher wages, from $70,000 up to six figures."[2] Of course, a median of $53,000 is perfectly consistent with some people earning $90,000 and some earning $30,000; that is how averages work! No evidence was actually provided that wages were in fact rising. So no shortage.

The evidence from the BLS's news release "Occupational Employment and Wages—May 2017" for plumbers, pipefitters, and steamfitters showed hourly wages of $26.94 in May 2016 and $27.44 in May 2017, up 1.9 percent. Earnings at the 90th percentile were $91,800 versus $31,500 at the 10th percentile.[3] No evidence was provided in the *Wall Street Journal* article that employers were having to raise the wages of plumbers although some apparently were offering extra beer. I don't buy it. Not much gushing going on, I am afraid.

Interestingly, the study from which the quote beginning this chapter is taken saying there is a shortage of workers cites a survey of firms taken by the Federal Reserve that I discuss in more detail below. The Fed has continued to report only modest wage growth. Even in October 2018 in its Beige Book the Fed reported that "wage growth was mostly characterized as modest or moderate, though Dallas reported robust growth. Most businesses expected labor demand to increase modestly in the next six months, and looked for modest to moderate wage growth."[4] We have had the same story for at least a decade. No wage growth means no labor shortage. A few local hiring difficulties that will always exist does not mean there is a national shortage of workers, skilled or otherwise.

Wage Growth Has Been Benign

Wages were hit hard by the fall in activity in the Great Recession all around the advanced world. They picked up across the OECD as recovery took hold and as the unemployment rate came down. Even though unemployment has fallen sharply, especially in the UK and the United States, wage growth has not returned to the pre-recession rates.

In the years prior to 2008 an unemployment rate of 4 percent would have generated nominal wage growth—wage growth not adjusted for price changes—of 4 percent or higher. Now it generates wage growth nearer to 2.5 percent. For a long time, post-recession, wage growth was stuck at a norm of around 2 percent and has only picked up slightly in the UK and the United States as unemployment rates fell from 5 to 4 percent and lower. Wage growth is benign in Germany, where the unemployment rate is 3.4 percent.

In recessions young people tend to enter the job pyramid lower down than they would in normal times. College graduates are forced to take the jobs that normally would be held by high school graduates. In a very nice article Lisa Kahn finds that there are large negative wage effects of graduating from college in the United States in a worse economy. She also finds that cohorts who graduate in worse national economies are in lower-level occupations. Kahn concludes that "graduating from college in a bad economy has a large, long-run, negative impact on wages" (2010, 312). In recessions, as we will see, workers are forced to work fewer hours than they would like, and as a result many take part-time jobs even though they would prefer full-time jobs. This is especially true among the young, minorities, non-union workers, and women.

Underemployment is an additional amount of slack in the labor market. Even though the unemployment rate in the United States and the UK has returned to pre-recession levels, underemployment has not. In countries such as France, Spain, Italy, and Greece that continue to have high levels of unemployment, on top of that they also have high levels of underemployment.

The relationship between the unemployment rate and wage growth that existed pre-recession has been broken, apparently irretrievably. Figure 3.1 is probably the most important figure in this book. Along with the unemployment rate, it plots the annual growth rate of hourly wages of private-sector production and non-supervisory workers (PNSWs) in the United States. This is the longest and best monthly series on wages available in America, dating back to 1964. Hence, we have wage-growth data back to 1965. The picture is essentially the same if weekly wages are plotted. According to the BLS, in its labor market release of November 2018, there were just under 105 million private-sector PNSWs or around 82 percent of the private-sector workforce and around 70 percent of the total number employed.[5] The figure is helpful because the series isn't pulled upward by very high earnings of managers and executives at the top end and tells us about the earnings of ordinary working folk. Wage growth used to closely follow the unemployment rate but no longer. As the unemployment rate fell, wage growth rose and vice versa, but that pattern broke in 2008.

Since January 2016 there has been a steady pickup in the hourly wage growth of PNSWs, mostly in 2018 as the unemployment rate dropped from 4.9 to 3.7 percent. As the economy moves toward full employment wage growth will rise. Hourly wage growth has ticked up from 2.4 percent in Janu-

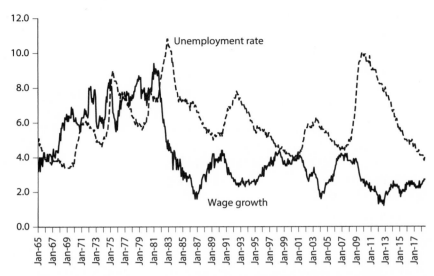

Figure 3.1. Annual hourly wage growth of U.S. private-sector production and non-supervisory workers, and the unemployment rate, January 1965–June 2018. *Source:* BLS.

ary 2016, when the unemployment rate was 4.9 percent, to 3.2 percent in the most recent data for October 2018 with a 3.7 percent unemployment rate. This contrasts with hourly wage growth of 3.8 percent for PNSWs in January 2008 when the unemployment rate was 5 percent.

Since 1965 when the data series started to be published, other than two months in 2018 there have been eight occasions when the unemployment rate was also 3.7 percent. They were as follows with their associated rates of hourly wage growth of PNSWs, which averaged 5.6% across the eight months.

September 1966	4.2%
October 1966	4.1%
January 1968	5.4%
March 1968	5.7%
June 1968	6.0%
July 1968	5.9%
September 1969	6.5%
October 1969	6.8%

Policymakers appear to believe wage growth of 4, 5, or even 6 percent is just around the corner. They are wrong; it is not. It is clear that something has broken in the United States in the relationship between average hourly pay growth of private-sector PNSWs and the unemployment rate. Times have changed.

Wage Growth Has Been Consistently Weak on Every Measure

There are a number of other wage measures available in the United States, and they tell a broadly consistent story of flat wage growth from 2009 through 2016 that picked up a little in 2017 and 2018. It is always a good idea to check for consistency.

The annual percentage growth rate of private-sector hourly and weekly earnings in the United States, based on Current Employment Statistics (CES) of employers, is published monthly by the BLS. This data series only goes back to 2006. In March 2007, hourly earnings growth was 3.4 percent and weekly earnings growth was 4 percent. Weekly earnings started tumbling first, as hours started to fall. Hourly earnings didn't start falling until January 2009, noting of course that the United States went into recession at the end of 2007.[6] Hence the slowing jobs market took a year or so to feed through to wages, which clearly are a lagging indicator.

A second set of wage data published quarterly is from the U.S. Current Population Survey on median usual weekly earnings of full-time wage and salary workers. This series has been available since 1980 and tends to be volatile quarter on quarter. It also shows a marked decline in wage growth since 2008 and a pickup since 2014. The series averaged a growth rate of 4 percent from 1980 to 1999, 3 percent from 2000 to 2008, and 2 percent from 2009 onward. The latest growth rate at the time of writing was 3.3 percent in the third quarter of 2018, up from 2 percent in the second quarter.

A third measure of compensation, the quarterly Employment Cost Index, shows broadly the same path but did not pick up in 2016.[7] A decline from a growth rate of total compensation of 3–4 percent prior to the recession and then a slowing to 2–3 percent is apparent here also. The latest data for the last two quarters of 2018 show a growth rate of 2.8 and 2.9 percent, versus 2.8 percent in the previous quarter.

The Board of Governors of the Federal Reserve (2017) reported on the magnitude of pay raises among employed workers using data from the 2016 Survey of Household Economics and Decision Making. They noted that 5 percent of all workers received a raise that exceeded the change in their living expenses, whereas 19 percent of workers said that it fell short of rising expenses. Hence, nearly three-quarters of workers "either did not receive a raise or received one that was less than the change in their expenses."

The Fed also found evidence that those with greater levels of education were more likely to have received a raise and to have received one that exceeded the change in their expenses. Among employed respondents with a bachelor's degree or above, 48 percent received a raise and 8 percent received one that exceeded the change in their expenses. In contrast, among employed respondents with a high school degree or less, 38 percent received a raise and just 2 percent received one that exceeded the change in their expenses. That doesn't look much like full employment to me. Ninety-eight percent of the less educated had a pay raise lower than inflation.

The box below summarizes reports from the twelve federal reserve banks in the October 2018 Beige Book on wages in several major cities. The economist Gary Schilling suggested to me at a conference we were both speaking at that I should look at it, as it was entirely consistent with the evidence of muted wage growth. He was right. The words "moderate" and "modest" are used frequently. Rather surprisingly the most bullish reports on wages came from the Cleveland Fed, which covers Ohio, western Pennsylvania, eastern Kentucky, and the northern panhandle of West Virginia. This seems rather unlikely. It is notable though that there is some sign toward the end of 2018 of some pickup in wage pressures in Dallas and San Francisco, but wage growth remains moderate in New York, Chicago, Minneapolis, and other areas. There is not much exploding.

Federal Reserve Beige Book, October 24, 2018

On balance, wage increases were *modest* to moderate, with some differences across sectors; a couple of Districts cited a pickup in the pace of wage growth.

Boston

Wage increases accelerated somewhat but remained moderate.

Federal Reserve Beige Book, October 24, 2018 (cont.)

New York

Wage pressures have remained fairly widespread. While businesses in most industries noted that wage growth has remained moderate thus far, a growing proportion reported that they plan to raise wages in the months ahead.

Philadelphia

On balance, wage growth continued at a moderate pace.

Cleveland

Overall wage trends were comparable to those of recent survey periods, with many contacts reporting wage increases that were slightly above the rate of inflation. In every industry, contacts noted that increased competition was requiring their firms to boost wages to retain workers.

Richmond

Wage increases remained modest.

Atlanta

A growing number of firms over the reporting period experienced an uptick in merit increases for workers; several contacts reported average merit raises in the 3 to 3.5 percent range.

Chicago

Wage growth remained modest overall.

St. Louis

Wages have increased modestly since the previous report. Multiple contacts reported wage increases for entry-level workers. Furthermore, wages grew in manufacturing and trucking sectors and were generally flat in the hospitality sector. Wages for small business in St. Louis rose slightly.

Minneapolis

Wage pressures were moderate since the last report.

Kansas City

Wage growth accelerated since the previous survey, with wages rising moderately in most sectors.

Federal Reserve Beige Book, October 24, 2018 (cont.)

Dallas

Upward wage pressure was generally pervasive and strong, according to contacts. Some businesses were implementing non-wage strategies to recruit and retain workers, such as giving sizable signing bonuses, offering part-time and/or flexible work schedules, and keeping employees on the payroll during periods of slower business. Also, a staffing firm reported that employers were willing to accept candidates that met only 60 percent of the qualifications rather than the usual 80 percent.

San Francisco

Wage growth picked up broadly. Contacts across the District noted continued upward compensation pressures for a variety of skilled occupations, including finance professionals, health-care providers, and business consultants. A contact in the retail industry raised starting wages in anticipation of intensifying labor shortages during the holiday season. A few contacts noted that some businesses increased benefits like vacation allowances and one-time bonuses rather than wages.

Figure 3.2, which is also hugely important for the UK, uses a long annual time series on weekly wages on the left-hand side and the unemployment rate on the right-hand side from 2001 through 2018. It uses the total pay measure of Average Weekly Earnings (AWE), which is the UK National Statistic. The unemployment rate for March 2018 was 4.2 percent and wage growth was 2.3 percent. In 2003 the unemployment rate was 5 percent and wage growth was 3.2 percent. In both 2004 and 2005 the unemployment rate was 4.8 percent and wage growth was 4.4 and 4.7 percent, respectively. Wage growth in the UK in 2010 was 2.3 percent with an unemployment rate of 7.9 percent.

The Great Recession changed everything. Of note is that the relationship between wage growth and the unemployment rate shifted similarly in the UK and the United States. The unemployment rate post-recession is associated with a lower wage growth than the same rate was associated with pre-

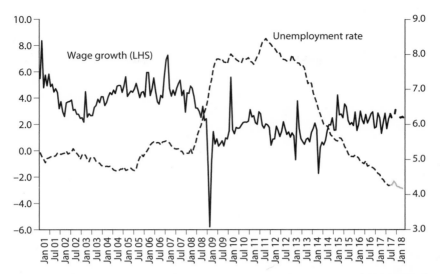

Figure 3.2. UK wage growth and the unemployment rate, January 2001–May 2018. LHS = left-hand side. *Source:* ONS.

recession. The unemployment rate in both countries appears to underestimate the level of slack in the labor market in 2019.

A 2–3 Percent Pay Norm Is a New Phenomenon in Many Countries since the Great Recession

Neither the wage data nor the employment rate suggests the United States is anywhere close to full employment. If it were, wage growth would be picking up and it isn't. It isn't in the UK either. Japan has seen nominal wages grow only 1 percent in nearly three decades and real wages are down 11 percent over that period. This may be the precedent going forward when price and wage growth surprise on the low side.

There are new regularities in the wage data around the world that were not there before the Great Recession. It seems the big economic shock scared the living daylights out of workers. A 2 percent pay norm is now operating around the world. There have been small ups and downs, as in the United States as noted above, but even when wage growth looks to be headed inexorably upward it then falls back. Central bankers get all excited that at long last normality is returning only to see their hopes fall by the wayside a couple of months later. I recall being told in the UK in 2007 and 2008 by the Governor of the Bank of England Mervyn King that wage growth was about to explode. I am still waiting. There is weak wage growth everywhere even in countries where the unemployment rate is low.

In 2008 I went to see Brendan Barber, the head of the Trade Union Congress in London, and asked him if there was any chance that wages were set to take off. He above all people should have known. He told me there was no chance at all of that. Workers, he told me, cared mostly about job security in tough times. They also cared about the flexibility of their job and how it fit into their busy family schedules of dropping off and picking up kids from school and other daily activities. They knew that their employer could move production abroad or hire migrant workers or simply subcontract the work to India or China. Or they could hire (non-union) subcontractors. Globalization had weakened workers' bargaining power and the big decline in 2008 and 2009 made that obvious for all to see. In the recovery, even if employers had the ability to pay more, they had no need to. What was true then is true now. Workers care about job security, fear losing their jobs, and have little bargaining power. That is why wage growth isn't rocketing.

In June 2018 more than 1 million workers in the UK's National Health Service settled for a pay raise of around 6.5 percent over the following three years.[8] The small rise came after seven years of a 1 percent cap on salaries. A lack of pay growth in the public sector feeds through to a lack of pay growth in the private sector and vice versa. Still waiting for Godot.

Wage data are also available from the UK Labour Force Survey (LFS) at the individual level on the gross weekly earnings of full-time employees and show a decline in wage growth from averages around 2.7 percent pre-recession to 1.4 percent subsequently. Mean annual weekly wage growth using these data was 2 percent for the latest time period of July–September 2018.

Annual wage data are also available from the UK Annual Survey of Hours and Earnings (ASHE) from 2002 to 2018. ASHE is based on a 1 percent sample of employee jobs taken from HM Revenue and Customs Pay As You Earn records. Given the survey reference date in April, the survey does not fully cover certain types of seasonal work, for example, employees taken on for only summer or winter work. Information on earnings and hours is obtained from employers. The data refer to earnings in the prior financial year. Median annual growth rates of weekly earnings for full-time employees according to ASHE averaged 4.2 percent from 1997 to 2007 and 1.75 percent for the years 2008–18.[9] Here we go again.

Bell (2015) has noted that even though there has been a notable increase in non-wage compensation, this rise consists largely of special payments to fund deficit gaps in "defined benefit" pension schemes—and most of these schemes have been closed to new members for years. Bell notes that there is no reason to suppose that non-wage compensation is distributed across the workforce in exactly the same pattern as wages. Indeed, he points out, high earners are more likely to have been in defined benefit schemes and in particular to benefit from the final salary aspect of such schemes. In addition, and more specific to the issue at hand, the increase in non-wage compensation may provide no, or few, benefits to the currently employed. Because a substantial part of these payments is to cover deficits in pension schemes for previous workers and those already in retirement, current workers benefit little from these payments.

Wage Growth Internationally Has Been Benign Also

Even in Germany where the unemployment rate is only 3.8 percent and underemployment is well below pre-recession levels, wage growth is weak. According to the Federal Statistical Office DESTATIS, the change in gross hourly earnings for industry and services for 2017 in Germany was only 2.2 percent, down slightly from 2.3 percent in 2016. Earnings in 2017 Q4 were up 1.9 percent while labor costs were up 1.5 percent compared with the same quarter a year earlier.

In part this seems to be because of the Hartz labor reforms that made the labor market more competitive and also because of changes in collective bargaining. Rinne and Zimmermann claim that a "substantial part of the country's success story during the Great Recession is its recent reform efforts that have helped put Europe's " 'sick man' back on track" (2012). In a subsequent article the same authors argue that "the German success story is mainly due to a combination of structural labor market reforms and the absence of fiscal austerity" (2013, 724).

Since the 1990s Germany has seen a big decline in union coverage rates, from 83 percent in 1995 to 58 percent in 2016. This fall has been accompanied by a rise in decentralization of wage setting, from the sectoral to the firm level. Kügler and coauthors argue that "the low wage growth in

Germany . . . is in part a consequence of an unprecedented decentralization of the wage setting process" (2018, 1).

So, the combination of labor market reforms and decentralizing of wage bargaining has meant wage growth has remained contained in Germany despite unemployment rates below 4 percent.

In France, the statistical bureau INSEE reports that nominal wage growth of monthly pay in both 2015 and 2016 was 1.2 percent. Wage growth in France has been below 2 percent every year since 2012 and at 1.1 percent for the last seven quarters. Hourly labor costs, according to Eurostat, grew by 1.1 percent in France between 2016 and 2017 in enterprises with ten or more workers excluding agriculture and public administration. As Quévat and Vignolles note in relation to France, "The rise in unemployment during the financial crisis of 2008–2009 clearly held back wage growth."[10]

The first two columns of table 3.1 provide the latest comparable evidence from the OECD of nominal annual earnings changes, not adjusted for changes in prices, for the thirty-five OECD member countries in the period prior to recession (2000–2007) and subsequently (2008–16). Nominal wage growth was markedly lower after the Great Recession. For example, in the UK in the former period average nominal wage growth rates were 4.1 versus 1.7 percent in the later period; in the United States they were 3.8 and 2.2 percent, while in France they were 3 and 1.7 percent. Greece had averaged 5.7 percent pre-recession but then –1.7 percent in the later period. Japan saw a slight pickup from –0.8 to –0.2 percent but still had falling wages. Germany is the one major country with a pickup from an average of 1.6 to 2.3 percent.

According to Statistics Canada, hourly and weekly wage growth in Canada from 1998 through 2004 averaged 2.5 percent. From January 2005 through April 2009 it averaged 3.6 percent. Since then it has averaged 2.3 percent and dropped to only 1.2 percent in the first three months of 2017. Statistics Canada noted that average weekly earnings rose 0.4 percent in 2016, the slowest rate of annual earnings growth since comparable data became available in 2001.[11] This follows an annual increase of 1.8 percent in 2015 and 2.6 percent in 2014. In 2016, they noted that annual rate of consumer inflation was 1.4 percent, so real earnings fell 1 percent.

Wage growth remained weak in 2017 across other advanced countries. In the first quarter of 2017, New Zealand had annualized wage growth of

Table 3.1. Annual Average Wage Changes, 2000–2016

	Nominal		Real	
	2000–2007	2008–2016	2000–2007	2008–2016
Australia	4.2	2.9	1.3	0.6
Austria	2.8	2.3	0.8	0.4
Belgium	2.5	1.7	0.1	0.3
Canada	3.5	2.6	1.7	1.2
Chile	4.9	7.0	1.3	2.7
Czech Republic	6.9	2.4	4.6	1.1
Denmark	3.4	2.7	1.5	1.1
Estonia	13.2	4.2	8.1	1.4
Finland	3.4	2.4	1.8	0.5
France	3.0	1.7	1.1	1.0
Germany	1.6	2.3	0.2	1.1
Greece	5.7	−1.7	2.6	−2.2
Hungary	10.9	2.9	4.3	0.1
Iceland	7.8	5.0	3.1	0.0
Ireland	5.9	1.2	2.4	1.2
Israel	1.8	2.3	0.2	0.5
Italy	3.1	1.2	0.4	−0.1
Japan	−0.8	−0.2	−0.1	0.0
Korea	5.6	2.7	2.5	0.5
Latvia	16.5	3.9	8.9	1.7
Lithuania	9.8	4.0	8.2	1.3
Luxembourg	3.8	1.8	1.4	0.7
Mexico	7.8	3.6	2.3	−0.7
Netherlands	3.5	1.8	1.0	0.7
New Zealand	4.3	2.3	2.5	0.8
Norway	4.7	3.6	2.8	1.3
Poland	4.8	3.8	1.2	2.0
Portugal	3.4	0.6	0.0	−0.4
Slovak Republic	8.9	3.2	3.6	1.7
Slovenia	8.0	2.1	3.0	0.9
Spain	3.3	1.8	−0.1	0.7
Sweden	3.5	2.7	2.2	1.3
Switzerland	1.9	0.5	−1.0	0.6
United Kingdom	4.1	1.7	2.7	−0.3
United States	3.8	2.2	1.5	0.7

Note: Average annual wages per full-time equivalent dependent employee are obtained by dividing the national-accounts-based total wage bill by the average number of employees in the total economy, which is then multiplied by the ratio of average usual weekly hours per full-time employee to average usually weekly hours for all employees. Real wage growth is in constant 2016 prices in national currencies. For more details, see www.oecd.org/employment/outlook.

1.6 percent with an unemployment rate of 4.9 percent. This was the same rate as reported in Australia in their latest estimate for average weekly earnings for all employees in November 2016 when they had an unemployment rate of only 5.9 percent.[12] This was the third quarter in a row with wage growth at 1.6 percent.[13] Analogously, hourly wages in the Netherlands saw an annual increase of 2.3 percent in October 2018.[14]

Japan has had little or no wage growth, in nominal or real terms, for years. Over the period since January 2008 nominal wage growth has averaged −0.45 percent. Nominal wage growth is up 1 percent over the period 1990–2017. Real wages are down 11 percent over the same period. The real wage index number of 99.9 in November 2017 is still 7 percent below its peak of 107.1 in April 2010.

As Michelle Lam has noted, the unemployment rate in Japan is at its lowest level since 1993, plus the ratio of job offers to applicant has surpassed its 1993 peak. But that still hasn't translated into wage growth.[15] It seems in Japan the unemployment rate also understates the amount of slack as women have entered the labor force, which has pushed down wages. Indeed, even though employment has risen, total hours have remained broadly flat because these women tend to work shorter hours. The latest data at the time of writing from the Monthly Labor Survey show nominal wage growth including bonuses of 0.9 percent in Japan in the year from November 2016 to November 2017.[16] Japan may be the precedent.

Maybe it's time to get used to the fact that wage growth, both nominal and real, going forward is going to be benign, just as it has been in Japan for years.

The Worst Decade for Real Earnings Growth in 210 Years?

It is appropriate to adjust nominal earnings growth by changes in prices to determine changes in living standards. If prices rise by 2 percent and wages rise by 3 percent workers are better-off. The problem is when prices rise by 2 percent and wages rise by 1 percent, which means workers are worse off.

The last two columns of table 3.1 provide the latest comparable evidence from the OECD of real annual earnings changes from 2008 to 2016 for the same thirty-five countries in the period prior to recession and subsequently.

Data also show a marked slowing in most countries with the major exceptions of Chile, Switzerland, and Poland, which saw major increases. Israel, Germany, Spain, and Belgium saw small improvements while the rest saw declines.

Real weekly earnings for the United States for production and non-supervisory workers in 1982–84 dollars have not recovered to 1972 levels. Weekly earnings are what matters as this is about take-home pay. Real weekly earnings were $341.36 in 1972 compared with $311.80 in April 2018, down 9 percent. In fact, real weekly earnings for most workers are approximately what they were fifty years ago. However, they are up 8.4 percent since the start of 2008 when the recession started. This contrasts sharply with the UK, which has seen real wage falls since 2008 but sharp rises before that.

We do know that the growth paths of earnings and incomes for all workers have been rather different. According to the Census Bureau median household income rose 27.5 percent between 1967 and 2015 whereas mean household income rose 60 percent.[17] Over the same period median household income in the top decile was up 82 percent while median first decile earnings were up 30 percent. Between 2005 and 2015 top decile earnings were up 6.5 percent but first decile incomes were down 3.2 percent; median incomes were up only 0.5 percent.

Real AWE weekly earnings in the UK of total pay including bonuses were £493 in constant 2015 pounds in September 2018, down 5.5 percent from a high of £522 in February 2008. They were also £493 in June 2010 when austerity was first implemented. To place this in context, a report for the Resolution Foundation in March 2017 looks at estimates of how real earnings in the UK have grown over the past three centuries.[18] It measures decadal real-terms earnings growth since the 1700s and measures changes in average pay between the last ten years and ten years before (CPI and predecessors-adjusted). The slight deterioration in the real pay outlook at the end of 2016 when combined with falling real pay at the beginning of this decade and only a couple of recent recovery years means the UK is on course for average pay across the decade to 2020 to be lower than the average for the decade before. That, they suggest, if the official outlook for pay of the UK government's forecaster, the Office of Budget Responsibility, were to come true, "would represent the worst decade for real earnings growth in 210 years" (Clarke et al. 2017, 27).

Between January 2005 and January 2008, for example, real wages in the UK rose by 7 percent compared with a rise of 0.5 percent in the United States over the same period, so there has been a catching up by U.S. workers. By April 2018 U.S. private-sector weekly wages of production and non-supervisory workers in the United States were up 9 percent compared with where they were in January 2005, whereas in the UK real weekly wages were up only 2 percent.

The self-employed in the UK, whose numbers have risen from 3.6 million in March 2005 to 4.85 million by October 2018, have seen their earnings fall sharply. The Resolution Foundation used data from the Family Resources Survey to chart movements in real earnings of employees and the self-employed from 2000.[19] Remarkably, the evidence showed that typical earnings for the self-employed were lower in 2014–15 than in 1994–95, twenty years earlier. A fall of 15 percent compares to a rise of 14 percent in typical employee earnings. From peak (2006–7) to trough (2013–14), typical self-employment earnings fell by 32 percent—£100 per week. In my paper with Costa and Machin (2017) we found that the self-employed without workers have seen their median real weekly income drop significantly since 2007–8, experiencing close to a 20 percent loss in real terms by 2014–15. Both employees and the self-employed with workers have had milder drops compared with individuals in independent self-employed work arrangements. It is not obvious by any means that more self-employment is better. Most countries other than the UK and the Netherlands have seen falling self-employment rates.[20]

Real net national disposable income in the UK is down: from £23,503 in 2007 to £22,786 in 2014.[21] It is interesting also that the real disposable income of retired households continued to rise while that of the non-retired did not. Between 2007–8 at the start of the recession and 2015–16, real disposable income of retired households rose 13 percent. In contrast, that of non-retired households fell by 1.1 percent.[22] Retired households have benefited from government policies on uprating state pensions and from rises in equity values and house prices, as well as all the fruits of quantitative easing. If we do the same calculation by quintile, the lowest quintile saw its real incomes rise by 13.2 percent; the second by 6.6 percent; the third by 3.9 percent; and the fourth by 4 percent; the top quintile real incomes fell 3.3 percent. This is of interest given that the poor, the retired, and older folks disproportionately voted for Brexit.

Productivity and Employment

Employment growth has picked up as productivity has slowed.[23] Employment growth rates in the UK, according to the ONS, were as follows (where we calculate the average annual growth rates of employment).

1970s	0.4%
1980s	0.6%
1990s	0.2%
2000–2007	1.0%
2008–10	−0.1%
2011–17	1.3%

The Great Recession saw a fall in employment from 2008 through 2012. By January 2012 employment was still 300,000 below the employment levels of January 2008. After that employment rose at a record average annual pace of 1.3 percent and by January 2018 was about two and a half million higher. Of note is that over the period January 2010 through January 2018, the employment rate rose from 58 to 60.9 percent, while real average weekly wages fell from a high of £522 in February 2008 to £488 in January 2018, or by over 6 percent. In contrast in the United States employment rates fell from 62.9 to 60.4 percent while real weekly wages of the private sector, in 1982–84 dollars, rose from $343.72 to $369.72.

As background we should note that productivity growth has declined steadily over time in the UK. According to the ONS, productivity rates in the UK were as follows:

1960s	2.88%
1970s	2.48%
1980s	2.07%
1990s	2.04%
2000s	1.01%
2010–17	0.73%

To put this in context, UK productivity was 17 percent below the average for the rest of the G7 in 2015.[24] By 2015, the UK produced in five days what it took the United States, Germany, and France to produce in four. There is little or no sign of catch-up. It is hardly surprising that wages have not risen—something structural has happened. Productivity growth is a third of what it was from 1960 to 2000.

Higher productivity tends to lead to higher real wages and is associated with higher consumption levels and better health.[25] It seems that wage growth has fallen as productivity has fallen and employment growth has slowed. The very low wage-growth rates in the last few periods have occurred when output per head was growing at less than 1 percent and employment growth was slowing.[26] Low-paid workers were hired. There was an industry-wide slowdown in business investment during the crisis and subdued growth since, which helps explain the productivity slowdown.

Consistent with this is the recent work by Haltiwanger et al. (2018), in the United States, who found strong evidence of a firm wage ladder that was highly procyclical. During the Great Recession, this firm wage ladder collapsed, with net worker reallocation to higher-wage firms falling to zero. They found that in the Great Recession, movement out of the bottom rung of the wage ladder declined by 85 percent, with an associated 40 percent decline in earnings growth. They find that upward progress from the bottom rung of the job ladder declines by 40 percent in contractions, relative to expansions.

Productivity is low when wage growth is low. A pay freeze in the public sector that has existed in the UK since 2010 has not helped to motivate staff. Workers on low pay are not motivated to work harder. In addition, in contrast to the United States, the employment rate in the UK has recovered to post-recession levels, in large part due to the hiring of more, low-paid, less productive workers.[27] In both countries private-sector unionization rates have collapsed, so workers appear to have less bargaining power than in the past.[28]

Blundell, Crawford, and Jin (2014) have noted that the supply of workers in this recession was higher than in previous recessions: the UK labor supply curve shifted to the right. However, despite the increase in supply occurring among groups toward the lower end of the jobs market, they found there is strong evidence against the composition or quality of labor hypothesis as a potential explanation for the reduction in wages and hence productivity that we observe. They found that there are more individuals willing to work at any given wage and thus that there is likely to be greater competition for jobs. As a consequence, Blundell and coauthors argue, workers are likely to have lower reservation wages than in the past and seem to attach more weight to staying in work (because their expected time to find another job is longer than in the past) than on securing higher wages and are thus willing to accept lower wages in exchange for holding onto their job.

Stansbury and Summers (2017) find evidence of a link between productivity and compensation in the United States: over 1973–2016, 1-percentage-point higher productivity growth has been associated with 0.7–1 percentage point higher median and average compensation growth and with 0.4–0.7 percentage point higher production/non-supervisory compensation growth. They further find the relationship between average compensation and productivity in Canada, West Germany (pre-unification), the UK, and the United States to be strong and positive with the effects somewhat weaker for France, Italy, and Japan.

A Mystery Not a Puzzle, but the Puzzle Is Solved!

Of interest, though, is that the path of wage growth appears to have befuddled policymakers who don't think Japan is the model. Not least because they expected productivity to take off and it hasn't, but it will any minute now although no explanation is ever given in answer to the question, "Why now?" On September 9, 2014, Mark Carney, the governor of the Bank of England, gave a speech at the 146th annual Trades Union Congress in Liverpool, titled "Prospects for the UK Labour Market," where he argued as follows:

> Specifically, the Bank's latest forecast expects real wage growth to resume around the middle of next year and then to accelerate as the unemployment rate continues to fall to around 5.5% over the next three years. By the end of our forecast, we see 4% nominal pay growth on average across the economy.[29]

That didn't happen. Table 3.2 presents the last twenty hopeless wage-growth forecasts from the Monetary Policy Committee (MPC) at the Bank of England. People are incredulous when I show them this chart. Reading downward I report each of the forecasts, noting that the MPC has a number of forecasts for the same year. The first forecast for 2015 was made in 2014 Q1 of 3.75 percent. The MPC has another seven goes at it and as time goes by it lowers the forecast, eventually getting to 2.5 percent in 2015 Q4, which is about right. The forecasts roughly go as follows. The current rate is

Table 3.2. Twenty Successive MPC Wage Forecasts, 2014–20 (%)

	2014	2015	2016	2017	2018	2019	2020
2014 Q1	2¾	3¾	3¾				
2014 Q2	2½	3½	3¾				
2014 Q3	1¼	3¼	4				
2014 Q4	1¼	3¼	3¾	3¾			
2015 Q1		3½	4	4			
2015 Q2		2½	4	4			
2015 Q3		3	3¾	4½			
2015 Q4		2½	3¾	4	4¼		
2016 Q1			3	3¾	4¼		
2016 Q2			3	3¾	4		
2016 Q3			2¾	3	3½		
2016 Q4			2½	2¾	3¾	3¾	
2017 Q1				3	3¾	3¼	
2017 Q2				2	3½	3¾	
2017 Q3				2	3	3¼	
2017 Q4				2¼	3	3¼	3¼
2018 Q1				2½	3	3¼	3½
2018 Q2					2¾	3¼	3½
2018 Q3					2½	3¼	3½
2018 Q4					3½	3	3¼
Outcome	1.6	2.4	2.4	2.3	2.8		

Source: Conditioning assumptions for Inflation Reports and AWE Total Pay annual averages.

2 percent but it will be 4 percent in a couple of years. As time goes by the forecast is lowered to around 2 percent as the data from the real world come in. But there is no learning as every forecast looks much like all the others. It is 2 percent now but it will be 4 percent despite the fact that it never is. I always get asked why the MPC keeps making these terrible forecasts and I have no answer.

In his exit interview after six years on the MPC in August 2018, Ian McCafferty argued that "labour shortages would lead to an acceleration in wage growth to close to 4% next year."[30] Five days after the interview was published on August 14, 2018, the ONS released new data on wage growth showing that it fell sharply in July 2018. AWE Total Pay growth fell from 2.5 percent in May 2018 to 2.1 percent in June 2018. XpertHR, which reports pay settlements (www.xperthr.co.uk), said on August 23, 2018, that pay settlements in the three months through the end of July 2018 in the UK slipped back from 2.5 percent to 2.3 percent. Four percent wage growth still seems a long way off.

Andy Haldane, chief economist and MPC member, Bank of England, in a speech called "Pay Power" given on October 10, 2018, argued, "A year ago, prospects for pay were cloudy. . . . Signs of a pay pick-up had, to that point, proved to be false dawns. A year on, I think there is more compelling evidence of a new dawn breaking for pay growth." Sir Jon Cunliffe, another member of the MPC, a week later in written testimony to the Treasury Select Committee (TSC) on October 17, 2018, argued that "pay growth has established itself in the 2.5–3 percent range. But the latest readings do not signal strongly that pay growth will make the next step to establish itself firmly in 3 percent territory in line with the May forecast." Cunliffe said, in verbal testimony to the TSC that day, that he was "not yet convinced that pay growth would exceed the 3 percent level the BoE predicted, adding that there had been many false dawns on pay in the past."[31]

The ONS released a new set of wage-growth data on November 13, 2018. It showed that AWE annual wage growth measured using single-month data, year on year, was as follows.

	Whole economy	Private sector	Public sector
July 18	3.3%	3.4%	3.0%
August 18	3.1%	3.3%	2.7%
September 18	2.8%	2.8%	2.7%

Down, not up.

Most other forecasters, including the Federal Open Market Committee (FOMC) in the United States, have also been overly optimistic about how quickly wage growth was set to reach 4 percent. That cry was often used by the hawks as a reason to raise rates as cost-push inflation, they claimed, was just around the corner, but it never was. Tomorrow and tomorrow and tomorrow creeps in this petty pace from day to day . . . but never did.

Fed chair Jerome (Jay) Powell, talking to Kai Ryssdal on NPR on July 12, 2018, said that the lack of wage growth was a mystery but not a puzzle: "We would have expected wages to move up fairly significantly. We now just in the last year or so, we have seen wages move up. But there is still a bit of a puzzle in that we're hearing about labor shortages now all over the country in many, many different occupations in different geographies. And one would have expected, I would have expected, that wages would move up a little bit more. So again, there's no—I wouldn't call it a mystery, but I would say that it's a bit of a puzzle given how tight labor markets appear to be. And what we're hearing from employers really is that they can't find workers, and you're wondering, well, why aren't wages going up faster?"

In response, Pedro Nicolaci da Costa in a column called "There's One Simple Explanation for the Wage Stagnation 'Puzzle' Confounding Top Fed Officials" in *Business Insider* on August 29, 2018, argued that "the Fed chairman should take a look at a new paper from David Bell of Stirling University in Scotland and David Blanchflower, former Bank of England member and Dartmouth College professor. There, Powell will find a simple and convincing answer to his puzzle. The job market is really not as hot as the headline unemployment figure makes it look, leaving workers without the requisite bargaining power to ask for raises." I agree! More on this below.

Most commentators and forecasters followed the roly-poly toy school of economics in terms of their predictions as to what was going to happen to the economy in general, especially the labor market. The round-bottomed doll, tilting doll, or wobbly man is a toy that rights itself when pushed over. Since 2008 forecasters have assumed the economy is just a toy that will soon right itself, within about eighteen months, when nudged. That has been the case especially in relation to wage growth, both in the UK and the United States. The MPC and the FOMC have both wrongly assumed reversion to an unreachable pre-recession mean. Knock the economy doll down and it didn't bounce back. In large part this appears to have been because of their mistaken belief that both economies were close to full employment, given the low unemployment rate. It turns out those were bad calls.

As recently as July 2016, when the unemployment rate was 4.9 percent, the FOMC said most participants thought the United States was close to full employment, when it clearly was not.

> Although most participants judged that labor market conditions were at or approaching those consistent with maximum employment, their views on the implications for progress on the Committee's policy objectives varied. Some of them believed that a convergence to a more moderate, sustainable pace of job gains would soon be necessary to prevent an unwanted increase in inflationary pressures. Other participants continued to judge that labor utilization remained below that consistent with the Committee's maximum-employment objective. These participants noted that progress in reducing slack in the labor

market had slowed, citing relatively little change, on net, since the beginning of the year in the unemployment rate, the number of persons working part time for economic reasons, the employment-to-population ratio, labor force participation, or rates of job openings and quits.[32]

But it remains clear they are conflicted. In the minutes from the January 2018 meeting when they kept rates constant it was clear there were divergent views on the labor market in general and wage growth in particular.

Many participants reported that labor market conditions were tight in their Districts, evidenced by low unemployment rates, difficulties for employers in filling open positions or retaining workers, or some signs of upward pressure on wages. The unemployment rate, at 4.1 percent, had remained near the lowest level seen in the past 20 years. It was noted that other labor market indicators—such as the U-6 measure of unemployment or the share of involuntary part-time employment—had returned to their pre-recession levels. A few participants judged that while the labor market was close to full employment, some margins of slack remained; these participants pointed to the employment-to-population ratio or the labor force participation rate for prime-age workers, which remained below pre-recession levels, as well as the absence to date of clear signs of a pickup in aggregate wage growth.

During their discussion of labor market conditions, participants expressed a range of views about recent wage developments. While some participants heard more reports of wage pressures from their business contacts over the intermeeting period, participants generally noted few signs of a broad-based pickup in wage growth in available data. With regard to how firms might use part of their tax savings to boost compensation, a few participants suggested that such a boost could be in the form of onetime bonuses or variable pay rather than a permanent increase in wage structures. It was noted that the pace of wage gains might not increase appreciably if productivity growth remains low. That said, a number of participants judged that the continued tightening in labor markets was likely to translate into faster wage increases at some point.[33]

By the January 30, 2019, FOMC meeting participants had changed their minds.

> In light of global economic and financial developments and muted inflation pressures, the Committee will be *patient* [italics mine] as it determines what future adjustments to the target range for the federal funds rate may be appropriate to support these outcomes.[34]

Something has changed when there is no wage growth when the unemployment rate is so low. Wage growth is the thermometer of the labor market; it tells you if and when it is running hot. At the time of writing, around the world benign wage growth suggests that labor markets are only running lukewarm.

Long-Term Unemployment Has the Same Impact on Wages as Short-Term Unemployment

Adam Posen and I (2014) also examined the impact of long-term unemployment in the United States in a series of hourly and weekly wage equations using data from the Current Population Survey pooled across state and year cells, for the period 1990–2013. We found no evidence that long-term unemployment had a smaller wage-reducing effect than short-term unemployment. In a recent paper, Kiley considered this issue using the Consumer Price Index (CPI) in each metropolitan area by year. Kiley concluded that "long-term unemployment has exerted similar downward pressure on inflation to that exerted by short-term unemployment in recent decades" (2014, 15).

Alan Krueger (2015) argued that the long-term unemployed (LTU) in the United States in essence aren't there as they have effectively withdrawn from job search. Hence, wage growth was set to explode, which, as we know, it didn't. If the LTU have no impact on wage pressure, and thus can safely be ignored, that would lower the effective unemployment rate even further. The prediction would then be that wage growth would be higher for any given unemployment rate. For example, if the unemployment rate was 6 percent and a third were LTU, if the theory was right, then a third of the unemployment rate can be discounted, meaning effectively the unemployment rate was 4 percent, implying higher wage growth.

Krueger's claims were countered in a series of papers from within the Federal Reserve System, which suggested there is no consistent evidence for the United States that the long-term unemployed have a different impact on wages than the short-term unemployed.[35] Or anywhere else for that matter.

I should note that this issue isn't new, as there was a major debate on exactly this point in Europe in the 1980s and 1990s, which did have lots of long-term unemployment while the United States did not. Layard and Nickell (1987), for example, argued that the long-term unemployed imposed much less wage pressure than the short-term unemployed. They found evidence that a long-term unemployment term, defined as the number of those who had been unemployed expressed as a proportion of total unemployment, had less of an impact on wages than short-term unemployment.

Using microdata for the United Kingdom, Oswald and I (1990) showed that this was not the case in the UK and that long-term unemployment did not play an independent role in wage determination. The problem was that high long-term unemployment is highly correlated with high unemployment. We concluded that "the British evidence does not support the view that long-term unemployment is an important element in the wage determination process" (1990, 232). That conclusion appears to apply everywhere; the long-term unemployed appear to have statistically identical impacts on wages as the short-term unemployed.

If the long-term unemployed don't count and all that matters are the short-term unemployed, there should be lots of wage pressure because the effective unemployment rate should be smaller. Long-term unemployment in the United States has continued to decline rapidly without an obvious surge in wage growth.

Work/Life Balance

Maybe things are much better than the data suggest, and people are really doing OK because they have more stuff. My colleague Bruce Sacerdote (2017) has argued that the finding of very little real wage growth since the 1970s for the United States is driven in part by the choice of the Consumer Price Index for All Urban Consumers (CPI-U) as the deflator. A similar argument could be made for other countries such as the UK, of course. Bruce notes that the number of cars per household with below median income has doubled since 1980 and the number of bedrooms per household has grown 10 percent despite decreases in household size. Plus, median square footage in these families' homes has risen about 8 percent. In 1960, 35 percent of households below the 25th percentile of household income did not have indoor plumbing. By 1970 this measure of deprivation shrank to 12 percent, and by 2015 virtually all households at all income groupings had indoor plumbing. Bruce shows that using a different deflator such as the Personal Consumption Expenditures (PCE) index yields modest growth in real wages and in median household incomes throughout the time period. PCE-adjusted wages according to his calculations grew 0.5 percent per year during 1975–2015 while other adjustments grew even more. Maybe.

Sacerdote argues there are at least four important explanations as to why Americans feel worse off even though consumption is actually rising. First, he argues, he is examining consumption within very large sections of the income distribution and there may be specific groups (e.g., men with less than a high school education) for whom consumption is actually falling. Second, it's possible, he argues, that the quality of some services such as public education or health care could be falling for some groups. Third, the rise in income inequality coupled with increased information flow about other people's consumption may be making Americans feel worse off in a relative sense even if their material goods consumption is rising. Fourth, changes in family structure (e.g., the rise of single-parent households), increases in the prison population, or increases in substance addiction could make people worse off even in the face of rising material wealth. A further factor is likely to be that men's real earnings growth is well below that of women.

If Sacerdote is right, then we probably should not see the discontent that is in the air. Despite the rise in the amount of stuff people have, the work/life balance appears to have been negatively impacted. It isn't just about what you have. Bianchi (2010) has pointed out that time-diary evidence suggests that work/life conflicts lead to a reduction in time spouses spend together and the time people have for themselves. Working mothers in particular give up leisure and sleep, compared to mothers not in the labor force, to meet the demands of childcare and jobs. Longer working hours mean higher income but not necessarily greater happiness. The OECD (2016b) has also noted that children of poor families often lack the opportunity to do better than their parents because they do not have access to high-quality schools and tend to drop out of college. For those lacking skills demanded by employers, the OECD suggests, vocational training and continuing education have had mixed results.

Americans have a poor work/life balance and it is worsening. I examined data from two sweeps of the International Social Survey Programme (ISSP) on "Family and Changing Gender Roles" in 2002 and 2012. The question I looked at was: "How often . . . during the past three months . . . [have you been] too tired from work to do duties at home—several times a week; several times a month; once or twice a year; or never?" The proportions saying several times a week were as follows.

	2002	2012
Australia	17%	20%
France	21%	21%
Germany	16%	19%
Great Britain	24%	24%
United States	29%	33%

The proportion saying several times a week was highest in America in both years and the gap against other countries is rising over time. Americans are tired.

Obviously dividing through with a smaller denominator will raise real wage growth. But poverty is relative. If everything is so great, why is happiness falling in the United States? The concern also is that hedonic adjustments for quality matter less at the lower part of the distribution, where basic necessities form a larger part of the budget than they do higher up the distribution.

A recent Pew Research Center survey of adults employed full- or part-time with children under 18 found that half of respondents have difficulties balancing work and family life (Parker and Wang 2013). A 2013 survey by Workplace Options shows that 41 percent of Americans wished they had more boundary between work and family, 36 percent feel uncomfortable taking a few days off, 41 percent would feel uncomfortable taking off a full week of work, and 61 percent feel uncomfortable taking off more than a full week. Forty-eight percent said they had missed out on family obligations due to work constraints.[36]

The General Social Survey has asked U.S. workers every two years since 2000, "If you were to get enough money to live as comfortably as you would like for the rest of your life, would you continue to work or would you stop working?" In other words, if you won the lottery would you quit your job? Seventy percent of Americans reported that they would continue to work. In fact the proportion answering this way varied little by year even as the recession hit: 2000 = 67%; 2002 = 69%; 2004 = 70%; 2006 = 69%; 2008 = 72%; 2010 = 70%; 2012 = 70%; 2014 = 68%; and 2016 = 71%.[37]

Sawhill and Pulliam have also noted that Americans in particular value work. Data from the Pew Research Center's Global Attitudes survey of 2014 shows that 73 percent of Americans think that hard work is very important for getting ahead. In comparison, other advanced countries, such as Germany (49%), Israel (30%), Japan (42%), the UK (60%), and France (25%), have a much lower percentage of people who think hard work is very important for getting ahead.[38]

Some of the story is that much of the rise in consumption has been debt fueled. Garriga, Noeth, and Schlagenhauf (2017) calculated that in the early post–World War II years, credit was not widely used, and the debt-to-income ratio was around 31 percent; in 2000 it was 81 percent. During the housing boom of the early 2000s, the debt-to-income ratio increased significantly, growing approximately 50 percentage points between 1990 and 2008. At the peak of the boom, household debt—which includes mortgages, automobile loans, unsecured debt (e.g., credit cards), and student loans—was around 1.2 times larger than personal income (or slightly higher if one considers disposable income). The Great Recession curtailed the growth of credit and household debt. As a result, household debt has declined since 2008 and once again fell below 100 percent after 2010.

Hacker (2008) suggests the "decline of the American dream" may very well turn out to be closely related to people's sense of insecurity and their awareness of being in a precarious situation. Hacker and coauthors (2014) combined data from multiple surveys and created an integrated measure of volatility in available household resources, accounting for fluctuations in income and out-of-pocket medical expenses, as well as financial wealth sufficient to buffer against these shocks. They found that insecurity—the share of individuals experiencing substantial resource declines without adequate financial buffers—has risen steadily since the mid-1980s for virtually all subgroups of Americans.

Of particular concern is their finding that individuals with the least education were impacted the most. The differences are large: on average, 26 percent of Americans in households headed by someone lacking a high school degree suffered a major economic loss each year between 2008 and 2010, compared to 16 percent of those in households headed by someone with post-college education using data from the Current Population Survey. For the period 1985–96, 20 percent of those with less than a high school education suffered a major economic loss versus 12 percent of those with post-college education. For 1997–2007 the estimates were 23 and 14 percent, respectively.

Four in ten U.S. adults were unable to meet an emergency expense in 2017 without borrowing from a friend or carrying a credit card balance, a Federal Reserve survey found.[39] The annual Survey of Household Economics and Decision Making, released in May 2018, found that 2 in 5 adults faced what the Fed judged to be a "high likelihood of material hardship," such as an inability to afford sufficient food, medical treatment, housing, or utilities. About 4 in 10 said they could not meet an unexpected expense of $400 without carrying a credit card balance or borrowing from a friend. Even without an unexpected expense, 22 percent of adults anticipated forgoing payment on some of their bills in the month of the survey. Most frequently, this involves not paying, or making a partial payment on, a credit card bill. In the government shutdown of 2018–19 it was shocking to see how many federal workers who were not being paid lined up for food.

Respondents were also asked if they had savings sufficient to cover three months of expenses if they lost their job. Half of the people in the Fed survey had set aside dedicated emergency savings of this level. Another one-fifth said that they could cover three months of expenses by borrowing or selling assets. In total, 7 in 10 adults could tap into savings or borrow in a financial setback of this magnitude. Tellingly, 3 in 10 could not.

As Pedro Nicolaci da Costa of *Business Insider* noted in the spring of 2018, if things were truly as rosy as the Fed's overall outlook suggests, "there's no way so many millions of families would feel as precariously as the central bank's own survey indicates."[40] Up to the start of 2019 the Fed was on a rate-raising path as they, wrongly in my view, claimed the U.S. labor market was at full employment. In the minutes of the May 2018 FOMC meeting it was stated that participants "noted a number of economic fundamentals were currently supporting continued above-trend economic growth; these included a strong labor market, federal tax and spending policies, high levels of household and business confidence, favorable financial conditions, and strong economic growth abroad."[41]

Da Costa noted that the Fed's own Community Advisory Council (CAC) in May warned that policymakers "should pay attention to the labor force participation rate, rates of involuntary part-time employment, labor share of income, and persistent wage stagnation to see how much room remains for the economy to grow." The report added that "when the Federal Reserve chooses to raise interest rates, among the other results is higher unemployment levels and preservation of racial inequities in employment. There should be a very high standard with respect to raising interest rates for fear of inflation since the consequences are dire for the most vulnerable in our society."[42] The CAC's conclusion is especially interesting: "A recurring theme in this section on labor markets, witnessed by every single Council member in their own communities, is the divergence between aggregate economic indicators, which highlight tight labor market conditions, and the actual experiences of individual populations—particularly rural, African American, Latino, and Native American populations."[43]

In May 2017 a Eurobarometer survey (#87.3) was taken in every EU country, which asked respondents, "How would you judge the financial situation of your family?" Possible responses were very good; rather good; rather bad; and very bad. Overall 32 percent of respondents and 25 percent of workers said their finances were rather bad or very bad. The estimates by country for workers were France, 28 percent; Germany, 15 percent; Italy, 37 percent; Greece, 71 percent; Spain, 37 percent; and the UK, 16 percent.

Respondents in the same survey were also asked, "To what extent do you agree or disagree with [the following statement?] Overall, regarding your quality of life—it was better before?" Options were as follows: totally agree; tend to agree; tend to disagree; and totally disagree. Below I report the proportion that said they "totally agree" or "tend to agree."[44]

	Overall	Workers
France	60	57
Belgium	60	55
Netherlands	24	20
Germany	35	36
Italy	79	75

	Overall	Workers
Luxembourg	49	44
Denmark	28	23
Ireland	56	55
UK	55	51
Greece	94	94
Spain	67	66
Portugal	70	69
Finland	34	28
Sweden	30	24
Austria	58	53

In several countries—Austria, Belgium, France, Italy, Ireland, Spain, Greece, Portugal, and the UK—the majority, including the majority of workers, report that life had been better "before." In 1957 UK prime minister Harold Macmillan famously said, "You have never had it so good." Not today.

Periods of economic instability often lead to greater work pressures and an increased sense of job insecurity, exacerbating conflicts between work and family life. There is evidence that this rise in economic insecurity has had negative consequences on people's well-being in diverse ways.[45] Increased obesity,[46] rising suicide rates,[47] a deterioration of mental health,[48] and long-lasting serious deficits in child and youth development[49] have all been attributed, at least in part, to the devastating impact of increased economic insecurity.

The question is, why has this happened? Why has wage growth been so weak? Why do people feel so insecure? That is what I turn to next.

CHAPTER 4

The Semi-Slump and the Housing Market

Why has wage growth been so weak? The simple answer is labor demand has been too low. At the time of writing it is eleven years since the United States entered recession in December 2007. It took until December 2008, a year after the recession started, for the National Bureau of Economic Research Business Cycle Dating Committee, which maintains a chronology of the U.S. business cycle, to work that out.[1] In September 2010 they concluded that the recession had ended in June 2009. In most other advanced countries, including the UK, France, Japan, and Italy, it started a few months later, around the second quarter of 2008. Almost all of the major advanced countries had two successive quarters of negative growth in 2008, which meets the usual definition of recession. For many of them it took a long time for the recession to end, measured by restoring lost output. In 2018 in the United States, the proportion of the population that was employed had still not returned to pre-recession levels.

If we simply use the more mechanical rule (because other countries don't have recession dating committees) that entering recession implies two successive negative quarters, then twenty-nine of thirty-five OECD countries entered recession in the period 2008 Q1 to 2009 Q1: Austria, Belgium, Canada, Czech Republic, Chile, Denmark, Estonia, Finland, France, Germany, Greece, Hungary, Iceland, Ireland, Italy, Japan, Latvia, Luxembourg, Mexico, Netherlands, New Zealand, Portugal, Slovenia, Spain, Sweden,

Switzerland, Turkey, the UK, and the United States. Norway had negative growth in the second and fourth quarters of 2008. Australia, Israel, and Poland only had negative growth in 2008 Q4. Korea had negative growth in 2008 Q4, of 3.34 percent in that quarter alone! The Slovak Republic had an astonishing 9 percent drop in output in 2009 Q1. The economic collapse was widespread.

There has been a lost decade since in the West. In 1931 John Maynard Keynes had warned of the "long, dragging conditions of semi-slump," directly after the Great Crash of 1929 at the onset of the Great Depression.

> For it is a possibility that the duration of the slump may be much more prolonged than most people are expecting, and much will be changed both in our ideas and in our methods before we emerge. Not, of course, the duration of the acute phase of the slump, but that of the long, dragging conditions of semi-slump, or at least sub-normal prosperity, which may be expected to succeed the acute phase. No more than a possibility, however. For I believe that our destiny is in our own hands and that we can emerge from it if only we choose—or rather if those choose who are in authority in the world. (3–4)

That quote sends shivers down my spine every time I read it. Ten years in we still haven't emerged from the long, dragging conditions of semi-slump.

I warned this was likely coming to advanced countries if policymakers didn't act in a couple of articles I published in the *Guardian*.

In a 2009 article I argued that if we are to avoid the long, dragging conditions of semi-slump, "public spending cuts make absolutely no sense. The government should be increasing spending now—and by a lot—not least because it can borrow at such a low long-run rate of interest. In such circumstances, infrastructure and education are smart investments for all our futures. Most of the self-proclaimed experts calling for public spending cuts missed the recession in the first place."[2]

In a 2011 article I reasoned as follows: "Even though we have now moved from the acute phase of the Great Recession, which occurred in the fall of 2008, the long, dragging conditions of semi-slump and sub-normal prosperity have arrived—and they aren't going away any time soon, as Keynes warned. The whole idea of an expansionary fiscal contraction was always fanciful in the extreme; now, it's time for a change of course—given that

austerity has failed. Growth is going to be low for many years, living standards are not going to rise, and the high levels of income inequality are all
likely to contribute to increasing levels of social unrest. Much, indeed, will
need to be changed."[3]

The *Guardian* editorial board in September 2009 even got in on the act
but nobody much was listening. It argued that "a year on from the collapse
of US investment bank Lehman Brothers and the height of the banking
crisis, it does look as if the economy has avoided a rerun of the Great Depression—but it does not follow that from here on the UK is in for either a
constant or a strong recovery. . . . The probable outlook for the UK economy
in 2009 is the same as described by Keynes in 1930: we are in for 'the long,
dragging conditions of semi-slump, or at least sub-normal prosperity.' "[4]
They were right.

Unsurprisingly, the recoveries that ensued after the Great Recession were
slow and feeble. Countries entered an extended semi-slump, of subnormal
prosperity, that a decade later still continues.

The response around the world after a burst of monetary and fiscal policy
easing was to revert to austerity—that is, to raise taxes and reduce spending,
which meant that monetary and fiscal policy were fighting one another. The
claim was that growth would come if the public sector got out of the way.
According to that theory public spending was supposed to crowd out private
spending, causing "contractionary fiscal expansion," so the thinking went. It
turned out that public spending crowded *in* private spending and austerity
resulted in a contractionary fiscal contraction; it didn't crowd it out, so one
down all down. Keynes would not have been shocked.

Lord Skidelsky, who is Keynes's biographer, made clear in a speech in the
House of Lords in 2018 what had gone wrong: "The economics of the matter
is straightforward. If the private sector reduces its own spending, government
has to increase its spending to plug the gap. If it cuts its own spending as
well, it deepens and prolongs the Recession. The only counter-argument is
that austerity was needed to give confidence to 'the markets.' But the evidence is clear that any confidence boosting effect of cutting spending on the
poor was overwhelmed by its depressive effect on total spending."[5]

It took longer for the UK to restore output than had been the case in any
recession in the previous three hundred years. The UK experienced negative
GDP growth in each of the five quarters from 2008 Q2 through 2009 Q2
of –0.7, –1.6, –2.2, –1.6, and –0.2 percent, so output fell by 6.3 percent. It

took sixteen quarters for output to be restored, that is, until 2013 Q2. The United States also had five quarters of negative growth from 2008 Q1 through 2009 Q2, with a quarter of positive growth in 2008 Q2: –0.7, +0.5, –0.5, –2.1, –1.4, and –0.1 percent, making a drop of 4.3 percent. This took eight quarters—to 2011 Q2—to be restored.

The UK's recovery was the third-slowest peacetime recovery in six hundred years. The South Sea Bubble, which was a speculation mania that ruined many British investors in 1720 when the South Sea Company collapsed, was the next slowest. The Black Death, from 1347 to 1351, which resulted in the deaths of more than 75 million, was the slowest. It was good for productivity, though. Recovery from the Great Recession was even slower than it was from the year without a summer, which occurred in 1816. Severe climate abnormalities caused global temperatures to drop, resulting in major food shortages. These weather conditions appear to have been caused by a huge volcanic eruption in 1815 by Mount Tambora, in the Dutch East Indies, which was the largest eruption in 1,300 years. Policymakers didn't learn the lessons of history and down we all went. It was as bad as that.

In the United States growth recovered more quickly after the Great Recession, but the employment rate of 60.7 percent in January 2019 was still well below its pre-recession level of 63.3 percent in March 2007, or the 64.7 percent found in March 2004. So, employment has still not recovered. It has numerically, because the population has risen, but not when the population is used as the denominator.

Table 4.1 shows the decline in GDP in the five quarters from 2008 Q2 to 2009 Q2 across the OECD. It also reports cumulative growth over the 41 quarters from 2008 Q2 to 2018 Q2 and the prior 41 quarters from 1998 Q1 to 2008 Q1.[6] The final column reports the most recent quarterly growth rates available for 2018 Q3. Every country except Australia, Poland, and Israel had a fall in output over the five quarters of recession. The United States was less hard hit than many, dropping 3.4 percent, with Canada down 3.4 percent and France 4 percent. This contrasts with 6–7 percent drops in Sweden, Germany, Mexico, Japan, Iceland, Ireland, and the UK.

It is apparent that recent growth has been worse than in the earlier period, by a factor of around two in the United States, Sweden, and Japan, and three in the UK, Iceland, the Netherlands, Denmark, and France. Italy and Greece experienced negative growth in the later period. Data for 2018 Q2 show

Table 4.1. Cumulative GDP Growth, 1998–2018 (%)

	2008 Q2– 2009 Q2	2008 Q2– 2018 Q2	1998 Q1– 2008 Q1	2018 Q3
Australia	2.1	26	36	0.3
Austria	−5.4	10	27	0.3
Belgium	−3.7	9	24	0.3
Canada	−3.4	18	30	0.5
Chile	−2.9	30	41	0.3
Czech Republic	−4.9	16	40	0.6
Denmark	−7.2	6	21	0.7
Estonia	−15.5	15	58	0.4
Finland	−9.9	1	36	0.3
France	−4.0	8	24	0.4
Germany	−7.0	12	17	−0.2
Greece	−4.1	−28	37	1.0
Hungary	−7.2	14	37	1.3
Iceland	−7.2	18	54	0.0
Ireland	−6.9	52	59	2.5*
Israel	0.6	36	39	0.6
Italy	−8.2	−5	14	−0.1
Japan	−6.8	6	11	0.3
Korea	−0.4	30	50	0.6
Latvia	−18.1	5	72	1.7
Lithuania	−15.6	15	64	−0.3
Luxembourg	−8.0	19	49	0.0*
Mexico	−7.0	22	24	0.8
Netherlands	−3.9	9	27	0.2
New Zealand	−2.5	23	35	1.0
Norway	−1.5	13	23	0.6
Poland	1.9	33	44	1.7
Portugal	−4.3	0	20	0.3
Slovak Republic	−4.1	24	52	1.1
Slovenia	−8.7	7	45	0.8
Spain	−4.3	3	38	0.6
Sweden	−6.2	17	32	−0.2
Switzerland	−2.7	15	25	−0.2
Turkey	−11.2	48	46	0.9
United Kingdom	−6.4	10	29	0.6
United States	−3.4	17	29	0.9

* = 2018 Q3.

Source: OECD data: https://data.oecd.org/gdp/quarterly-gdp.htm#indicator-chart; Eurostat data: https://ec.europa.eu/eurostat/documents/2995521/9437650/2-07122018-AP-EN.pdf/eadec005-b37c-42e2-a8e7-a8bfc2e74f1d.

every country growing, but in 2018 Q3, Germany, Italy, Lithuania, Sweden, and Switzerland now have negative growth.

Recoveries do not die of old age. The recovery in the United States became the second longest ever at 107 months in May 2018. It will become the longest ever in June 2019 at 120 months. Recoveries in the past have died because the Federal Reserve in the United States raised rates too soon and/or the oil price rose. The Fed cut rates to 0.25 percent in December 2008, which was the lowest Fed funds rate they believed was achievable, although other central banks including the European Central Bank (ECB) and the Bank of Japan (BOJ) have subsequently gone negative. The Monetary Policy Committee at the Bank of England cut the bank rate down to 0.25 percent. At the time of writing the Fed had raised rates seven times: in December 2015 to 0.5 percent; December 2016 to 0.75 percent; March 2017 to 1 percent; June 2017 to 1.25 percent; December 2017 to 1.5 percent; March 2018 to 1.75 percent; and for the seventh time since 2014 to 2 percent in June 2018. The Fed had been signaling more rises to come; President Trump turned his ire toward them, and they changed their tune in 2019. I have to say I agree with him.

The fall in output around the world appears to have shaken up the labor market in general and wage growth in particular in unprecedented ways. The long, dragging conditions of semi-slump, of subnormal prosperity, are continuing. The question is, why?

Why Did the Long, Dragging Conditions of Semi-Slump Happen?

There is a wide set of possible causes. How they have interacted with the recession is critical to an understanding of the fall in wage growth from 2008 onward. For example, the increase in self-employment in the UK has been associated with greater labor market flexibility, but the increasing share of the self-employed in the UK workforce has been on a steady upward trend during the first two decades of this century. This trend was not affected by the recession. Therefore, unless there was a marked change in the nature, rather than the volume, of self-employment around the time of the recession, it is difficult to link the sudden drop in wage settlements to the evolution of self-employment. The gig economy is a phenomenon that has been developing for a couple of decades at least. In addition, union representation in the private sector in advanced countries has been declining steadily for decades.

The main reason that real wages haven't risen is presumably that labor productivity has also been flat. There are obviously a number of deep factors driving the labor productivity puzzle, but we have to accept that real wages and labor productivity are closely linked. In addition, the labor share has been remarkably stable in this period. The nominal part of the wage story is presumably connected to the attainment of price stability. We simply do not expect price inflation to hit 10 percent anymore, and this may partly explain why a pay norm seems to have been anchored around 2 percent for several years around the world.

In reality, the high level of labor market slack and the weakness of worker bargaining power are keeping pay and price inflation down. Full employment is a long way off. If it were anywhere close, wage growth would be back to pre-recession levels of 4 percent or even higher.

There is some evidence that migration flows and potential migration flows keep wage growth in check. In the UK, if wages were to rise, more East Europeans and especially Poles would, legally, show up, containing that wage pressure. Similarly, in the United States, with increased flows of illegals across the southern border.

Jens Weidmann, president of the Bundesbank, the German central bank, has argued that "migration from other EU member states partially accounts for damped wage pressures in Germany."[7] Chris Shadforth and I (2009) examined the influx from Eastern Europe into the UK when it opened its borders in 2004. We concluded that "the inflow of workers from Eastern Europe has tended to increase supply by more than it has increased demand in the UK, and thereby acted to reduce inflationary pressures and reduce the natural or equilibrium rate of unemployment over the past few years" (F136). Migration flows are one way in which the forces of globalization keep a lid on wage pressure.

The onset of recession in 2007 and 2008 resulted in a rise in the unemployment rate. The Great Recession started in the U.S. housing market in 2005 and 2006 and spread like a pandemic. Countries that experienced the biggest increases in unemployment

- had large financial sectors (UK and United States);
- had major rises and subsequent collapses in house prices (UK, United States, Ireland, and Spain);

- did not have their own central banks and currencies (France, Italy, Spain, Greece);
- had limits on the mobility of labor especially in the housing market (Greece and Spain had the highest levels of homeownership rates and the highest unemployment rates in Europe, while Germany and Switzerland had the lowest homeownership rates and the lowest unemployment rates); and
- did not have fully functioning capital, product, and/or housing markets (Spain, Italy, and Greece).[8]

Mobility mattered. As we will discuss, a very high proportion of young adults in countries with high youth unemployment rates still lived with their parents even into their late twenties, especially in Greece, Spain, and Italy. The housing market controls, including rent controls, prevented youngsters from striking out on their own. It was easier to go abroad than to move across town. The proportion of youngsters living with their parents and not striking out on their own to form households increased sharply around the world including in the United States after the Great Recession.

The conventional explanation of the causes of unemployment did not predict this. The claim, made in the OECD Jobs Study (1994) and by Layard, Nickell, and Jackman (1991), for example, was that labor market inflexibility was the big problem, driven by overly generous unemployment benefits, job protection, and trade union practices. Despite the received wisdom, high unemployment does not seem to be primarily the result of job protection, labor taxes, trade union power, or wage inflexibility.[9] This was all wrong and nothing has been heard of those who argued that the labor markets were the crux of all evil. Countries with flexible labor markets like the UK and the United States were hit hardest. Those with protective labor market institutions like Germany and Austria did best.

The ILO, for example, argued rightly even before the onset of recession as follows: "Labour market rigidities have not been an underlying cause of past labour market performance. Labour market performance has deteriorated since the first oil shock irrespective of differences in labour market regulation, suggesting that a more fundamental common factor (or factors) has been at work" (1995, 20).

Contrary to what many have claimed, labor market institutions do not tend to cause unemployment. The major exception is changes in the replacement rate, which, in some specifications, do appear to be negatively correlated with changes in the unemployment rate. Blanchard and Wolfers, for example, argued that "one can indeed give a good account of the evolution of unemployment across countries and times by relying on observable shocks and interactions with labour market institutions" (2000, 31). It turns out this result told us nothing whatsoever about what was going to happen in the Great Recession.

Howell and coauthors econometrically examined the impact of these labor market rigidity variables, or what they call Protective Labor Market Institutions (PLMIs), and concluded that "while significant impacts for employment protection, benefit generosity, and union strength have been reported, the clear conclusion from our review of these studies is that the effects for the PLMIs is distinctly unrobust" (2007, 58).

Indeed, in his published comments on the Howell et al. article, Economics Nobel Laureate Jim Heckman argues that the authors "are convincing in showing the fragility of the evidence on the role of labor market institutions in explaining the pattern of European unemployment, using standard econometric methodology" (2007, 1). Richard Freeman also finds the evidence for the impact of these institutional variables less than convincing: "Despite considerable effort, researchers have not pinned down the effects, if any, of institutions on other aggregate economic outcomes, such as unemployment and employment" (2007, 20).

What the researchers missed was that mobility mattered. The housing market is central. It turns out that a major part of how low unemployment can go is likely driven by labor market mobility—that is, how easy it is to move around the country. It is notable in the United States that the proportion of people who move locations—within or across states—has halved in the last fifty years as homeownership rates have risen. Immigrant flows, especially when the workers are skilled, turn out to grease the wheels of the labor market. This is what happened in the UK when it began to allow entry of workers from Eastern Europe in 2004. Several million showed up, principally from Poland, and they were free to move around the country and that is exactly what they did—they went to where workers were needed.

My limo driver taking me to a TV studio in Naples, Florida, one day told me he moved to southwest Florida in 2007 and can't move even if he wanted

Table 4.2. Annual U.S. Geographical Mobility Rates, by Type of Movement, 1950–2016 (%)

	Total movers	Same county	Different county	Different state	Abroad
2016–17	11.0	6.8	2.1	1.7	0.4
2015–16	11.2	6.9	2.4	1.5	0.4
2008–9	12.5	8.4	2.1	1.6	0.4
1980–81	17.2	10.4	3.4	2.8	0.6
1950–51	21.2	13.9	3.6	3.5	0.2

Source: U.S. Census Bureau, https://www.census.gov/data/tables/time-series/demo/geographic-mobility /historic.html.

to because the value of his house has fallen dramatically and is still well below the size of his mortgage. He is stuck.

Table 4.2 shows the big decline in mobility in the United States. In part this has to do with having negative equity. The table shows that the proportion of adults who move in any one year has essentially halved since 1950. This is true for movements within the same county, between counties in the same state, and to different states. Indeed, on November 16, 2016, the U.S. Census Bureau reported that the percentage of Americans moving over a one-year period fell to an all-time low of 11.2 percent in 2016.[10] Among those who moved, 42 percent said they moved for a housing-related reason, such as wanting a new or better home/apartment. In comparison, 27 percent said they moved for a family-related reason, 20 percent said they moved for an employment-related reason, and 10.2 percent said they moved for some other reason.

Mobility works. Another excellent example of looking at how the real-world works and the value of moving is a study by Raj Chetty, Nathan Hendren, and Larry Katz (2016), who examined the workings of the Moving to Opportunity (MTO) experiment, which offered randomly selected families housing vouchers to move from high-poverty housing projects to lower-poverty neighborhoods. They analyze MTO's impacts on children's long-term outcomes using tax data. They found that moving to a lower-poverty neighborhood when young (before age 13) increases college attendance and earnings and reduces single parenthood rates. Moving as an adolescent had slightly negative impacts, perhaps because of disruption effects. The decline in the gains from moving as children get older, they argue, suggests that the duration of exposure to better environments during childhood is an important determinant of children's long-term outcomes.

High Homeownership Rates Have Bad Consequences

The housing market appears to be central. A rising homeownership rate reduced the rate of mobility in the years before the Great Recession. The decreased mobility of homeowners has been widely reported in the literature.[11] As Beugnot and coauthors note (2014), less mobility inhibits search strategies and may translate into poor matching between workers and jobs. Lower mobility, they suggest, may translate into homeowners earning lower wages. My research shows that homeownership is bad for job growth and increases unemployment.[12] High homeownership rates often involve NIMBY rules, which make it hard for firms to set up in an area, which reduces job growth and raises unemployment. I recall being on a TV debate with former New Hampshire governor and senator Judd Gregg, who was not impressed with this result, declaring that "this theory was un-American." I tried to explain I was just reporting what the data showed.

The Germans have low homeownership and low unemployment rates. They also commute long distances cheaply and quickly. Oswald and I (2013) found evidence consistent with the view that the housing market plays a fundamental role as a determinant of the rate of unemployment. The findings may go some way toward explaining why nations like Spain (78 percent homeownership rate and 20 percent unemployment rate), Greece (75 and 24 percent, respectively), Switzerland (43 and 5 percent, respectively), and Germany (52 and 4 percent, respectively) in 2016 had such different mixtures of homeownership and joblessness. Figure 4.1, which uses Eurostat data, shows that there is a strong positive correlation across European countries between their homeownership rates and the latest unemployment rates. The two data points at the top are Greece and Spain and the two at the bottom left are Germany and Switzerland.

Using data on two million randomly sampled Americans, Andrew Oswald and I (2013) modeled unemployment, employment, the number of weeks worked, the extent of labor mobility, the length of commuting times, and the number of businesses and found they were all impacted by homeownership rates. We came to several conclusions. We document a strong statistical link between high levels of homeownership in a geographical area and later high levels of joblessness in that area. We show that this result is robust across subperiods going back to the 1980s. The lags from ownership levels to unemployment levels are long; they can take up to five years to be

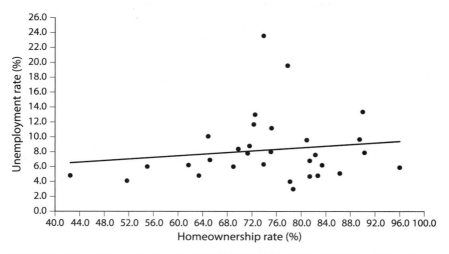

Figure 4.1. Unemployment rate and the homeownership rate in 29 EU countries plus Switzerland and Iceland, 2016. *Source:* Eurostat, https://ec.europa.eu/eurostat/statis tics-explained/index.php/Housing_statistics#Tenure_status.

evident. This suggests that high homeownership may gradually interfere with the efficient functioning of a labor market.

We find that rises in the homeownership rate in a U.S. state are a precursor to eventual sharp rises in unemployment in that state. A doubling of the rate of homeownership in a U.S. state is followed in the long run by more than a doubling of the later unemployment rate. We have experimented a lot to find other variables that explain unemployment at the state level and it is a struggle. We have found some evidence that the level of out-of-work benefits matters, but we do not find that unionization rates have any impact. It is hard to find any other competing variables to explain movements in unemployment rates across U.S. states or countries.

Green and Hendershott (2001) examine state-level U.S. data on home-ownership and unemployment between 1970 and 1990 and find similarly sized effects. Interestingly, they find the relationship doesn't exist for young and old households but does for middle-aged ones. Young households, they suggest, have accumulated little wealth and have had less time to become attached to the geographical area than middle-aged households and thus are more likely to respond to unemployment by relocating. Older households' employment cannot be greatly affected by homeownership because their members are largely not in the labor force. Belot and van Ours (2001) also found, in a study of eighteen OECD countries, that a 10-percentage-point rise in the homeownership rate raised the unemployment rate by around 2 percentage points.

Andrew Oswald and I (2013) also showed that rises in homeownership rates lead to three problems: (1) lower levels of labor mobility, (2) greater commuting times, and (3) fewer new businesses. Our argument is not that owners themselves are disproportionately unemployed but that the housing market can impose negative "externalities" upon the labor market. The time lags are long, so the gradualness may explain why these important patterns are so little known.

It turns out that long commuting times make people especially unhappy. Kahneman and Krueger interviewed a sample of nine hundred working women in Texas and found that the activity that made them the least happy was the morning commute: "Commuting in the morning appears particularly unpleasant" (2006, 12). In contrast, the activity that made these women the most happy was "intimate relations."

Both within and across U.S. states, high homeownership areas have lower labor mobility. Importantly, this is not due merely to the personal characteristics of owners and renters. We are unable to say exactly why, or to give a complete explanation for the patterns that are found, but the results of my 2013 study with Andrew Oswald on homeownership are consistent with the unusual idea that the housing market can create dampening externalities upon the labor market and the economy. We also demonstrate that states with higher rates of homeownership have lower rates of business formation. This might be the result of zoning restrictions and NIMBY effects. In Lyme, a town close to where I live in New Hampshire, they passed an ordinance mandating that any new building lots had to be a minimum of 25 acres. People are smart; the effect of the ordinance was to raise the price of swamp land. Twenty-four acres of swamp and one acre of building land was just fine. Or five houses built close together on five acres and 120 acres of useless land next to a little cul-de-sac. They then called the giant swamp a nature preserve.

Oswald and I found that the lower the mobility rate (how many individuals moved residence in a particular year), the higher the homeownership rate and the higher the unemployment rate.[13] In addition, the higher the level of joblessness in a particular state, the more people are likely to move. The rate of movement in a state is nearly 18 percentage points lower in a place with double the homeownership rate of another area. These results are broadly consistent with an earlier study by Hämäläinen and Böckerman (2004), who find that net migration to a region of Finland appears to be depressed by a greater level of homeownership in that region.

We found evidence that states with higher rates of homeownership have longer commute times. This phenomenon is likely to reflect greater transportation congestion that goes with a less mobile workforce, and it will act to raise costs for employers and employees. The higher the homeownership rate in a state, the longer the average commuting time, which is consistent with the idea that moving for an owner-occupier is expensive and that as a result places with high homeownership will see more workers staying put physically but working further from their family home. Because roads, in particular, are semipublic goods in which individuals can create congestion problems for others, this pattern in the data is consistent with the existence of unpriced externalities. Homeownership likely unwittingly impairs the labor market by deterring people from moving in search of work, a process that is time-consuming and expensive; long commuting times might also discourage a householder from taking a particular job. This suggests that, without politicians being aware of it, high homeownership may slowly erode a country's industrial base.

The U.S. homeownership rate peaked in 2004 Q4 at 69 percent while the unemployment rate peaked in 2009 Q4 at 9.9 percent exactly five years later. In 2016 Q4 the homeownership rate had fallen to 63.7 percent, back to its level in 1990. Declining homeownership may have contributed to the rising malaise. The wave of foreclosures that occurred in the Great Recession caused a decrease in well-being. The American Dream meant you could own your own home, but it increased unemployment and lowered mobility.

Recent work by Hsieh and Moretti (2018) attempted to quantify the amount of spatial misallocation of labor across U.S. cities and its aggregate costs and showed they are enormous. Misallocation arises because high-productivity cities like New York and the San Francisco Bay Area have adopted stringent NIMBY restrictions to new housing supply, effectively limiting the number of workers who have access to such high productivity. Instead of increasing local employment, productivity growth in housing-constrained cities primarily pushes up housing prices and nominal wages. The resulting misallocation of workers lowers aggregate output and the welfare of workers in all U.S. cities. The authors found that these constraints lowered aggregate U.S. growth by more than 50 percent from 1964 to 2009. They conclude that "local land use regulations that restrict housing supply in dynamic labor markets have important externalities on the rest of the country. Incumbent homeowners in high productivity cities have a private incentive to restrict housing supply. By doing so, these voters de facto limit the number of US workers who have access to the most productive of American cities. In general equilibrium, this lowers income and welfare of all US workers" (2018, 3).

Negative equity may prevent people from moving because they are locked in. Moreover, even where there isn't negative equity it is perfectly possible that a lower credit score makes it hard for many individuals to obtain the mortgage they currently have on another property. Nationally, according to Zillow, five million homeowners, or 10.5 percent of those with a mortgage, were underwater at the end of 2016, down from 13.1 percent of homeowners a year earlier. More than 55 percent of homeowners in negative equity are more than 20 percent underwater.[14] Negative equity in 2016 was substantial in several rust-belt towns including East Stroudsburg, Pennsylvania (29%); Racine, Wisconsin (23%); Toledo, Ohio (14%); Battle Creek, Michigan (17%); and Scranton, Pennsylvania (17%).[15] Negative equity impacts mobility, making it hard, or even impossible, for people to move.

Chevalier and Lardeux (2017) found evidence of a positive correlation between the homeownership rate and the unemployment rate in France using the French census from 1968 to 2011. They found that a 10-percentage-point rise in local homeownership increased the unemployment rate by around 1 percentage point. They argue that part of the explanation is that spatial mismatch and workers' immobility reduce their access to information to new jobs, therefore limiting their ability to search for jobs and lowering the exit rate from unemployment.

Andrews and Sánchez (2011) have noted that homeownership rates have increased significantly in many OECD countries over recent decades. For example, Canada saw its homeownership rate rise from 61.3 percent in 1994 to 68.9 percent in 2004; and Austria, Belgium, Denmark, Italy, the Netherlands, and Spain all had increases from the early 1990s to the early 2000s. In contrast France, Luxembourg, and Australia all experienced decreases in the homeownership rate.

We now have data from Eurostat on the changes in homeownership rates since the Great Recession, and it seems the rises have reversed themselves, especially in the UK and Ireland, where there were major house-price collapses.[16] The main exception is France.

	2008	2016
Belgium	73.1%	71.3%
Denmark	66.5%	62.0%
Germany	53.3%*	51.7%
Ireland	77.3%	70.0%**
Greece	76.7%	73.9%
Spain	80.2%	77.8%
France	62.1%	64.9%
Italy	72.8%	72.3%
Sweden	68.8%	65.2%
United Kingdom	72.5%	63.4%
	* = 2005	** = 2015

A major story in the UK has been the arrival of 2.7 million East European workers, especially from Poland, since 2004, as well as another 900,000 from Bulgaria and Romania since 2014, who are free to move around the country. Flows of immigrants in other countries have also helped grease the wheels of the labor market. These newcomers are not as constrained by the housing market and family ties as the indigenous population; they have moved to where the work is and are highly mobile. Another example is the flow of illegal immigrants into the United States, which has slowed under the Trump administration; I will return to this issue. One concern about the slowing of the flow of foreign migrants is that it makes the labor market function less well, because the housing market restricts mobility as the mobile foreigners leave.

The characteristics of jobs have also changed with the march of technology, which has meant there has been a decline in manufacturing jobs in advanced countries. That isn't to say that the Luddites were right; technology has created many jobs too. But they are generally high-skilled ones. Manufacturing employment in the United States peaked at fourteen million jobs in April 2006, fell to a low of eleven million in March 2010, and rose to 12.8 million in January 2019. In addition, construction employment fell from a high of 7.5 million jobs in January 2007 to a low of 5.4 million in January 2011. It had picked back up to 7.5 million in January 2019. These industries supplied well-paying jobs principally to prime-age men without college degrees. Less-skilled manufacturing jobs moved to China and the Far East. Even if coal prices were to rise it is unclear that the number of jobs would increase at all because machines can do the work faster and more cheaply. There would be further substitutions of capital for labor.

It is my contention that the decrease in homeownership rates will eventually help improve mobility and lower the natural rate of unemployment. Lower homeownership rates are associated with lower unemployment rates ahead. Andrew Oswald and I (2013) found that high homeownership rates also lowered the participation rate.

Low Participation

The United States has had a lower participation rate after the Great Recession when other countries have not. Why? There is always the possibility that individuals who are not working and not unemployed, who are not members of the labor force, will change their minds and rejoin the labor force. The likelihood is that as the wages of available jobs rise, the attractiveness of those jobs increases. The most obvious example of that relates to young people who turn to education when job opportunities are not available. As labor market slack has fallen since 2009 the participation rates of prime-age and young workers have risen. At the same time the continuing upward trend of more labor force participation of those 55 and older has continued.

The very different post-recession trends in the United States versus those of other advanced countries can be shown in another way via the labor force participation rate (LFPR), or activity rate. The LFPR rose steadily from the end of World War II in the United States and elsewhere postwar as an increasing proportion of women joined the labor force. For example, the monthly LFPR in the United States for those of working age (16 and over) was 58.6 percent in January 1948, rising to 67.3 percent between February and April 2000. It fell slightly to 66.2 in January 2008 but declined sharply thereafter, falling to 62.7 percent in December 2014, only slightly below the 63.2 in the latest data for January 2019. The United States is different.

Most other OECD countries have seen LFPRs for men over the last decade or so remain roughly flat, as the table below illustrates. Canada's LFPR for women was flat whereas the other countries saw increases for women. The U.S. rates fell for both men and women. No other country had declines for either men or women.

	Men			Women	
	2007	2016		2007	2016
Canada	82	82		74	74
France	75	76		65	68
Germany	82	82		69	74
UK	83	84		70	73
United States	82	79		69	67

Source: OECD 2017, appendix table C.

In the United States, there has been an especially large increase in the number of people unable to work due to illness or disability, especially among prime-age men with less than a high school education.[17] In 2014, 14 percent of less-educated men ages 25–54 claimed they could not work because of either of these reasons; this rate was 12 percent in 2004. The corresponding percentages for less-educated women of the same age were lower and showed little change (12.8% and 12.7%, respectively). The number of people who reported being NILF because they were ill or disabled rose over this period by just under 4 million (+32%).

There is scant evidence of any pickup in the U.S. prime-age male rate of labor force participation. For women, LFPRs have risen in every country except the United States. Notable is the rise in the LFPR in Japan, which was targeted in Abenomics to get women back into the labor force.

Krueger has claimed that "the labor force participation rate has stopped rising for cohorts of women born after 1960"; but that doesn't seem to be right.[18] The latest data from the BLS suggest that isn't the case and show a rise for the younger two prime-age groups since the start of 2012. In the case of ages 25–34, the participation rate is now higher than it was at the start of the Great Recession.

Women age groups	25–34	35–44	45–54
January 2008	75.2	76.1	76.2
January 2012	73.9	74.9	75.2
September 2017	75.7	75.5	74.9
January 2019	76.7	75.3	75.9

For men there has been a recent increase in the participation rate for the two youngest age groups.

Men age groups	25–34	35–44	45–54
January 2008	91.7	91.7	89.7
January 2012	89.3	90.9	87.5
September 2017	88.9	90.8	87.8
January 2019	89.4	91.4	87.4

In a recent paper Yagan (2017) uses U.S. local areas as a laboratory to test whether the Great Recession depressed 2015 employment. He found that exposure to a 1-percentage-point larger 2007–9 local unemployment shock caused working-age individuals to be 0.4 percentage points less likely to be employed at all in 2015, evidently via labor force exit. These shocks, he found, also increased 2015 income inequality.

General human capital decay and persistently low labor demand, Yagan argues, each rationalize the findings better than lost job-specific rents, lost firm-specific human capital, or reduced migration. Simple extrapolation of the paper's local-shock-based estimate to the aggregate suggested that the Great Recession caused 76 percent of the 2007–15 age-adjusted decline in U.S. working-age employment. It is my contention that the labor market declines we have observed in the United States are mostly cyclical, not structural. A lagged homeownership rate enters negatively in a labor force participation rate equation.

In an article in the *New York Times* Ben Casselman wondered whether the scars Yagan identified will prove enduring. Maybe, but there is hope. Casselman interviewed Yagan, who said, "The signals say the recession is over, but employment's not back to normal. Recession effects aren't supposed to last this long."[19] That seems right. Larry Summers also commented helpfully on the article, saying it is "difficult to escape the conclusion that recessions now do permanent—or at least quasi-permanent—damage to the economy. That is, the recession may have been what pushed people out of the labor force, but recovery alone may not be enough to bring them back." That looks right, but it seems to me the non-participants are not lost forever and can come back if there are decent jobs available.

Table 4.3 presents data by each U.S. state on the employment rate in 2007 and 2016. With one exception, the District of Columbia, the former is higher than the latter. I simply calculate a new measure of slack, which is the number of jobs it would take to restore the 2016 employment rate to the 2007 rate, based on the 2016 employment number, which is also presented. I present the number and then express it as a percentage of 2016 employment.

The correlation between the two series—the unemployment rate and my new measure of slack—is .37. Overall, in 2016, it would take over 8 million jobs to get back to pre-recession levels, which is 5.5 percent of total employment. In Texas, the number is nearly half a million jobs, in Florida 830,000, and in California nearly a million. New Mexico has the highest proportion at 12.8 percent. Even states with unemployment rates under 5 percent have large slack rates. For example, Colorado has an unemployment rate of 3.3 percent but an employment slack rate of 7.4 percent. Even in my home state of New Hampshire, which has an unemployment rate of 2.8 percent, the employment rate in 2018 is still well below the 2007 rate.

An influential paper by researchers at the Federal Reserve argues that the declining participation rate in the United States "likely reflects the ongoing influence of an ageing population" (Aaronson et al. 2014, 198). They argue that the ongoing aging of the baby-boom generation accounts for nearly half of the decline in the U.S. participation rate. There is hope because in all likelihood they would rejoin the labor force if good jobs showed up. Without real-world evidence Aaronson and coauthors assumed there is no hope. They concluded that "while we believe some of the participation rate's current low is indicative of labor market slack, we do not expect the rate to substantially increase from current levels as labor market conditions continue to improve" (2014, 197). Fortunately, they were wrong. I recall sitting at a seminar when the paper was first presented by Bill Wascher at a conference at the Peterson Institute in Washington, D.C., and listening in disbelief. I complained that the results made no sense as they had simply assumed the decline in the LFPR was structural, without any basis in actual evidence—it was nothing more than simple extrapolation. There was a fall for a number of years and the authors essentially drew a straight line with a ruler, just extending the past exactly to the future. They hadn't bothered to do the economics of walking about. Young people, I suggested, would rush out of the education system in a heartbeat to take a decent-paying job. It seems lots of Trump-voting middle-aged adults, especially those with less education, would too. The Aaronson paper has been influential with members of the FOMC who have frequently argued that the fall in the U.S. participation rate is structural not cyclical. It isn't.

Table 4.3. State-Level Labor Market Slack Using Employment Rates, 2007 and 2016

	Employment rate		Employment	Slack#	Slack	Urate
	2007	2016	2016	2016	2016	2016
Alabama	58.7	53.4	2,038,775	202,350	9.9	6.0
Alaska	66.3	61.7	336,620	25,096	7.5	6.6
Arizona	61.3	57.1	3,066,264	225,540	7.4	5.3
Arkansas	59.9	55.8	1,288,994	94,711	7.3	4.0
California	62.1	58.9	18,065,043	981,462	5.4	5.4
Colorado	69.5	64.7	2,795,233	207,374	7.4	3.3
Connecticut	65.5	62.6	1,795,519	83,179	4.6	5.1
Delaware	64.1	59.8	451,973	32,500	7.2	4.4
DC	64.3	65.9	368,846	−8,955	−2.4	6.0
Florida	61.3	56.3	9,358,571	831,134	8.9	4.9
Georgia	65.0	59.0	4,656,255	473,517	10.2	5.4
Hawaii	64.1	60.8	664,690	36,077	5.4	3.0
Idaho	65.7	61.5	783,434	53,503	6.8	3.8
Illinois	65.0	61.4	6,154,867	360,872	5.9	5.9
Indiana	63.3	61.8	3,179,806	77,180	2.4	4.4
Iowa	69.4	67.0	1,638,288	58,685	3.6	3.7
Kansas	67.8	64.3	1,422,122	77,409	5.4	4.2
Kentucky	58.7	54.7	1,892,273	138,375	7.3	5.0
Louisiana	59.1	55.5	1,992,125	129,219	6.5	6.1
Maine	63.2	60.7	664,010	27,348	4.1	3.9
Maryland	66.3	64.2	3,034,131	99,247	3.3	4.3
Massachusetts	63.6	62.5	3,455,827	60,823	1.8	3.7
Michigan	59.9	58.2	4,599,049	134,336	2.9	4.9
Minnesota	69.1	66.8	2,884,091	99,303	3.4	3.9
Mississippi	56.4	52.8	1,205,779	82,212	6.8	5.8
Missouri	63.5	62.4	2,970,702	52,368	1.8	4.5
Montana	64.5	61.2	504,573	27,207	5.4	4.1
Nebraska	70.7	67.3	978,567	49,437	5.1	3.2
Nevada	65.6	58.6	1,346,008	160,786	11.9	5.7
New Hampshire	68.3	66.7	727,420	17,449	2.4	2.8
New Jersey	63.6	60.6	4,299,931	212,868	5.0	5.0
New Mexico	60.6	53.7	864,912	111,134	12.8	6.7
New York	59.8	57.7	9,121,323	331,972	3.6	4.8
North Carolina	62.5	58.7	4,629,329	299,684	6.5	5.1
North Dakota	71.7	69.2	403,067	14,562	3.6	3.2
Ohio	63.6	59.4	5,430,790	383,995	7.1	4.9
Oklahoma	60.9	58.2	1,739,362	80,692	4.6	4.9
Oregon	62.3	59.5	1,954,821	91,992	4.7	4.9
Pennsylvania	61.7	59.8	6,120,029	194,449	3.2	5.4
Rhode Island	64.9	61.0	522,812	33,426	6.4	5.3
South Carolina	59.4	56.3	2,186,740	120,407	5.5	4.8
South Dakota	71.1	67.0	440,299	26,944	6.1	2.8

Table 4.3. (*continued*)

	Employment rate		Employment	Slack#	Slack	Urate
	2007	2016	2016	2016	2016	2016
Tennessee	61.4	57.2	2,984,259	219,124	7.3	4.8
Texas	62.9	60.7	12,671,801	459,275	3.6	4.6
Utah	70.1	66.4	1,459,703	81,339	5.6	3.4
Vermont	67.6	64.8	333,640	14,417	4.3	3.3
Virginia	66.8	62.2	4,070,260	301,016	7.4	4.0
Washington	64.8	60.2	3,445,880	263,306	7.6	5.4
West Virginia	53.6	50.0	736,427	53,023	7.2	6.0
Wisconsin	67.4	65.4	2,991,033	91,469	3.1	4.1
Wyoming	69.0	63.5	286,373	24,804	8.7	5.3
USA	62.9	60.4	151,012,646	8,299,641	5.5	4.2

Note: Slack is just the 2007 employment rate over the 2017 rate, multiplied by the 2016 employment number, minus the 2016 employment number. So Alabama = [((58.7/53.4)*2,038,775)–2,038,775] = 202,350. Correlation between slack % and unemployment rate is .37. U.S. numbers relate to September 2017 and September 2007. The rest are the sum of the state numbers. *Source:* https://www.bls.gov/lau/staadata.txt.

An important new paper by John Abowd and coauthors (2018) contradicts that view. They found that, unlike in previous recessions, substantial numbers of people employed prior to the Great Recession did not return to employment even five or more years after the start of that recession. They also showed that such persons are attached to the labor force, as evidenced by their dynamic employment histories. Abowd found from administrative records that about 30 percent of those who are NILF had reported positive earnings within the previous four years, indicating that many had had some recent attachment to the labor market. They go on to argue that the exclusion of their inactive periods from earnings inequality measures understates the degradation at the bottom of the distribution. In private communications, John Abowd suggested to me that "we do see workers coming back in after two or more full calendar years of zero wages. And, of course, a full analysis of income inequality would have to treat the non-labor sources, still it is very misleading to do earnings inequality and leave out all of the zeros."

If we are to search for an explanation of the cause of the decline in the U.S. participation rate it makes sense to look at the experience of other countries, not least as it helps to rule out some possible explanations. If the reason had to do with technology, which is essentially common to other advanced countries, they should all observe the same patterns and they clearly don't. In an interesting speech, external MPC member Michael Saunders argued that various factors explain the *rising* participation rate in the UK "including rising life expectancy and improved health, the rising female retirement age and technological gains that facilitate flexible work."[20] To have a credible explanation of why the participation rate has fallen in the United States we need to look for explanations that don't apply in countries that have seen a falling participation or employment rate such as the UK and Canada.

Any explanation for the differences in these trends is not going to derive from characteristics that are common to both, such as an aging population or technology. For both men and women, it seems likely that the recent drops in participation that we have seen, all of which occurred at around the time the recession hit the United States in December 2007, are cyclical changes. They are driven by the fall in demand.

It seems unlikely that the differences, for example, in the time series of participation rates between Canada, the UK, and the United States have anything to do with aging. I went to the U.S. Census Bureau International Programs website and downloaded population data by age for the three countries. I found the share of the total population across six age groups, as a proportion of the population ages 15 and over. Canada and the UK, for example, have a higher proportion of individuals 65 and older. The proportions aged 35–44 are all about 15 percent. It certainly looks from these data that differences in participation rates between these countries have nothing to do with aging.

The United States does have a slightly higher proportion of those aged 15–34. Just as they have in the United States, youth participation rates have declined around the OECD, not least because youngsters have been pushed into higher education when there are fewer job opportunities. In the United States, there was a major jump in the number of students enrolled in college in the United States when recession hit in 2008, and that number continued to rise through 2011.[21] In 2008 there were 18.6 million, rising to 20.3 million in 2010 and falling back to 19.1 million in 2015. That rising trend went into reverse as the economy recovered through 2015. Part of the reason for the decline in college enrollment was because of a decline in cohort size.

It is possible to obtain data on demographics by single year of age for the United States in 2008 from the Census Bureau's International Programs International Database.[22] In 2008 the peak cohort size was of those who were

18 years old: 4.6 million. This was 350,000 higher than the number who were 22 years old and 390,000 higher than the number who were 14 years old. Alan Krueger (2015) also argues that the rise in school enrollment has largely offset the declining participation of younger workers. This is unlikely to be structural; more decent-paying jobs make college a less attractive option. The decline in the participation rate for youngsters also looks mostly cyclical.

President Obama's Council of Economic Advisers (CEA) examined the fall in male participation rates and came to exactly the opposite conclusion than did Aaronson and coauthors. The CEA concluded "no single factor can fully explain this decline, but analysis suggests that a reduction in the demand for less skilled labor has been a key cause of declining participation rates as well as lower wages for less skilled workers" (2016a, 43). That looks right. Labor demand is too low.

The CEA notes a series of important factors in understanding the decline in the male participation rate. They examined how prime-age men spent their time, using data from the American Time Use Survey. They found that prime-age men not in the labor force spend about the same amount of time as all prime-age men caring for household members. Non-participating prime-age men also do not spend meaningfully more time caring for non-household members, an activity on which all groups spend an average of less than ten minutes per day. Prime-age men not in the labor force spent more time, approximately twenty-six additional minutes per day, engaged in household activities and services than prime-age men overall.

The CEA went on to argue that one might expect differing patterns for married and non-married men, as married men are better able to specialize in household production while their spouse works. However, they found that non-participating prime-age men spent time comparably across most time-use categories regardless of whether they were married or single. This includes household activities, on which unmarried men spent 108 minutes per day while married men spent 112 minutes on average. When they examined men with children, they found that although non-participating prime-age men with children spend more time caring for household members (73 minutes) than prime-age men with children overall (58 minutes), the difference amounts to less than an additional half hour per day.

In another study, Tomlinson (2017) suggests, sensibly, that the UK has proved more adept at creating high-skilled jobs than has the United States.

Tomlinson notes that the reduction in midskill jobs is of relevance to participation because, as research by Foote and Ryan (2012) has shown, U.S. workers with a midskill level who become unemployed rarely reenter employment in either low- or high-skilled roles. Midskill workers in the United States are either more unwilling, or less able, to transition to jobs with different skill levels and are increasingly likely to move from unemployment to nonparticipation rather than back into work. Taken together, Tomlinson suggests, these factors are all likely to have contributed to falls in prime-age participation rates in the United States and the inverse outcome in the UK. Good stuff.

The CEA (2016b) also noted that the rise of mass incarceration and the associated rise in the fraction of the population that was formerly incarcerated look to be part of the explanation for the reduction in prime-age participation rates. The number of men behind bars in the United States has increased substantially, growing from 564 per 100,000 in the population in 1990 to 890 per 100,000 in 2014. Those who emerge from the criminal justice system, the CEA argues, suffer stigma and hiring restrictions, potentially reducing their ability to work, and thus reducing the demand for their labor. So stigma and hiring restrictions reduce the ability to get a job. It may be a very big deal in Florida in the 2020 presidential election given that a ballot initiative was passed in 2018 allowing a million ex-felons to vote.

There are over 1,000 mandatory license exclusions for individuals with records of misdemeanors and nearly 3,000 exclusions for those with felony records. Even in the absence of legal restrictions, employers are less likely to hire someone with a criminal record.[23] Recent estimates suggest that 6.4 to 7.2 percent of the prime-age male population in 2008 were ex-offenders.[24] Eberstadt (2016) estimated that among white men 45–54 years old who had been arrested or imprisoned, the odds of being out of the workforce were 35 percent, which is four times the odds for white men with no history in the criminal justice system. Among those 45–54, a high school graduate with no criminal history had a one-in-seven chance of being NILF, compared with odds of one in three for those with a history of incarceration.

Bucknor and Barber (2016) have examined the adverse impact time in prison or a felony conviction has on a person's employment prospects. The authors estimate that the employment penalty is around a 1-percentage-point reduction in the overall employment rate, equivalent to a loss of around 1.8 million workers. Black men suffered a 4.7- to 5.4-percentage-point reduction in their employment rate, while the equivalent for Latino men was 1.4–1.6 percentage points, and for white men it was 1.1–1.3 percentage points. They found that 6–6.7 percent of the male working-age population were former prisoners, while 13.6–15.3 percent were people with felony convictions, which seems incredibly high. Other advanced countries don't use mass incarceration and don't prevent ex-prisoners from working after their sentences are completed; they have figured out that rehabilitation works.

In terms of GDP, Bucknor and Barber calculate that the population of former prisoners and people with felony convictions led to a loss of $78–87 billion in GDP in 2014. Holy smokes! This is a major difference compared to other advanced countries, which have been more willing to wipe the slate clean after usually shorter prison spells.

The Gig Economy and Zero-Hours Contracts

Also of interest is the very different trend in the UK and the United States in their self-employment rates.[25] The OECD defines self-employment as the employment of employers, workers who work for themselves, members of producers' cooperatives, and unpaid family workers. The latter are unpaid in the sense that they lack a formal contract to receive a fixed amount of income at regular intervals, but they share in the income generated by the enterprise. Unpaid family workers are particularly important in farming and the retail trade. In the UK, non-participants have been pushed into low-paying self-employed jobs as a matter of public policy.

All persons who work in corporate enterprises, including company directors, are considered employees. The self-employment rate is usually measured as the percentage of employment. The U.S. self-employment rate has declined steadily from 18 percent in 1955 to under 7 percent in 2015. In contrast, the self-employment rate in the UK has increased steadily since 2002, rising from 13 to 15 percent in 2014.[26]

Many of the people who recently moved to self-employment in the UK had few hours and low earnings.[27] Approximately 40 percent of the self-employed in the UK earned less than £5,000 ($7,000) in 2011–12. The UK statistical agency, the ONS, reported that between 2008–9 and 2012–13 real self-employed earnings fell by 22 percent.[28] In the most recent year for which there were data available, 2012–13, they fell by 12 percent. In the UK, there is some evidence that the rise in the number of self-employed since 2008 has some equivalence to a rise in non-participation in the United States. It turns out, though, that the self-employed are happy, so encouraging self-employment via tax incentives in the United States may help the left-behinds.

One major source of insecurity in the UK has been the rise in the number of people employed on contracts where they are not guaranteed any hours in a given week, also known as zero-hours contracts. According to the ONS the number of people employed on zero-hours contracts in their main job has risen steadily over the last decade. During the period October–December 2017 there were 901,000 in this category, representing 2.8 percent of all employed people.[29]

People who report being on a zero-hours contract are more likely to be women, young, in full-time education, or working in hotels and restaurants. As Pennycook and coauthors note, "For those individuals who require a minimum number of working hours per week to ensure their family is financially secure or those who, confronting severe power imbalances in the workplace, fear that turning down hours as and when offered will result in future work being withdrawn, life on a zero-hours contract is one of almost permanent uncertainty" (2013, 21). It should be said, though, that this type of contract does fit into some workers' lifestyles as it gives them flexibility.

The Chartered Institute of Personnel and Development (CIPD) (2013) in a survey found that 28 percent of workers on such contracts having no minimum contracted hours were very satisfied; 19 percent were satisfied; 23 percent were neither satisfied nor dissatisfied; 11 percent were dissatisfied; and 16 percent were very dissatisfied, with 2 percent saying they didn't know.

Datta et al. (2018) found in another survey of workers on zero-hours contracts that there was an almost even split between workers who were satisfied with their number of hours (40 percent) and workers who would rather work more hours (44 percent), while a remaining 16 percent wanted to work fewer hours. Of those wanting to work more hours, 74 percent pointed to the lack of available work.

Katz and Krueger (2017) reported that in the United States the percentage of workers engaged in alternative work arrangements—defined as temporary help agency workers, on-call workers, contract workers, and independent contractors or freelancers—rose from 10.1 percent in February 2005 to 15.8 percent in late 2015. In an update Katz and Krueger (2019) walked those conclusions back somewhat based on new BLS data for 2017 arguing any upward trend was in fact more modest. They found a slight *decline* in the incidence of alternative work arrangements from 10.7 percent in 2005 to 10.1 percent in 2017.

Rising Inequality: Let Them Eat Cake

The CEA (2016a) concludes that the trends in the labor force participation rate for prime-age men are associated with other economic trends such as rising inequality. They modeled the association between a $1,000 increase in annual wages at different percentiles of the wage distribution in a state and its prime-age male labor force participation rate, controlling for time-invariant state differences as well as national time trends. The correlation they found was strongest at the bottom of the wage distribution: at the 10th percentile, a $1,000 increase in annual wages, or a roughly $0.50 increase in hourly wages for a full-time, full-year worker, is associated with a 0.17-percentage-point increase in the state labor force participation rate for prime-age men.

Higher up in the wage distribution, the correlation between wages and participation, the CEA found, becomes weaker, with a $1,000 increase in annual wages at the median corresponding to just a 0.05-percentage-point higher participation rate. This suggests that the decline in the LFPR is driven by the cycle. More high-paying jobs means higher male LFPRs. "When the returns to work for those at the bottom of the wage distribution are particularly low, more prime-age men choose not to participate in the labor force" (2016a, 3). This looks to be demand driven.

Inequality makes people unhappy. People compare themselves to others and don't like what they see. It is well known that inequality, especially in the United States, has risen sharply over time. It turns out that is true whether one examines wages, income as well as non-labor income, and wealth. But that is not true in many other OECD countries. Income inequality in the United States tends to be higher than in other OECD countries.

Table 4.4 reports on changes in the earnings dispersion between 2008 and 2016 using the 90–10 differential.[30] That is the ratio of earnings at the 90th percentile compared to earnings at the 10th percentile. A few facts stand out. First, on this measure earnings inequality is highest in the United States at both points in time than in any other country, and second, it rose over the eight-year period from the start of recession. Wage dispersion rose

Table 4.4. Earnings Dispersion: 9th to 1st Deciles, 2008 and 2016

	2008	2016		2008	2016
Australia	3.34	3.32	Japan	3.02	2.83**
Austria	3.32	3.27	Korea	4.93	4.30**
Belgium	2.25	2.36*	Mexico	3.93	3.33
Canada	3.75	3.71	Netherlands	2.87	3.02
Denmark	2.43	2.57	New Zealand	2.91	2.82**
Finland	2.57	2.50	Norway	2.26	2.55
France	2.81	2.81	Portugal	4.25	3.95
Germany	3.21	3.33	Spain	3.10	3.12
Greece	3.26	3.27	Sweden	2.31	2.28
Iceland	3.21	2.99*	Switzerland	2.70	2.72
Ireland	3.75	3.79	United Kingdom	3.63	3.42
Italy	2.27	2.25	United States	4.89	5.07**

Note: *2015 **2017. Data for France, Spain, and the Netherlands are for 2010 and 2014.
Source: OECD, http://www.oecd.org/employment/emp/employmentdatabase-earningsandwages.htm.

in nine of the twenty-four countries and fell in fourteen of them and was unchanged in France. Finally, wage inequality was low in the latest data, and especially so in the northern European countries of Belgium (2.36), Denmark (2.57), Finland (2.50), Norway (2.55), and Sweden (2.28). These countries are well known for scoring high on happiness rankings. Italy also had low levels of inequality although it does not score high in happiness rankings.

If we examine the 90–10 measure of household disposable income rather than wages there is even bigger dispersion. This measure consists of earnings, self-employment and capital income, and public cash transfers; income taxes and social security contributions paid by households are deducted. The income of the household is attributed to each of its members, with an adjustment to reflect differences in needs for households of different sizes. According to the OECD, in 2016 it was 6.3 in the United States versus 4.2 in the UK (in 2017), 3.7 in Germany in 2015, 3.5 in France, 3.3 in Sweden (in 2016), and 2.9 in Denmark (in 2015).[31]

Another measure of inequality is the Gini coefficient, which is available across countries for 2012. This shows that, across OECD countries, the United States and the UK rank #1 and #3 as the countries with the highest levels of inequality. Despite these relatively narrow income differences many in Europe think they are still too high.

Table 4.5. Government Should Reduce Income Differences: Percentage Saying "Strongly Agree" or "Agree"

Austria	77	Israel	77
Belgium	72	Netherlands	62
Germany	73	Russia	69
Finland	71	Sweden	64
France	75	Switzerland	65
Ireland	72	UK	64

Source: European Social Surveys Sweep 8, 2016 (variable = *gincdif*), weighted. http://www.europeansocialsurvey.org.

Respondents to the European Social Survey (ESS) were asked every two years from 2002 to 2016 whether they thought the government should reduce income differences. They were given five options: strongly agree, agree, neither, disagree, and strongly disagree. The proportions saying agree or strongly agree are tabulated in table 4.5. In Sweep 8 taken in 2016 three-quarters agreed in France and Austria, for example. The percentages are the lowest in the Netherlands, the UK, Switzerland, and Sweden.

Turning to the United States, in the General Social Survey, Americans were asked the following question:

QUESTION. Some people think that the government in Washington ought to reduce the income differences between the rich and the poor, perhaps by raising the taxes of wealthy families or by giving income assistance to the poor. Others think that the government should not concern itself with reducing this income difference between the rich and the poor. Here is a card with a scale from 1 to 7. Think of a score of 1 as meaning that the government ought to reduce the income differences between rich and poor, and a score of 7 meaning that the government should not concern itself with reducing income differences. What score between 1 and 7 comes closest to the way you feel? (CIRCLE ONE).

There were 32,000 responses over the period 1978–2016, with a mean score of 3.71, so people were right in the middle. Overall, 19.8 percent were 1s and 13.2 percent were 7s. There was little sign of much movement over time. In the years 1978–89, the mean was 3.66; 1990–99 = 3.79; 2000–

2008 = 3.70; and 2010–16 = 3.68. It was 3.50 in 2016. So, Americans aren't that hung up on inequality even though there is lots of it about. As you would expect, though, respondents with low levels of education are supportive and those with college educations less so, but the differences are not huge. In the years 2010–16 they had mean scores of 3.53 and 3.80, respectively.

Piketty argued that the explosion of wage inequality post-1980 helped trigger the financial crisis. The reason, he argues, was the virtual stagnation of the purchasing power of the lower and middle classes. This made it more likely they would take on debt, especially, he argues, because unscrupulous bankers and other financial intermediaries, freed from regulation, wanted to make good yields on the huge savings the well-to-do had. Hence, they offered credit on increasingly generous terms (2014, 373). And then everything went haywire.

Piketty, Saez, and Zucman (2018) combine tax, survey, and national accounts data to estimate the distribution of national income in the United States since 1913. They conclude that what they have seen is a tale of two countries. They find that for the 117 million U.S. adults in the bottom half of the income distribution, growth was essentially nonexistent for a generation while at the top of the ladder it has been remarkably strong. They also show that this stagnation of national income accruing at the bottom is not due to population aging. Quite the contrary. For the bottom half of the working-age population (adults under 65), income has in fact fallen. In the bottom half of the distribution, only the income of the elderly is rising. From 1980 to 2014, they show, none of the growth in per-adult national income went to the bottom 50 percent, while 32 percent went to the middle class (defined as adults between the median and the 90th percentile), 68 percent to the top 10 percent, and 36 percent to the top 1 percent.

This stagnation matters. Raj Chetty and coauthors (2016), as part of the Equal Opportunity Project, reported on what they called "the fading American Dream." They showed that there has been a big decline in the percentage of children earning more than their parents by year of birth. It was down from over 90 percent for those born in 1940 to around 50 percent for those born in 1985. They argue that reviving the "American Dream" of high rates of absolute mobility would require economic growth that is spread more broadly across the income distribution.

Average pretax national income per adult, Piketty and coauthors (2017) found, has increased 60 percent since 1980, but they found that it has stagnated for the bottom 50 percent of the distribution at about $16,000 a year. The pretax income of the middle class, adults between the median and the 90th percentile, has grown 40 percent since 1980, faster than what tax and survey data suggest, due in particular to the rise of tax-exempt fringe benefits. The authors found that income has boomed at the top: in 1980, the top 1 percent of adults earned on average 27 times more than the bottom 50 percent of adults, while they earn 81 times more today. The upsurge of top incomes was first a labor income phenomenon but has mostly been a capital income phenomenon since 2000, they argue. Since 1980, growth in real incomes for the bottom 90 percent of adults has been only about half of the national average on a pretax basis and about two-thirds on a posttax basis. Median pretax incomes have hardly grown since 1980. The government has offset only a small fraction of the increase in inequality.

According to Mishel and Sabadish (2013), "A key driver of wage inequality is the growth of chief executive officer earnings and compensation." Piketty agrees, noting that "the primary reason for increased income inequality in recent decades is the rise of the super-manager" (2014, 315). And he adds that "wage inequalities increased rapidly in the United States and Britain because U.S. and British corporations became much more tolerant of extremely generous pay packages after 1970" (2014, 332). Song et al. (forthcoming) disagree and show that the wage gap between the most highly paid employees within these firms (CEOs and high-level executives) and the average employee has increased only by a small amount. They examined data on earnings for a one-sixteenth percent representative sample of U.S. workers, matched to the (100 percent) population of U.S. firms, between 1978 and 2012. They found strong evidence that within-firm pay inequality has remained mostly flat over the past three decades. They conclude that firms matter. Although individuals in the top 1 percent in 2012 were paid much more than were the top 1 percent in 1982, they were paid less in 2012, relative to their firms' mean incomes, than they were three decades ago.

Data on the distribution of wealth in the United States shows a nation becoming ever more divided. This is the other really scary figure in the book! Something had to give. Figure 4.2 is from Saez and Zucman 2016 and Deutsche Bank[32] and shows differences in the proportion of U.S. wealth held

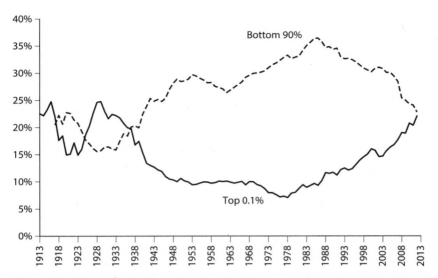

Figure 4.2. Share of U.S. household wealth by income level, 1913–2012. This figure depicts the share of total household wealth held by the 0.1 percent richest families and bottom 90 percent of households, as estimated by capitalizing income tax returns. In 2012, the top 0.1 percent includes about 160,000 families with net wealth above $20.6 million. *Sources:* Saez and Zucman 2016; Deutsche Bank.

by the top 0.1 percent of households and the bottom 90 percent. It shows that for the first time since before World War II the two groups have virtually the same amount of wealth—22 percent and 22.8 percent. The high point for the bottom 90 percent was a share of 36.4 percent in 1985 compared with 9.3 percent for the top 0.1 percent. Saez and Zucman conclude that "wealth concentration was high in the beginning of the twentieth century, fell from 1929 to 1978, and has continuously increased since then. The top 0.1% wealth share has risen from 7% in 1978 to 22% in 2012, a level almost as high as in 1929. Top wealth-holders are younger today than in the 1960s and earn a higher fraction of the economy's labor income. The bottom 90% wealth share first increased up to the mid-1980s and then steadily declined. The increase in wealth inequality in recent decades is due to the upsurge of top incomes combined with an increase in saving rate inequality" (2016, 519).

Balestra and Tonkin (2018) examine data from the OECD's Wealth Distribution Database and find that wealth concentration is twice the level of income inequality. Across the 28 OECD countries covered, the wealthiest 10 percent of households hold, on average, 52 percent of total household wealth, while the 60 percent least wealthy households own a little over 12 percent. Up to a quarter of all households report negative net worth (i.e., liabilities exceeding the value of their assets) in a number of countries. In addition, some countries feature large shares of households with high levels of debt relative to both their incomes and the assets that they hold; this potentially exposes such households to significant risks in the event of changes in asset prices or in their income. The authors also found that more than one-third of people are economically vulnerable, as they lack liquid financial assets to maintain a poverty-level living standard for at least three months.

Balestra and Tonkin also report on the distribution of household net wealth in 2015 (or latest available year) across OECD countries. They report the share of wealth owned by the top 1 percent. It is notable how much more unequal the wealth distribution is in the United States than elsewhere. The top 1 percent own 17 percent of the wealth in Canada; 21 percent in the UK; 19 percent in France; 24 percent in Germany; and 43 percent in the United States. The bottom 40 percent own 3 percent in Canada, France, and the UK; 0.5 percent in Germany; and –0.1 percent in the United States.

Garriga and colleagues (2017) used data from the Surveys of Consumer Finance to calculate 30–50 and 90–50 ratios for earnings, income, and net worth in the United States. In 1992, average earnings of median households were 3.62 times greater than those of households in the 30th percentile. From 1992 to 2007, this disparity declined to 2.68. For income, the 30–50 ratio is approximately constant, which may seem surprising. The 30–50 income ratio did not vary widely over that time because of government transfer programs, which prop up households in the lower part of the income distribution. Lower-income households, however, have more challenges in accumulating wealth. The 30–50 net-wealth ratio shows a slight increase in disparity, from 3.83 in 1992 to 4.53, in 2007. During the boom period, median households (probably homeowners) accumulated wealth more rapidly than households in the 30th percentile.

The Great Recession, Garriga and coauthors (2017) note, ended the decline in the United States in the 30–50 earnings ratio. In 2013, average earnings of median households were 3.3 times larger than those of households in the 30th percentile. In other words, the disparity reverted nearly to the 1992 level of 3.62. A more startling result is discovered for net worth: the Great Recession increased disparity. In 1992, net worth of median households was 3.83 times larger than that of households in the 30th percentile. By 2013, that number increased to 5.49. They suggest that the explanation is that households in the lower part of the income distribution (1) started with relatively little savings and (2) are hit harder by recessions.

The 90–50 ratios show an even starker story. In 1992, households in the 90th percentile had earnings 3.35 times larger than those of median households. For income in the same year, the 90–50 ratio was 2.94. For both earnings and income, the 90–50 ratios were relatively constant through 2007. However, starting in 2010, the 90–50 ratios for both earnings and income began to increase. By 2013, average earnings for a household in the 90th percentile were 4.07 times larger than those of median households and average income was 3.31 times larger. These increases in disparity, however, are small compared with the changes in the 90–50 net-worth ratio. Between 1992 and 2007, average net worth of households in the 90th percentile was approximately 7.55 times larger than that of median households. After 2007, the disparity grew substantially. In 2010, the 90–50 net-worth ratio reached 12.35 and then slightly declined to 11.58 in 2013.

A possible explanation, the authors suggest, for this large increase was the performance of the stock market, which benefited stockholders. The S&P 500 index increased 11 percent between 1990 and 2013. Research indicates that participation in the stock market increases wealth, with richer households being more likely to hold risky assets than poorer households. In 2013, the richest 10 percent of households owned over 80 percent of total stocks. It is reasonable to conclude, therefore, that the recent performance of the stock market is a factor in the increase of the 90–50 net-worth ratio.

In the UK median disposable income was £26,300 in the financial year 2016; this was £600 higher than the previous year and £1,000 higher than the pre-downturn value of £25,400 in 2007–8 (after accounting for inflation and household composition).[33] Looking separately at retired and non-retired households, the median income for retired households rose by 3.1 percent between 2014–15 and 2015–16, while the median income for non-retired households was broadly unchanged. The economic downturn had a larger effect on non-retired households, with median income in 2015–16 still 1.2 percent lower than pre-downturn levels in 2007–8, while the income for retired households grew by 13 percent over the same period.

According to Sir John Hills (2015), the dominant feature of austerity in the UK has been that non-pensioners with lower incomes on average lost more from benefit and tax-credit cuts than they gained from increased income tax allowances. The reverse was true for most income groups above the middle (but not those right at the top). These changes generally transferred income from those in the bottom half of the income distribution (and some right at the top) to those in the top half of the distribution, rather than contributing to deficit reduction.

Claudia Wells, the head of Household Income and Expenditure Analysis at ONS, has noted, "Household incomes are above their pre-downturn peak overall, but not everyone is better off. While retired households' incomes have soared in recent years, non-retired households still have less money, on average, than before the crash."[34] Interestingly, the old voted for Brexit while the young voted for Remain. As we will see, young people who voted Remain turned on the May government in the 2017 election. Relative things matter.

Part of the explanation for the rise in inequality is the decline of trade unions in the private sector around the world. In the United States, private-sector trade union membership rates declined from 24 percent in 1973 to 17 percent in 1983 and 6.5 percent in 2017. Public-sector rates rose from 23 percent in 1973 to 34 percent in 2017. In the UK, private-sector union density rates were 21 percent in 1995 but were 15 percent in 2017.[35] We have seen a dramatic fall in union representation in the United States especially in the rust belt. Private-sector union density rates fell more sharply in rust-belt states that voted for Trump than nationally. Public-sector unionization rates in the UK fell from 61 percent in 1995 to 51 percent in 2017.

The decline in private-sector unionism especially matches exactly the time period when inequality rises. There is some evidence in the literature that the decline in unionization rates is a modest source of the rise in wage inequality. David Card (2001), for example, found using Current Population Survey microdata for 1973–74 that falling unionization rates of men during the two sample periods, with bigger declines among lower-skill groups, account for 15–20 percent of the rise in male wage inequality.

Larry Mishel (2012) from the Economic Policy Institute found that the decline of U.S. unionization in the 1990s and 2000s put continued downward pressure on middle-wage men and contributed to the continued growth of the 90–50 wage gap between high- and middle-wage men. The erosion of unions, however, has also affected non-union wages, and the consequence has been a sizable increase in wage inequality among women as well as men. Another study examined the impact of unions on inequality in the United States, Canada, and the UK and found that unions systematically reduced the variance of wages in all three countries for men, but they found no such effects for women.[36]

Union density in the UK went from 21 percent in the private sector in 1995 and 61 percent in the public sector to 13.9 percent in the private sector in 2015 and 55 percent in the public sector. This contrasts with 10 percent in the private sector in the United States in 1995 versus 38 percent in the public and 6 percent and 35 percent, respectively, in 2015. Wages are higher in union jobs, so the loss of union jobs meant the loss of high-paying jobs. In the UK, based on hourly earnings, there was a raw premium for union jobs of 15 percent in 1995, which was down to 8 percent in 2015. Even controlling for characteristics there is a substantial union wage premium.[37] Union density in Italy has increased between 1999 and 2014, from 35 percent to 37 percent, but declined in Germany from 25 percent to 18 percent. It remained flat at 8 percent in France although coverage remains almost total.

It also appears that trade has contributed relatively little to the rise in inequality. Most economists agree that trade has not been a major factor in the shift in labor demand away from less skilled and toward more skilled workers. Other factors playing an important role seem to be demand shifts from skill-biased technological change, a deceleration in the growth of the skilled-labor supply, and institutional factors.[38]

Trade has certainly been getting a good deal of the blame recently for negatively impacting the labor market. It's all those foreigners taking American jobs away. Donald Trump has taken aim at trade by withdrawing from TPP and announcing he would renegotiate NAFTA to "get better deals" to protect workers. My Dartmouth colleague Doug Irwin, though, has argued that Trump's brand of economic nationalism "is just one step away from old-fashioned protectionism." He argues that "an 'America first' trade policy would do nothing to create new manufacturing jobs or narrow the trade deficit, the gap between imports and exports. Instead, it risks triggering a global trade war that would prove damaging to all countries" (2017, 45).

Colgan and Keohane summed it up well:

Working-class Americans didn't necessarily understand the details of global trade deals, but they saw elite Americans and people in China and other developing countries becoming rapidly wealthier while their own incomes stagnated or declined. It should not be surprising that many of them agreed with Trump and with the Democratic presidential primary contender Bernie Sanders that the game was rigged. (2017, 40)

People Compare Themselves to Others

Some social scientists, prominently the economist James Duesenberry (1949) nearly seventy years ago, argued that human beings care mainly about relative, rather than absolute, income. In a well-known essay my Dartmouth colleague Erzo F. P. Luttmer—to be distinguished from his cousin at the University of Minnesota, Erzo G. J. Luttmer—explored whether individuals feel worse when others around them earn more (2005). That is, do they care about their relative position? The answer was in the affirmative; higher earnings of neighbors are associated with lower levels of self-reported happiness. An increase in neighbors' earnings and a similarly sized decrease in own income have roughly the same negative effect on well-being.

Andrew Oswald and I (2004a) found that relative income impacts happiness even when absolute income is held constant. We find evidence that one's own income relative to the per capita income in a state has an independent, significant, and positive impact, over and above own income, on happiness. Absolute and relative income thus both matter for happiness.[39] Other research also shows the importance of relative income.[40] Concern for relative position generates imitative behavior where people follow one another's actions.[41] Happiness appears to be negatively related to others' incomes and to one's own past income.[42] People compare themselves to others.

Economics Nobel winner Vernon Smith once told me that economic models apply really well to monkeys but not necessarily to people. In group settings when people are offered choices, they don't behave in ways predicted by economic models. Here is an example of two choices. Would you choose (a) you get six and everyone else gets four, or (b) you get five and everyone else gets one? Monkeys mostly choose (a). There is transitivity. People choose (b) because they prefer five to six and more isn't better. Relative things matter. The implication is that people care about inequality.

There is evidence that individuals in Europe have a lower tendency to report themselves as happy when inequality is high, but this is not the case in the United States.[43] Another analysis was recently conducted at the zip-code, MSA, and state levels of the inequality well-being relationship using data from the Gallup Healthways Well-Being Index and income inequality data from the American Community Survey.[44] It found, in contrast, that the net relationship between income inequality and happiness in the United States is negative. A study that used the World Database of Happiness found a positive relationship in Latin America, Eastern Europe, and Asia but a negative one in Western Europe.[45]

Another study looked at the relationship between economic mobility and inequality across advanced countries.[46] It found clear evidence that as inequality rises, mobility declines. Countries with the highest mobility had the lowest inequality. Subsequent work suggests that there is limited mobility in the United States.[47] Children born in the bottom 20 percent of the income distribution only have a 7.5 percent chance of making it to the top 20 percent. Scarily, 47 percent of Americans say that they are so short of money that they could not cover a $400 emergency without borrowing money or selling something.[48] With the shrinking middle class and rising inequality one study suggests Americans are becoming more and more segregated by income and as a result less and less likely to interact with people who are dissimilar to themselves.

Data from the 2016 International Social Survey Programme (ISSP) suggest that even with the very high levels of inequality, Americans don't think it is the responsibility of the government to reduce the differences in income between rich and poor. Respondents in many countries were asked this question, with possible replies of definitely should be; probably should be; probably should not be; definitely should not be; and can't choose. Among the twenty-eight countries polled, the proportion saying governments definitely should be and probably should be was lowest among advanced countries— United States (54%) and Japan (57%)—and highest in Hungary (88%), Chile (91%), Croatia (91%), and Slovenia (91%). Other percentages were as follows: UK (68%); New Zealand (64%); France (78%); Germany (78%); Israel (85%); and Spain (86%).

This is what the long, dragging conditions of semi-slump, or at least subnormal prosperity, look like. Growth has disappointed. Falling home-ownership rates are likely to improve mobility and the prime-age participation rate is picking up, but these things are happening slowly in the United States. People compare themselves to others so rising inequality hurts.

CHAPTER 5

Underemployment

The most common way of measuring underemployment is to calculate the number and share of involuntary part-timers (IPT) in total employment. This is a relatively crude measure that only captures the number of part-time workers wishing to extend their hours. It carries no information on the number of additional hours these workers would prefer or on whether some other workers would prefer to reduce their hours. It turns out that there are significant numbers of the overemployed who want fewer hours.

The use of a measure of underemployment based solely on part-timers who can't find full-time jobs reflects the lack of alternatives, particularly in the United States. In Europe, involuntary part-timers are described as part-timers who want full-time jobs (PTWFT), whereas in the United States they are described as part-time for economic reasons (PTFER). In Europe, statistics on PTWFT are obtained from the individual-level European Labor Force Surveys (EULFS) and in the United States on PTFER from the Current Population Survey. I treat these measures analogously. Monthly data on these measures are published for the United States and the UK; quarterly data are available for Europe.

Figure 5.1 plots PTFER and PTWFT for the United States and the UK, respectively, in each case expressed as a proportion of total employment that David Bell and I have termed U7 (Bell and Blanchflower, forthcoming).

Monthly data are available for the United States from May 1955 through June 2018 and for the UK from April 1992 through April 2018. First the data for the United States show strong cyclicality with peaks of 6.3 percent in March 1958 and 6.7 percent in March 2010. The UK rate peaked at 4.9

Figure 5.1. Involuntary part-timers as percentage of workforce. *Sources:* BLS and ONS.

percent in April 2013 and in the latest data for January 2019 is 3.3 percent, having jumped 490,000 on the month. In the United States the post-2000 low was 2.3 percent in July 2000 while in the UK it was 1.9 percent in December 2004 and in the latest data release for October 2018 is 3 percent. In both the UK and the United States rates peaked after the Great Recession and fell back but have not returned to pre-recession levels. This rise and subsequent fall in U7, as I document in this chapter, were also the case in other advanced countries. Underemployment is an additional amount of labor market slack over and above the unemployment rate.

Policymakers Have Spotted the Rise in Underemployment

In the past underemployment tracked unemployment closely, but since the Great Recession that has not been the case. At the beginning of 2017 the *New York Times* editorial board argued as follows:

> Even now, the Fed should continue to keep rates as low as possible, for as long as possible, to help bring down underemployment: The number of working people who cannot find full-time hours remains elevated even as unemployment has declined.[1]

The minutes of the FOMC meeting in December 2016 argued that

> some participants saw the possibility that an extended period during
> which labor markets remained relatively tight could continue to
> shrink remaining margins of underutilization, including the still-high
> level of prime-age workers outside the labor force and elevated levels
> of involuntary part-time employment and long-duration
> unemployment.[2]

The European Central Bank, in its June 2016 Economic Bulletin No. 4,
got in on the act too:

> At the euro area level, the growth in part-time employment seems to
> have been driven to a significant extent by employers' preference for
> this type of contract. More than half of the increase in part-time
> employment since the first quarter of 2008 seems to reflect decisions
> taken on a voluntary basis, as workers willingly took advantage of new
> part-time opportunities. However, almost half is due to a rise in
> "underemployment" as workers involuntarily accepted part-time
> employment, although they would have liked to work more.[3]

Ignazio Visco, governor of the Bank of Italy, concurred on November
11, 2015:

> It is now quite generally held that the "potential" growth rate too has
> been lowered by the reduction in investment and the very high levels
> of long-term unemployment and underemployment.[4]

Chapter 2 of the IMF's *World Economic Outlook* for October 2017 looked
at recent wage dynamics. They concluded that "the bulk of the wage slowdown can be explained by labor market slack (both headline unemployment
and underutilization of labor in the form of involuntary part-time employment), inflation expectations, and trend productivity growth. While involuntary part-time employment may have helped support labor force participation and facilitated stronger engagement with the workplace than the
alternative of unemployment, it also appears to have weakened wage growth"

(2017, 1). The IMF found that in comparing the years since 2008 with 2000–2007 in economies where unemployment rates are still appreciably above their averages before the Great Recession, conventional measures of labor market slack can account for about half of the slowdown, with involuntary part-time employment acting as a further significant drag on wages.

In economies where unemployment rates are now below their averages before the Great Recession and measured slack appears low, slow productivity growth can account for about two-thirds of the slowdown in nominal wage growth since 2007. Even in these economies, the report suggests involuntary part-time employment "appears to be weighing on wage growth." The report says, "Subdued nominal wage growth has occurred in a context of a higher rate of involuntary part-time employment, an increased share of temporary employment contracts, and a reduction in hours per worker." They are right when they argue that "market slack may therefore be larger than suggested by headline unemployment rates" (2017, 85).

Dennis Lockhart, president of the Federal Reserve Bank of Atlanta, gave a speech called "A Potentially Momentous Year for Policy" in Atlanta on January 12, 2015, in which he argued that "the recent evidence on wages has been mixed. A number of measures of wage growth remained well below historical norms throughout most of last year, while others did tick up slightly in the second and third quarters. Based on research, my team has advanced the thesis that the elevated number of people working part-time involuntarily is restraining wage growth."[5] It turns out that is right, and I will return to the issue of the extent to which underemployment impacts wages.

Underemployment means workers are being pushed into part-time jobs when they would like full-time jobs—so-called involuntary part-timers. It can also mean that workers who voluntarily choose to be part-time or who are full-time have fewer hours than they would like. And the desire for a change in hours of voluntary part-timers and full-timers, along with involuntary part-timers, varies over time with the cycle in expected ways. In bad times workers of all three types want more hours and in good times they want less. At the same time, there are workers who feel overworked and would like fewer hours (overemployment). Simply using involuntary part-timers ignores how much voluntary part-timers and full-timers want to change their hours.

The Literature Says Firms Change Worker Utilization
Rates as Product Demand Changes

When the labor market is fully functioning, there are different jobs on offer, so workers can find jobs with the right number of hours to suit them. In the post-recession world, many workers and especially new entrants are hours constrained. They would take more hours at the going wage rate. This wouldn't happen if labor markets were at full employment. The levels of underemployment currently being experienced, even though they are below their recent peaks, are still higher than they have ever been at such low unemployment rates. Underemployment has to be added to unemployment to get a true measure of labor market slack. It should be said, though, that we do have evidence from the UK that in the years 2001–8, on the net, workers in the UK wanted fewer hours not more, so they were overemployed.

If aggregate demand were higher, our data suggest that more wage-hour combinations would be available that include extra hours, which would likely improve welfare and well-being. Low demand reduces the availability of such choices and generates underemployment. Given the fact that the data we present suggest that workers are prepared to work more hours at the going wage, a package with a higher number of hours in it would likely be profitable for firms.

What theoretical backing can we give to our claims to observe underemployment and overemployment, when the so-called "canonical" model of Pencavel (1986) suggests that workers are free to choose their hours of work, given the wage rate? In answer to this, first, we note that more recently Pencavel (2016) himself acknowledged that this model where workers select their hours, dominant in the literature since Lewis (1957), neglects the role of employer preferences in hours determination.[6] Even though Lewis himself stepped back from this position (1969), acknowledging that the preferences of employers are neglected in the canonical model, the assumption that workers select from a continuum of hours, while treating the wage rate as exogenous, continues to dominate research and teaching. This approach persists in economics, even though aggregate hours fluctuate in response to changes in demand and the organization of production requires employers to place some restrictions on working time (e.g., to ensure that a production line is fully staffed).

Some authors, acknowledging that observed hours and wage combinations reflect both supply and demand influences, have sought to identify these effects empirically. Feldstein (1967) and Rosen (1969) attempted to identify the supply and demand for worker hours using industry variation, with limited success. Pencavel (2016) questions why the issue of the identification of supply and demand for hours has been neglected for the last forty years. To put it technically, this literature weakens the assumption that workers are invariably located along their individual supply curves. The evidence suggests that large numbers of workers are off their labor supply curves.

This argument is reinforced by the literature that focuses on how firms adjust to a positive output shock, which dates back to the 1960s and 1970s.[7] Hart and Sharot, for example, argued that their results "hinge on the proposition that firms achieve short-run changes in labor requirements by varying their worker utilization rates, whereas . . . the response of employment is more sluggish and long-term" (1978, 307). Of course, the same applies to a negative shock.

Hart (2017) has noted that the peak-to-trough percentage change in hours in the Great Recession was greater than in employment. GDP fell in the UK by 6.3 percent and by 6.6 percent, peak to trough, in Germany. He notes that employment in the UK fell by a relatively modest 2.3 percent, while person-hours changed more, with a 4.3 percent drop. Germany's fall in employment was a trivial 0.5 percent, while that of person-hours was a much larger 3.4 percent. The U.S. GDP drop was not quite as severe, at 4.1 percent, but employment and person-hours reductions were considerably greater, at 5.6 percent and 7.6 percent, respectively. The three countries experienced a decrease in peak person-hours that preceded that of employment by at least one quarter.

Hart concludes as follows: "During economic downturns, adjusting person-hours contributes to wage-earnings losses among workers whose actual hours of work fall short of their desired hours. However, the costs of not achieving output requirements in a relatively speedy manner—associated with shortfalls or excesses in the production of goods and services—are likely to be considerably greater. As such, the response patterns of hours compared to employment during demand shocks provide substantial net benefits" (2017).

A key element of Hart's analysis is the relative costs of varying hours and employment. Where hiring, firing, and training costs are high, employers are more likely to rely on the internal labor market. Where they are low, there is likely to be more job turnover, implying greater reliance on the external labor market. This does not seem to be a situation in which employees are selecting a utility-maximizing combination of real wage and leisure; rather, it suggests workers' hours preferences being overridden in the interests of firm profitability.

Another version of this argument is that a firm might have some fully employed but not underemployed workers and some underemployed workers, the latter of whom may be a kind of reserve army that permits the firm to give lower raises to the fully employed. The very existence of underemployed workers at a firm alongside those with acceptable hours may well exert more downward wage pressure than would the unemployed.

For example, for unemployed workers to restrain a firm's wage increases, the firm has to know about the unemployed workers; however, underemployed workers are already there but must communicate their willingness to work longer hours at perhaps reduced wage rates. That presumably isn't hard given they are prepared to express such a willingness to a survey interviewer. It is also less costly for a firm to increase worker hours than it is to hire new workers. There seems to be no workplace-level analysis that would tell us the extent to which there is a mix of workers who are content with their hours at a workplace or if the underemployed group together in certain firms.

However, if employers are monopsonistic, they may be able to vary workers' hours in response to fluctuations in demand even if there is little joint investment in firm-specific skills.[8] Hours variations are invariably less expensive than rescaling the workforce, and firms may use such variations when they perceive the probability of inefficient separations is low. Bhaskar, Manning, and To (2002) suggest a number of explanations as to why labor markets are typically "thin," giving employers a degree of market power.

Manning, while also lamenting the preeminence of the canonical model, argues that under monopsony, utility-maximizing employees may be displaced from their supply curve and would express a desire to increase or decrease their current hours at the current wage rate (2003, 228). Using data from the British Household Panel Survey for the period 1991–98, he shows that the desire to reduce hours substantially exceeded desired hours increases. This finding is consistent with David Bell's and my analysis (Bell and Blanchflower 2018b) using the UK Labor Force Survey (UKLFS) for the early part of the following decade, but we find a subsequent reversal after the Great Recession.

One consequence may be that workers are forced to agree to contracts that give employers rights to vary working time on short notice without changing pay rates. Azar and colleagues (2017) show that product market concentration is high, and increasing concentration is associated with lower wages such that there is a negative correlation between labor market concentration and average posted wages in that market. Using data from the employment website CareerBuilder.com, they calculate labor market concentration for over 8,000 geographic-occupational labor markets in the United States. They show that going from the 25th percentile to the 75th percentile in concentration is associated with a 15–25 percent decline in posted wages, suggesting that concentration increases labor market power.

Underemployment is an additional labor resource that can be used by firms when demand rises. The fact that underemployment existed in 2017 at levels much higher than existed pre-recession helps explain why there is weak wage growth. If labor demand were adequate, it would inevitably increase the hours of those who desired more, especially as this is likely a more cost-effective response than hiring more people.

One other thing that does tend to happen in a recession is that young people enter the job market on a lower rung on the jobs pyramid than they would have in good times.[9] College graduates take the jobs that would previously be taken by high school graduates and so on. This is especially hard in current circumstances, when college is so expensive and many are carrying high levels of student debt. This adds to the difficulty of striking out on one's own without the bank of mom and dad. This should be considered another form of labor underutilization. The concern is that young people feel they are overeducated, though the extent of overeducation is disputed in the literature. Wilkins and Wooden (2011) provide a good summary.

Cajner and coauthors (2014) concur that the rise in involuntary part-time employment is dominantly cyclical. They argue that although the number of persons working part-time involuntarily remains unusually high, this primarily reflects continued weak labor market conditions and the share of part-time employment will likely diminish as the labor market improves.

Underemployed individuals are significantly more likely to be "struggling" (54%) than employed Americans (38%), based on data from the

Gallup Healthways Well-Being Index. Worry and stress are pervasive among the underemployed. Nearly half said they experienced worry the day before the survey compared with 29 percent of the employed. The underemployed are also more likely than the employed to report experiencing stress and sadness and almost twice as likely to have been told by a doctor or nurse that they suffer from depression (21% versus 12% of employed Americans).

A San Francisco Fed study confirmed that the PTFER depends heavily on cyclical variation in labor market conditions.[10] However, the study also identified slower-moving market factors, reflected mainly in industry employment shares and population demographics, which account for ongoing elevation in PTFER despite the cyclical recovery in the labor market. These market or structural factors account for about a percentage point or more of the elevated PTFER share of total employment through 2014. The contribution of these factors declined only slightly during the recovery period following the recession. The study's results suggest that the incidence of PTFER employment may remain well above its pre-recession lows as the labor market expansion continues.

There is also a suggestion that employers' anticipation of the Affordable Care Act (ACA) health benefit mandate explains almost all the rise in PTFER. Using data from the Current Population Survey (CPS) between 1994 and 2015, Even and Macpherson (2016) find that PTFER employment in 2015 was higher than predicted based on economic conditions and the composition of jobs and workers in the labor market. Importantly, they find that the increase in the probability of involuntary part-time employment since passage of the ACA has been greatest in the occupations with a larger share of workers affected by the mandate. Their estimates suggest that up to 700,000 additional workers without a college degree between the ages of 19 and 64 are in PTFER employment due to the ACA employer mandate.

The Behavior of the Underemployed

There is a growing literature on the behavior of the underemployed. Valletta, Bengali, and van der List (2018) found that persistent market-level forces, most notably changing industry composition, explain sustained elevation in the rate of involuntary part-time work in the United States. Borowczyk-Martins and Lalé (2016) compare transitions between full- and part-time work including involuntary part-time work in the UK and the United States.

In a later article (2018) the same authors show that involuntary part-time work generates lower welfare losses relative to unemployment. This finding relies critically on the much higher probability of return to full-time employment from part-time work, especially at the same employer. They interpret it as a premium in access to full-time work available to involuntary part-time workers.

Feldman (1996) treated "underemployment" more broadly, incorporating education, work duties, field of employment, wages, and permanence of the job and includes a mismatch between education and training. He also suggested that underemployment may be a continuous as well as a dichotomous variable. I do not attempt to extend into these other dimensions of underemployment but rather focus on extending measures such as PTWFT and PTFER that treat underemployment as a dichotomous variable.

Interestingly, Cajner and coauthors (2014) found that one-third of the increase in part-time employment for economic reasons in the United States during the recession represented a shift from voluntary part-time to involuntary part-time employment. They speculate that this merely represents a measurement issue: for example, in times with a weak labor market, CPS respondents became more likely to attribute their part-time hours to economic reasons than to non-economic reasons (e.g., family obligations or other personal reasons). On the other hand, they argue it could be that the increased flow from voluntary to involuntary part-time work during the recession represented a real behavioral change: for example, if a household's primary earner experienced a spell of unemployment, the secondary earner, who had previously been working part-time for non-economic reasons, might have wished to work longer hours and thus reported working part-time for economic reasons.

Golden (2016) reports that involuntary part-time work and its growth in the United States are concentrated in several industries that more intensively use part-time work, specifically, retail and leisure and hospitality. The retail trade (stores, car dealers, etc.) and the leisure and hospitality industries (hotels, restaurants, and the like) contributed well over half (63.2 percent) of the growth of all part-time employment since 2007 and 54.3 percent of the growth of involuntary part-time employment. These two industries, together with educational and health services and professional and business services, account for the entire growth of part-time employment and 85 percent of the growth of involuntary part-time employment from 2007 to 2015.

There is evidence that involuntary part-timers are disproportionately young, less educated, and minorities. Valletta, Bengali, and van der List (2018) reported that in the United States, men and women under the age of 24, the single, the least educated, blacks and Hispanics, and the unincorporated self-employed are most likely to be IPT. Glauber (2017) noted that workers without a high school degree are more likely to be IPT. Eurofound (2017) reported on the distribution of involuntary part-time work across the EU28 in 2015, finding that they were disproportionately female, young, less educated, and on temporary contracts and in elementary occupations.

There are composition effects by adding more involuntary part-time workers because they suffer a wage penalty. Golden (2016) found that among those who are paid by the hour in the United States, voluntary part-time workers earned $15.61 per hour on average compared with only $15.11 for those working part-time involuntarily. Among those who could "find only part-time work," their hourly earnings were even lower, $14.53. In Bell and Blanchflower 2018a, using UKLFS data, we found that individuals who reported that they wanted more hours, over and above whether they were PTWFT, had lower wages. Individuals who were PTWFT had lower hourly wages than voluntary part-timers and full-timers. Veliziotis and coauthors (2015) found the same for the UK and also reported the same result for Greece. This implies that wages will be depressed the greater the willingness of workers to provide more hours at the going wage rate. Part-timers who want extra hours are paid less than part-timers who are content with their hours. It seems that having workers in jobs where they want more hours keeps wages down as they accept lower pay, conditional on their characteristics. Underemployment impacts wages.

Glauber (2017) has noted that involuntary part-time workers in the United States are more than five times more likely than full-time workers to live in poverty. She also notes that they earn 19 percent less per hour than full-time workers in similar positions. Women experienced a 14 percent wage penalty for involuntary part-time employment, men 21 percent. These wage penalties are net of differences in workers' occupations, industries, regional and metropolitan areas of residence, educational attainment, and age. So being underemployed conveys a wage penalty.

Sum and Khatiwada (2010) estimate that the lost earnings in 2009 Q4, when there were nearly 9 million PTFER, compared with 2007 Q4, when there were around 4.2 million, yields an aggregate value of slightly under $68 billion in lost earnings. All told, they calculate the combined aggregate annualized earnings, payroll tax, and other non-wage compensation losses associated with higher levels of underemployment at an estimated $78 billion. They note that the lower-income groups of underemployed workers especially are more likely to depend on in-kind transfers such as food stamps, rental subsidies, and Medicaid to support themselves and their families, thereby imposing fiscal costs on the rest of the taxpaying public.

Larrimore and coauthors reported that in the United States the 2017 Survey of Household Economics and Decision Making showed that more than one-third of non-retirees working part-time for economic reasons in 2017 had an irregular work schedule set by their employer.[11] One-quarter of non-retired individuals working part-time for non-economic reasons, and 12 percent of full-time workers, have such a schedule. This, the authors suggest, means that many of the part-time workers who would potentially work more hours and thus are not currently at their full employment also face the challenge of unpredictable hours. As another sign of differences in employees' status, only 3 in 10 of those working part-time for economic reasons received a raise in the previous year versus more than half of full-time workers.

The Evidence on Underemployment

By the start of the Great Recession in December 2007 in the United States and April 2008 in the UK, involuntary part-time employment was off its lows, both in levels and rates, and then it climbed fast. The number of PTFER in the United States hit a high of 9.25 million in September 2010, up from a low of 3.14 million in July 2000 and 4.85 million in January 2008. U7 reached a high of 6.4 percent at the peak in December 2010. This compares to a low of 3.1 million or 2.3 percent of employment in July 2000 and 2.7 percent in April 2006. The latest data for October 2018 show 4.62 million with a U7 of 2.95 percent.

The number of workers who were PTWFT in the UK was as low as 555,000 in January 2003, and 671,000 in April 2008, rising to a peak of 1.46 million in June 2013. As a percentage of employment in the UK, PTWFT now also represents 2.9 percent of total employment; it rose to a peak rate of 4.88 percent in June 2013 versus a low of 1.87 percent in December 2004. In the latest data there were 916,000 workers in August 2018 who were PTWFT, giving a U7 rate of 2.83 percent.

The numbers of PTFER are large as compared, for example, to the number of unemployed people, which in the latest data for the United States in January 2019 is 6.5 million while in the UK in October 2018 there were 1.38 million unemployed. In January 2019 there were around 5.1 million PTFER in the United States, down from a peak of over 9 million in March 2009, or three-quarters of the unemployment stock. In contrast they are around two-thirds of the unemployment stock in the UK. Thus, the additional level of labor market underutilization they represent is substantial.

The European Statistical Office Eurostat reports annually a more expansive definition of underemployment among part-timers than U7. It reports data on the number—and the rate as a proportion of employment—of underemployed part-time workers who *want more hours*.[12] That includes not only part-timers who say they want full-time jobs but also part-timers who don't want full-time jobs but want more hours. As a consequence the numbers they report are larger than using PTFER and the rates they report are higher than U7. The Eurostat numbers across ten major European countries are as below for 2008, 2012, and 2017, in thousands. For the UK the numbers reached a peak of 1.92 million in 2012 and then fell back in 2017 to 1.51 million. This contrasts with an average for U7 published by the ONS of PTFER of only 1.45 million and 1.02 million, respectively, on those two dates.

	2008	2012	2017
EU28	7,688	9,358	8,972
Belgium	37	158	171
Denmark	68	88	108
Germany	2,449	1,758	1,373
Greece	99	189	259
Spain	814	1,398	1,359
France (metropolitan)	1,254	1,346	1,518
Italy	400	587	731
Netherlands	97	148	453
Austria	134	145	182
Sweden	215	237	171
United Kingdom	1,269	1,920	1,511

In nine of the eleven countries the numbers rose from 2008 to 2012 and then fell back and in 2017 were above 2008 levels. The exceptions are Ger-

Table 5.1. Underemployed Part-Time Workers Who Would Prefer to Work More Hours as Percentage of Employment (Ages 15–74)

GEO/TIME	2008	2012	2017
Austria	3.4	3.6	4.3
Belgium	0.8	3.5	3.7
Cyprus	2.0	5.3	7.8
Denmark	2.4	3.3	3.8
Estonia	0.7	1.7	0.7
Finland	2.9	3.0	3.9
France	—	—	5.9
France (metropolitan)	4.8	5.2	5.8
Germany	6.4	4.5	3.3
Greece	2.1	5.1	6.9
Hungary	0.2	2.2	0.8
Ireland	—	8.1	4.8
Italy	1.7	2.6	3.2
Latvia	2.2	5.0	3.1
Lithuania	1.2	2.9	1.2
Luxembourg	0.7	2.2	2.0
Malta	1.9	2.4	1.4
Netherlands	1.1	1.8	5.3
Norway	3.0	3.1	2.6
Poland	1.6	2.2	1.5
Portugal	1.9	5.6	4.3
Romania	2.3	2.5	2.4
Slovakia	0.8	1.6	2.2
Slovenia	1.4	2.0	3.0
Spain	4.0	7.9	7.2
Sweden	4.7	5.1	3.4
United Kingdom	4.3	6.5	4.7

Source: Bell and Blanchflower, forthcoming.

many, which saw a steady fall, and Sweden, which had a pickup but the 2017 number was below the 2008 number.

In several A10 East European countries, which had large outward migration flows, especially to the UK—Bulgaria, Romania, Poland, Lithuania, and Latvia—the numbers in 2016 were little different from those in 2008. If you wanted more hours and you lived in an A10 Accession country, you moved westward, especially to the UK.

Table 5.1 reports underemployment rates based on the numbers reported above for part-timers who want more hours, whether they want full-time jobs or not, expressed as a proportion of total employment for twenty-six countries for 2008, 2012, and 2017. Rates spiked as high as 7.9 percent in

Spain and 8.1 percent in Ireland in 2012. In Germany, Norway, and Sweden the 2017 rate is lower than the 2008 rate.

Countries with high unemployment rates like Spain and Greece even in 2017 have high Eurostat underemployment rates. Italy has a relatively low rate given they have such high unemployment rates of over 10 percent. The Netherlands has a noticeably high PTFER in 2017 even though the unemployment rate is 4.9 percent. Some of these contrasts reflect structural differences in national labor markets. In 2017, 46.6 percent of employment in the Netherlands was part-time, while in Portugal and Poland the equivalent rates were substantially lower at 8.6 percent and 8.3 percent, respectively. These differences in the share of part-timers in total employment obviously constrain possible variation in the underemployment rate derived from reports of part-timers, without necessarily fully reflecting differences in labor market slack.

Of note also is that the rise in U7 has accompanied only small changes in average hours worked in both the United States and the UK. In the U.S. private sector, average weekly hours, according to the BLS, were 34.4 in January 2008 versus 34.5 in January 2019. For production and non-supervisory workers, it was unchanged at 33.7 on both dates. In the UK, average actual hours at the start of the recession in March–May 2008 were 37.1 for full-timers and 15.6 for part-timers. This compares to 37.1 and 16.3, respectively, for September–November 2018. Overall average actual hours were 32.0 at both dates. In Germany average hours declined slightly from 35.6 to 35.2. Usual weekly hours fell in the European Union, according to Eurostat, from 37.9 in 2008 to 37.1 in 2016.

The Bell/Blanchflower Underemployment Index

In a series of papers David Bell and I used data from the UKLFS to show that measuring underemployment using the number of part-time workers who want full-time jobs does not fully capture the extent of worker dissatisfaction with currently contracted hours.[13] This is due to its focus on a particular group of workers—involuntary part-timers—rather than all workers. Eurostat's coverage inclusion of voluntary part-timers who want more hours but don't want a full-time job is an obvious improvement, but it doesn't take account of the desires of full-timers to change their hours. It turns out that, over the Great Recession years and subsequently, not only do involuntary part-timers who say they would prefer full-time jobs appear to be underemployed but so also do voluntary part-timers who wish to remain part-time and some full-timers.[14] Some workers, mostly full-timers, say they would like to work fewer hours, which also varies over time, both in terms of how many workers report this and the aggregate number of hours they report. We can use these data to determine who is overemployed and who is underemployed.

In the UKLFS, workers report whether they would like to change their hours *at the going wage rate* and how many extra or fewer hours they would like to work. A desired hours variable can be constructed for each individual. It is set to zero for workers who are content with their current hours. It is negative for those who wish to reduce their hours (the overemployed) and positive for those who want more hours (the underemployed). Equivalent questions are asked in the European Labor Force Survey (EULFS) in twenty-five countries including three non-EU countries—Switzerland, Iceland, and Norway—and the UK.[15] We do not have microdata on Bulgaria, Slovenia, Slovakia, or the Czech Republic. None of the major U.S. surveys asks workers whether they wish to increase or decrease their hours. Hence the calculations that we report below are not available for the United States. We use annual data for European countries rather than quarterly data for the UK to avoid having to calculate rather complicated seasonal adjustments by country.

Our underemployment measure is more general than the unemployment rate because it is affected by the willingness of current workers to vary their hours at the current pay rate—underemployment. For any given unemployment rate, a higher underemployment index implies that reductions in unemployment will be more difficult to achieve because existing workers are seeking more hours—there is excess capacity in the internal labor market. We define our underemployment index in hours rather than people space.

Our index gives a more complete picture of excess demand or excess supply in the labor market than does the unemployment rate. It may also offer advantages over the unemployment rate as a means of calibrating the output gap. It is not affected by equal-sized increases and reductions in desired hours. If the underemployment index is high relative to the unemployment rate and there is an upturn in demand, cost-minimizing producers will offer existing workers longer hours, thus avoiding recruitment costs and the costs of uncertainty associated with new hires. Plus, the unemployment rate will not fall so rapidly in a recovery if the underemployment index is relatively high at the start of the recovery. This is what may have happened in the 1980s in the United States and in the post–Great Recession period.

We also use the EULFS microdata to estimate aggregate employment, unemployment, and average hours of work. All of these statistics are converted to national aggregates using weights supplied with the EULFS. We include the employed, self-employed, family workers, and those on government schemes when calculating total employment and average working hours. Together these calculations provide all of the components necessary to create our underemployment index.

Note that unemployment rates peaked in most countries around 2013. They were especially high in Greece and Spain, where they reached over 25 percent. The annual unemployment rate peaked between 15 and 20 percent in Estonia, Ireland, Croatia, Cyprus, Latvia, Lithuania, and Portugal. In the UK it peaked at 8.1 percent compared with 9.6 percent in the United States. Poland, which had seen an unemployment rate of 20 percent in 2002, saw a steady fall in its rate after its accession to the EU in 2004. Other Accession countries—both the A8 that joined in 2004 and the A2 that joined in 2007—saw much lower unemployment rates in 2017 than prior to the Great Recession.[16] By 2017 over 2.65 million people from the A8 and around one million from the A2 had registered to work in the UK.[17] According to the OECD the annual unemployment rate peaked in Canada at 8.4 percent in 2009 and at 6.1 percent in Australia in both 2014 and 2015, at 6.4 percent in New Zealand in 2012, and at 3.7 percent in Japan in 2010, which is the same level it reached in 2016 and 2017.[18]

Table 5.2 reports the number of weekly hours of those who say they want fewer hours and those who say they want more hours for thirteen major European countries. (Data for a further thirteen countries and for more years are provided in Bell and Blanchflower, forthcoming.) The numbers of people who want more hours moved sharply upward in the recession. The number who want fewer hours is more stable but does show some increase; that is, the numbers are less negative. They become more negative again in 2016.

The final three columns report the difference between our calculated underemployment rate and the unemployment rate for each of these thirteen countries, for 2007, 2012, and 2016. Fewer and more hours in table 5.2 are added together and divided by average actual hours in the country*year cell to create unemployment equivalents that are added to our estimate of the

Table 5.2. Excess Hours

	#Fewer Hours			#More hours			Difference		
	2007	2012	2016	2007	2012	2016	2007	2012	2016
Belgium	4.0	4.9	4.7	-0.1	-0.1	0	2.3	2.8	2.6
Finland	7.5	7.5	7.7	-6.7	-4.8	-5.0	0.8	2.7	2.8
France	73.0	69.2	77.8	-15.6	-13.7	-17.4	5.5	5.2	5.6
Germany	39.2	78	63.4	-53.2	-38.5	-37.4	2.5	2.7	1.7
Greece	8.8	11.5	12.7	-9.3	-6.4	-6.6	-0.2	2.4	3.0
Ireland	2.1	5.4	4.3	-0.2	0	-0.2	0.8	6.1	4.4
Italy	10.4	16.3	16.7	-9.9	-3.7	-4.8	0.1	1.4	1.3
Netherlands	20.1	19	19.8	-28.1	-20.5	-20.0	-0.1	0.8	0.2
Portugal	8.7	20.5	18.4	-8.9	-7.0	-4.9	0.9	9.3	8.1
Spain	23.2	41.7	33.4	-18.5	-7.1	-7.2	0.5	3.9	3.1
Sweden	15.7	16.1	15.7	-7.8	-8.0	-8.5	4.4	4.4	3.7
Switzerland	8.8	7.7	8.2	-15.8	-18.0	-20.1	-4.7	-6.5	-7.1
UK	28.0	43.1	39.7	-30.8	-28.0	-34.2	-0.2	1.6	0.6

Note: The difference is the underemployment rate minus the unemployment rate.
Source: Bell and Blanchflower, forthcoming.

unemployment rate. In the case of the UK, we use the UKLFS to construct underemployment estimates because the EULFS data file does not contain the numbers who wish to reduce their hours.

These underemployment rates are mostly higher than the equivalent unemployment rates, and especially so in recent years, but in some cases, they are lower. This occurs when, in aggregate, workers wish to reduce their hours rather than increase them. In 2016 the difference was positive everywhere except Switzerland and Lithuania. It makes sense to compare the most recent data with what was occurring well before the onset of recession. In most cases the difference is well above pre-recession levels. Of note is that the difference in the UK was negative pre-recession and positive subsequently. The difference in 2016 is especially high in Portugal.

Germany is of particular note. It experienced a steady decline in the underemployment rate over time from 2004. Switzerland had a negative rate in all years except 1999, showing workers there wanted fewer hours. In almost every other case the rate rose through around 2012 or so and then fell back. This includes Belgium, Denmark, Spain, France, Greece, Ireland, the Netherlands, Portugal, Sweden, Cyprus, Estonia, Croatia, Hungary, Iceland, Lithuania, Malta, Poland, and the UK.[19] In a couple of other countries, the drop came later; for example, Finland and Romania didn't see a decline until 2016. Austria and Norway saw steady rises from 2011 and 2012 onward. Luxembourg's rate reached a peak in 2008. Underemployment rates remain elevated in many countries.

There are obvious biases apparent from table 5.1 in excluding voluntary part-timers and full-timers from any calculation of underemployment in a country. The U7 is a downward-biased estimator of the extent of labor market slack in the period after the Great Recession. The extent of the bias will move over the business cycle and remains uncertain; the United States does not have such data, but it does seem there are consistent time-series patterns across countries. The Eurostat measure is a halfway house and less biased as it uses data from all part-timers but still excludes full-timers. As the recession hit all three groups of workers, involuntary and voluntary part-timers were more likely to say they would like more hours. The table does show also considerable variation across countries, which means it isn't simple to work out for the United States, which does not have continuous desired hours data. In the UK the three groups each account for about one-third of excess hours in each of the three years. This seems to be a major omission. We will

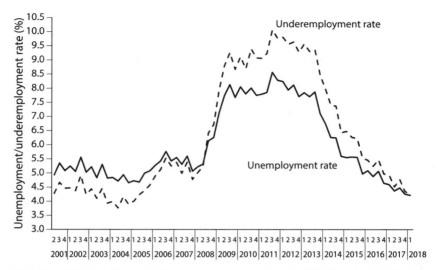

Figure 5.2. UK underemployment and unemployment rates. *Source:* Bell and Blanch-flower 2018b.

show that the U7 plays a hugely significant role in wage determination in the United States.

Figure 5.2 is taken from Bell and Blanchflower 2018b and shows how the UK quarterly underemployment and unemployment rates have moved. In the years before 2008 the UK underemployment rate was below the unemployment rate. In the years after 2008 the underemployment rate rose more than the unemployment rate and recently the gap has closed. Figure 5.3, also for the UK, shows why. It plots the number of hours of those who say they want more hours and the number who say they want fewer at the going wage. The more hours series was broadly flat until recently but was always above the fewer hours series before 2008. That suggests there is still a good deal of underutilized resources in the labor market available to be used up before the UK reaches full employment. It is notable that post-recession in the UK both lines in figure 5.3 have moved upward.

Our index allows for the possibility that not just part-time workers are underemployed. Questions on desired hours are asked of the part-timers who are voluntary and want full-time jobs and full-timers.[20] In general full-timers want fewer hours, but both groups of part-timers want more hours. Involuntary part-timers in the UK desire an average of about ten extra hours while

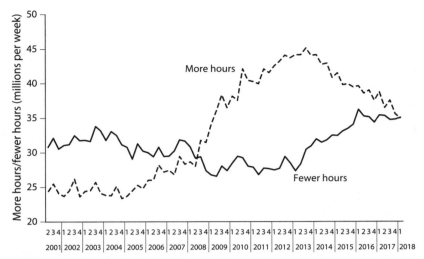

Figure 5.3. UK more hours and fewer hours in millions of hours. *Source:* Bell and Blanchflower 2018b.

voluntary part-timers wanted fewer—around one hour. But there were many more of them. In the years 2001–8 the former group in the UK averaged 2.2 percent of workers versus 4.1 percent in the subsequent period while voluntary part-timers were 18 percent in both periods. It turns out that post-2008 the underemployment rate is more important than the unemployment rate in terms of its impact on wages.

Table 5.3 decomposes the net variation in aggregate desired hours between countries into components from voluntary and involuntary part-timers, and full-timers. It is clear that U7 is a biased estimator of the extent of labor market slack in the period after the Great Recession. The extent of the bias will move over the business cycle and remains uncertain—the United States does not have such data, but it does seem there are consistent time-series patterns across countries. As the recession hit all three groups of workers, involuntary and voluntary part-timers were more likely to say they would like more hours. In the UK, Germany, France, and Ireland, for example, in 2016, involuntary part-time employment accounted for only around a third of excess hours. There is considerable variation in these groups across countries, implying that there is no straightforward relationship that could be exploited to predict the U.S. underemployment rate. This seems a major omission.

Table 5.3. Share of Excess Hours (%)

	2008			2012			2016		
	Voluntary	Involuntary	Full-time	Voluntary	Involuntary	Full-time	Voluntary	Involuntary	Full-time
Belgium	25	33	43	35	19	45	37	21	43
Finland	14	33	53	16	24	59	15	39	47
France	11	21	68	13	23	64	12	27	61
Germany	27	70	2	34	39	27	49	38	13
Greece	36	115	-51	15	59	26	13	70	17
Ireland	18	13	69	21	35	45	20	32	48
Italy	22	152	-74	7	70	22	5	99	-4
Netherlands	237	58	-195	138	62	-100	280	167	-347
Portugal	8	23	69	10	21	69	11	20	70
Spain	24	74	2	9	74	17	10	91	-1
Switzerland	-8	-8	117	-3	-9	112	-1	-10	110
UK (2007 not 2008)	38	22	41	31	37	32	37	32	31

As an economy moves toward full employment opportunities should increasingly present themselves for underemployed workers who want more hours and overemployed workers who want fewer hours to overcome their hours constraints. Full employment opens up possibilities as more jobs become available. One possibility for those who want more hours is to obtain a second job. A further possibility would be for employees to switch to self-employment, where they could choose their own hours. Self-employment could be a secondary or primary job. This should be especially apparent as the economy moves closer to full employment. There is no evidence in the data so far to support such a claim in the United States or the UK on either front in the recent period when the unemployment rate dropped below 5 percent to 4 percent and lower.

There is no evidence of any rise in either the United States or the UK in multiple job holding as the unemployment rate dropped below 5 percent. In the UK in April 2008 there were 1.12 million workers with more than one job or 3.8 percent of total employment. In October 2018 there were also 1.12 million at a rate of 3.42 percent. In the United States there were 7.6 million multiple job holders in January 2008 (5.2% of jobs) versus 7.8 million in January 2019 (4.9%). Hirsch, Husain, and Winters (2016) find no relationship in the United States between multiple job holding and unemployment. Lalé (2015) finds similarly. Pouliakis (2017) finds that the multiple job holding rate in the EU28 has remained roughly constant over the last fifteen years.

Just as there is no evidence of a rise in multiple job holding in the United States or the UK as the unemployment rate has fallen below 5 percent, there is also no evidence of a significant rise in self-employment in either country as that happened. The self-employment rate in the UK, measured as self-employment as a percent of total employment, *rose* from 13.1 percent in April 2008 to 15.1 percent in September 2016 when the unemployment rate was last 5 percent. In the period since then through August 2018 when the unemployment rate dropped to 4.0 percent, the self-employment rate fell back to 14.9 percent in October 2018.

In the United States the seasonally adjusted number of unincorporated self-employed was 10.2 million in January 2008 and 9.6 million in January 2019. The unadjusted number of incorporated self-employed, which is the only number the BLS reports, rose from 5.8 million to 6.0 million over the same period. The unemployment rate was last 5 percent in September

2016. The self-employment rate in the United States, obtained by adding the incorporated and unincorporated numbers together, fell from 10.8 percent in January 2008 to 10 percent in September 2016 when the unemployment rate was last 5 percent. The unemployment rate dropped further to 4.0 percent in January 2019, up from 3.7 percent in November 2018, and the self-employment rate remained unchanged at 10 percent.

If the United States or the UK were anywhere close to full employment I would have expected to see evidence from both self-employment and multiple job holding that the underemployed were starting to move their actual hours closer to their desired hours. None is apparent in the data.

Wage Growth and the Lack of It, Explained

This section establishes some key stylized facts for a range of labor markets before and after the Great Recession. Our first piece of evidence concerns low wage growth internationally.

A major part of this lack of wage response post-recession is because of globalization. This includes the fear that migrants may come and take away jobs. It also includes the possibility that a firm will move production abroad or subcontract parts of its work abroad. The weakening of labor unions, which have seen their membership decline around the world, means workers have little bargaining power. Some of the story for flat wage growth also turns out to be because of underemployment, which continues to remain elevated. In some ways the very existence of underemployment arises because of the weakness of worker bargaining power. Underemployment is less prevalent in the union than in the non-union sector.

Important recent work by Hong et al. (2018) from the IMF across thirty countries has shown that the involuntary part-time rate (IPTR)—expressed as a percent of total employment—significantly lowers wage growth.[21] They find that, on average, a 1-percentage-point increase in the involuntary part-time employment share is associated with a 0.3-percentage-point decline in nominal wage growth.

Importantly Hong et al. find that the effect is more pronounced in countries where the unemployment rate is below pre–Great Recession averages—the Czech Republic, Germany, Japan, Israel, the Slovak Republic, the UK, and the United States. Within this group of countries, a 1-percentage-point increase in the involuntary part-time employment share is associated with a

0.7-percentage-point decline in wage growth. The estimated effect is only 0.2 percentage point for countries with unemployment appreciably above the pre–Great Recession averages. The authors conclude that "involuntary part-time employment appears to have weakened wage growth even in economies where headline unemployment rates are now at, or below, their averages in the years leading up to the recession" (2018, 2).

Hong et al. kindly provided their data to David Bell and me; we then mapped onto the data our underemployment rates for nineteen of the countries.[22] We found that for the whole period covering both pre- and post-recession, both the unemployment rate and the underemployment rate significantly lower wage growth. Post-2008 only the underemployment rate lowers pay growth while the unemployment rate has no effect. David and I find similar results below with the IPTR for the United States.

David Bell and I (2018b) created a balanced panel of twenty regions by sixty-two quarters for the UK from 2002 Q2 to 2017 Q3 using data from the LFS. We found the unemployment rate had no impact on pay over this period. In contrast we found that our "under hours" variable significantly lowered wages. On top of that we found some evidence that "over hours" raised pay; workers who wanted fewer hours received a compensating differential. Underemployment lowers wages and overemployment raises them, while unemployment does not have an impact in the UK.

In a subsequent work David Bell and I (forthcoming) examined hourly and weekly wages using state-level data from the BLS matched by state and year to data from the Merged Outgoing Rotation Group files of the CPS for 1980–2017. We take the microdata in each year and collapse it to the state*year cell to calculate wages as well as personal characteristics including schooling, age, race, and gender. The personal controls are measured across all individuals while the wage data are calculated for employees only, and part-time for economic reasons variables are calculated for all workers. We mapped that onto state-level data from the BLS on the unemployment rate (U3) as well as data on U4 through U6, which are alternative measures of labor market slack, from 2003 through 2017.[23] Bell and I found that the unemployment rate lowered wage growth in the period 1980–2007, consistent with the earlier findings for the 1960s, 1970s, and 1980s in Blanchflower and Oswald 1994.

We then restricted the period to the years since the onset of the Great Recession, which the NBER's Business Cycle Dating Committee

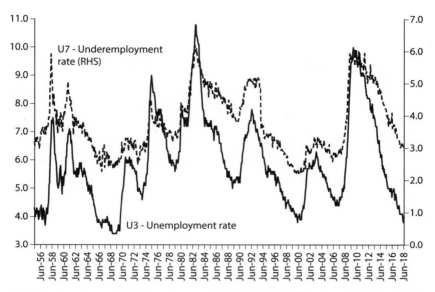

Figure 5.4. U.S. unemployment and underemployment rates, June 1955–June 2018. RHS = right-hand side. *Source:* BLS.

categorized as starting in December 2007. There is no wage curve in hourly wage*unemployment space in the post–Great Recession period. We then added the part-time for economic reasons, defined as a proportion of total employment, which has a significant negative coefficient with or without the presence of the unemployment rate. So, there is a wage curve in wage*underemployment space. We also included the change in the homeownership rate as a control, which was negative in every year from 2005 but became positive in 2017. The variable enters significantly negative: a falling homeownership rate lowered wage pressure in the period since 2008.

Figure 5.4 plots the U.S. unemployment rate (U3) and the underemployment rate (U7) since May 1955, which shows that the latter remains above its pre-recession low of 2.2 percent, last observed in October 2000. An unemployment rate of 3.9 percent was last seen in December 2000. The low of the unemployment rate series was 3.4 percent, which was last seen in May 1969.

This new U7 variable significantly lowers wage growth while the unemployment rate (U3) has no effect. We also created two new variables we call U8 and U9, which identify the discouraged and marginally attached worker rates, expressed as a percentage of the civilian labor force. To be clear then, as constructed, U7a + U8 + U9 = U6, where here the denominator of U7a is the labor force, not employment. U8 and U9 are both insignificant. In terms of wage growth, the U7 variable is driving all the action in the U6 variable and in the years since 2008, U3, U8, and U9 are irrelevant. Underemployment matters these days as a measure of labor market slack in wage determination while unemployment does not.[24]

In the later period the significant and negative U7 variable allows us to calculate the long-run underemployment elasticity, which is –.03. So, there is still a well-defined wage curve in wage underemployment space. The change in the homeownership rate is once again significantly negative. Wage responsiveness post-recession to a change in labor market slack has fallen. We found similar results for the UK (Bell and Blanchflower 2018b).

Underemployment Has Replaced Unemployment as the Main Measure of Labor Market Slack

In the post-recession period underemployment has replaced unemployment as the main indicator of labor market slack. Notably, underemployment has not returned to its pre-recession level in many countries whereas unemployment has. In the past, at the low levels of the unemployment rate existing in countries like the UK, Germany, and the United States, there was a pay norm growth rate of 4 percent in the years before the Great Recession and 2 percent or a little higher subsequently. Wages grew by 4 percent and more a year before the Great Recession and 3 percent and less after it: it's as simple as that. The reason is that in 2018 underemployment is pushing down on wages while the unemployment rate contains little or no information at such low levels in either the UK or the United States. At the very least the unemployment rate is having much less impact than it did before the Great Recession.

David Bell and I in a series of papers have constructed an underemployment index that is preferable to using the data on part-timers who can't get full-time jobs. We found evidence across European countries that voluntary part-timers also report wanting more hours and Eurostat now uses this in their definition of underemployment. In contrast, if full-timers say they want to change their hours it is usually to decrease them. During the recession the number of additional hours part-time workers wanted, whether voluntary or involuntary, increased sharply. There was also a fall in the number of hours full-timers wanted their work weeks to be reduced by. In the recovery, just as the number of involuntary part-timers fell, so did our index. The extent of the bias in only having the number of PTFER as in the United States remains unclear. Trends in our series and the involuntary part-time rate, whether expressed as a percent of total employment or the labor force, seem to vary by country.

We find evidence (Bell and Blanchflower, forthcoming) that in the years after the Great Recession underemployment predicts what is happening to wage growth, whereas unemployment does not. Existing levels of underemployment are predictive of low wage growth because they do not suggest economies are at full employment. The low levels of the unemployment rate suggest much higher levels of wage growth than are being observed and appear to be giving policymakers a false signal. Underemployment matters; unemployment does not.

Declines in the homeownership rate appear to have lowered the Non-Accelerating Inflation Rate of Unemployment (NAIRU) in the United States and likely have done the same in other countries such as the UK that have also seen sharp declines in homeownership rates. Oswald and I (2013) estimate that implies that a 10-percentage-point rise in the homeownership rate in the United States will equate to an extra 1.5 percentage points in the unemployment rate. Hence a 5- to 6-point move downward in the homeownership rate, which is what we have seen, implies a fall of 0.8 percentage points in the natural rate of unemployment, or the NAIRU. A lower NAIRU implies less wage growth at a given unemployment or underemployment rate. The wage curve in the years since the Great Recession in the United States exists in wage underemployment space.

Even though the unemployment rate is at historic lows in many countries, this does not suggest that these countries' labor markets are anywhere close to full employment. Full employment likely does not mean excessively high underemployment rates where workers are willing to work more hours at the going wage.

David Bell and I also found in a further paper (2018c) that workers do not seem to like underemployment. In part, as noted above, the reason is likely to come from their irregular work schedules and lower pay. There is some evidence from the UK from well-being surveys that supports that contention. The ONS in the UK collects data on happiness, life satisfaction, anxiety, and whether life is worthwhile as a supplement to the Labor Force

Survey. Below I report well-being rates for various groups of workers: these are all scored from 0 (not at all happy) to 10 (completely happy) and the data cover the years 2013–17.

	Happiness	Life satis- faction	Worth- while	Anxious
Unemployed	6.9	6.7	7.1	3.4
Workers only				
Full-timers	7.5	7.7	7.9	2.8
Voluntary part-timers	7.7	7.9	8.2	2.8
Involuntary part-timers	7.2	7.2	7.6	3.1
Under hours = 0	7.5	7.8	8.0	2.8
Under hours > 0	7.3	7.3	7.7	3.2
Under hours ≥ 20	7.3	7.5	7.8	3.3
PTWFT 7 under hours ≥ 10	7.0	6.8	7.2	3.2
Fewer hours > 0	7.4	7.7	7.9	3.2

For each of these measures involuntary part-timers are less content than voluntary part-timers or full-timers. However, they do not have the low levels of well-being of the unemployed. The underemployed do not want to be underemployed. The overemployed are anxious.

Bell and I (2018c) found remarkable evidence that depression in the UK, using the Labour Force Surveys, has risen since 2010, when it was 1.6 percent, to 3.6 percent in 2018. The rise was especially apparent among the underemployed, whose incidence of depression rose from 1.5 percent in 2010 to 4.8 percent in 2018. This was a bigger proportionate rise than experienced by the unemployed (2.9 to 8 percent).

It would make sense for the BLS to include a question on workers' desired hours in its Current Population Survey given the importance of the involuntary part-time variable in explaining U.S. wage growth. It remains uncertain how much additional information would be obtained from being able to construct our measure, because in the analysis we performed the results from using our index are broadly similar to those using an involuntary part-time measure in the UK. The extent of any bias is uncertain, though, given the rather different results by country in terms of the share of underemployment accounted for by the involuntary part-timers.

In the post–Great Recession years, measures of underemployment replace unemployment as the primary indicators of labor market slack in many countries and help provide a more convincing explanation of wage growth. The fact that underemployment has not returned to pre-recession levels is a big part of the benign wage-growth story.

PART II

The Response to the Great Recession

CHAPTER 6

Something Horrible Happened

I joined the Monetary Policy Committee (MPC) at the Bank of England in July 2006. I didn't apply for the job. I read in the *Financial Times* that the UK government was looking for a replacement for Professor (now Sir) Steve Nickell, whom I had known for years. I eventually got a call from (now) Lord Nick Macpherson, Permanent Secretary of the Treasury, asking if I was interested.[1] A couple of weeks later I was on holiday at the Boulders Resort in Arizona and got the call that they wanted to offer me the job. I accepted and served on the MPC from 2006 to 2009. During the second half of that term, from around October 2007 onward, I started to vote for rate cuts, all on my own. Believe me, it was the worst time of my life. Eight people on the MPC had the same opinion and I had a different one, so there were only two opinions. I have to admit that I felt like I had the weight of the British people on my shoulders. I felt totally isolated. As the famous Liverpool FC battle cry from the Kop End, the old Gerry and the Pacemakers song goes, "Walk on with hope in your heart and you'll never walk alone." I had no hope and felt like I was walking alone. Some years later Gordon Brown, who was absolutely excellent during the crisis, called me up and apologized for appointing me "to that awful job." I still believe Gordon Brown and Ben Bernanke saved the world.

I commuted to the UK every three weeks from my home in New Hampshire, and during 2007 and the early part of 2008 I watched as shops started closing in the towns in the Upper Valley—Lebanon, White River Junction, Claremont, and Windsor.[2] The housing market started slowing and house prices turned downward. The patterns I saw where I lived suddenly started to appear in the UK. The pandemic had started to spread. Too few people were watching. Nouriel Roubini, otherwise known as Dr. Doom, had also spotted that a downturn was coming. Some years later he and I commiserated on what had happened and that nobody much had listened to our warnings on a beach in Bahrain after we both gave talks there, waiting for our delayed long-haul flights home.

While Rome Burned

Turning points are especially hard for forecasters to spot. When the good times roll they think they will continue forever, and vice versa when the downturn comes they are too optimistic. This is what happened in 2008. Policymakers in government and central banks missed the big one because economists whose job is to warn of impending doom failed to do so. The job of volcanologists is to predict when a volcano will erupt. Weathermen are supposed to be able to predict when hurricanes will hit. Macroeconomists are supposed to spot recessions.

It is instructive to examine the economic projections reported by members of the FOMC during 2008. For simplicity, I report the central tendencies, which exclude the three highest and three lowest projections. In January the projections for GDP growth were, as percentages, as follows:

	2008	2009
January 2008	1.3 to 2.0	2.1 to 2.7
April 2008	0.3 to 1.2	2.0 to 2.8
June 2008	1.0 to 1.6	2.0 to 2.8
October 2008	0 to 0.3	−0.2 to 1.1
January 2009		−1.3 to −0.5
April 2009		−2.0 to −1.3

The actual quarterly GDP outcomes reported in 2018, after a long series of revisions, were as follows:

Q1 2008	−0.68
Q2 2008	0.50
Q3 2008	−0.48

Q4 2008	-2.11
Q1 2009	-1.39
Q2 2009	-0.14
Q3 2009	0.33
Q4 2009	0.97

The FOMC missed the big one; the central tendencies had no negatives for 2008, and they were unduly pessimistic for 2009. The transcript of the Fed's meeting on September 16, 2008, when it kept the federal funds rate at 2 percent, only has a couple of mentions of a recession. The most notable quote is from Chairman Ben Bernanke, which has a hint of something coming: "I think what we saw in the recent labor reports removes any real doubt that we are in a period that will be designated as an official NBER recession. Unemployment rose 1.1 percentage points in four months, which is a relatively rapid rate of increase. The significance of that for our deliberations is, again, that there does seem to be some evidence that, in recession regimes, the dynamics are somewhat more powerful, and we tend to see more negative and correlated innovations in spending equations. So, I think that we are in for a period of quite slow growth."[3]

The transcript makes clear at the very outset that there was deep trouble on Wall Street: "The markets are continuing to experience very significant stresses this morning, and there are increasing concerns about the insurance company AIG. That is the reason that Vice Chairman Geithner is not attending."[4] On Saturday, September 13, 2008, Timothy Geithner, then the president of the Federal Reserve Bank of New York, called a meeting on the future of Lehman, which included the possibility of an emergency liquidation of its assets. Lehman Brothers filed for bankruptcy protection on September 15, 2008, the day before the FOMC meeting.

Boston Fed president Eric Rosengren told my Dartmouth class "Financial Crisis of the Noughties" some years later that it would have been possible to rescue Lehman Brothers over the several months after Bear Stearns collapsed in March 2008. By September 15 when Lehman filed for chapter 11 bankruptcy protection it was too late as they were already insolvent. The job of the central bank is to help solvent but illiquid banks, not the insolvent. Clearly opportunities were missed.

I got into big trouble at the start of 2008 when I did an interview with Ashley Seager, at the *Guardian*, where I said the MPC was "fiddling while

Rome burns."[5] In testimony to the Treasury Select Committee in the House of Commons that oversees the MPC, I worried on March 28, 2008, about what might happen: "My concern would be one should make sure one is ahead of the curve so that later one is not in a position where something horrible happens, I do not want that to occur. My risks are to the downside and I have concerns that *something horrible might come* and I do not want that to happen."[6] Sadly, something horrible did happen.

Mervyn King, the governor of the Bank of England, made it clear throughout 2007 and 2008 that the United States was irrelevant to the UK. At the Treasury Select Committee MP Andrew Love asked King whether he was concerned that U.S. recession might spread to the UK (Q38, March 26, 2008). "For us, far more important than the United States in terms of the impact on demand in the UK is the impact on the euro area because they have a weight three times larger than the United States in our trade-weighted index, so what happens in the euro area is much more important to us directly than the US economy." The governor of the Bank of England had no idea what was going on in the British economy in 2008 as the biggest recession in a hundred years hit. The two countries had not decoupled. It turned out that when the United States sneezed, the UK caught pneumonia, from which it still hasn't fully recovered.

Lord King even said this, sitting two seats from me on March 28, 2008, three days before the Great Recession started, giving testimony to the Treasury Select Committee at the House of Commons: "I do not think we really know what will happen to unemployment. At least, the Almighty has not vouchsafed to me the path of unemployment data over the next year. He may have done to Danny, but he has not done to me."[7]

It wasn't just in the UK that forecasters were hopeless. The International Monetary Fund (IMF), for example, in their October 2008 report, forecast world output to grow in 2009 by 3.9 percent. Country forecasts were: United States, 0.5 percent; Germany, 0 percent; France, 0.2 percent; Italy and Spain, –0.2 percent; Japan, 0.5 percent; UK, –0.1 percent; and Canada, 1.3 percent. It didn't turn out that way. Moises Schwarz, the IMF's Independent Evaluation Officer, argued that "the IMF's pre-crisis surveillance mostly identified the right issues but did not foresee the magnitude of the risks that would later become paramount" (2016, 1).

Larry Kudlow, President Trump's director of the National Economic Council, called it precisely wrong in December 2007, the month that the United States entered recession.

Yesterday's tremendous ADP jobs report puts the dagger into the very heart of the recession case. The fact is, America is working. Look at how close the reports parallel one another. So here's my point: Jobs aren't folding. Jobs aren't plummeting. Jobs are strengthening. Now I'm not smart enough to know what the jobs number is going to be tomorrow, but you could easily have a blockbuster 200,000 jobs report. I don't know, it could be 150K, it could be minus 600K, but I highly doubt that folks. When you see this kind of ADP report, you've got a whole new situation. . . . There ain't no recession.[8]

The same day Kudlow's comments were published the official data release from the BLS showed that the unemployment rate rose from 4.7 percent to 5 percent and the number of unemployed rose by 474,000. Non-farm payrolls were +18,000 while private non-farm payrolls fell 13,000.[9]

Kudlow was at it again in November 2018, arguing that "the basic economy has reawakened and it's gonna stay there. I mean, I'm reading some of the weirdest stuff, how a recession is around the corner—nonsense. My personal view, our administration's view, recession is so far in the distance I can't see it."[10] Maybe he is right this time, but maybe he isn't.

The MPC produced a forecast in August 2008 that I have to admit I signed on to—and the main inflation report that accompanied it never made any mention of recession. I am so embarrassed. A couple of weeks earlier the first estimate of quarterly GDP growth was reported by the ONS for 2008 Q2 of +0.2 percent. I had expected the number to be negative and that number threw me for a loop. By that point I had started to doubt that I was right. I went home after the meeting in early August with the intention of resigning as I was clearly so wrong.

Figure 6.1A is the MPC's forecast for quarterly GDP growth. The first vertical line in 2008 is where we were at the time of the forecast. The shaded bands depict the probability of various outcomes for GDP growth. To the left of the first vertical dashed line, the distribution reflects the likelihood of revisions to the data over the past; to the right, it reflects uncertainty over the evolution of GDP growth in the future. If economic circumstances identical to those during the time the forecast is made were to prevail on 100 occasions, the MPC's best collective judgment is that the mature estimate of GDP would lie within the darkest central band on only 10 of those occasions. The chart is constructed so that outturns are also expected to lie within each pair of the lighter areas on 10 occasions. Consequently, GDP

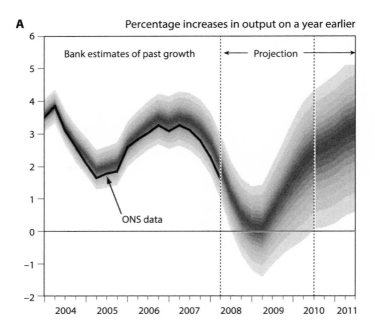

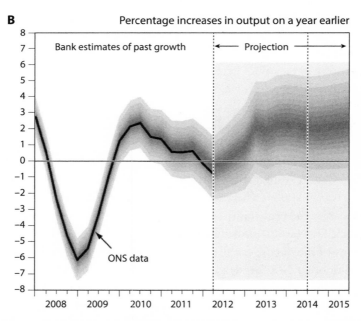

Figure 6.1. (A) MPC August 2008 GDP projection based on market interest rate expectations. *Source:* Bank of England. (B) MPC August 2012 GDP projection based on market interest rate expectations. *Source:* Bank of England.

growth is expected to lie somewhere within the entire fan on 90 out of 100 occasions.

The fan narrows to the left, as data revisions occur and we become more certain about the actual data. The black line shows the official data. The fact that the majority of the shaded fan in the backcast is above the line means the MPC expects data revisions to pull up the data. The forecast to the right has a trumpet shape as it is harder to forecast further into the future. The forecast horizon is where the MPC is focused on given that it takes about two years for its actions to have an effect. The forecast suggests that the MPC is 90 percent confident that GDP growth on a year earlier will be in the interval from around 0.5 percent to just over 5 percent. The saddest thing is that it predicted that there would be no recession—and no quarters of negative growth.

GDP data are subject to revision, especially at turning points. Growth in 2008 Q2 was revised down a lot; as I noted earlier, GDP fell by 6.3 percent, peak to trough. In the table below I report the revisions for four quarters of data in 2008. I present the initial estimate and those prevailing in May 2018, as well as a couple of intermediate dates.

	2008 Q1	2008 Q2	2008 Q3	2008 Q4
April 2008	0.4			
July 2008	0.3	0.2		
August 2008	0.3	0		
October 2008	0.3	0	–0.5	
January 2009	0.4	0	–0.6	–1.5
August 2011	0	–1.3	–2.0	–2.1
August 2012	0.1	–0.9	–1.8	–2.1
May 2018	0.3	–0.7	–1.6	–2.2

It took until May 2009 for the 2008 Q2 estimate to be revised to a negative number and confirm the start of the recession, given that the third quarter was always negative. By May 2018 the 2008 Q2 figure had been revised from +0.2 to –0.7 percent. The third and fourth quarters had downward revisions also. By May 2018, 2009 Q1 and 2009 Q2 are confirmed as being negative at –1.5 percent and –0.2 percent. It is also difficult to estimate upturns; the initial estimate for 2009 Q3 in October 2009 was –0.4 percent; by May 2018 the number had been revised to +0.2%. At upturns the statistical authorities are more likely to underpredict what is happening.

Figure 6.1B, taken from the August 2012 inflation report, shows what happened. Output collapsed and there were five negative quarters. It is also apparent from this figure that in August 2008 the UK was already in recession. We didn't know where we were. We didn't know where we had been, and we didn't know where we were going. Same as now.

Northern Rock

It is not as if there weren't adequate warnings. During my time on the MPC I watched as thousands of people lined up outside Northern Rock when its website failed. The world was treated to the scenes of a good old bank run. Depositors waiting in line around the country to withdraw their cash. Shin (2009) has noted that the last time that happened was at Overend, Gurney, a London bank that got in trouble in the railway and docks boom of the 1860s.

Britain's deposit-insurance scheme guaranteed fully only the first £2,000 of deposits, and then 90 percent of only the next £33,000. It was sensible to run to the bank to get your money. Northern Rock relied on wholesale markets rather than on retail deposits to finance most of its lending.[11] In January 2007, it announced record pretax profits of £627 million for 2006, up 27 percent on the previous year. As the MPC was pushing interest rates up, from 4.5 percent in July 2006 to 5.75 percent in August 2007, Northern Rock had agreed to issue a tranche of mortgages at interest rates lower than those it eventually had to pay to finance them. Northern Rock was in trouble.

The Bank of England emphasized the concerns over moral hazard. They wanted to send a message that if bankers took excessive risks they could not look to the central bank to rescue them from the consequences. On September 13, 2007, Alistair Darling, the Chancellor of the Exchequer, had little choice but to agree that the central bank should provide emergency funding to Northern Rock. The run started on the evening of September 13, following the news that a well-known bank had gone to the Bank of England for help.

Northern Rock had seventy-two branches in total, and only four branches in London. Many branches had only a couple of counters because the bank did not normally conduct much of its retail business over the counter. Because of money laundering requirements, large withdrawals could take several minutes to be completed. As the Treasury Select Committee (TSC) noted, these factors together explained why it did not take many customers seeking to withdraw their funds for queues to extend out the front door and into the street—and into the public consciousness.[12]

Lines started to form outside branches of Northern Rock on Friday, September 14, as the share price fell 31 percent on the day. Lines continued to form the next day, Saturday.[13] On Monday, September 17, shares opened 31 percent lower. With lines forming again. Alistair Darling intervened, pledging that the government would guarantee all deposits. Northern Rock was eventually nationalized on February 17, 2008. The run was halted. The man in the street was rightly upset at the failure to stop a bank run. The Bank of England knew well before it failed that Northern Rock was in trouble and did nothing about it.

It was obvious that if Northern Rock, which depended on access to wholesale money markets and had relatively few depositors, was in trouble so would be others that were dependent on that source of funding. At the top of that list were two building societies, Alliance and Leicester (A&L) and Bradford and Bingley (B&B), but nothing was done by the Bank of England. A&L was taken over by Santander in 2008 after its shares fell by more than 80 percent.[14] The latter was eventually sold to Abbey National, after running into "difficulties." Henry Wallop at the *Telegraph* made clear how bad things were, noting that in 1999 shares in B&B were 247 pence. By mid-September 2008 they "were worth just 20p, as the full scale of the UK housing market crash, and the global financial turmoil, made the headwear of choice for B&B shareholders a tin hat rather than a bowler."[15] DeAnne Julius, a former member of the MPC, was reported in the *Economist* on October 18, 2007, as saying, in relation to Northern Rock, that "the first duty of a central bank is to retain confidence in the banking system, especially at a time of illiquidity, and our central bank didn't do that."[16]

Sleeping in the Back Shop

Lord John McFall, chairman of the TSC, famously accused Sir John Gieve, the deputy governor at the Bank of England in charge of financial stability, at a hearing about Northern Rock on September 20, 2007 (Q6), of having a sleep in the back shop while a mugging was taking place in the front. The TSC was also particularly scathing about the governor of the Bank of

England's inaction, due to fears of moral hazard. This was economic theory speaking; it would surely have never been said by an experienced banker. It was time to act, not dither. Michael Fallon, at the time an MP and subsequently UK defense secretary, had it right when he suggested at the hearing that the problem was that the Bank of England failed the practical.

Alistair Darling (as reported in Darling 2011) rescued the Royal Bank of Scotland (RBS) in October 2008. At the time, it was the biggest bank in the world by assets and one of the largest companies in the world. He was told, on October 7, 2008, that if he didn't rescue RBS, which couldn't make a large payment, there was a significant chance that every cash machine and credit card in the world would stop working the following day. The next day, October 8, 2008, the MPC committee I was on had an emergency meeting and, in an unprecedented move, cut rates by 50 basis points in a coordinated easing in monetary policy with six other central banks—the Bank of Canada, the European Central Bank, the U.S. Federal Reserve, Sveriges Riksbank, the Swiss National Bank, and the Bank of Japan. When central banks act together in a surprise move there is good news and bad news. The good news was that they acted together and did something. The bad news was that something was obviously up, and the likelihood was that there had been a bank failure.

From September 2008 on the central banks eventually got it. They cut rates close to zero and started quantitative easing. The models were saying that there was a thing called the "zero lower bound" that interest rates couldn't go below, so if you couldn't lower the price of money then you had to raise the quantity. Only later did we discover that rates could go negative. Plus, the fiscal authorities threw the kitchen sink at the crisis by cutting taxes and offering cash for clunkers and fridges and lots of stimulus money. And it worked, and economies started to grow. Then the fiscal authorities around the world imposed austerity, which Mark Blyth called a "dangerous idea" (2015, 245), while Martin Wolf called it a large unforced error: "The fact that the economy grows in the end does not prove that needlessly weakening the recovery was a sound idea. This has been an unnecessarily protracted slump. It is good that recovery is here, though it is far too soon to tell its quality and durability. But this does not justify what remains a large unforced error."[17]

Central banks were desperate to raise rates and continued to tell anyone who would listen that they were about to, although they didn't because recovery was so tepid. The European Central Bank (ECB), though, did so twice in 2011 as did the Swedish central bank, which caused its economist, Deputy Governor Lars Svensson, to resign in 2013. Swift about-faces were to follow. By the end of 2018 the MPC had raised rates twice in ten years, once in November 2017 from 0.25 to 0.5 percent and then in August 2018 to 0.75 percent. Growth never did happen at the rate it had in past recoveries. It turned out that zero was not even the lower bound as several central banks, including the ECB, the Swiss, Swedish, and Japanese central banks, cut their rates to negative. It still remains unclear how low rates could go.

At the end of August 2008, I decided I was right, and that the UK economy was headed for disaster. I did an interview with Sumeet Desai and Matt Falloon of Reuters that got me into big trouble. I said that two million Britons might be out of work by Christmas and big cuts in interest rates were needed then and there to stop the economy from heading into a deep and prolonged slump. I take no pleasure in the fact that we now know officially from the ONS that unemployment hit two million in November 2008. I argued that the Bank of England could no longer be complacent because the economy was already shrinking, and a rate cut of more than 25 basis points was probably needed. I said that our forecast (figure 6.1A) was wishful thinking and that things could get much worse.

> The fears that I have expressed over the last six months have started to come to fruition. I've obviously voted on quite a number of occasions now for small cuts but we need to act and we probably need to act in larger amounts than that. We need to actually get ahead of the game and it appears that we are now behind. We are going to see much more dramatic drops in output. The way to get out of it is to act, by interest rate cuts and fiscal stimulus and other things to try [to] help people who are hurt through this. Sitting by doing nothing is not going to get us out of this and hoping that a knight in shining armor will come and lift us out of this is optimistic in the extreme.[18]

The MPC meeting was the following Wednesday and Thursday, September 3 and 4, 2008. We would always meet to be briefed on the previous Friday, which was August 29, the day after my interview appeared. I had my hand slapped, which if it had been carried out by Margaret Thatcher would have been called a "severe hand-bagging," about what I had said in the interview. But I made clear I was not impressed by the rest of the MPC's inability to spot the greatest recession in a generation. I had nothing to apologize for.

At that meeting I voted for a rate cut of 50 basis points while the rest voted to leave rates at 5 percent, which they argued was necessary "if inflation was to be brought back to the target in the medium term. That would continue to balance the upside and downside risks to inflation appropriately." In contrast this is what I said: "For one member, the prospects for UK demand had clearly worsened over the month, increasing substantially the downside risk to inflation in the medium term. There was no evidence that inflation expectations were pushing up nominal pay growth. The slowdown might be amplified by financial institutions' responses to increased financial fragility. A significant undershooting of the inflation target, in the medium term, at a time when output and employment would be well below potential, risked damaging the credibility of the monetary framework."[19]

Rates were cut by 50 basis points at the next meeting. They were cut by 150 basis points in November; 100 in December; and 50 in January, February, and March 2009 to 0.50 percent. Seventy-five billion pounds of asset purchases were made in March 2009 and a further £50 billion in May that I voted for. By May 2018 £435 billion of government bonds and £10 billion of corporate bonds were held by the MPC. Quantitative easing started at least a year too late.

The failures of Lehman Brothers, RBS, and Lloyds, the latter two of which were secretly rescued by the UK government, were the turning points. Things might well have been worse if the authorities hadn't acted. In a CBS *60 Minutes* program on March 15, 2009, Ben Bernanke argued that if AIG had failed it would have brought down the financial system. On December 3, 2010, he was interviewed again on *60 Minutes* and was asked about the counterfactual.

> Scott Pelley: What would unemployment be today?
> Ben Bernanke: Unemployment would be much, much higher. It might be something like it was in the Depression. Twenty-five percent. We saw what happened when one or two large financial firms came close to failure or to failure. Imagine if ten or twelve or fifteen firms had failed, which is where we almost were in the fall of 2008. It would have brought down the entire global financial system and it would have had enormous implications,

very long-lasting implications for the global economy, not just the U.S. economy.

I got into even more trouble when I tried to explain what the counterfactual was in the UK. On September 24, 2009, I wrote in the *New Statesman* that "if spending cuts are made too early and the monetary and fiscal stimuli are withdrawn, unemployment could easily reach four million. If large numbers of public sector workers, perhaps as many as a million, are made redundant and there are substantial cuts in public spending in 2010, as proposed by some in the Conservative Party, five million unemployed or more is not inconceivable."[20] The word "if" here was crucial.

I was simply trying to understand the counterfactual—what the world would have looked like if the MPC hadn't acted. In a speech on December 6, 2015, Mark Carney argued that the Bank of England estimated that unemployment would have been 1.5 million higher at its peak, of 2.5 million or so, if the MPC hadn't acted.[21] In 2018 Treasury Secretary Hank Paulson explained what happened in the fall of 2008: "What we were trying to do was to prevent Armageddon. We were looking at a situation where if we felt we had one more big institution go down, it would have taken the whole system down. We were focused on staving off disaster."[22]

Trust in Economists, Rightly, Is Low

Economists and policymakers were looking at what was going on in entirely the wrong way. They were focused on what happened in the 1970s, as I will explain later, which was most unlikely to repeat, and on largely untested theoretical models that amounted to little more than mathematical mind games. Their best defense was that nobody could possibly have expected us to spot the biggest crisis in a generation. That wasn't good enough, of course. We had experienced the Great Depression. The experts were just looking in the wrong places.

I went to a meeting of the Canadian Learned Societies in Newfoundland in May 1997 to present a paper. I arrived at the airport and asked the taxi driver to take me to the Learned Society meetings. He told me that the participants called them "the learneds" and that the locals had another name for the meetings and those who went to them: "the stupids." I didn't realize at the time what an important insight that was.[23]

The reputation of economists and other experts has taken a big hit. As the Queen said at the London School of Economics in November 2009 when she was opening the new Department of Economics, "Why did no one see this coming"? The answer of course was they were working on something else that was more important, which they weren't.

A three-page response from the British Academy to the Queen in July 2009 signed by around thirty distinguished economists, economic journalists, and politicians didn't help. In my view, the letter made it worse: "In summary, Your Majesty, the failure to foresee the timing, extent and severity of the crisis and to head it off, while it had many causes, was principally a failure of the collective imagination of many bright people, both in this country and internationally, to understand the risks to the system as a whole."[24]

Ex–Bank of England deputy governor Charlie Bean astonishingly argued, in a speech in October 2010, that "no one should expect to be able to predict the timing and scale of these sorts of events with any precision."[25] I recall Gordon Brown, the British prime minister, saying that the UK government in September 2007 had simulated what would happen if a bank failed but not if the whole financial system came tumbling down. "We always liked to plan for any eventuality and so we thought it would be very useful to play through the scenario of a bank failure. . . . Would the fall of a bank or a building society raise systemic issues? Could we allow such a bank or building society to fail? What was the point at which such a collapse became a threat to the entire system?" (2010, 17). He continued: "At the time the simulation was not set up to ask what might happen if a combination of banks might be in difficulty" (2010, 19).

Economics itself is in a sorry state.[26] It has overemphasized the importance of theory and "mathiness," as former World Bank chief economist and 2018 Economics Nobel Laureate Paul Romer (2015) has argued. His claim is that economists have made use of mathematics principally to persuade or mislead rather than to clarify. I have a good deal of sympathy with his view that mathiness allows academic politics to masquerade as science. Romer is right that in the end, the test of a model is its "correspondence with the world."[27]

In his presidential address to the American Economic Association in December 1970, Wassily Leontief argued that "in no other field of empirical inquiry has so massive and sophisticated a statistical machinery been used with such indifferent results" (1971, 3). Nothing much had changed four decades later.

Wolfgang Münchau has argued that the curse of our time is fake math. "Think of it," he says, "as fake news for numerically literate intellectuals: it is the abuse of statistics and economic models to peddle one's own political prejudice. . . . Fake maths has given us, the liberal establishment, the illusion of certainty."[28] He may well be right.

Thomas Piketty has argued that "to put it bluntly, the discipline of economics has yet to get over its childish passion for mathematics and for purely theoretical and often highly ideological speculation, at the expense of historical research and collaboration with other social sciences. Economists are all too often preoccupied with petty mathematical problems of interest only to themselves. This obsession with mathematics is an easy way of acquiring the appearance of scientificity without having to answer the more complex problems posed by the world we live in" (2014, 41). That is exactly what I address in this book: the complex problems posed by the world we live in, specifically in relation to jobs.

It is perhaps not surprising that macroeconomists missed the Great Recession. The profession had become complacent. In his 2003 presidential address to the American Economic Association, Bob Lucas denied the possibility of a Great Recession, arguing that "macroeconomics in this original sense has succeeded: Its central problem of depression prevention has been solved, for all practical purposes, and has in fact been solved for many decades" (2003, 1). It hadn't. The view was that stabilization of output, even if possible, should not be a macroeconomic priority because the gains are trivially small. Future Fed chair Janet Yellen and George Akerlof (2006) countered by arguing there is a solid case for stabilization policy, which can produce non-negligible gains in welfare.

John Rapley has it right: "We should have read the warning signs. If history teaches us anything it's that whenever economists feel certain they've found the holy grail of endless peace and prosperity, the end of the present regime is nigh. . . . No sooner do we persuade ourselves that the priesthood has finally broken the old curse than it comes back to haunt us all: pride always goes before a fall" (2017, 399). It sure does.

Economic Forecasting Is Broken

John Kenneth Galbraith once said that economic forecasting makes astrology look good. Ex-president of the Minnesota Federal Reserve and voting member of the FOMC Narayana Kocherlakota, now a professor at the University of Rochester, has argued that macroeconomic forecasting is still broken. Kocherlakota suggests that the point of forecasting is to get a sense of possible outcomes and allocate probabilities to them.[29] The problem is the probabilities have been way off.

In December 2007, the Federal Reserve estimated that there was a less than 5 percent chance that the unemployment rate would be above 6 percent in two years. It eventually rose to 10 percent. Kocherlakota says he has seen little response from academics to fix the problem over the last decade. This, he suggests, matters as "the central bank remains set on raising interest rates because it sees downside risks, such as a sharp decline in growth and hiring, as being relatively small. But there are good reasons to worry that, just as in 2007, any model-based assessment of those risks is overly optimistic—and perhaps wildly so."[30]

Many forecasters have simply assumed that what has come to be known as the productivity puzzle will simply vanish into the ether. For example, the Office for Budget Responsibility (OBR), which produces forecasts for the UK government, assumed that productivity growth would simply return to pre-recession levels. Their forecasts have been wildly inaccurate. Figure 6.2, taken from the OBR's 2017 Forecast Evaluation Report, shows successive and essentially unchanging and inaccurate OBR productivity forecasts and the actual data. No wonder the public is skeptical of elites.

The black line in the figure shows the outcome over the period from 2009 through 2017 along with sixteen successive forecasts. Each forecast implausibly slopes up sharply, and all the forecasts are basically parallel to each other. Each of them forecasts an explosion of productivity growth, which never happened, but there was no learning and no change. The latest March 2017 report showed a very slight shallowing. Each assumed the productivity puzzle was solved when it wasn't. How could they keep making the same mistake? How could they claim productivity was about to take off even though it hadn't for ages and every one of their prior forecasts had been terrible?

Of interest is the timing of the collapse of productivity growth. This follows almost exactly from the introduction of austerity in the UK budget of June 2010. The changes took a little time to have an impact, so if we assume 2011 Q2 as a reasonable starting point for the effects of austerity, output per hour was 103.7, with 2009 = 100. By 2017 Q2 it was 103.9. Austerity killed productivity. The elites got it wrong but took no responsibility. There was no accountability for this abject failure. Nobody fired the forecasters. This is not unique to the UK. Both the U.S. Federal Reserve and the MPC's forecasts

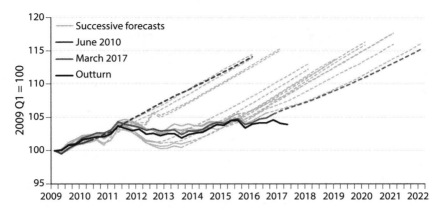

Figure 6.2. Successive OBR productivity forecasts (output per hour). Solid lines represent the outturn data that underpinned the forecasts at the time (the dashed lines). *Source:* Office for Budget Responsibility, Forecast Evaluation Report, October 2017, chart 1, https://obr.uk/fer/forecast-evaluation-report-october-2017/.

were equally hopeless. Each continued to assume all would be well tomorrow, but tomorrow never came. We are now ten years into the crisis.

In October 2017, in its Forecast Evaluation Report (FER), the OBR produced a mea culpa admitting it had been wrong all along; the productivity puzzle had not been solved and the UK economy was not set to mean revert to pre-recession levels: "One recurring theme in past FERs has been productivity falling short of our forecasts. . . . Our rationale for basing successive forecasts on an assumed pick-up in prospective productivity growth has been that the post-crisis period of weakness was likely to reflect a combination of temporary, albeit persistent, influences. And as those factors waned, so it seemed likely that productivity growth would return towards its long-run historical average."[31]

And later: "While we continue to believe that there will be some recovery from the very weak productivity performance of recent years, the continued disappointing outturns, together with the likelihood that heightened uncertainty will continue to weigh on investment, means that we anticipate significantly reducing our assumption for potential productivity growth over the next five years in our forthcoming November 2017 forecast."[32]

In January 2017 Andy Haldane, the Bank of England's chief economist and MPC voter, expressed his concerns about the state of economics. He said it was "a fair cop" that economists had missed the financial crisis.[33] David

Miles, who replaced me on the MPC, took a rather different view, arguing that to the extent that economics says anything about the timing of such events like the Great Recession it is that they are virtually impossible to predict.[34] I don't think so.

The State of Macro Is Bad

The paper mentioned in chapter 1, written by Olivier Blanchard (2009) just before the crash of Lehman Brothers that claimed the state of macroeconomics is "good," made no mention of any real-world data and was seemingly unaware that almost every EU country and the United States had been in recession for several months. The paper argued that macroeconomics was going through a period of great progress and excitement: "A macroeconomic article today often follows strict, haiku-like rules. It starts from a general equilibrium structure, in which individuals maximize the expected present value of utility, firms maximize their value, and markets clear. Then, it introduces a twist, be it an imperfection or the closing of a particular set of markets, and works out the general equilibrium implications. It then performs a numerical simulation based on calibration, showing that the model performs well. It ends with a welfare assessment."

I have no idea what "haiku-like" rules are or how they can help us understand how an economy works. The man on the Clapham omnibus would, rightly, likely think it was worthless mumbo-jumbo. I have been especially struck by claims celebrating that the practice of macroeconomics is firmly grounded in the principles of economic theory.[35] It would have been much better if macroeconomics had been well grounded in the muddy waters of the data. Difficulties arise when a subject emphasizes theory over empirics. Theory is fine, but we need to test it against data from the real world to see if a theory fits the data and how well it works compared with competitors. Just like selling new cars. If economics is not what Arnold Harberger (1993) called an observational discipline, it is nothing. Macroeconomic theory has proved itself to be largely irrelevant.

I have a great deal of sympathy with Nobel Laureate Bob Solow's view (2008) that because modern macro has paid very little rigorous attention to data there is essentially nothing in the empirical performance of these models that could come close to overcoming a modest skeptic. Hence, they shouldn't be used for serious policy analysis. The problem was they were, and that contributed to the big mess in 2008.

In a recent blog post Russ Roberts, the host of the podcast *Econ Talk*, even goes as far as arguing that "most economics claims are really not verifiable or replicable." He suggests that "economics provides the illusion of science, the veneer of mathematical certainty."[36] Adam Ozimek responded, noting that even when empirical economics doesn't settle questions definitively or provide reliable point estimates, it narrows the scope of debate and rules out obviously wrong answers.[37] Maybe.

Noah Smith goes further, arguing that the alternative to empiricism in economics is not agnostic humility but intuitionism—the idea that we can know about the world by thinking about how it works and that exposure to evidence will only pollute the truths that we divine from our own minds. And that's something he argues—and I agree—that economists need to avoid.[38] John Cochrane in response to Roberts argues that "PhD training in economics focuses on theory and statistical technique, and prepares you well to do academic research . . . PhD training really is vocational training to do research, not to advise public policy. . . . Actually we need more math."[39] That may be what economists do, but in the long run it isn't sustainable as university presidents will soon realize it is better to hire folks working on pressing real-world issues, such as a cure for cancer. Economists need to do more empirical testing not less. Mathiness doesn't do it. Economists have incentives to publish in top-tier journals rather than to solve real-world problems. But there is hope.

Famously, Ronald Coase in his Nobel Prize lecture argued that "inspiration is most likely to come through the stimulus provided by the patterns, puzzles, and anomalies revealed by the systematic gathering of data, particularly when the prime need is to break our existing habits of thought" (1992, 718).

In a recent column celebrating the award of the 2017 Sveriges Riksbank Nobel Economics prize to Richard Thaler, Robert Shiller, who won the prize in 2013, noted that there had been antagonism within the profession to the research agenda of the behavioral economists, which includes him. Shiller notes that "many in economics and finance still believe that the best way to describe human behavior is to eschew psychology and instead model human behavior as mathematical optimization by separate and relentlessly selfish individuals, subject to budget constraints." Shiller notes that people have trouble resisting the impulse to spend a $10 bill they might find on the sidewalk; as a result of such mistakes they save too little for retirement. Shiller concludes persuasively that "economists need to know about such mistakes that people repeatedly make."[40] Amen to that. Fortunately trying to understand how the world actually works is on the rise and is increasingly an honorable estate. This is what I call the economics of walking about.

Mohammed El-Arian noted that even after the Great Recession hit the elites were lost and stuck in the irrelevant past: "Despite the enormity of the ongoing dislocations, many were still hostage to the conventional cyclical mindsets that had served policy making well for many decades—that is the notion that advanced economies follow business cycles around a rather robust and stable path. As such they wrongly believed that the sharp down-turn in 2008–9 would be followed by an elastic-band like rebound" (2016, 69).

Some had even convinced themselves, wrongly, that the housing bubble in the early 2000s was entirely sustainable. This time was different. In the words of ex–MPC member Sir Stephen Nickell, "There are good reasons for believing that the equilibrium ratio of house prices to earnings is currently well above the average ratio of house prices to earnings over the last two decades."[41] By July 2007 the house-price to earnings ratio in the UK reached a peak of 5.81, well above its long-run peak, and down it all came. It didn't stop tumbling until April 2009. Things were supposed to be different this time around; the models said so. They didn't.

Sir Charles Bean, also a member of the MPC, agreed that a higher house-price to earnings ratio compared to the past was likely sustainable as everything had changed. Sadly, it hadn't.

> An average house today costs about six times average annual earnings, whereas the historical multiple is somewhat below four. Now there are good reasons why house prices should have risen relative to earnings. The transition to a low inflation, low interest rate environment has shifted the real burden of repayments for a typical mortgage into the future, so making it easier initially for cash-strapped households to service a loan of a given size. Demographic and social developments mean the number of households has been rising, while until recently the rate of house building has been low. And disillusion with the performance of the stock market and concerns about the value of pension promises may have boosted the demand for property as a vehicle for retirement saving. Nevertheless, it is difficult to rationalize the full extent of the increase in house prices and it is likely that the ratio of house prices to earnings

will probably continue to ease for a while, though a return to historical norms seems unlikely.[42]

It's no wonder the public has become disillusioned with experts in general and economists in particular. The elites were stuck in the past.

A survey conducted in the UK by YouGov in April 2017 found that there is a big problem of trust in the opinions of economists, particularly among people who have not studied economics (55%), among older age groups (54% of 65+ age group), among residents of the North of England (44%), and among Leave voters in the EU referendum (54%). Half of the respondents thought that economists expressed views based on personal and political opinion rather than on verifiable data and analysis. When asked what economists do, nearly two-thirds of respondents chose forecasting. Only 26 percent saw economists advising government on policies and 33 percent on industry regulation. When asked to name economists in the public eye, only 16 percent were able to provide any names.

Intent on Repeating the Mistakes of the 1930s

Soon after the crisis economists recommended reckless and unnecessary austerity. Policymakers jumped on board, as it was a great opportunity to reduce the size of the state. Nothing much more. As Mark Blyth noted in 2013, "Much of Europe has been pursuing austerity consistently for the past four years. The results of the experiment are now in, and they are equally consistent: austerity doesn't work. . . . The only surprise is that any of this should come as a surprise." Blyth said it well: "Austerity now insanity later" (49). Austerity, Blyth argued, is a delusion. Austerity continues to be a delusion.

Ryan Cooper recently argued that during and immediately after the crisis, neoliberal and conservative forces attacked the Keynesian school of thought from multiple directions.

Stimulus couldn't work because of some weird debt trigger condition, or because it would cause hyperinflation, or because unemployment was "structural," or because of a "skills gap," or because of adverse demographic trends.

Well going on 10 years later, the evidence is in: The anti-Keynesian forces have been proved conclusively mistaken on every single argument. Their refusal to pick up what amounted to a multiple-trillion-dollar bill sitting on the sidewalk is the greatest mistake of economic policy analysis since 1929 at least.[43]

In the UK, the Tory Chancellor of the Exchequer George Osborne imposed austerity in June 2010 that crushed the fragile recovery. Osborne had backed all the spending plans of the previous Labour government and advocated for more deregulation. He blamed Labour for the global recession, arguing they failed to fix the roof as the sun was shining. This was the most important factor in the Brexit vote: the hurt who didn't cause the recession but were the target of Tory austerity weren't taking it lying down. By 2017 the dispossessed had more or less given up on many aspects of capitalism and at the same time support for a renationalization program for the commanding heights of the economy rose sharply. Even those with jobs in the UK over the previous decade have struggled to make ends meet as real wages in 2018 are still 5.5 percent below pre-recession levels.

In the June 2010 budget, the official forecast by the Office for Budget Responsibility was that GDP growth would take off and the deficit would fall to zero by 2015–16. Growth disappointed and didn't live up to the hyperbole. The debt-to-GDP ratio was forecast to be 67.4 percent (83.6%) in 2015–16 with average earnings growth of 4.4 percent (1.9%). The actual (bad) outcomes are in parentheses.[44]

When Margaret Thatcher resigned, it was reported she had made more trips as prime minister to the United States than she had to places north of the Watford Gap, eighty miles north of London. You can't get there from here. People outside the big cities were hurting and the elites didn't notice. They didn't go there.

On March 23, 2011, George Osborne in his budget speech set out his plan for growth: "We want the words: 'Made in Britain', 'Created in Britain', 'Designed in Britain', 'Invented in Britain' to drive our nation forward. A Britain carried aloft by the march of the makers. That is how we will create jobs and support families. We have put fuel into the tank of the British economy."[45] Not exactly what happened.

Subsequently, the UK lost its AAA credit rating, and despite claims at the outset that the UK government would deliver a "march of the makers," that didn't happen, and manufacturing employment declined further. Public-sector pay freezes were imposed and public-sector employment fell sharply. Other governments around the world pursued tight fiscal policy, which meant that central banks were the only show in town. Low interest rates and many billions of asset purchases followed. House and equity prices rose but real wages fell.

The number of workforce jobs in UK manufacturing was 2.57 million in June 2010 compared to 2.72 million in September 2018. As a share of all workforce jobs in the UK, it fell from 8.2 percent in June 2010 to 7.7 percent in the latest data. Chancellor Osborne didn't keep his promises. There has been no march of the makers, just a march of the unemployed ex-makers.

In the United States, manufacturing employment in January 2019 was 12.8 million, down from 14 million in January 2007. Manufacturing employment was 9.9 percent of total non-farm employment in December 2007 versus 8.5 percent in 2019. Coal-mining jobs are down over the same period by a third and in January 2019 there were 52,700 miners, up from 50,800 in January 2017.

Cut Government Budgets and Lay People Off until They Get Jobs

The slowness of recovery from the Great Recession in large part is explained by the misplaced imposition of reckless austerity. Populism was a response to the lack of decent jobs, especially outside the big cities. The white working class took the heat.

Austerity that came in 2009 meant reversing the stimulus that fiscal authorities had undertaken that had successfully turned downturn into recovery. Cash for fridges and old cars was stopped, tax reductions were reversed, and public spending was cut, including public investment, with disastrous consequences. These measures, just as Keynes expected, almost instantly stalled recovery. "Look after unemployment and the Budget will look after itself," was John Maynard Keynes's advice. This may not always be true but, as Lord Skidelsky, Keynes's distinguished biographer, and I argued in an op-ed in the *New Statesman* in 2011, it is better than the coalition's stance of: "Look after the Budget and unemployment will look after itself."[46] It didn't.

The fact that austerity has never worked mattered not. It was a unique political opportunity for the right to reduce the size of the state and never mind the social and economic consequences. They did a reverse Robin Hood, taking from the poor and giving to the rich. I always found it hard to understand the view that you paid the rich more and that made them work harder and paid the poor less to make them work harder.

There was a widespread view among mostly left-leaning economists, largely ignored by mostly right-leaning policymakers, that austerity was a really bad idea in a slump. I wrote endless articles in my weekly columns in the *Independent* and the *New Statesman* declaring it was a really dumb idea that would hurt ordinary people and wouldn't generate an expansionary fiscal expansion but rather a contractionary fiscal contraction, which is what happened. Nobody listened.

Economics Nobel Laureate Joe Stiglitz has noted, "Take the central issue of austerity: it has never worked. Herbert Hoover tried it and converted the 1929 stock market into the Great Depression. I saw it tried in East Asia, when I was the World Bank's chief economist: downturns became recessions, recessions depressions. The austerity medicine weakened aggregate demand, lowering growth; it reduced demand for labour, lowering wages and pushing up inequality; and it damaged public services on which ordinary citizens depend. In the UK, sharp cuts to public investment do not merely weaken the country today, but also ensure it will be weaker in the future."[47]

As the economic historian Barry Eichengreen noted, "After a brief period in 2008–9 when the analogy to the Great Depression was foremost in the minds of policy makers, and the priority was to stabilize the economy, the emphasis shifted. The priority now was to balance budgets. For central banks, it was preventing an outbreak of inflation, however chimerical. The shift occurred despite the fact that the recovery continued to disappoint. Rather than avoiding the mistakes of the 1930s, policy makers almost seemed intent on repeating them" (2015, 284).

Paul Krugman argued that austerity "was not at all grounded in conventional macroeconomic models. True, policy-makers were able to find some economists telling them what they wanted to hear, but the basic Hicksian approach that did pretty well over the whole period clearly said that depressed economies near the zero lower bound should not be engaging in fiscal contraction. Never mind, they did it anyway" (2018, 165).

As the *Financial Times'* Martin Wolf noted, "Austerity has failed. It turned a nascent recovery into stagnation. That imposes huge and unnecessary costs, not just in the short run, but also in the long term: the costs of investments unmade, of businesses not started, of skills atrophied, and of hopes destroyed."[48]

Harvard economist Alberto Alesina told the Austerians what they wanted to hear, that in the aftermath of the Great Recession, many OECD countries needed to reduce large public-sector deficits and debts. He claimed that "fiscal adjustments, even large ones, which reduce budget deficits, can be successful in reducing relatively quickly debt over GDP ratios without causing recessions. Fiscal adjustments based upon spending cuts are those with, by far, the highest chance of success" (2010, 15). That didn't work out so well.

In the Mais lecture on February 24, 2010, called "A New Economic Model," the soon to be Chancellor of the Exchequer, George Osborne, quoting work by Reinhart and Rogoff (2010), warned that "the latest research suggests that once debt reaches more than about 90% of GDP the risks of a large negative impact on long term growth become highly significant."[49] This was used as a justification in the UK and elsewhere for austerity.

It turns out that result was entirely false, as shown by University of Massachusetts graduate student Thomas Herndon. He came to talk to one of my classes at Dartmouth and showed the result arose because of a series of spreadsheet errors. Countries with high debt-to-GDP ratios were simply omitted from the calculations. When they were included the results completely disappeared.[50] The 90 percent number was wrong. Mark Blyth (2013) has called this "Excelgate."

Stephen Colbert was unmerciful in an episode of the *Colbert Report* on April 23, 2013, where he discussed the spreadsheet errors with Thomas Herndon as a special guest. Colbert succinctly summarized how austerity was supposed to work: "We have to keep cutting government budgets and laying off people until those people get jobs." Funny but sad. The justification for all that austerity disappeared into the ether. And it was all down to a smart graduate student.

Alesina has now more or less gone back on his earlier findings where he concluded, for example, that "fiscal consolidations implemented mainly by raising taxes entail large output costs." Alesina and coauthors punted on whether austerity was the right thing to do: "Our results however are mute on the question whether the countries we have studied did the right thing implementing fiscal austerity at the time they did" (2015, 1).

Simon Wren-Lewis argues that

the reason why economists like Alesina or Rogoff featured so much in the early discussion of austerity is not because they were influential, but because they were useful to provide some intellectual credibility to the policy that politicians of the right wanted to pursue. The influence of their work did not last long among academics, who now largely accept that there is no such thing as expansionary austerity, or some danger point for debt. In contrast, the damage done by austerity does not seem to have done the politicians who promoted it much harm, in part because most of the media will keep insisting that maybe these politicians were right, but mainly because they are still in power.[51]

The consequences of this lack of understanding of how the real world operates led to Western economies being unprepared for what was coming, especially because of their narrow focus on inflation. Of relevance here is Paul De Grauwe's well-known comment that macro models were as useful as the line of defense France built on its borders with Switzerland, Luxembourg, and Germany in the 1930s.[52] Macro models in central banks, he claimed, in the 2000s operated like a Maginot line. They were built to fight inflation, but that was the last war. They weren't prepared to fight the new war against financial upheavals and recession. The macroeconomic models, De Grauwe suggests, do not provide central banks with the right tools to be successful. Mervyn King, in a speech on the tenth anniversary of the formation of the MPC, argued that "there is no more important challenge than keeping inflation and inflation expectations anchored on the target."[53] It turns out there was.

Lord Skidelsky argued in October 2008 that to understand how markets can generate their own hurricanes there was a need to return to John Maynard Keynes.[54] He noted that over the past quarter century economists devoted their intellectual energy to proving that such disasters cannot happen. The models, Skidelsky noted, failed to take account of greed, ignorance, euphoria, panic, herd behavior, predation, financial skullduggery, and politics—the forces that drive boom-bust cycles. The Big Short couldn't possibly be true. This meant that mainstream theory had absolutely no explanation for why things had gone so horribly wrong. Bubbles apparently hardly ever happen, but they do. The *Financial Times* columnist Wolfgang Münchau went as far as to argue that macroeconomists are no longer considered experts on the macroeconomy![55]

Simon Wren-Lewis has claimed, though, that some bits of macroeconomic theory in some ways have had a good crisis in that Keynesian macro theory says not to worry about borrowing in a recession as interest rates will remain low and they have.[56] Keynes, the Master, was right.[57] New Keynesian theory said that creating lots of money via quantitative easing would cause runaway inflation and it hasn't. Macro theory, Simon suggests, predicts that the move to austerity would delay and weaken the recovery, and it did. He probably has a point. There were winners and losers.

Economists as Engineers, Dentists, and Plumbers: There Is Hope!

Greg Mankiw argued that the problem that gave birth to macroeconomics was the Great Depression. God, he suggested, put macroeconomists on earth not to propose and test elegant theories but to solve practical problems, which were not modest in dimension. He suggested that economists needed to be more like engineers.

> My premise is that the field has evolved through the efforts of two types of macroeconomist—those who understand the field as a type of engineering and those who would like it to be more of a science. Engineers are, first and foremost, problem-solvers. By contrast, the goal of scientists is to understand how the world works. The research emphasis of macroeconomists has varied over time between these two motives. While the early macroeconomists were engineers trying to solve practical problems, the macroeconomists of the past several decades have been more interested in developing analytic tools and establishing theoretical principles. These tools and principles, however, have been slow to find their way into applications. As the field of macroeconomics has evolved, one recurrent theme is the interaction—sometimes productive and sometimes not— between the scientists and the engineers. The substantial disconnect between the science and engineering of macroeconomics should be a humbling fact for all of us working in the field. (2006, 29–30)

Very good. Esther Duflo (2017) later argued that economists should seriously engage with plumbing! She suggests as economists increasingly help governments design new policies and regulations, they take on an added responsibility to engage with the details of policymaking and, in doing so, to adopt the mind-set of a plumber. Plumbers, Duflo suggests, try to predict as well as possible what may work in the real world, mindful that tinkering and adjusting will be necessary since our models give us very little theoretical guidance on what (and how) details will matter. Economists as engineers and plumbers seems fine to me.

Larry Summers, ex–Harvard president and Treasury secretary, summarized it so well: "Good empirical evidence tells its story regardless of the precise way in which it is analyzed. In large part, it is its simplicity that makes it persuasive. Physicists do not compete to find more elaborate ways to observe falling apples. Instead they have made progress because theory has sought inspiration from a wide range of empirical phenomena. Macroeconomics could progress in the same way. But progress is unlikely, as long as macroeconomists require the armor of a stochastic pseudo-world before doing battle with evidence from the real one" (1991, 146).[58]

Olivier Blanchard (2016) argued that the dynamic stochastic general equilibrium (DSGE) models used by macroeconomists that failed so badly in the Great Recession are improvable. Economics Nobel Laureate Paul Krugman responded to this by saying what makes a modeling approach truly useful is when it offers "surprising successful predictions." He asks, "Were there any interesting predictions from DSGE models that were validated by events?" and answers his own question: "If there were, I'm not aware of it." He concludes, "At the very least we should admit to ourselves how very sad the whole story has become."[59]

In contrast, Reis argues, "Current macroeconomic research is not mindless DSGE modeling filled with ridiculous assumptions and oblivious of data. Rather, young macroeconomists are doing vibrant, varied, and exciting work, getting jobs, and being published," but, he concedes, "macroeconomics informs economic policy only moderately" (2017, 132). There is the rub. It didn't in 2008 and hasn't since. DSGE models look awfully like mindless modeling to this empirical labor economist.

Joe Stiglitz has suggested, rightly, that the most important function of any macro model is to provide insights into the deep downturns that have occurred repeatedly and what should be done in response. He suggests, "The DSGE models fail in explaining these major downturns, including the source of the perturbation in the economy which gives rise to them; why shocks, which the system (in these models) should have been able to absorb, get amplified with such serious consequences; and why they persist, i.e., why the economy does not quickly return to full employment, as one would expect to occur in an equilibrium model. These are not minor failings, but rather go to the root of the deficiencies in the model" (2018, 71). This is a devastating critique of the state of macroeconomic modeling. Krugman went as far as to argue that "while there was a failure to forecast the crisis, it did not come down to a lack of understanding of possible mechanisms, or of a lack of data, but rather through a lack of attention to the right data" (2018, 156).

Who Needs Bloody Experts?

A UK government minister even compared economists to Nazis. Michael Gove, UK secretary of state for justice, made clear in 2016 why voters in the EU referendum should not listen to the economic organizations warning about the impact of a Leave vote. "I think the key thing here is to interrogate the assumptions that are made and to ask if these arguments are good," Mr. Gove said during an interview with LBC Radio. "We have to be careful about historical comparisons, but Albert Einstein during the 1930s was denounced by the German authorities for being wrong and his theories were denounced and one of the reasons of course he was denounced was because he was Jewish. They got 100 German scientists in the pay of the government to say that he was wrong, and Einstein said 'Look, if I was wrong, one would have been enough.' "[60]

Aditya Chakrabortty, senior economics editor at the *Guardian*, was right when he told me in private communication that politics has now become the art of promising the impossible. Aditya suggests we are now in the world of fantasy politics, which allows politicians to say you shouldn't believe experts. Michiko Kakutani summarizes the strategy employed by the populist politicians in regard to policies on, for example, climate science or gun control and in the UK the impact of Brexit that run counter to expert evaluation and the polls: "Dig up a handful of professionals to refute established science or argue that more research is needed; turn these false arguments into talking points and repeat them over and over and assail the reputations of the genuine scientists on the other side" (2018, 74–75). As Joseph Goebbels, Hitler's minister of propaganda, noted, "A lie told once remains a lie, but a lie told a thousand times becomes the truth."

The experts said that the banks were rock solid, wages were going to rise, the economy was going to grow, austerity would work beautifully, and the deficit would be paid off tomorrow. When none of that happened, ordinary

folk held up their hands and ended up believing populist messages that offered hope. The failure of the elites played a big part in the rise of fantasy
politics. All of this hurt those most in need.

The experts also said that Donald Trump wasn't going to win and that
the British people would not vote for Brexit. My friend Sir Steve Smith, who
is the excellent vice-chancellor of Exeter University, whose field is international relations, told me with economists failing to spot the Great Recession
there were similarities in that experts in his field failed to spot the fall of the
Berlin Wall! The experts did miss the big one though. Why did no one see
this coming? They were working on something else.

CHAPTER 7

Sniffing the Air and Spotting the Great Recession

Today, the economist who wanders into a village to get a deeper sense of what the data reveals is a rare creature.

—JOHN RAPLEY, *Twilight of the Money Gods*

Economics isn't magic. My PhD supervisor, Bernard Corry, taught me to try to understand the low-side risk of any policy prescription, by which I mean always worry about the consequences if you are wrong. I remember him telling me on numerous occasions that I should be concerned about the welfare of the man or woman commuting on the train or bus or, as he put it, worry about the welfare of the "man on the Clapham omnibus."[1]

In part this was to ensure that economists did no harm, and also because Bernard understood that this bus passenger was paying his salary. Interestingly, Clapham is now a pretty prosperous part of London. Bernard always encouraged me to look at the data carefully and to sniff the air. To adopt a more "investigative" approach, if you like: to put the data before the theory. People know what's going on: just ask them.

I first coined the phrase "the economics of walking about" in a lecture I gave on May 30, 2007, at Queen Mary College in honor of Bernard.[2] He encouraged me to look at the data carefully and to look for patterns in the data. This is in direct contrast to much of economics that apparently believes the real world is a special case and uninteresting. In my view economics is not just about understanding mathematics or elegant theoretical models. Statistics and statistical analysis are not the be-all and end-all of course. What matters is the interpretation and the questions that are asked.

The timing was pretty good. The economics of walking about (EWA) gave an early indication that a major recession was coming in 2007 and 2008 in advanced countries. It is the articulated vision of experience. The people know what is happening around them. Taking seriously what firms and individuals were saying gave an early indication that something horrible was coming.

The Economics of Walking About

An early example of EWA was one of the first papers Andrew Oswald and I published together (1988) that reported on what personnel managers said when they were asked what factors influenced the level of pay in the most recent pay settlement. We reported results separately for blue- and white-collar workers. In the case of blue-collar workers, the influences were different between union and non-union sectors. Non-union sector respondents were much more likely to say merit payments were important.

I recall economists at the time being highly critical of using this sort of data. One commentator at a seminar when I first presented the paper asked me, "What would personnel managers know about the setting of pay?" My response was, "Everything," which seemed to take him by surprise. Despite the opposition of economists, the working paper was apparently one of the Centre for Labour Economics' most requested ever. Those who did the economics of walking about liked it. Most economists hated it. I recall the seminar audience really didn't like the paper. I still really like it, mostly for its simplicity. Pay, the paper showed, is set by an intricate blend of insider and outsider forces and I still believe that.

Ins and outs, as Bob Solow pointed out, are "as old as the hills" and were well known by the old generation of labor economists like Sumner Slichter, John Dunlop in the United States, Sidney and Beatrice Webb in the UK, and more recently Sir George Bain and Willie Brown. We did a couple of econometric papers that confirmed what the personnel managers said.[3]

During the 1970s the UK unemployment rate rose inexorably. The overall unemployment rate, though, remained below 6 percent to the end of the 1970s. It hit 6 percent in March 1980 and by the summer of 1981 had reached 10 percent, eventually reaching 11.9 percent in the spring of 1984. The unemployment rate didn't get back below 6 percent until May 1999 under Tony Blair's Labour government, having been in double digits between September 1992 and January 1994.

My sense at the time was that as the overall unemployment rate started to rise, the situation facing young people was worsening rapidly. I had been teaching in schools and colleges from 1974 through 1979 and had the sense that the job opportunities were diminishing. This was my first time doing the economics of walking about. I didn't buy that youth unemployment by 1982 was not a growing problem. I wrote my master's thesis at University College, Cardiff, in Wales on youth unemployment. Layard (1982) had argued that the UK didn't have a youth labor market problem and sought to explain why youth unemployment in the UK was so low, relative to U.S. rates. He reported data from 1959 through 1977 for the two countries. He argued the difference came down to higher U.S. incomes and the fact that income maintenance in the United States was lower. Plus, he claimed, "apprenticeship programs provided a strong incentive for British youths to be employed" (1982, 500). I didn't buy it.

My conclusion from interacting with young people as a teacher and lecturer through the 1970s was that by 1980 youth unemployment had become a big problem in the UK. Increasingly my students, who were based in the South of England in and around London, were struggling to find jobs. Some of my former students wrote and told me they were losing their jobs in the City of London. Jobs for young people were becoming hard to find.

A paper from the U.S. Bureau of Labor Statistics in September 1981 by Constance Sorrentino suggested that by the start of the 1980s there was change in the air. Sorrentino had two more years of data than Layard, with data adjusted to U.S. concepts, and showed that UK unemployment rates for those under 25, as Layard found, were everywhere below the U.S. rate from 1960.[4] But by 1977, which was Layard's stopping point, the situation had begun to reverse itself, at the same time as the UK aggregate unemployment rate plotted in figure 1.1 overtook the U.S. rate. Layard didn't see this coming. The age-specific unemployment rates are set out below.

	United States			Great Britain		
	All	Age < 25	Age ≤ 25+	All	Age < 25	Age ≤ 25
1960	5.5	11.2	4.4	1.9	2.4	1.7
1970	4.9	11.0	3.3	3.9	6.1	3.3
1974	5.6	11.8	3.6	3.1	5.7	2.5
1975	8.5	16.1	6.0	4.6	9.3	3.6
1976	7.7	14.7	5.5	6.0	12.7	4.5
1977	7.0	13.6	4.9	6.4	13.5	4.8
1978	6.0	12.2	4.0	6.3	13.7	4.6
1979	5.8	11.7	3.9	n/a	n/a	n/a

We do not have good data for the period 1980–82, but we do have comparable monthly data ever since January 1983 for both the United States and the UK for those under 25. By January 1983 youth unemployment rates, for those 16–24 in the UK, reached 20 percent versus 18.5 percent in the United States. Over subsequent years the monthly youth unemployment rate for those under 25 in the UK was mostly above the U.S. rate. Things can change quickly in the labor market. Despite the fact that the overall unemployment rate in the United States reached 10 percent versus 8.5 percent in the UK, youth unemployment rates in the UK during the Great Recession were always higher than in the United States, peaking at 22.3 percent in October 2011 versus 19.7 percent in the United States in May 2010.

The economics of walking about is fundamental to this book. There are many ways of doing so. Some commentators even track the color of Mario Draghi's tie. It is usually blue when he announces a policy change. There is even a "lipstick index," which is a term coined by Leonard Lauder, chairman of the board of Estée Lauder, who noted an increase in sales of cosmetics in the early 2000s recession. Women buy lipstick in tough times when they can't afford to buy clothes. In the 2010s there was talk of a nail polish index. Economic downturns have a wide range of effects on medicine; in recessions the volume of both elective and non-elective procedures decreases. Interestingly, however, vasectomies increase during recessions.[5] According to the American Society of Plastic Surgeons, in 2008 fewer cosmetic surgical procedures were performed than were in 2007: breast augmentations were down 12 percent; tummy tucks were down 18 percent; liposuction was down 19 percent; and facelifts were down 5 percent.[6]

Bloomberg's Richard Yamarone, whom I knew and fished with on occasion and who sadly died recently, was famous for noting that an important indicator of how the economy was doing was the previous quarter's sales of women's dresses (2012, 2017). His argument was that women tend to determine most household—and therefore consumer—spending and that their dress purchases are uniquely dictated by themselves. Yamarone explained that these resulting "luxury" purchases tell us a lot about discretionary income in the American home. Other indicators include the amount that Americans are spending on dining out, jewelry and watches, and casino gambling.

Yamarone argued in his *Economic Indicator Handbook* that his dress sales index shouldn't be confused with the hemline index, a theory propounded by George Taylor in 1926. The idea is that hemlines on women's dresses rise along with stock prices. In good economies, we get such results as miniskirts as seen in the 1920s and the 1960s. In poor economic times, as shown by the 1929 Wall Street Crash, hems can drop almost overnight. Van Baardwijk and Franses (2010) collected monthly data on the hemline for 1921–2009 and evaluated these against the NBER chronology of the economic cycle. Their main finding is that "the economic cycle leads the hemline with about a three-year lag." We should probably take this research with a major pinch of salt, though, given that ten years in I see little evidence of ankle-length skirts.

As Tamar Lewin reported in a column in the *New York Times* in 2008, Leo Shapiro, chief executive of SAGE, a Chicago-based consulting firm, has suggested that buying patterns can be predicted in economic downturns: "During a recession, laxatives go up, because people are under tremendous stress, and holding themselves back. During a boom, deodorant sales go up, because people are out dancing around. When people have less money, they buy more of the things that have less water in them, things that are not so perishable. Instead of lettuce and steak and fruit, it's rice and beans and grain and pasta. Except this time the price of pasta's so high that it's beans and rice."[7]

More seriously, Yamarone suggests that women don't make cuts to the kids' dance classes, soccer, baseball, or piano lessons. They will, he suggests, reduce expenditures of a self-purchase before reducing expenditures on their family and there is no greater self-purchase than a dress. Yamarone's famous chart is the annual percentage year-on-year change in the value of sales of

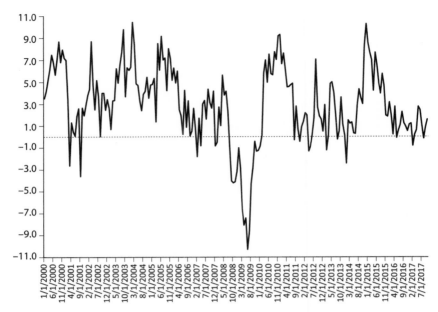

Figure 7.1. Yamarone's year on year % change in the U.S. sales of women's and girls' clothes, 2000–2017.

women's and girls' clothes shown in figure 7.1.[8] It plunged in 2008 and has fallen steadily since the end of 2014.

Two stories from the UK from the fall of 2016 are illustrative of what can be learned from the economics of walking about. The *Washington Post* reported on an already gathering economic storm for Britain. It reported that Brexit was already spooking some British companies, including a 122-year-old British firm based in Gainsborough, Lincolnshire, called Smiffys. On their website (www.smiffy.com) they report they have been in the business of fancy dress since 1894, becoming a global organization with offices and showrooms worldwide: "As the leading fancy dress, Halloween and Carnival manufacturing company in the UK, we distribute nearly 5,000 products to over 5,000 stockists around the world, with over 26 million items shipped every year." Their mission, they say, is "to be the best, most liked, trusted and respected company in our industry." The *Washington Post* reported that, due to Brexit uncertainty, Smiffys are leaving the UK to head to Amsterdam, the capital city of the Netherlands, and inside the EU. Elliott Pecket, the company's director, argued, "One word sums up the issue: uncertainty. Any business needs as much certainty as it can get around the cost of goods or the markets you can trade in. But right now, you don't know where you are from one day to the next."[9]

Smiffys was the first of many firms that are likely to quit the UK if there is a disorderly Brexit. In many ways, the economics of walking about is nothing more than market intelligence. The question is, how much slowing in the UK economy will result from Brexit, especially as the UK government doesn't seem to have a plan and is tied up in litigation? It will be crucial to watch carefully what Keynes called "animal spirits" and how economic sentiment changes. I suspect there may be more Smiffys.

Rivington Biscuits, the maker of Pink Panther wafers, went into administration in December 2016, blaming the fall in the value of the pound following the Brexit vote.[10] The company, a key employer in Wigan, which voted to leave the EU by nearly 64 percent, said it would cut 99 of its 123 staff to fill remaining orders. Rivington Biscuits' financial position worsened in the wake of the June referendum, as the slump in the value of the pound pushed up the cost of ingredients used to make its biscuits.

Up to 1,000 bankers working for JP Morgan in the City of London are to be relocated to Dublin, Frankfurt, and Luxembourg. Standard Chartered told their shareholders at its annual meeting in London in 2017 it was talking with regulators in Frankfurt about setting up a new subsidiary in Germany. Deutsche Bank warned in 2017 that up to 4,000 UK jobs could be moved to Frankfurt and other locations in the EU as a result of Brexit.[11] Barclays has chosen Dublin as its post-Brexit hub. Goldman was one of the first financial institutions to announce it was moving staff away from the UK. In 2017 Goldman decided to close some of its hedge fund operations in London and move the staff to New York. The world's biggest specialist insurance market, Lloyds, announced it would be seeking a new Brussels-based subsidiary the day after UK prime minister Theresa May invoked Article 50, the official EU exit clause.[12]

In June 2018 aerospace giant Airbus said that the "severe negative consequences" of withdrawal from the EU could force it to leave Britain.[13] Airbus said it might ditch plans to build aircraft wings in British factories over concerns that EU regulations will no longer apply as of March 2019 and uncertainty over customs procedures, instead opting to transfer production to North America, China, or elsewhere in the EU. Airbus directly employs 14,000 people at 25 sites in Britain and supports more than 100,000 jobs in the wider supply chain.[14] At Broughton in north Wales, the Airbus plant has 6,000 staff, Aditya Chakrabortty notes, "in an area that 40 years ago was pretty much stripped of its steel industry. If it loses that giant factory, the local economy will be back on the floor for decades. Some will doubtless point out the irony of the leave voters of north Wales now paying for their votes with their jobs."[15] Wales voted for Brexit.

Lloyds of London says the government's plan for relations with the EU after Brexit will speed up the departure of firms from the UK. On July 14, 2018, Inga Beal, its CEO, said the government's white paper on Brexit would see the three-hundred-year-old insurance market go "full speed ahead" to set up its subsidiary in Brussels—and spur others on as well. Lloyds (not in) London. On July 4, 2018, Britain's biggest car maker, Jaguar Land Rover (JLR), warned that a hard Brexit would cost £1.2 billion a year in trade tariffs and make it unprofitable to remain in the UK.[16] Ralf Speth, JLR chief executive, said, "We have to decide whether we bring additional vehicles, and electric vehicles with new technology with batteries and motors into the UK." He added, "We have other options. If I do it here and Brexit goes in the wrong direction, then what is going to happen to the company? If I'm forced to go out because we don't have the right deal, then we have to close plants here in the UK and it will be very, very sad."[17] Votes have consequences.

CNN Money has a "Brexit Jobs Tracker" that identifies companies moving jobs or investment from the UK because of Brexit.[18] As of November 12, 2018, there were twenty-five on the list. After being praised by Boris Johnson for moving to London five years earlier, Japanese pharmaceutical firm Shionogi announced in March 2019 that it was moving its headquarters to Amsterdam. According to the Netherlands Foreign Investment Agency, in January 2019 more than 250 companies were in discussions about Brexit-driven relocations.[19]

The Literature on Walking About and Not Sniffing the Wine

Orley Ashenfelter from Princeton University is another believer. He is famous for his controversial but correct work on modeling the quality of red Bordeaux using data (2008, 2017). He is no slouch; he was editor of the *American Economic Review*, the main journal of the American Economic

Association and the most prestigious journal in economics. He looks at the location of the vineyard and the weather and can predict the quality of the wine via a simple equation. Facing south at an angle of forty-five degrees is important, as there are vineyard fixed effects; some locations are just better than others. He finds no evidence for any separate effect from the winemaker. His prediction doesn't change over time. Orley predicted the 1989 Bordeaux would be "the wine of the century" and claimed the 1990 vintage was going to be even better. His method has the great benefit that you don't have to open bottles of unripe wine to see how the wine is maturing. You don't have to sniff undrinkable wine with Orley's method so there is more wine to drink. You can save it for a later day. Brilliant.

Britain's *Wine* magazine said, "The formula's self-evident silliness invite[s] disrespect." But they would say that, wouldn't they, because if Ashenfelter is right, which I suspect he is, wine critics are largely out of a job. In his case, he doesn't have to sniff the wine; he just looks at how much sun and rain there is and when.[20] Ashenfelter writes, "There is now virtually unanimous agreement that 1989 and 1990 are two of the outstanding vintages of the last 50 years" (2008, F181). He also suggests the 2000 and 2003 vintages are in a league similar to the outstanding vintages of 1989 and 1990. The weather was also exceptional in those years. A great example of the economics of walking about and up and down those steep vineyards.

In a new paper (2017) Ashenfelter argues that if the relation between weather and grape quality is known for each grape type in existing growing areas, then it is possible to predict the quality of grapes that would be produced in other locations, or in the same location with a changed climate. This permits the optimization of grape type selection for a location and also provides an indication of the value that a particular planting should produce. The relation of grape quality to the weather is reported by Ashenfelter for several well-known viticultural areas, including Burgundy, Bordeaux, Rioja, and the Piedmont.

Ashenfelter applied this method to a new vineyard area, Znojmo, in the Moravian province of the Czech Republic following the demise of communism. His main finding is that the highest-quality vintage in Znojmo would have been about 83 percent of the quality of a top Burgundy vintage. On the other hand, the worst Znojmo vintage would have been twice the quality of the worst Burgundian vintage in the period from 1979 to 1992. On average, the typical Znojmo vintage would have been about 75 percent of the quality of the typical Burgundian vintage. Ashenfelter concludes that there is considerable potential for producing high-quality pinot noir wines in the Czech Republic. Nice.

Ashenfelter also has written about the art market, the value of life, hospital mergers, and McWages, to name but a few other data-driven projects. He has published on how to not lie with statistics, as well as on lawyers as agents of the devil in a Prisoner Dilemma game and pendulum arbitration. He also examined the behavior of identical twins using data from the Twins Days Festival at Twinsburg, Ohio. Looking at the data is an honorable estate. Others walk about too. Phew.

Another study that looks at the data is David Card's famous article on the effect of the Mariel Boatlift of 1980 on the Miami labor market (1990). The Mariel immigrants increased the Miami labor force by 7 percent, and the percentage increase in labor supply to less-skilled occupations and industries was even greater because most of the immigrants were relatively unskilled. Nevertheless, the Mariel influx appears to have had virtually no effect on the wages or unemployment rates of less-skilled workers, even among Cubans who had immigrated earlier. The author suggests that the ability of Miami's labor market to rapidly absorb the Mariel immigrants was largely owing to its adjustment to other large waves of immigrants in the two decades before the Mariel Boatlift.

Still another fine example of working out what was happening in the real world is the 2004 case study by Alan Krueger and Alexandre Mas of the effect of labor relations on product quality. This was economic detective work. They examined whether a long, contentious strike and the hiring of permanent replacement workers by Bridgestone/Firestone in the mid-1990s contributed to the production of an excess number of defective tires. Using several independent data sources, the authors found that labor strife in the Decatur, Illinois, plant was closely correlated with lower product quality. They found significantly higher failure rates for tires produced in Decatur during the labor dispute than before or after the dispute, or than at other plants.

Monthly data suggest that the production of defective tires was particularly high around the time wage concessions were demanded by Firestone in early 1994 and when large numbers of replacement workers and permanent workers worked side by side in late 1995 and early 1996. The stock market valuation of Bridgestone/Firestone fell from $16.7 billion to $7.5 billion in the four months after the recall of tires was announced and the top management of Bridgestone/Firestone had been replaced. The company also closed the Decatur plant in December 2001.

In a path-breaking book titled *Myth and Measurement* (1995), David Card and Alan Krueger examined data from a series of recent episodes, including the 1992 increase in New Jersey's minimum wage, the 1988 rise in California's minimum wage, and the 1990–91 increases in the federal minimum wage.[21] They found evidence showing that increases in the minimum wage led to increases in pay but no loss in jobs. Increases in the minimum wage led to productivity growth as tenure rates rose and quit rates fell.

A big question in economics is why wages and salaries don't fall during recessions. Truman Bewley (2002) explored this puzzle by interviewing over three hundred business executives and labor leaders, as well as professional recruiters and advisors to the unemployed, during the recession of the early 1990s. He found that the executives were averse to cutting wages of either current employees or new hires, even during the economic downturn when demand for their products fell sharply. They believed that cutting wages would hurt morale, which they felt was critical in gaining the cooperation of their employees and in convincing them to internalize the managers' objectives for the company.

Golf handicap also seems to matter for CEOs.[22] A study based on publicly available data from the United States for the years 1998, 2000, 2002, 2004, and 2006 examined the relationship between golf handicaps of CEOs and corporate performance and CEO compensation. The study found that golfers earn more than non-golfers and CEO pay increases with golfing ability. Despite that, the authors find that there is no relation between golf handicap and corporate performance.

A London limo driver in January 2017 told me the problem in Britain, and the reason there was a vote for Brexit, was that ordinary people had no hope. He told me he had to balance the need to spend time with his kids (ages 6 and 13) with the need to drive many more hours than he had in the past to make enough money to live. He told me it was tough for him to have lost hope as he had always been an optimist. Another limo driver in Southampton told me he had voted for Brexit as a protest vote, not expecting it would win. Once Brexit won he immediately regretted his vote.

Applying EWA to the Crisis: London Cabbies, Delivery Trucks, and Jingle Mail

There are many ways to sniff the air out and about. A taxi driver in early January 2008 was driving me down Oxford Street. It is full of clothes stores and big department stores like Selfridges and Debenhams and John Lewis, and in the January sales it should have been a frenzy of activity. My cabbie pointed out something unusual about the shoppers that year: they had no bags and were only window shopping. People didn't have any money to spend.

I spoke to other London taxi drivers during the first half of 2008. London cabbies, I find, are always a good source of information on what is happening in London. At first, they were big supporters of the new mayor of London, Boris Johnson, but then they quickly turned against him. A number told me that they were having to work more hours to make their money every week. Some of them told me that they were fortunate because they could increase their hours but many of their friends and family weren't as lucky. Hours of work were falling, and people were being laid off.

The cabbie's hunch likely was correct, but there were other possibilities to explain the decreased presence of shopping bags. One possibility was that people were less likely to be shopping on the high streets, where rents tend to be high, leading to higher prices, and more likely to be browsing there but buying in large stores further out that offered lower prices due to lower rents and greater economies of scale. Another possibility is that people were moving away from purchasing at brick-and-mortar stores and increasingly buying online, with the convenience of having items delivered to one's home. From the simple observation that people were not carrying shopping bags, multiple possible explanations exist. The taxi driver offered a telling anecdote, but its meaning was open to interpretation. It turns out the economy was slowing and the published economic data hadn't caught up.

A couple of weeks after the cab driver spoke to me an owner of a company in the UK that operated a tire service called me. This firm had taken over a fleet and serviced all their tire needs. If tires needed replacing or had a puncture out on the road, the firm would sort it. As part of that every delivery truck they serviced had tachometers in them to record how many miles were being driven. He called to tell me he had noticed that the mileage on the delivery trucks he serviced was way down.

In the United States a new phenomenon emerged (which economists failed to spot) around 2007 as the housing market started to slow and subprime mortgages began to fail: "jingle mail." By early 2007 a growing number of mortgage holders were failing to make their monthly payments, especially among subprimes, which induced a wave of selling. As a result, prices fell and continued to do so. John Rapley explained it well: "So prices fell further, and more borrowers missed payments—or simply walked away from their homes, leaving their keys in the bank's night deposit boxes. Bankers soon began to dread this 'jingle mail'" (2017, 362).

Economists, including those in academia, Wall Street, and Canary Wharf, as well as in central banks around the world, of course had no clue this was happening. But it isn't as if this hadn't happened before. This term was first used to describe the surprise mailings that mortgage lenders received following the savings and loan debacle of 1990–91.

A 2010 paper from the Richmond Fed found that the probability of default on a mortgage loan was 32 percent higher at the mean value of the default option at the time of default in nonrecourse states than in recourse states.[23] There are eleven nonrecourse states: Alaska, Arizona, California, Iowa, Minnesota, Montana, North Carolina, North Dakota, Oregon, Washington, and Wisconsin. In these eleven states, banks' recourse in collecting on residential "purchase" mortgages after default is limited to the value of the collateral (the home). If the debt is larger than the value of the home, usually determined by proceeds from the foreclosure sale, the lender is generally barred from trying to collect the remainder of the debt from the borrower. So, mortgage holders who were underwater walked away especially in these states.

As Paul Krugman noted,

Economists were also under-informed about the surge in housing prices that we now know represented a huge bubble, whose bursting was at the heart of the Great Recession. In this case, rising home prices were an unmistakable story. But most economists who looked at these prices focused on broad aggregates—say, national average home prices in the United States. And these aggregates, while up substantially, were still in a range that could seemingly be rationalized by appealing to factors like low interest rates. The trouble, it turned out, was that these aggregates masked the reality, because they averaged home prices in locations with elastic housing supply (say, Houston or Atlanta) with those in which supply was inelastic (Florida—or Spain); looking at the latter clearly showed increases that could not be easily rationalized." (2018, 158)

Duh!

A further method of sniffing the air is simply to "eyeball the data." It has been said that the plural of anecdote is data and that statistics is simply the collection of anecdotes. The benefit of statistics is that it allows multiple possible explanations to be tested against the evidence, or the collection of anecdotes. These data generally involve sampling firms or individuals, asking their opinions and summing them together into some sort of score. Examples are surveys of firms as conducted, for example, by Markit, which talks to purchasing managers to produce Purchasing Manager Indices (PMIs) for many countries and sectors. The Bank of England's agents talk to contacts and produce scores of what firms think about all sorts of variables including employment, investment, prices, and turnover.

Consumers are surveyed about their views on the economy. The most well-known of these individual-level surveys is the consumer confidence index. In the United States, the two most famous are those of the Conference Board and the University of Michigan. In the UK, the EU consumer confidence index is the most well-known, conducted monthly in all twenty-eight member countries of the EU by the European Commission. These are not the sort of data that academic economists look at. They spend their academic lives looking at the past, not the present.

The statistics show that both the taxi driver and the tire-service owner were on to something. What they noticed was that consumer confidence was down and people were spending less because they were worried about the future. Consumer confidence, as it turns out, is something that can be measured. What was evident by January 2008, and probably even before that, was that consumer confidence was headed sharply down.

Look at table 7.1, which plots what Keynes called "animal spirits." It plots consumer confidence indices—which show how confident consumers are about the economy—for the United States and the UK along with the respective unemployment rate. For the United States, it is from the Conference Board's measure and for the UK it is from the EU Commission. I do need to do some housekeeping with these qualitative surveys. Sometimes the index

Table 7.1. Animal Spirits: Consumer Confidence and Unemployment, United States and United Kingdom

	United States		United Kingdom	
	Consumer confidence	Unemployment rate	Consumer confidence	Unemployment rate
Jan-07	110.2	4.6	−6.8	5.5
May-07	108.5	4.4	−3.3	5.4
Sep-07	99.5	4.7	−2.9	5.2
Jan-08	87.3	5.0	−7.0	5.2
May-08	58.1	5.4	−15.0	5.4
Aug-08	58.5	6.1	−24.8	5.9
Oct-08	38.8	6.5	−27.4	6.2
Average	96.2 (1978–2009)		−8.5 (1985–2009)	

Source: Blanchflower 2008.

is reported as a number, as with the Conference Board, which has 1985 = 100. In other instances, which include the EU Commission survey, they are reported as a balance. So, if the respondent is asked if something was worse (20%), the same (25%), or better (55%), the balance is calculated as better minus worse = +35. It is useful to compare to the long-run survey average. To put it simply, more is better, less is worse.

It is clear that the two data series moved down sharply together and appear to have done so before the unemployment rate rose. In the United States, the high point was 111.9 in July 2007 and the unemployment rate started picking up in December 2007. These are the data the NBER Business Cycle Dating Committee determined showed the start of the Great Recession. It was pretty obvious by spring 2008 consumer confidence had collapsed and the unemployment rate was climbing in both countries. Animal spirits were plunging but nobody much noticed.

In the UK case, the consumer confidence index appears to have started falling sharply from the beginning of 2008 and was falling fast by April 2008, which, based on the GDP data, was the start of the UK recession. The unemployment rate started to rise around July 2008. What happened in the United States spread to the UK within a very few months and from there to the rest of Europe and beyond.

Figure 7.2 shows the Economic Sentiment Index (ESI) for the UK and the European Union as a whole, including the UK. This is a combination

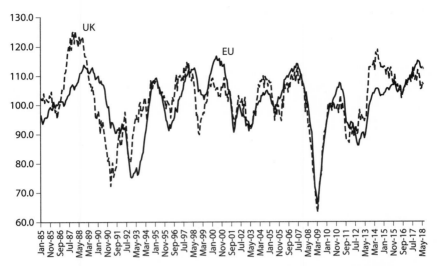

Figure 7.2. European Commission's monthly Economic Sentiment Index, EU and UK, 1985–2018.

of surveys taken monthly by the European Commission in every country, combining reports from consumers, retail, construction, services, and industry. I like to think of this series as a perfect example of the economics of walking about—it summarizes the timely views of people and businesses. Sadly, academic economists pay little or no attention to such series, but they should. I plot the ESI from 1985 through 2018. It is clear that the two series move closely together. It turns out that France, Germany, and the UK all reached a peak around June 2007. A similar story of a big drop in the ESI by September 2008 was to be found in other major European countries, including Austria, Belgium, Denmark, Finland, Greece, Italy, the Netherlands, Portugal, Spain, and Sweden. By the summer of 2008 it was apparent that something bad was amiss in Europe as well as the United States. Few spotted it.

Other qualitative series showed similar patterns. This includes the Purchasing Manager Indices that are reported monthly for manufacturing, services, and construction. In the UK, the Bank of England's agents report a series of scores they calculate from their visits to business contacts.[24] Their scores for turnover, profitability, capacity constraints, and investment and employment intentions all started tumbling from around May 2007. Nobody much noticed. Well, some did.

Figure 7.3. The Baltic Dry Index, 2006–17.

Of special note here is the Baltic Dry Index (BDI), which collapsed in the fall of 2008 and has hardly recovered (figure 7.3).[25] The Baltic Dry Index is issued daily by the London-based Baltic Exchange. The index covers Handysize, Supramax, Panamax, and Capesize, massive dry bulk carriers of a range of commodities around the world including coal, iron ore, and grain. BDI covers 100 percent of dry bulk cargo in transit on the world's oceans but does not include ships transporting freight via container or transport of energy liquids by tanker.[26] On May 20, 2008, the index reached its record-high level since its introduction in 1985, of 11,793 points. By September 1 it had dropped to 6,691 and nobody much noticed. Trade credit was increasingly becoming unavailable. Three months later, on December 5, 2008, the index had dropped by 94 percent, to 663 points, the lowest since 1986. At the time of writing, in November 2018, BDI was at 1,031, up from a low of 297 on February 5, 2016. It remains unclear what to make of this low level of the index or of its trebling over the last couple of years, but keep watching. It is a bad sign when economic indicators fall by 95 percent in a few weeks.[27]

Another example of EWA is the regular report by the Bank of England agents. This report used to be monthly but has become less regular since the

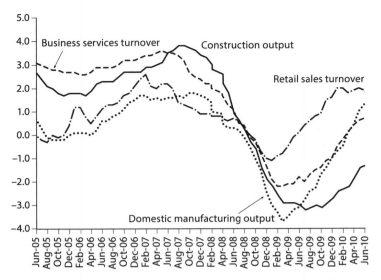

Figure 7.4. Bank of England agents' scores, 2005–10. *Source:* Bank of England, https://
www.bankofengland.co.uk/about/people/agents.

MPC stopped meeting monthly. These reports are roughly equivalent to the
Beige Book in the United States, which reports on conditions on the ground
from talking to firms. In 2007 and 2008 the scores they reported were plunging but nobody was taking much notice. At the time I recall saying to the
staff who were gathered to brief the MPC at one of our Friday pre-MPC
meetings in the spring of 2008 that the problem with the agents is they don't
believe the agents. They had been so pounded by the economists. In the
regular Friday briefing they would have ten minutes or so at the end. They
spotted early that recession was coming.

Figure 7.4 illustrates. It plots four scores out of the thirty or so the bank's
agents produce. These four are illustrative and the others follow a similar
pattern. They all plunged together from around June 2007. By August 2008
each was in free fall. The Bank of England's August 2008 Inflation Report
said, "Reports from the Bank's regional Agents point to broadly flat output
in the third quarter." No, they didn't. There was no mention of the plunge
in essentially all thirty scores including employment intentions, recruitment difficulties, capacity constraints, domestic prices, material costs and
investment intentions, turnover, and output. All of them. The evidence of a
sharp downturn was in plain sight. The data were moving fast to unprecedented territory.

The minutes of the MPC meeting of August 6–7, 2008, where I voted for a 25 basis point cut and everyone else voted to do nothing, said, "The main questions for the Committee were the likely degree of persistence in inflation and how much spare capacity would be needed to offset that persistence."[28] That was not the main question. My view was different: "For another member, the downside risks to activity growth were greater than the majority view expressed in the Inflation Report. For this member, there was less risk of inflation being persistent and more risk of undershooting the inflation target in the medium term, because of rapidly slowing activity, so an immediate cut in Bank Rate was warranted."[29]

Spotting the Recession

By the spring of 2008 I was becoming increasingly frustrated that nobody much else had spotted the fact that the major economies were slowing fast. What was happening in New Hampshire was starting to happen in the UK and other European countries I was visiting. There was some benefit of my flights every three weeks across the Atlantic. I decided to give a speech to the David Hume Institute at the Royal Society in Edinburgh on April 29, 2008, setting out my thoughts. In the speech I essentially said that recession had arrived in the United States and the UK using the economics of walking about. At the dinner afterward in Edinburgh participants from various financial firms wanted to talk about the possibility that one of Nicholas Taleb's black swan events was coming to the United States, the UK, and globally. The discussion was prescient. Lots of people, including members of the MPC, said, who could have known recession was coming? The speech is still downloadable from the Bank of England's website.[30]

At the start of the speech I said that I am a strong believer in Hume's own view that we should not seek to solely explain events and behavior with theoretical models; rather, as Hume wrote in 1738 in his *Treatise of Human Nature*, we should use "experience and observation," that is, the empirical method. My theme was that the UK was exhibiting broad similarities to the U.S. experience, essentially drawing on the evidence from the economics of walking about. I argued this suggested that in the UK we were also going to see a "substantial decline in growth, a pick-up in unemployment, little if any growth in real wages, declining consumption growth driven primarily by significant declines in house prices. The credit crunch is starting to hit and hit hard."

I set out four phases of the downturn the United States had already been through and suggested the same was true of the UK, which was already in stage three and approaching stage four. I presented the data that I had available at the time, which are in the appendix (table A.1). This is relevant as it tells us what I knew at the time. It seemed clear to me that the United States was already in recession and the UK was heading there: "For some time now, I have been gloomy about prospects in the United States, which now seems clearly to be in recession," and "I believe we face a real risk that the UK may fall into recession." With hindsight, it looks broadly right. The United States went into recession in December 2007; the UK and most of the rest of Europe followed in April 2008.

I repeat here, verbatim, what I wrote in April 2008, the month we now know the UK went into recession.

> **Phase 1 (January 2006–April 2007).** The housing market starts to slow from its peak around January 2006 (columns 1 and 2). Negative monthly growth rates in house prices start to appear from the autumn of 2006.
>
> **Phase 2 (May 2007–August 2007).** Substantial monthly falls in house prices and housing market activity including starts (column 3) and permits to build (column 4) are observed from late spring/early summer of 2007. Consumer confidence measures (columns 5 and 6), alongside qualitative labor market indicators, such as the proportion of people saying jobs are plentiful (column 7), started to drop precipitously from around September 2007.
>
> **Phase 3 (September 2007–December 2007).** Average hourly earnings growth (column 8) starts to slow from September 2007 as does real consumption (column 11). The growth in private nonfarm payrolls starts to slow (column 8). House price and activity declines speed up.
>
> **Phase 4 (January 2008–).** By approximately December 2007 the housing market problems have now spilled over into real activity. The United States seems to have moved into recession around the start of 2008. There have been big falls in house prices. In March 2008 housing starts were at a seventeen-year low. Foreclosure fil-

ings jumped 57 percent in March compared with the same month last year. One out of every 139 Nevada households received a foreclosure filing last month. California was second with a rate of one in every 204 homes, with Florida third with a rate of one in every 282 being hit with a foreclosure filing. Mortgage application volume fell 14.2 percent during the week ending April 18, according to the Mortgage Bankers Association's weekly application survey. Refinance volumes fell 20.2 percent on the week.

Nominal retail sales (column 10) and real personal disposable income (column 12) have both fallen sharply since the start of the year. Real annual GDP growth in 2007 Q4 is now down to +0.1 percent, from 1.2 percent in 2007 Q3.

Spending on big-ticket items in the United States is tumbling. For example, Harley-Davidson, the biggest U.S. motorcycle maker, is cutting jobs and reducing shipments to dealers amid declining sales. Harley sold 14 percent fewer bikes in the United States in the first three months of the year [2008] than in the same period in 2007. U.S. automakers such as GM and Ford reported double-digit U.S. sales declines in March [2008] as demand for trucks and sport utility vehicles plummeted, with consumers holding back because of concerns about gas prices, the housing slump, and tightening credit. Even McDonald's Corp., the world's biggest restaurant company, has seen U.S. comparable-store sales fall 0.8 percent in March 2008, the first decline since March 2003.

The most recent labor market data release for the United States, for March 2008, showed the biggest drop in payrolls in five years, while applications for unemployment benefits are on the increase. The benefit claims average for the past two months has already risen to a level similar to where it was at the start of the 2001 recession and with no sign of bottoming out. Unemployment jumped from 4.8 to 5.1 percent with particularly large increases for the least educated.

Declines in employment to this point in the United States have been concentrated in manufacturing, construction, and financial activities. The numbers below report the declines by industry grouping and are in thousands, seasonally adjusted between November 2007 and December 2008. Private-sector non-farm payrolls over this period have fallen by three hundred thousand with a decline of more than 60 percent of the job loss from construction, even though it accounted for only 6.5 percent of the stock at the start of the period.

	November 2007	March 2008	Change
Private non-farm	115,759	115,459	−300
Manufacturing	13,794	13,643	−151
Construction	7,520	7,338	−182
Financial activities	8,260	8,228	−32
Government	22,278	22,387	+109

I then showed similar evidence for the UK, with the data presented in the appendix (table A.2).

Phase 1 (August 2007–October 2007). House prices start to slow in 2007 Q2 and 2007 Q3 (columns 1, 2, and 3). Housing activity measures also slow (columns 4 and 5) from around October 2007.

Phase 2 (November 2007–January 2008). Consumer confidence measures start slowing sharply also from around October 2007 (columns 6, 7, 8, and 9). The qualitative labor market measures such as the REC Demand for Staff index also start slowing from around October 2007.

Phase 3 (February 2008–). In early 2008 the Halifax index and the Royal Institute of Chartered Surveyors (RICS) survey both suggest that house-price falls have started to accelerate. The Council of Mortgage Lenders (CML) recently announced that mortgage lending in March was down 17 percent on the year. Loan approvals are down, and the RICS ratio of sales to stocks is down from .38 in September 2007 to .25 in March 2008. Bradford and Bingley, Britain's biggest buy-to-let lender, has recently reported that some borrowers are finding it hard to repay their loans, so mortgage arrears are growing, reminiscent of what has been happening in the United States.

The latest figures showed that the number of people whose homes were repossessed in 2007 went up by 21 percent. The CML said 27,100 homes, the highest figure since 1999, were taken over by lenders after people fell behind with repayments. According to data published by the British Bankers' Association the number of mortgages granted to homebuyers dropped last month by 47 percent below the same month last year to its lowest level in more than a decade. Some 35,417 mortgages were approved for home purchase in March, compared with 43,147 in February, a drop of 18 percent.

Hourly earnings growth is sluggish—both the AEI and LFS measures are slowing. Total hours and average hours started to fall in early 2008. Claimant count numbers for February 2008 are revised up from a small decline to an increase. There is a growth in the number of part-timers who say they have had to take a full-time job because they couldn't find a part-time job—up 37,000 in March alone. Even though the number of unemployed has fallen, the duration of unemployment appears to be rising, which means that the outflow rate from unemployment has fallen. The number unemployed over six months in March 2008 was up 22,000 while the number unemployed for less than six months was down 47,000.

As in the United States, recent declines in employment in the UK are concentrated in manufacturing, construction, and financial activities. The numbers presented below are in thousands, seasonally adjusted, and relate to the number of workforce jobs. The quarterly data relate to the period September–December 2007 while the annual data refer to December 2006–December 2007.

	Change on quarter	Change on year
All jobs	+13 (0.0%)	+208 (0.7%)
Manufacturing	29 (−0.9%)	−53 (−1.6%)
Construction	−19 (−0.9%)	−7 (−0.3%)
Finance & business services	−5 (−0.1%)	+149 (2.3%)

Phase 4 is coming. More bad news is on the way. I think it is very plausible that falling house prices will lead to a sharp drop in consumer

> spending growth. Developments in the UK are starting to look eerily
> similar to those in the United States six months or so ago. There has
> been no decoupling of the two economies: contagion is in the air. The
> United States sneezed and the UK is rapidly catching its cold. . . . I
> have identical concerns for the UK. Generally, forecasters have tended
> to underpredict the depth and duration of cyclical slowdowns.

At his Mansion House speech of June 18, 2008, with the UK in its third
month of recession, Bank of England governor Mervyn King had it totally
wrong. No mention of recession and inflation was about to plummet like a
rock. Oh dear.

> The fact that growth and inflation are heading in opposite directions
> has led some commentators to question our monetary framework.
> Target growth not inflation is the cry. I could not disagree more. This
> is precisely the situation in which the framework of inflation targeting
> is so necessary. Without it, what should be a short-lived, albeit sharp,
> rise in inflation, could become sustained. Without a clear guide to the
> objective of monetary policy, and a credible commitment to meeting
> it, any rise in inflation might become a self-fulfilling and generalised
> increase in prices and wages. And surely the lesson of the past fifty
> years is that, when inflation becomes embedded, the cost of getting it
> back down again is a prolonged period of sluggish output and high
> unemployment. Price stability—returning inflation to the target—is
> a precondition for sustained growth, not an alternative.

Price stability was not a precondition for anything, let alone sustained
growth. It turns out targeting inflation meant too many policymakers failed
to spot the biggest recession in a generation. Since then we have continued
to have a growth problem and a "too little" inflation problem. Deflation
replaced inflation as the new problem central bankers faced, but they have
failed to adapt. The crisis was totally predictable using the EWA. Focusing
on inflation meant policymakers took their eyes off what was happening in
the real world. The CPI, which was the measure the MPC was supposed to
target and keep at 2 percent, was 5.2 percent in September 2008 but only
1.1 percent in September 2009.

Reading the speeches of central bankers and examining the minutes of their meetings along with forecasts, especially during 2007 and 2008, doesn't give one confidence that they know what they are doing. Things have not been much better since.

What Has Been Learned from the Crisis?

Not much. Same old, same old.

I was on a panel at the beginning of 2018 where the two other participants forecast that GDP growth in the United States would be well over 4 percent, as claimed by Trump, driven by the GOP tax cut. I noted that the December 2017 forecasts of the FOMC, the OECD, the IMF, and the World Bank that came out the next day were all up slightly from earlier in 2017.[31] All were around 2.5 percent or so and slowing to about 2.2 percent by 2020 and 2021. The problem since 2010 is that central bank forecasts have been too optimistic; now the claim is they are overly pessimistic. Nobody trusts economic forecasters anymore. They prefer guesswork.

In April 2018 the markets had fully priced in a rate rise by the MPC at their May 2018 meeting. This was based on comments by members including Mark Carney. It was clear, though, that there were no actual data to back up the need for a rate rise; it was being driven by results from their (hopeless) models. The same ones that failed to spot the Great Recession in the first place, and likely the same modelers too. By the meeting itself, held in May, probabilities of a rate rise fell to 8 percent and the MPC did nothing. In the meantime, data turned bad with GDP growth of 0.1 percent for 2018 Q1 and weak PMIs as well as declining inflation, investment, and retail sales. GDP in the UK grew 1.1 percent in the first three quarters of 2018, but quarterly GDP growth in Q4 was only 0.2 percent. Brexit uncertainty appears to have slowed activity, and by 2019 talk of rate raises has gone.

There remains some disagreement among central bankers on what is happening, but when it comes to votes on rate rise they are almost always unanimous. In a speech on June 4, 2018, new external MPC member Silvana Tenreyro discussed the importance of models, although she didn't mention how awful their forecasting record has been: "I expect that the narrowing in labour market slack we have seen over the past year will lead to greater inflationary pressures, as in our standard models," despite the fact that the MPC has been saying that for the last five years and it hasn't happened. She concluded that "we should keep working on our models because they do help

our thinking—even though they will never predict everything in advance—
we might know better how to respond to events once they occur."[32] The
models were great, but sadly the real world didn't comply.

Sir Jon Cunliffe, deputy governor at the Bank of England, took a somewhat more dovish tone, arguing in a November 2017 speech that there was
likely more capacity in the UK labor market because of underemployment:

> A straightforward explanation of why pay growth is subdued at very
> low levels of unemployment is that we are under-measuring the
> amount of spare capacity—or "slack"—in the labour market. Recent
> trends in the world of work have meant greater (voluntary and
> involuntary) self-employment and part-time employment. Measures
> incorporating under-employment as well as unemployment—i.e.,
> how much more people who are in work would like to work—may
> give a better indication of the amount of spare capacity in the labour
> market. In such a world, low pay is simply telling the policy maker
> that there is more labour market slack than the unemployment
> indicators are registering, that the output gap is larger than thought
> and that the economy can grow at a faster rate without generating
> domestic inflation pressure.[33]

Inexplicably, in the end he voted for a rate rise in August 2018.

The MPC vote to raise rates on August 2, 2018, from 0.5 to 0.75 percent
was unanimous, 9–0. The FOMC vote to raise the interest rates on required
and excess reserve balances to 2.2 percent, effective September 27, 2018, was
also unanimous, 9–0. Groupthink is back in town. In my view there were
no data from the real world to justify either rate rise. In both cases I would
have dissented.

Based on weak PMIs and slowing GDP growth the Eurozone (EZ) appears to be slowing. However, the Harmonised Index of Consumer Prices
(HICP) inflation in the EZ picked up due to a rise in energy prices to 2.2
percent but only to 1.3 percent excluding energy in October 2018, the same
as it was in August and September. Eurostat data releases in October 2018
showed production in the EZ construction was down 0.5 percent. The flash
estimate of GDP growth in the euro area was 0.2 percent in 2018 Q3, down
from 0.4 percent in the previous two quarters.[34] The annual growth in wages
in the EZ in the second quarter of 2018 was 1.9 percent, versus 1.8 percent

in 2018 Q1, 1.6 percent in 2017 Q4, and 1.7 percent in 2017 Q3. In Germany in 2018 Q2 wage growth was 2 percent and in France it was 1.8 percent.[35]

The *Financial Times* reported that, despite the fact there was no evidence in the data of any rise in wage growth in the EZ, Peter Praet, ECB chief economist, said the "underlying strength" of the Eurozone economy has bolstered his confidence that inflation will move toward the central bank's objective, highlighting policymakers' view that recent weakness is transitory.[36] The ECB executive board member said there is "growing evidence that labour market tightness is translating into a stronger pick-up in wage growth," according to prepared remarks to the Congress of Actuaries in Berlin. So, a 2 percent wage norm means that rates should rise?[37]

The *Financial Times* also quoted Jens Weidmann, president of Germany's Bundesbank and a member of the ECB's governing council, who echoed Mr. Praet's bullish take on inflation, claiming it is "now expected to gradually return to levels compatible with our target." He added that market expectations that the ECB will halt its vast bond-buying program by the end of this year "are plausible."[38] Inflation in the Eurozone in January 2019 was 1.4 percent, while only three out of nineteen member countries had inflation rates of over 2 percent. The clueless hawks haven't gone away.

A speech from Sabine Lautenschläger, member of the executive board of the ECB and vice chair of the supervisory board of the ECB, gave me hope. I am not sure that she can be confident that the euro area is not at a turning point, as that is hard to call even when you are at one as we found in 2007 and 2008. It is worth quoting a chunk of her speech in full as it looks broadly right.

So we are seeing that the pace of growth has become more moderate, but we are not seeing a turning point. We remain confident in the strength of the economy.

After all, the things that are currently holding back growth seem to be temporary. There was the early timing of the Easter break, there was a strong outbreak of flu in some parts of the euro area, there was cold weather and there were strikes in some countries. All this weighed on growth, but it won't do so permanently.

We need to keep a close eye on all this, and we will. But for now, there is no need to rewrite the story. The economic expansion remains solid and broad-based. Financing conditions are good, the labour market is robust with a historically high increase in jobs, and income and profits are growing steadily. In short: the real economy is doing well.

By contrast, inflation so far does not seem to be recovering as convincingly. This has left many observers scratching their heads as to why the current level of low inflation does not match the current state of the real economy. It seems that inflation is responding less to the slack in the economy than would be expected. This disconnect between the real and nominal sides of the economy is the subject of intense debate. In very general terms, there might be two forces at play. First, the Phillips curve might have changed. It might, for instance, have flattened, or it might have shifted downwards. Empirically, it is very hard to determine which—if either—of the two things has happened.

And that brings me to the second point, which is that we cannot be sure whether we are measuring slack correctly in the first place. The unemployment rate, for instance, is based on a narrow definition. Just think of people who work part-time. Officially, they are employed, but they could work more, of course. So, the amount of slack could be larger than we think. If that is the case, it's no surprise that inflation has not kicked in.[39]

Sabine Lautenschläger at least has got it.

There are one or two EWA indicators that were flashing amber in the United States in mid-2018. The U.S. yield curve plots Treasuries with maturities ranging from four weeks to thirty years. The gap between long and short yields turning negative has been a reliable indicator of recession. The yield curve was flattening during the first few months of 2018. Ed Yardeni's Boom-Bust Barometer, which measures spot prices of industrial inputs like copper, steel, and lead scrap divided by initial unemployment claims, fell before or during the last two recessions. Housing starts and building permits have fallen ahead of some recent recessions. The Census Bureau reported in October 2018 that in the United States private-owned housing units authorized by building permits in September 2018 were down 0.6 percent compared with August. Privately owned housing starts were down 5.3 percent on the month. Privately owned housing completions were 4.1 percent down on the month.[40] Megan Davies also notes that risk premiums on investment-grade corporate bonds over comparable Treasuries have topped 2 percent during or just before six of the seven U.S. recessions since 1970. Spreads on Baa-rated corporate bonds rose to 2 percent in July 2018.[41]

Nic Fildes has reported on difficulties since the Brexit vote in June 2016 in the UK high street.[42] Spending, which held up after the Brexit vote through dis-saving and borrowing, has now started to fall. This is to be expected given that real wages in the UK are down 5 percent since 2008 and didn't change at all between March 2016 and March 2018, which are the latest data available.

According to the ONS, in 2017 UK households saw their outgoings surpass their income for the first time in nearly thirty years. On average, each UK household spent or invested around £900 more than they received in income in 2017, amounting to almost £25 billion (or about one-fifth of the annual National Health Service [NHS] budget in England). Households' outgoings last outstripped their income for a whole year in 1988, although the shortfall was much smaller at just £0.3 billion. Even in the run-up to the financial crisis of 2008 and 2009—when 100 percent (and more) mortgages were offered to home buyers without a deposit—the ONS noted, the country did not reach a point where the average household was a net borrower.[43]

House of Fraser and Marks and Spencer are expected to shed dozens of stores in 2018, while Next, the clothing retailer, is looking at inserting a clause into its property leases to lower its rent. Toys "R" Us, Calvetron Brands, which owns women's wear chains including Jacques Vert and Precis, and the electronics retailer Maplin have all entered administration. Mothercare and Carpetright are also in trouble. The children's goods retailer revealed plans to close fifty stores while Carpetright, Fildes reports, has been forced to pursue a rescue rights issue after closing ninety-two stores. Fast-fashion chain New Look also plans to close up to sixty stores while food chains Prezzo, Jamie's Italian, and Byron Burger have also closed outlets. N. Brown, a Manchester-based company that has been operating since the 1850s, has begun a consultation process to close its remaining twenty high street stores.[44] Not good.

The collapse of the Wolverhampton-based Carillion, the UK's second-biggest construction company (whom I used to work for when they were called Tarmac), at the start of 2018, with its 45,000 workers, of whom

20,000 were in the UK, sent shock waves around the UK.[45] It holds a number of government contracts, including for the construction of a high-speed rail link and for the maintenance of roads.[46] Carillion found it harder and harder to borrow. This feels like 2008 all over again.

The liquidation threatens the jobs of more than 43,000 British workers, including those who are in partnership with Carillion, which suggests still others may go under. Carillion as well as hundreds of contractors and subcontractors.[47] Its shares had dropped 90 percent in 2017, it issued profit warnings, and it was on its third chief executive within six months.[48] Carillion had been awarded large public-sector contracts of over £2 billion by the UK government and an open question is why, given that it was under investigation by Britain's financial watchdog.[49]

I suspect this isn't going to go down well with the general public. A *Guardian* editorial on what they call "reaping the consequences of corporate greed" noted the extent of the impact the failure of Carillion is likely to have on jobs. The government has promised that Carillion's public-sector contracts will continue to operate, under the Official Receiver's control, following the liquidation. But private-sector contracts—which make up 60 percent of Carillion's business—are only guaranteed for forty-eight hours. After that, they could be terminated. Maybe this is a one-off, but it probably isn't. Four Seasons Health Care, the UK's second-largest home health-care business, reported large third-quarter losses, blaming public spending cuts and a Brexit-related shortage of nurses.[50] The question is, are these two cases the start of something big and bad?

Worryingly, on January 29, 2019, the Conference Board released their Consumer Confidence Index for the United States, which decreased in January, following a decline in December. The index now stands at 120.2 (1985 = 100), down from 126.6 in December and 136.4 in November. The Present Situation Index—based on consumers' assessment of current business and labor market conditions—declined marginally, from 169.9 to 169.6. Of particular concern is that the Expectations Index—based on consumers' short-term outlook for income, business, and labor market conditions—decreased from 112.3 in November to 97.7 in December and 87.3 in January. The question is whether this decline is the start of a trend downward as occurred at the start of the Great Recession.

This generally isn't what happens at full employment. Nothing much has changed since 2008. More fiddling about by policymakers. This was all eminently foreseeable. But the biggest downturn wasn't spotted until many months *after* it had started, and as a consequence people suffered. The economic forecasting models failed and continue to fail. Policymakers ignore the economics of walking about at their peril. Why should we trust any of them now? I don't.

CHAPTER 8

The People Have Lost Their Pep

The Great Recession is the twenty-first century's bubonic plague. If the Great Depression was anything to go by, there were inevitably going to be consequences from the crisis that started in the U.S. housing market and just spread around the world like an economic pandemic. The Great Crash of 1929 was followed by what Keynes called the long, dragging conditions of semi-slump. Unemployment in the 1930s hit 25 percent, living standards fell, and right-wing populist movements emerged in Austria, Germany, and Italy and in many other countries. That led to war. Rearmament spending in the UK at the end of the 1930s and war spending itself brought full employment. Women workers were central to the war effort.

John M. Barry, in his classic *The Great Influenza: The Story of the Deadliest Pandemic in History*, documents how the 1918 flu pandemic "reached everywhere . . . even a mild to moderate pandemic is something to worry about" (453, 456). Older people had built up antibodies to the flu from previous milder infections; it mostly impacted the young who had no immunity. The later the disease attacked the lesser the blow (372).

Young men infected with the disease joined the armed forces and were not isolated, and the flu spread as they went from camp to camp, troop ship to troop ship. Then they went back to their hometowns and passed the disease on to women. Soldiers were posted around the world by generals who refused to isolate them, and the disease spread even wider. The most conservative estimate is that it killed twenty million people. "New York City was panicking, terrified" (276). The spreading pandemic was driven by ignorance and the failure of public (health) authorities. There were too few nurses, and "the federal government was giving no guidance that a reasoning person could credit. Few local governments did better. They left a vacuum. Fear filled it" (410, 333). In the end science prevailed. But war and the flu especially impacted men.

Barry reported that Cincinnati Health Commissioner Dr. William Peters told the American Public Health Association meeting almost a year after the epidemic that phrases like "I am not feeling right," "I don't have my usual pep," and "I am all in since I had the flu" had become commonplace (392).

Months after recovering from the flu, Dartmouth's Robert Frost wondered, Barry reported, "what bones are they that rub together so unpleasantly in the middle of extreme emaciation . . . ? I don't know whether or not I'm strong enough to write a letter yet."[1]

Barry's final three paragraphs in his magnum opus seem especially apt.

> So, the final lesson of 1918, a simple one yet one most difficult to execute is that those who occupy positions of authority must lessen the panic that can alienate all within a society. Society cannot function if it is every man for himself.
>
> By definition society cannot survive that. Those in authority must retain the public's trust. The way to do that is to distort nothing, to put the best face on nothing, to try to manipulate no one. Lincoln said that first, and best.
>
> A leader must make whatever horror exists concrete. Only then will people be able to break it apart. (461)

In 2018 many people have lost their "usual pep." The effects of the Great Recession and the long, dragging conditions of semi-slump and subnormal prosperity that follow have lingered.

The Great Recession of 2008 and 2009 started in the U.S. housing market and spread, just like the bubonic plague, to the rest of the advanced world and beyond. People lost their houses, their jobs, and their pensions. Many just lost hope. Thankfully the authorities put in fiscal and monetary stimulus in 2008 and 2009 that prevented the unemployment rates in most countries from reaching the levels seen in the 1930s. The exceptions were Greece and Spain, which saw rates rise to interwar levels with youth unemployment rates even higher. Recovery started in 2009 and it seemed that the battle had been won.

Sadly, though, the imposition of austerity from 2010 onward meant that there was going to be slow progress from there. Policymakers found Keynes for a short while and then ditched him all in the name of debt. GDP growth since then has been weak and living standards have been hit hard. The UK recovery was the slowest in three hundred years. Simon Wren-Lewis was absolutely right when he said "without austerity in the UK we could have had a recovery that was *strong and long*" (2018, 285). In a tweet to me Simon argued, and I agree, "I just don't think enough people realise how different everything would have been with strong and long recoveries." I asked him if he thought that recovery had been long and weak and whether he thought austerity led to Brexit. In a subsequent tweet he replied, "In the US yes. In the UK it has been more standstill, weak and now very weak. In the Euro-zone there was of course a double dip recession. Given the narrow margin of victory, probably austerity did help cause Brexit." The United States has an employment rate that is 3 percentage points below its level at the start of recession.

Public spending cuts hit the weak, the disabled, and the vulnerable. Coal jobs, construction jobs, manufacturing jobs were gone, and nothing replaced them especially outside the big cities. Flyover America did badly while the exam-taking classes prospered. It is clear there was going to be a price to pay for too many years of hurt. In the United States the real earnings of workers in 2018 were still 10 percent below those of their parents in 1973. The American Dream is certainly broken and maybe gone.

In this chapter I look at the consequences of the Great Recession that hit in 2008 and the lost decade that followed. The first piece of evidence we look at suggests that people are in pain. Their mental and physical health has deteriorated, and life expectancy in the United States and the UK has fallen. There has been a rise in what Anne Case and Angus Deaton (2017b) have called "deaths of despair" in the United States, and an exploding opioid crisis shows no signs of abating. Of particular concern are the bad outcomes we observe for less-educated prime-age adults, especially whites, in the United States. This includes increases in deaths from drug overdoses, liver disease, and suicide.

When people are in pain they need to find someone to blame. Immigrants fit the bill, and that is the subject of chapter 9. Pain has inevitably had an impact on politics, which is the subject of chapter 10. Recessions and long periods of semi-slump, of subnormal prosperity, have consequences. It remains unclear the extent to which the recession caused these changes.

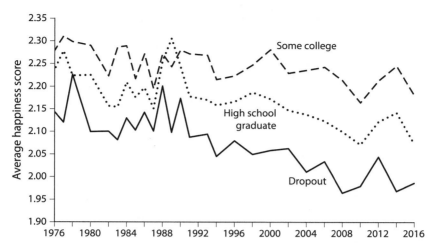

Figure 8.1. Declining happiness in the United States from the General Social Survey, 1976–2016. The figure plots average happiness "scores" based on answers to the question, "Taken all together, how would you say things are these days—would you say that you are very happy (= 3), pretty happy (= 2), or not too happy (= 1)?" (GSS question 157). *Source:* Blanchflower and Oswald 2018.

More likely it exposed deep underlying wounds. The people most affected by these changes disproportionately voted for Trump, who offered hope from despair.

Over the last few decades measured happiness has fallen in the United States. Figure 8.1 illustrates; it shows the decline in happiness by education groups using self-reported happiness data from the General Social Survey. It measures responses to the question, "Taken all together, how would you say things are these days—would you say that you are very happy (= 3), pretty happy (= 2), or not too happy (= 1)?" In 2016, the average happiness score was 2.12 versus 2.14 in 1972 and 2.21 in 2000. This is especially notable among high school dropouts.

Other countries have seen rising levels of happiness. For example, in the UK happiness has risen, using a scale of 1–10, from 7.3 in the period April 2011–March 2012 to 7.5 between July 2016 and June 2017.[2] Germany saw a rise from 2.9 to 3.2 in 2017. UK life satisfaction over this period rose from 3.2 in 2006 to 3.4 in 2017. France saw flat life satisfaction on a 4-point scale, using Eurobarometer surveys, at 3.0. Italy saw a fall—from 2.9 to 2.7, as did Greece from 2.71 to 2.23—but these countries all had high levels of unemployment. According to Helliwell et al. (2019) writing in the 2019 World

Happiness Report, the United States ranks nineteenth in the world happiness rankings, ahead of the Czech Republic (twentieth) and the United Arab Emirates (twenty-first). Germany is seventeenth, the UK fifteenth, Canada ninth. The top seven countries, in order, were Finland, Denmark, Norway, Iceland, Netherlands, Switzerland, and Sweden, where the distribution of income is relatively flat. The United States looks different.

Pain, Depression, and Despair

Pain in the United States is especially high compared with other countries, and its incidence has risen sharply over time. One-quarter of patients seen in primary care settings in the United States say they suffer from pain so intense that it interferes with the activities of daily living. There has also been a dramatic rise in opioid prescriptions in the United States but not elsewhere. Sadly, the evidence shows that opioids are ineffective in treating pain; it is better to take Advil or Tylenol. Plus, opioids are highly addictive; withdrawal is extremely difficult.

Dr. Donald Teater of the National Safety Council, founded in 1918 and chartered by Congress, examined the evidence on the effectiveness of opiates and non-opiates in treating pain. He concluded, "Opioids have been used for thousands of years in the treatment of pain and mental illness. Essentially everyone believes that opioids are powerful pain relievers. However, recent studies have shown that taking acetaminophen and ibuprofen together is actually more effective in treating pain." Teater cites a couple of review articles with supporting evidence. First, Moore and Hersh (2013, 898) in the *Journal of the American Dental Association* addressed the treatment of dental pain following wisdom tooth extraction and concluded that 325 milligrams of acetaminophen taken with 200 milligrams of ibuprofen provides better pain relief than oral opioids. Second, a review article in the *Spine Journal* (Lewis et al. 2013) looked at multiple treatment options for sciatica (back pain with a pinched nerve with symptoms radiating down one leg) and found that non-opioid medications provided some positive global effect on the treatment of the disorder, while the opioids did not.

My endodontists have a similar view about managing dental pain (Blicher and Pryles 2017). They only prescribe Advil after root canals, trust me! Their view is that opioids are not in fact the best means to manage dental pain: "800mg of ibuprofen is demonstrably more effective in managing severe dental pain than other available prescription analgesics, including narcotic

compounds. Furthermore, the combination of ibuprofen (Advil) and acetaminophen (Tylenol) offers greater pain relief than either medication alone
and significantly more than the combination of acetaminophen and opioid
medication both following endodontic treatment and third molar extraction"
(2017, 56). In his brilliant book Sam Quinones noted that in the last decade
or so entire families grew up on Social Security Disability Insurance (SSI),
which paid only a few hundred dollars a month. SSI had a major benefit: it
came with a Medicaid card and that made all the difference when Oxycontin
arrived. Having a Medicaid card, Quinones pointed out, allowed you to get
a monthly supply of pills worth several thousand dollars. With Oxycontin,
"a Medicaid card became [a license] to print money" (2015, 211). A Medicaid card provides health insurance, and part of that insurance pays for
medicine, whatever pills the doctor determines appropriate. For a three-
dollar Medicaid co-pay, an addict got pills priced at a thousand dollars with
a street value of ten thousand dollars: "Some of the most potent early vectors
were newly christened junkies from eastern Kentucky, where coal mines were
closing, and SSI and Medicaid cards sustained life" (Quinones 2015, 242).

Ethicist Travis Rieder told his own story of addiction after a devastating
injury. Rieder had a serious motorcycle accident, necessitating multiple
surgeries. He documents the heart-rending nightmare of trying to deal
with withdrawal from the pain killers he was given. The doctors just kept
prescribing.

> Physicians are the gatekeepers of medication for a reason: They are
> supposed to protect their patients from the harm that could come
> from unregulated use of those medications. Physicians, public health
> officials, and even the Centers for Disease Control and Prevention tell
> us that we are in the midst of an "opioid epidemic," due to the incred-
> ible addictive power of these drugs. Yet when people become addicted
> to painkillers after suffering a trauma, the best advice they might get
> from physicians when coping with withdrawal is to go back on it to
> feel better. Can we really do no better than that? (Rieder 2017)

In private communication with me, Travis Rieder noted that the United
States has 5 percent of the global population and 80 percent of its opioid
use. As we shall see, this is much less of a phenomenon in Europe. In the
United States, there were over 62,000 deaths due to opioid overdose in 2017,
which is more than the number of people killed in homicides or auto acci-

dents. The states with high drug-poisoning deaths, obesity rates, and low happiness levels disproportionately voted for Trump. West Virginia ranks worst on almost all dimensions. Why is this not happening in the UK? One reason is that prescription medicines cannot be advertised directly to the public. My doctor friends tell me they think the big reason for the difference is that British patients can't shop doctors if their general practitioner refuses to oblige with a prescription whereas they can in the United States.

Andrew Oswald and I (2004a, 2008, 2009, 2016, 2017) have found that those in middle age tend to suffer more than other age groups when it comes to such measures as happiness, enjoyment, pain, the number of "bad mental health days," worry, stress, fatigue, depression, sadness, and anxiety. The use of antidepressants peaks in middle age, as does the difficulty in paying bills and the incidence of obesity. In the United States, the number of bad mental health days is especially high and peaks in middle age, particularly for the nonworking, least educated.

The rise in the prevalence of pain has been apparent for some time, and its incidence is highest among those with less education. The Institute of Medicine (IOM) reported (2011) a marked rise in pain between 2000 and 2009, especially for those ages 45–64 and for white non-Hispanics. The IOM found that in 2009 there was little difference in knee, shoulder, neck, finger, and hip pain between those with less than a high school diploma and those with some college. But there were marked differences in the incidence of low back pain and severe headaches between the least and most educated groups.

Non-Hispanic whites had a higher incidence of back and neck pain than other racial groups.[3] Older adults, women, Caucasians, and people who did not graduate from high school were all more likely to report frequent or constant pain.[4] The prevalence of chronic, impairing lower-back pain in the United States has risen significantly over time.[5] Increases were seen for all adult age strata (men and women, white and black).

Data from England also suggest a rise in back pain,[6] although data from Finland[7] and Germany[8] showed little change. It is unclear why there are such marked differences across countries or whether the differences are real and there has been an increase in back pain in the United States and the UK just in self-reports.

To try to put the high levels of pain observed in the United States into perspective, Andrew Oswald and I (Blanchflower and Oswald, forthcoming) examined microdata from the 2011 International Social Survey Programme

(ISSP), which is a survey of thirty-two countries. Respondents in the United States reported the most pain. Respondents were asked, "How often during the past 4 weeks have you had bodily aches or pains? Never (= 1); seldom (= 2); sometimes (= 3); often (= 4); very often (= 5); or can't choose (set to missing)?" The proportions saying "often" or "very often" were 22 percent for France; 21 percent in Germany; 22 percent in Italy and the Netherlands; 17 percent in Spain; 28 percent in Great Britain; and 32 percent in the United States.[9]

Case and Deaton (2015) examined data from the U.S. National Health Interview Survey and looked at changes between the mean for 2011–13 and 1997–99 for those ages 45–54 with regard to neck pain, facial pain, chronic joint pain, and sciatica, all of which showed significant increases. One in three white non-Hispanics aged 45–54 reported chronic joint pain in the 2011–13 period. This rise in pain is correlated with the rise in pain medication prescriptions. They found that the prevalence of pain was highest for those ages 35–54 with less than a high school education.

The U.S. 2015 National Health Interview Survey also reported on levels of pain, including lower-back, neck, and face pain. It turns out that lower-back pain is especially prevalent with a mean of 30 percent, compared with 16 percent for neck pain and 4 percent for face pain. It is notable that lower-back pain varies by education and is especially high for dropouts (35%) compared with high school graduates (31%) and those with some college (28%).

Nahin (2015) reported that a remarkable 126 million or 56 percent of American adults experienced some type of pain in 2012. Of these, 20 percent had pain daily (i.e., chronic pain). Women were more likely than men to have such pain. White non-Hispanics had the highest incidence of pain versus other minorities. In both sexes, lower-back pain was most common. Krueger (2016) found that about half of prime-age men who are not in the U.S. labor force (NILF) may have a serious health condition that is a barrier to work. Nearly half of prime-age NILF men, he found, take pain medication daily, and in nearly two-thirds of cases they take prescription pain medication. The extent of the feelings of bodily pain is an obvious problem given that Muhuri and coauthors (2013) document that it leads to heroin use.

Tsang and coauthors (2008) found that the prevalence of any chronic pain condition was higher among women than men in both developed and developing countries. The prevalence of any chronic pain condition in the preceding twelve months in developed countries was highest in France

(50%), followed by Italy (46%) and the United States (44%), with Germany (32%) and Japan the lowest (28%).

Diener and Chan (2011) show that there is evidence in the literature of a relation between pain and well-being. They cite four intriguing papers. Pressman and Cohen (2005) discovered that positive emotions, by which they mean happiness, joy, excitement, enthusiasm, and contentment, are related to lower pain and greater tolerance of pain. They argue there is considerable evidence linking positive emotions to reports of fewer symptoms, less pain, and better health. In a meta-analysis, Ryan Howell et al. (2007) reported that there was a strong association between measures of well-being and pain tolerance. Tang and coauthors (2008) found that, in patients with chronic back pain, experimentally induced negative mood increases self-reported pain and decreases tolerance for a pain-relevant task, with positive mood having the opposite effect.

Depression, feelings of hopelessness, and stress are also on the rise in the United States and elsewhere. Data for 2009–12 show that 7.6 percent of Americans aged 12 and over had depression in the two weeks prior to being interviewed.[10] This was up from 5.4 percent during the period 2005–6. Consistent with these data, table 8.1 reports the extent to which antidepressants for depression and related disorders were used in the previous thirty days in the United States, in 1999–2002 and 2009–12. There has been a sharp increase in the prevalence of antidepressant use for all ages and for both men and women.[11]

Assari and Lankarani (2016) found that depressive symptoms accompany more hopelessness among U.S. whites than blacks. Hopelessness, they found, positively correlates with depression and suicidality and negatively correlates with happiness. Whites are less resilient, had higher suicide rates, and reported higher levels of pain in their daily lives than blacks did. This finding may explain, they suggest, why blacks with depression have a lower tendency to commit suicide.

Graham and Pinto (2016) found the odds of experiencing stress were highest among poor whites, who were 9 percent more likely to have stress than middle-class whites. Poor blacks were half as likely to experience stress. They also found that reported pain is higher in rural areas than in urban areas, where optimism about future life satisfaction is significantly lower.

A new article by Goldman and colleagues (2018) investigates whether the psychological health of Americans has worsened over time, as suggested

Table 8.1. Antidepressants (Depression and Related Disorders) Used in the Past 30 Days, United States (%)

	Men		Women	
	1999–2002	2009–2012	1999–2002	2009–2012
All ages	4.4	6.0	8.3	11.8
18–44 years	3.6	5.9	8.5	10.8
45–64 years	7.0	9.6	13.8	18.6
65 years and over	7.2	10.3	10.8	18.7
65–74 years	5.8	10.8	12.1	19.1
75 years and over	9.2	9.6	9.4	18.3

Source: Centers for Disease Control and Prevention, National Center for Health Statistics," table 80, "Health, United States, 2015," https://www.cdc.gov/nchs/data/hus/hus15.pdf.

by the "deaths of despair" narrative, linking rising mortality in midlife to drugs, alcohol, and suicide. The results show that distress is not just a midlife phenomenon but a scenario plaguing disadvantaged Americans across the life course. They investigated whether mental health had deteriorated since the mid-1990s, a time period known for increased opioid use and rising mortality from suicide, drugs, and alcohol. They used data from two cross-sectional waves of the Midlife in the U.S. Study (MIDUS) to assess trends in psychological distress and well-being. MIDUS conducted interviews with national samples of adults in 1995 and 1996 and another sample again between 2011 and 2014, which closely spans the period of rising substance abuse. The researchers looked at measures of distress and well-being to better capture overall mental health.

Distress was represented by two measures: depression and what's called "negative affect," which includes reports of sadness, hopelessness, and worthlessness. Well-being was assessed by four measures that reflect emotions such as happiness, fulfillment, life satisfaction, and meaning in life. The results revealed the influence of socioeconomic status. In both time periods studied, disadvantaged Americans reported higher levels of distress and lower levels of well-being compared to those of higher socioeconomic status. Importantly, between the two different waves of people studied, distress increased substantially among disadvantaged Americans, while those of higher socioeconomic status saw less change and even improvement.

In the UK, the report "Prescriptions Dispensed in the Community" for 2005–15 shows that the number of antidepressant items prescribed and dispensed in England has more than doubled in the last decade.[12] In 2015, there were 61 million antidepressant items prescribed—32 million more than in 2005 and 3.9 million more than in 2014. Between 2015 and 2016 the number of prescriptions for antidepressants rose 6 percent, from 61 million to 65 million.[13] The UK government noted this was the biggest single growth rate of any prescription medication.

Vandoros and coauthors (2018) examined whether the number of prescriptions for antidepressants in the UK increased after the Brexit referendum, benchmarking them against other drug classes. They used general practitioners' prescribing data to compile the number of defined daily doses per capita every month in each of the 326 voting areas in England over the period 2011–16. They found that antidepressant prescribing continued to increase after the referendum but at a slower pace. Therapeutic classes used as controls showed a decrease. The authors argue that "major political and economic shocks may have unanticipated consequences on population health, even before they directly affect employment, business or migration patterns" (2018, 7).

David Bell and I (2018c) examined data from the UK Labour Force Surveys where respondents report on whether they have a health problem and if so what it is. It is possible to report more than one, but respondents determine which problem is the main one. One of the options was "mental illness, or suffers from phobia, panics, or other nervous disorders." We found that there was no evidence of any rise over time in these serious forms of mental ill health. We did find evidence of a rise in the proportion who reported having "depressions, bad nerves or anxiety" as their main health problem. The incidence was broadly flat from 2004 through 2010 but then more than doubled between 2010 and 2018 with the implementation of austerity.[14]

The consumption of antidepressants around the world has been little studied in the economics literature.[15] One article does show that job loss caused by plant closure leads to greater antidepressant consumption; another argues that an increase in sales of one antidepressant—selective serotonin reuptake inhibitors (SSRIs)—by one pill per capita produces a large reduction (of 5%) in a country's suicide rate. A further exception in the wider literature examines data on the timing of people's Google searches on antidepressants' side effects.[16] For Europe, Knapp et al. (2007) document a near-doubling of antidepressant consumption in the ten years from 1990 to 2000.

Recent data on antidepressant medication usage from the OECD reveal a continuing upward trend across all countries. Antidepressant consumption in daily doses per thousand population rose, in the UK, for example, from 20 in 1995 to 87 in 2014. This rate, in 2014, was higher than in France (50 in 2008), Italy (47), or Germany (55).

Well-Being, Health, Healing, and Longevity

This all matters. It turns out that happy people heal faster. A meta-analysis assessed the impact of stress on the healing of a variety of wound types in different contexts, including acute and chronic clinical wounds, experimentally created punch biopsy and blister wounds, and minor damage to the skin caused by tape stripping.[17] The results reveal a robust negative relationship whereby stress is associated with the impairment of healing and disregulation of biomarkers associated with wound healing. This is broadly consistent across a variety of clinical and experimental, acute and chronic wound types in cutaneous and mucosal tissue. The relationship was evident across different measures of stress.

Later work also concluded that evidence from experimental and clinical models of wound healing indicate that psychological stress leads to clinically relevant delays in wound healing.[18] Dental students who were given a standardized wound healed more quickly during the summer than during final exams.[19] It has also been found that surgical patients heal more quickly if they report high levels of life satisfaction.[20]

Hemingway and Marmot (1990) found that depression and anxiety predicted coronary heart disease in healthy people. Analogously, Zaninotto, Wardle, and Steptoe (2016) studied a national representative sample of English men and women age 50 and over and examined measures of enjoyment of life. Subsequent mortality was inversely correlated with the number of occasions on which participants reported high enjoyment of life. Chida and Steptoe (2008) conducted a meta-analysis and found that positive psychological well-being was related to lower mortality. Joy, happiness, and energy, as well as life satisfaction, hopefulness, optimism, and a sense of humor, lowered the risk of mortality.

Obesity is also correlated with depression, but the direction of causation is not obvious.[21] Obesity makes people depressed, or depression makes people eat, which causes depression or possibly both in a downward spiral. Luppino et al. (2010) addressed this issue with a meta-analysis of studies using longitudinal data and examined whether depression is predictive of the development of overweight and obesity and, in turn, whether overweight and obesity are predictive of the development of depression. Importantly they found the direction of causation ran from depression to obesity; depression was found to be predictive of developing obesity. This was especially strong in American studies, where the average BMI is higher than in other countries.

Obesity, depression, and pain seem to go together. Obesity has trended up over time, in the United States, from 30.7 percent in 1999–2000 to 37.7 percent in 2013–14.[22] State rankings show that West Virginia has the highest rate of obesity, as well as the highest incidence of drug-poisoning deaths of any state according to the NHCS. The ten states with the highest obesity rates voted for Trump.[23] Pratt and Brody (2014b) found that 53 percent of U.S. adults with depression were obese. Fifty-five percent of adults who were taking antidepressant medication, but still reported moderate to severe depressive symptoms, were obese.

Relative things also appear to matter for obesity. The United States has far and away the highest BMI of any OECD country. According to the OECD, 40 percent of the adult population in 2016 in the United States was obese, measured by whether their BMI is 30 or over, which is the highest in the OECD. This compares with 28 percent in Canada; 26 percent in the UK; 24 percent in Germany; 17 percent in France and Spain; and 4 percent in Japan.[24] Obesity levels are one indicator of poor physical and mental health.

There Is Growing Evidence of a Midlife Crisis for the Jobless

A good deal of the evidence in this chapter suggests there is an ongoing midlife crisis. This is especially apparent for white, less-educated people.

Happiness is U-shaped with regard to age while unhappiness has the opposite shape. The rates of depression and antidepressant usage according to age have an inverted U-shape as do the incidence of obesity and pain (including neck and lower-back) and the rates of fatigue and stress. It also turns out that views on many other variables, including household finances and the state of the economy, have a U-shape according to age.

Pain is highest in middle age. Drug-poisoning deaths are also highest among those in middle age. There was an especially large jump in the U.S. suicide rate of white non-Hispanic men ages 45–64 between 1999 and 2014.

Deaths of despair, due to drug and alcohol poisoning and suicide, are up in the United States, particularly for white non-Hispanics with low education levels, but they are not for Hispanics, Asians, or blacks.

In a 2008 article Andrew Oswald and I showed that happiness is U-shaped with regard to age in seventy-two countries around the world.[25] In many countries, the U-shape can be found without any control variables. The United States does not have a well-being U-shape in age until control variables are included.[26]

In a 2017 paper Andrew and I reexamined the U-shape pattern for happiness in six data sets. These include the UK with data on life satisfaction, happiness, and worthwhileness from the Well-Being Supplement to the Labour Force Survey for 2011–15, as well as data from the EU28 from the Eurobarometer Surveys and the European Social Surveys from 2002–14, plus the multicountry International Social Survey Programme (ISSP) for 2012. All six surveys, for around seventy countries, show a convincing U-shape. Happiness also rises with income level. Those with the lowest incomes are the least happy. The unemployed are especially unhappy.

Andrew Clark and I have examined the unexpected finding in the happiness literature that children lower happiness. In a study of a million Europeans we find that children actually raise happiness once account is taken of the difficulty parents have in paying their bills.

In the 2016 European Social Survey taken across eighteen European countries, approximately 35,000 respondents were asked about their life satisfaction as well as their satisfaction with the economy; the national government; the way democracy works in their country; the state of education; and the state of health services in their country. Answers were recorded on a 1–10 scale where 1 = extremely dissatisfied and 10 = extremely satisfied. In all six cases satisfaction followed a U-shape in age, all of which had satisfaction levels minimizing around age 55.[27]

Just to extend the idea that the U-shape in well-being broadens beyond simply happiness and life satisfaction, there are also data in a large number of Eurobarometer surveys on other topics. As an example, a survey taken in May 2017 asked about life satisfaction: "On the whole, are you very satisfied (= 4), fairly satisfied (= 3), not very satisfied (= 2), or not at all satisfied (= 1) with the life you lead?" The approximately 33,000 respondents in the survey were also asked: "How would you judge the current state of a) the situation of the national economy, b) the financial situation of your household, c) the employment situation in your country, d) the provision of public services in your country?" Responses were very good (= 4), rather good (= 3), rather bad (= 2), and bad (= 1). In every case responses followed a U-shape in age, with a low point in age ranging from 44 to 56.[28]

A Eurobarometer survey conducted between February and March 2010 asked respondents in thirty European countries the following question: "How often over the past four weeks did you feel a) tired and b) worn out?" Responses were never (= 1), rarely (= 2), sometimes (= 3), most of the time (= 4), and all the time (= 5). Tiredness and being worn out both maximize in the mid-40s and then fall away. There was also a question in the survey about depression, which also had an inverted U-shape in age.

Graham and Pozuelo (2017) found that stress had an inverted U-shape in age in 34 out of 46 countries they studied, including Germany, the UK, and the United States. The question used was: "Did you experience the following feelings during a lot of the day yesterday? How about stress?" A recent U.S. study using Gallup Healthways data on over 1.5 million respondents analyzed a question asking about stress felt the previous day and found that ratings of daily, perceived stressfulness rose from age 20 through to about age 50, followed by a precipitous decline after age 70.[29] Data from the American Time Use Survey also confirmed that the level of stress rose to around age 54 and then declined.

Another study using the Gallup Healthways data file reported results on the relationship between stress and age. The study showed there was a correlation between stress and age in high-income English-speaking countries for men but not women; however, it was present for both genders in sub-Saharan Africa, in countries of the former Soviet Union, and in Latin America and the Caribbean (their figure 3).[30] The researchers also found evidence of an inverted U-shape in age for whether respondents had experienced "a lot of worry yesterday" in English-speaking countries, Latin America, and the Caribbean.[31]

A recent study used data from a telephone survey conducted in 2008 by the Gallup organization to examine well-being in the United States.[32] The authors found that enjoyment showed a U-shaped pattern in age, along with happiness, with the low point at age 50. Sadness and worry both had an inverted U-shape in age. Stress, though, rose from the youngest age group (18–21) to ages 22–25 and then fell steadily thereafter; anger also declined after the mid-20s.

There is evidence of a U-shape curve in relationship satisfaction. Specifically, it decreases during the first years of a relationship but increases subsequently.[33] It also turns out that happiness with one's marriage is U-shaped in age as well. In the U.S. General Social Survey from 1973 to 2016, respondents were asked how happy they were with their marriage: not too happy (= 1); pretty happy (= 2); and very happy (= 3). I examined how this varied by age and restricted the sample to those who were married; with a sample of 29,500 it turns out that happiness minimizes at age 47.[34]

It is also possible to look at the number of bad mental health days people report having in one month. I examined microdata files for the United States from the 2000 and 2016 Behavioral Risk Factor Surveillance System (BRFSS). The BRFSS asks respondents how many bad mental health days they have experienced over the previous month. These data were reported on by Case and Deaton (2015), who found that men and women ages 45–54 for the periods 1997–99 and 2011–13 reported an additional day of bad mental health on the month. It turns out that the states with the highest number of bad mental health days in 2015 were Kentucky (47), Alabama (48), West Virginia (49), and Tennessee (50).[35] Hawaii and South Dakota had the lowest number of bad mental health days.

I plotted the number of bad mental health days by single year of age separated out by low and high levels of education and whether the respondent was working or not working. Here low education is defined as a high school graduate/GED or less and high education is at least some college. Figure 8.2 shows, for 2016, that the number of bad mental health days declines with age for those who work. There is a clear inverted U-shape for those who are not working, whether with a low or a high education. Both peak around age 50. The peak for the less educated is 12 bad mental health days, whereas it is nearly 9 for the more educated. Figure 8.3 is for 2000 and also shows the same pattern although the minimum is further to the left.

Not working is bad for mental health, especially for those with less than a high school education. There were markedly fewer people employed as a proportion of the population in 2016 than there were in 2000. In 2000 the employment rate was 64 percent. In 2016 it was just under 60 percent.

In another article I wrote with Andrew Oswald (2016), we found that antidepressant use took the form of an inverted U-shape in age across twenty-seven EU countries. We also found that, despite the advantages of modern living, one in thirteen Europeans had taken an antidepressant in the previous

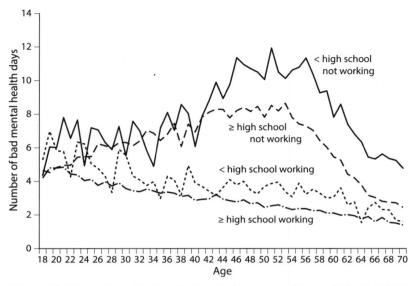

Figure 8.2. U.S. number of bad mental health days by age. *Source:* Behavioral Risk Factor Surveillance System 2016, https://www.cdc.gov/brfss/data_documentation /index.htm.

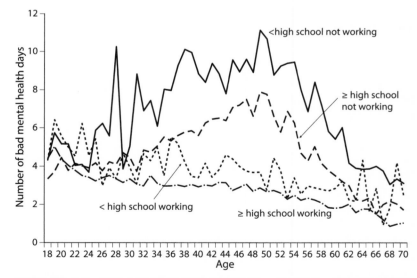

Figure 8.3. U.S. number of bad mental health days by age. *Source:* Behavioral Risk Factor Surveillance System 2000, https://www.cdc.gov/brfss/data_documentation /index.htm.

twelve months. The rates of antidepressant use are greatest in Portugal, Lithuania, France, and the UK. Rather robustly, the probability of using an antidepressant attains a maximum in the late 40s. This seems to suggest that mental distress is particularly acute in midlife. In addition, the probability of taking antidepressants is also greater among those who are female, unemployed, poorly educated, or divorced or separated.

Cumulative Disadvantage and Deaths of Despair

Anne Case and Angus Deaton documented rising mortality rates for white non-Hispanic men and women ages 45–54 in the United States between 1999 and 2013 (Case and Deaton 2015). Death rates for this group rose both absolutely and relative to other racial and ethnic groups. The rising rate of "deaths of despair," as they call them, is due to drug and alcohol poisoning and suicide, which disproportionately impact the middle-aged but especially white non-Hispanic middle-aged.

Table 8.2 reports death rates from drug poisoning by age in 1999, 2008, and 2015. It shows the white non-Hispanic rate more than tripled between 1999 and 2015. The rate for blacks and Hispanics rose by a lot less. The increase for white non-Hispanic women and men aged 45–54 was especially marked (8 to 32% for women and 13 to 41% for men). Among patients receiving opioid prescriptions for pain, higher opioid doses were associated with increased risk of opioid overdose death.[36] Specifically, the risk of drug-related adverse events is higher among individuals prescribed opioids at doses equal to 50 milligrams per day or more of morphine. More is worse, less is better.

Table 8.2. Age-Adjusted Death Rates (%) Due to Drug Poisonings: United States, 1999–2015

	Non-Hispanic whites				Blacks	Hispanics
	All ages	35–44	45–54	55–64	All ages	All ages
1999	6.2	14.1	10.5	4.0	7.5	5.4
2008	14.8	26.8	29.1	13.6	8.4	5.8
2015	21.1	38.6	36.3	23.4	12.2	7.7

Source: Centers for Disease Control and Prevention, National Center for Health Statistics, "Drug Poisoning Mortality in the United States, 1999–2016," https://www.cdc.gov/nchs/data-visualization/drug-poisoning-mortality/#tables.

Over the fifteen-year period, midlife all-cause mortality fell by more than 200 per 100,000 for black non-Hispanics, and by more than 60 per 100,000 for Hispanics. By contrast, white non-Hispanic mortality rose by 34 per 100,000. Case and Deaton (2015) find that the change is largely accounted for by an increasing death rate from external causes, mostly increases in drug and alcohol poisonings and in suicide. In contrast to earlier years, drug overdoses were not concentrated among minorities. In 1999, poisoning mortality for ages 45–54 was 10.2 per 100,000 higher for black non-Hispanics than white non-Hispanics; by 2013, poisoning mortality was 8.4 per 100,000 higher for whites. Death from cirrhosis and chronic liver diseases fell for blacks and rose for whites.

After 2006, death rates from alcohol- and drug-induced causes for white non-Hispanics exceeded those for black non-Hispanics; in 2013, rates for white non-Hispanics exceeded those for black non-Hispanics by 19 per 100,000. Case and Deaton found that all education groups saw increases in mortality from suicide and poisonings, as well as an overall increase in external-cause mortality; those with less education saw the most marked increases. This increase in all-cause mortality for those ages 45–54 was not seen in Australia, Canada, France, Germany, Sweden, or the UK.

In a follow-up paper Case and Deaton (2017b) noted that increases in all-cause mortality continued unabated to 2015, with additional increases in drug overdoses, suicides, and alcoholic-related liver mortality, particularly among those with a high school degree or less. The decline in mortality from heart disease, they reported, has slowed and, most recently, stopped, and this combined with the three other causes is responsible for the increase in all-cause mortality. Their main finding is that educational differences in mortality among whites are increasing, but mortality is rising for those without, and falling for those with, a college degree. This is true for white non-Hispanic men and women in all age groups from 25–29 through 60–64. Mortality rates among blacks and Hispanics continue to fall; in 1999, the mortality rate of white non-Hispanics aged 50–54 with only a high school degree was 30 percent lower than the mortality rate of blacks in the same age group; by 2015, it was 30 percent higher.

Alcohol-poisoning deaths are high for two distinct groups: (1) men ages 45–54, and (2) white non-Hispanics, although markedly lower than for drug poisonings.[37] Using the most recent data we have available for the United States, we can track changes in death rates due to alcohol poisoning between 1999 and 2014.[38] The number of deaths from chronic liver disease for those ages 45–54 rose from 17.4 to 19.9 per 100,000, with the biggest rise for those ages 55–64, from 23.7 to 31.9. Death rates from chronic liver disease in the United States were 18 per 100,000 for white non-Hispanic men versus 9.5 for black men and 4.1 for Asians. Rates were second highest in West Virginia (14.3), behind New Mexico (22.5).

Eurostat provides evidence on death rates from alcohol between 2011 and 2013 for the UK plus France, Germany, and Italy. These have not changed much over time and remain at low levels. Drug-poisoning deaths are a lot higher in the UK than the other three countries, confirming the findings of Case and Deaton that trends in mortality due to drugs, alcohol, and suicide were especially high in other English-speaking countries. They found that the UK, Ireland, Canada, and Australia stand alone among the comparison countries in having substantial positive trends in mortality from drugs, alcohol, and suicide over this period. However, their increases are dwarfed by the increase among U.S. whites.

Suicide is a leading cause of death in the United States. The Centers for Disease Control (CDC) has found that since 1999 there has been a steady climb in the rate of Caucasian suicides, from 11.5 in 1999 to 15.4 in 2014.[39] Age-adjusted suicide rates for females rose from 4.0 in 1999 to 5.8 in 2014.[40] For males, the rate rose from 17.8 to 20.7. A majority of Caucasian suicide victims were male, with a rate of 24 per 100,000 (compared to a rate of 7 for women). There was an especially large jump in the suicide rate of white non-Hispanic males aged 45–64 between 1999 and 2014, from 7.0 to 12.6. There also appears to be an inverted U-shape in age in suicide especially among females in the United States, although not so obviously for men.[41]

Between 1999 and 2015, suicide rates increased across all levels of urbanization, with the gap in rates between less urban and more urban areas widening over time, most conspicuously over the later part of this period. Geographic disparities in suicide rates, Kegler, Stone, and Holland (2017) suggest, might reflect suicide risk factors known to be prevalent in less urban areas, such as limited access to mental health care, social isolation, and the opioid overdose epidemic, because opioid misuse is associated with increased risk for suicide. The gap in rates began to widen more noticeably after 2007–8, which might reflect the influence of the economic recession, which disproportionately had less impact on urban areas.

In June 2018 the CDC reported that nearly 45,000 lives were lost due to suicide in 2016, a few days after the suicides of fashion designer Kate Spade and chef and raconteur Anthony Bourdain. Suicides were up 25 percent

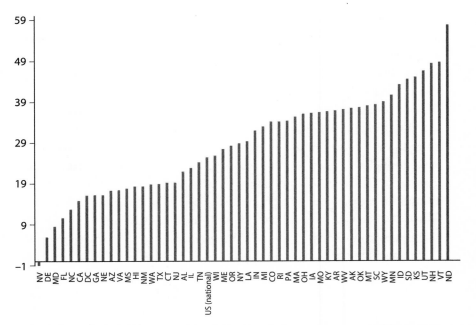

Figure 8.4. Suicide rate changes by state, 1999–2016. *Sources:* https://www.cdc.gov
/vitalsigns/suicide/; https://www.cdc.gov/vitalsigns/suicide/infographic.html#graphic1.

nationally and by more than 30 percent in half of the states since 1999 and
were only down in Nevada. More than half of the people who died by suicide
did not have a known mental health condition, which may just show the
inadequacy of mental health care provision. Figure 8.4 reveals the suicide
rate changes by state; North Dakota had the highest change in the suicide
rate, followed by Vermont and New Hampshire. According to the U.S. Department of Veterans Affairs, an average of twenty veterans a day committed
suicide in 2014.[42] These data are scary.

Stuckler and Basu (2013) have argued that austerity kills. They estimate
that 4,750 "excess" suicides, that is, deaths above what preexisting trends
would predict, occurred from 2007 to 2010. Rates of such suicides were
significantly greater in the states that experienced the greatest job losses.
Deaths from suicide, they note, in the UK overtook deaths from car crashes
in 2009.

Mary Daly, who has recently become the president of the Federal Reserve
Bank of San Francisco Federal and who in 2018 had a vote on interest rates,
and her coauthors (2011) present evidence to suggest that others' happiness

may be a risk factor for suicides. Using international and U.S. data, they note a paradox: the happiest places tend to have the highest suicide rates. Denmark and Sweden have a positive correlation between suicide rates and life satisfaction levels. What they call "dark contrasts" may in turn increase the risk of suicide. This is comparable to the finding that in Italy, suicide rates of the unemployed seem to be higher in low-unemployment regions.[43]

As one might expect, happy people themselves are less likely to commit suicide. At baseline, Koivumaa-Honkanen et al. (2003) found that in a sample of 29,000 adult Finns, unhappiness was associated with older age groups, being male, sickness, living alone, smoking, heavy alcohol consumption, physical inactivity, and belonging to an intermediate social class. The risk of suicide over the next twenty years increased with decreasing happiness.

Case and Deaton in their 2015 article examine the relationship between suicide, age, and well-being and find that suicide has little to do with own life satisfaction. However, they do find at the county level that suicide rates are higher where life evaluation is higher, confirming the findings of the 2011 Daly et al. paper. They note that suicides are most likely to occur on Mondays: 16 percent of suicides occur on that day of the week. The Boomtown Rats were right when they sang, "I don't like Mondays." Apparently mental health episodes are more likely to occur at holiday times as well.[44] In addition, Case and Deaton (2015) find that the prevalence of pain, which is increasing in middle-aged Americans, is strongly predictive of suicides.

A recent study explored the relationship between mortality and a plausibly exogenous change in U.S. trade policy in October 2000: granting Permanent Normal Trade Relations (PNTR) to China that differentially exposed U.S. counties to increased international competition via their industry structure.[45] The authors of the study found that counties more exposed to trade liberalization exhibit higher rates of suicide among whites and especially white men.

Case and Deaton argue that the rise in mortality of prime-age, less-educated whites in the United States is explained by cumulative disadvantage, which they suggest is "rooted in the steady deterioration in job opportunities for people with low education. Ultimately, we see our story as about the collapse of the white, high school educated, working class after its heyday in the early 1970s, and the pathologies that accompany that decline" (2017b, 438–39). Cherlin concurs, arguing that what he calls the fall in the working-class family occurred because less-educated people lack strong connections to mainstream institutions such as marriage, the labor market, and organized religion: "The hollowing out of the labor market—the loss of industrial jobs to offshoring and computerization—has removed the economic foundation of the kind of working-class lives their mothers and fathers led" (2014, 175).

Case and Deaton's conclusions have been attacked by Auerbach and Gelman for aggregating the data too much by race.[46] In addition, Harris[47] criticized Case and Deaton for disaggregating the data too much by education levels and ignoring selection effects. Noah Smith effectively disposes of these criticisms, arguing that they are overblown and concluding that these critiques "don't invalidate the result." Smith argues that "most of the critics have overstated their case pretty severely. The Case-Deaton result is not bunk—it's a real and striking finding." He suggests that a lot of the eagerness to discredit Case and Deaton's results stems from political reasons. He concludes, "The critiques of Case-Deaton are overdone. Maybe Case and Deaton should have focused less on disaggregating by education, and more on disaggregating by gender, age, and region. But those are quibbles. The main results are real and important."[48] I agree.

Things Are Worse in Rural Areas

There is a big contrast between rural areas and the big cities. In an interesting column Paul Overberg identifies several factors distinguishing rural from urban areas, not least that few immigrants are moving to rural areas. Most seek work and neighbors in places that are familiar, which largely means urban areas.[49] This, Overberg argues, has opened a cultural gulf between diverse, growing cities and mostly white, aging small towns. Rural areas have only 3.8 percent of their populations that are foreign born versus 22 percent in large metro areas.

Overberg notes that in the 1990s, a few rural areas began to record more deaths than births. Then the recession of 2007–9 lowered U.S. birth rates and slowed migration and immigration. Rural America now faces the "grim prospect" of natural decrease, meaning more deaths than births over time. More jobs, especially full-time jobs with benefits, require a bachelor's or advanced degree. Without a larger share of college graduates, small towns have little hope of closing the income gap. Rural America seems to be anti-immigrant even though they have relatively few immigrants. Rural America voted for Trump.

There is new evidence from the CDC that the death rate in rural areas from the five leading causes of death—heart disease, cancer, unintentional injury, chronic lower respiratory disease, and stroke—is much higher than in urban areas.[50] Moy and coauthors (2017) note that it is well known that residents in rural areas have higher rates of health risk factors for the leading causes of death, including factors such as cigarette smoking, obesity, physical inactivity during leisure time, and not wearing seatbelts. They also tend to have less access to health care and preventive services.

The authors examine "excess death," which the CDC defines as deaths among persons less than 80 years old over the number that would be expected if the age-specific death rates of the three states with the lowest rates (i.e., benchmark states) occurred across all states. They find that approximately half of deaths among persons less than 80 years old from unintentional injury (57.5%) in nonmetropolitan areas were potentially excess deaths, compared with 39.2 percent in metropolitan areas. Over the period 1999–2014 deaths from unintentional injury rose in metropolitan and nonmetropolitan areas, and in all years, they were approximately 50 percent higher in rural areas than urban areas.

Garcia et al. (2017) suggest that several factors explain the wide gap in rural-urban death rates from unintentional injuries. First, unintentional injury burden is higher in rural areas because of severe trauma associated with high-speed motor vehicle traffic-related deaths. Second, rates of opioid analgesic misuse and overdose death are highest among poor and rural populations. Third, behavioral factors (e.g., alcohol-impaired driving, seatbelt use, and opioid prescribing) contribute to higher injury rates in rural areas. Fourth, access to treatment for trauma and drug poisoning is often delayed when the injury occurs in rural areas. For life-threatening injury, higher survival is associated with rapid emergency treatment. Because of the geographic distance involved, emergency medical service (EMS) providers who operate ambulances take longer to reach injured or poisoned patients in rural areas.

Moreover, the authors note, ambulatory transport to the optimal treatment facility also can take longer because of increased distance to the treatment facility. Most life-threatening trauma is best treated in advanced trauma centers, which are usually located in urban areas; care at these centers has been associated with 25 percent lower mortality.[51] Folks in rural areas, whose health care has been left behind, voted for Trump.

In October 2017 the CDC noted that in 2015, approximately six times as many drug-overdose deaths occurred in metropolitan areas than occurred in nonmetropolitan areas (metropolitan: 45,059; nonmetropolitan: 7,345). Drug-overdose death rates (per 100,000 people) for metropolitan areas were higher than in nonmetropolitan areas in 1999 (6.4 versus 4.0); however, the rates converged in 2004, and by 2015, the nonmetropolitan rate (17.0) was slightly higher than the metropolitan rate (16.2).[52]

In November 2018 the CDC released new data showing that life expectancy at birth in the United States in 2017 was 78.6 years, down from 78.7 in 2016 (Murphy et al. 2018). The CDC also reported (Hedegaard, Miniño, and Warner 2018) that there were 70,237 drug-overdose deaths in the United States in 2017. The age-adjusted rate of drug overdoses was 9.6 percent higher in 2017 compared with 2016. There was a sharp increase in overdose deaths involving synthetic opioids, such as fentanyl, fentanyl analogs, and tramadol, from 2016 to 2017. The age-adjusted rate of drug-overdose deaths involving synthetic opioids other than methadone increased by 45 percent. While the average rate of drug-overdose deaths involving synthetic opioids increased by 8 percent per year from 1999 to 2013, the average rate increased by 71 percent per year from 2013 to 2017. West Virginia (57.8 deaths per 100,000 people), Ohio (46.3), and Pennsylvania (44.3) had the highest age-adjusted drug-overdose rates.

The suicide rate among the U.S. working-age population increased 34 percent during 2000–2016 (Hedegaard, Curtin, and Warner 2018). In 2012 and 2015, suicide rates were highest among males in the "construction and extraction" occupational group (43.6 and 53.2 per 100,000 civilian noninstitutionalized working persons, respectively), who were especially hard hit by the housing crash in the Great Recession.[53] The age-adjusted suicide rate for urban counties in 2017 was 16 percent higher than the rate in 1999, whereas in rural counties in 2017 it was 53 percent higher. By 2017 the suicide rate in rural counties (20 per 100,000) was nearly double that of urban counties (11.1).

Globalization, automation, and falling real wages do seem to be the cause of the long-term patterns of mortality and morbidity I have documented. The Great Recession didn't cause them but simply exposed underlying trouble. Alarmingly, life expectancy in the United States at 78.6 years in 2017 was down 0.1 percent from 2016, which was the second year in a row of a 0.1 percent decline.[54] After decades of steady improvements in the UK, in the most recent data for 2015–17 life expectancy at birth saw no improvement from the previous national life tables.

A lack of well-paying jobs was always going to have consequences. Joblessness worsens mental health. Rural areas in the United States have been hit especially hard. Rural areas voted for Trump. Society cannot function if it is every man for himself. By definition society cannot survive that. Those in authority must retain the public's trust.

CHAPTER 9

Somebody Has to Be Blamed

When people are hurting they seem to want someone to blame. Immigrants will do. In tough times the outsider is easy to blame. Immigration is a divisive political issue around the world. Bloody foreigners. As Bob Dylan sang, "pity the poor immigrant."

Mexicans, Poles, and Muslims will do. The Jews were the scapegoats in the 1930s. There is clearly a perception among those who voted for Trump that the influx of foreigners from Mexico and elsewhere took jobs away. In the UK there was considerable opposition to the flow of immigrants to the UK led by the UK Independence Party (UKIP), and this was central to the Brexit campaign—keep Britain British. There were growing fears of terrorism and the fear that refugees might do bad stuff.

As can be seen in the table below calculated from the OECD's "International Migration Outlook, 2018" (table 1.1), the inflow of permanent immigrants in 2016 compared to 2010 was up in percentage terms, nearly fourfold in Germany, and more than doubled in Austria and Sweden. Countries are ranked by the percentage change in the flow. They have fallen substantially in Italy, the UK, Spain, and Portugal.

Germany	372	Denmark	62	Canada	5
Poland	161	Netherlands	51	Norway	2
Greece	143	Mexico	32	Belgium	–14
Austria	130	France	17	Portugal	–18
Sweden	107	New Zealand	15	United Kingdom	–22
Ireland	79	United States	13	Spain	–23
Korea	78	Switzerland	9	Italy	–52
Japan	71	Australia	7	Slovakia	–71

There was a huge public outcry when the Trump administration implemented a policy to separate immigrant children from parents crossing the southern border illegally. Pictures of crying youngsters who had been separated from their parents and imprisoned didn't go over well. Former First Lady Laura Bush in an op-ed in the *Washington Post* argued that "our government should not be in the business of warehousing children in converted box stores or making plans to place them in tent cities in the desert outside of El Paso. These images are eerily reminiscent of the Japanese American internment camps of World War II, now considered to have been one of the most shameful episodes in U.S. history."[1] Michael Steele, former Republican National Committee chairman, called them concentration camps.[2] General Michael Hayden, former director of the CIA, tweeted a picture of a Nazi concentration camp and the words "other governments have separated mothers and children." Emotions are running high.

Majorities in most countries, though, including the UK and the United States, do remain supportive of immigration, but there is significant and vocal opposition. Support for immigration tends to be highest in the big cities where the immigrants live. Paris voted against Frexit; Washington, D.C., and New York voted for Clinton; and London voted to Remain. Most opposition is found where the immigrants don't live, for example, in rural areas in the United States. In European countries with more asylum seekers from Iraq and Syria—Germany and Sweden—people tend to view immigrants as less threatening. There is a good deal of concern about the big rise in Muslim asylum seekers, especially given the terror attacks that have taken place in France, Germany, and the UK. Terrorism is a growing concern.

Migrants, who are a highly selected, mobile, and motivated group, add more to an economy than they take from it. In general, there is a mover's premium; the best move. In academia the best people are able to get offers at other institutions to raise their salaries, and you have to pay people more to move to compensate for the disruption and an adjustment period. Movers grease the wheels of the labor market, as they are more mobile and often more productive than the indigenous population and can move to where the work is. Immigrant populations have likely improved the workings of the labor markets in host countries and have kept prices down for a number of items, for example, fruit and vegetables, which benefits everyone. But the left-behinds with low skills are threatened as they are the most impacted. The gainers didn't compensate the losers enough.

Unsurprisingly, the central plank of populist uprisings in the years after the Great Recession has been an opposition to immigration. Immigration is a prime example of where there is a striking juxtaposition between perception and reality. Crime among immigrants, for example, is lower than among the indigenous populations, but the majority of the public seems to believe the reverse. There is a widely expressed fear that immigrants are taking high-paying jobs away as they are prepared to do them more cheaply than would indigenous workers.

I am an immigrant. I have been in the United States for nearly thirty years but have never lost my accent. I am asked all the time where I am from. I know what it's like to be told to go home—well, a bit.

I arrived in the United States with my two daughters on July 3, 1989. The Irish writer George Bernard Shaw once said: "England and America are two countries separated by a common language." It took a long time to work out where to buy things. There were no public toilets or fish and chip shops. I couldn't find a tire shop in the phone book as I kept looking up "tyre." Nobody could help me find an ironmongers. The supermarket was a huge culture shock as we had no idea what brands to buy. I couldn't work out why nobody came to collect the rubbish and I missed gritting lorries and pubs. I can only imagine how hard it is for those who don't speak the lingo. It took me many months to understand the rules of baseball. After a couple of months at Dartmouth my secretary asked me if they celebrate Christmas in Britain. Geraint Johnes, professor of economics at Lancaster University with whom I shared an office in graduate school in Cardiff, tells me his culture shock story involved going to the post office in 1984 to send a telegram and being told they didn't do that—he had to find a florist.

I am proud to be an immigrant too. I have been told on a few occasions to go back to England if I don't like the way things are done here. I have a son who was born here who is an officer in the U.S. Army Reserve and is a proud American. My U.S. passport is the same as everyone else's. I remember before I became a citizen I had a green card. I was chatting with a very nice immigration officer at the Boston airport who told me that a green card was an important document. "Anyone can get a passport," he told me, "but we checked you out!"

I do recall, though, at the interview for the green card, the INS officer asked my three-year-old and five-year-old daughters whether they were promised brides. Both started crying. I wasn't happy, and my attorney told me to be quiet! My eldest daughter was sixteen in November 2001 and took drivers ed at school that term and went with everyone else to the local test center. She was mortified to be told that she couldn't take the test there as she was an alien and had to go to the Alien Driving Test Center in the state capital, Concord. It apparently had been established after 9/11. The guy giving the driving tests asked her if she had ever driven in Concord, and she replied that she hadn't. He told her to park the car and that she had passed the test and loved her English accent. They never actually left the test center. It isn't easy being an alien though.

My final green card story involves the border patrol. I picked up my twelve-year-old daughter from school on a winter's night in my truck, towing a trailer with two snowmobiles on the back, headed down one exit on I-91 to the local place in Vermont to get them serviced. Post-9/11 border patrol had a checkpoint on the freeway watching for terrorists coming from Canada. I arrived at the checkpoint and the officer asked where I was going, and I said that I was going to the next exit to drop my snow machines off. He then asked if we were U.S. citizens and when I told him we were green card holders he asked to see them. Then the trouble really started. I had mine, but I had left my daughter's card at home. The officer became rather angry and told my daughter she had to have her green card on her at all times and if not, she was subject to arrest. More tears. (Every parent knows what a great plan it would be to send a green card to school with a child each day.) Eventually the supervisor, who had kids of his own, apologized and let us go. There was a long line of cars on the freeway behind us. They never did catch any terrorists and they aren't there anymore. The barrier was almost always closed when it was raining and there was another road that ran parallel to the freeway between the two exits that I always took after that. Brilliant. After all that nonsense, I decided it was time for us to become citizens, so we did. I can only imagine how hard it would be for an illegal immigrant who doesn't speak the language.

Immigration was a huge issue in the Brexit campaign, not least when it was announced just before the vote that net migration had hit a record level of 333,000 in 2015. Prime Minister David Cameron had pledged to get that number down to under 100,000. Feelings are very strong in the United States about immigration and refugees. Donald Trump promised to build a wall along the Mexican border, that Mexico would pay for the deportation of 11 million illegal immigrants, and that he would ban Muslims from entering the United States. Mexicans who came to the United States were rapists, apparently. Immigration was also a major issue in the recent French presidential election.

The reality is a long way from the rhetoric. There is a lot of antipathy toward immigrants in the years of slow recovery after the Great Recession. Immigrants themselves disproportionately did not vote for Trump, Brexit, or Le Pen. Major towns and cities with high proportions of immigrants voted against also. The fear of immigrants appears to be highest in locations where they don't live. It seems the fear of the foreigner who is known is much less than the fear of the unknown foreigner.

Immigration in the United States: Build That Wall

On December 7, 2015, Trump released a statement saying, "Donald J. Trump is calling for a total and complete shutdown of Muslims entering the United States until our country's representatives can figure out what the hell is going on."[3] Trump also called for a wall to be built on the Mexican border; the frequent cry from his supporters at his rallies was "build that wall" once they were done with chants of "lock her up." Trump even claimed that Mexico was going to pay for it, which was always a non-starter and has now, conveniently, been dropped.

Not a single foot of new wall has been built since Trump took office in 2017. Ex-president of Mexico Vicente Fox Quesada made it clear to Trump on Twitter that Mexico was not going to pay for his "#f***ingwall."

On July 29, 2018, Donald Trump tweeted, "I would be willing to 'shut down' government if the Democrats do not give us the votes for Border Security, which includes the Wall! Must get rid of Lottery, Catch & Release etc. and finally go to system of Immigration based on MERIT! We need great people coming into our Country!" At that time the GOP controlled the House, the Senate, and the presidency. Shutting down the federal government to get funding for a wall in December 2018 didn't work out so well for President Trump, who reopened the government with no concessions from the Democrats.

In a speech on June 16, 2015, Donald Trump labeled immigrants from Mexico "rapists" and criminals. "When Mexico sends its people, they're not sending their best. They're not sending you. They're sending people that have lots of problems, and they're bringing those problems with us. They're bringing drugs. They're bringing crime. They're rapists. And some, I assume, are good people," he said.[4] Pity the poor immigrant, some of whom, presumably, are good people.

More than forty million people living in the United States were born in other countries, and almost an equal number have at least one foreign-born parent. The number of immigrants living in the United States increased by more than 70 percent, from 24.5 million or about 9 percent of the population, in 1995, to 42.3 million or about 13 percent of the population, in 2014. The native-born population increased by about 20 percent during the same period.

Immigrants are more geographically concentrated than natives. California, the state with the highest percentage of immigrants, hosts 25 percent of all U.S. foreign born but only 9 percent of its natives. New York, the metropolitan area with the highest percentage of immigrants, hosts 14.5 percent of all U.S. foreign born but only 5.5 percent of natives. Consequently, native individuals have a very different degree of exposure to immigrants depending on where they live. Among California residents, in 2011, for every two U.S. born there was one foreign born. At the other end of the spectrum, among West Virginia's residents, for every 99 natives there was one immigrant.[5]

A Pew Research Center report in November 2016 estimated that there were 11.1 million unauthorized immigrants in the United States in 2014, a total that is broadly unchanged from 2009.[6] The number peaked in 2012 at 12.2 million, or 4 percent of the U.S. population. The workforce includes around 8 million illegals. Six states accounted for 59 percent of illegal immigrants: California, Texas, Florida, New York, New Jersey, and Illinois.[7] In a recent report Pew noted that the number of U.S.-born babies with unauthorized parents has fallen since 2007. About 250,000 babies were born to unauthorized immigrant parents in the United States in 2016, the latest year for which information is available, according to a new Pew Research Center analysis of government data. This represents a 36 percent decrease from a peak of about 390,000 in 2007.[8]

The demographics of illegal migration on the southern border have changed significantly over the last fifteen years: far fewer Mexicans and single adults are attempting to cross the border without authorization, but more families and unaccompanied children are fleeing poverty and violence in Central America. In FY17, approximately 58 percent of U.S. Border Patrol apprehensions were individuals from countries other than Mexico—

predominantly individuals from Central America—up from 54 percent the previous year. Of the 310,531 apprehensions nationwide, 303,916 were along the southwest border. Of those, 162,891 were from El Salvador, Guatemala, and Honduras. Another 127,938 were from Mexico. Of those apprehended by the U.S. Border Patrol, 10 percent had been apprehended on at least one other occasion in FY17, down from 12 percent in 2016. Notably in 2017 Customs and Border Protection recorded the lowest level of illegal cross-border migration on record, as measured by apprehensions, which had averaged over 1 million per year between 1980 and 2016.[9]

It is also possible to determine how many people overstay their visas. In 2015, the Department of Homeland Security (DHS) determined that there were nearly 45 million non-immigrant admissions to the United States for business or pleasure through air or sea ports of entry who were expected to depart in FY2015. Of this number, DHS calculated a total overstay rate of 1.17 percent, or around half a million individuals. The overstay rate was especially high for visitors from Afghanistan (10%), Bhutan (24%), Georgia (12%), Iraq (6%), Sudan (7%), and Yemen (6%). It was 0.4 percent for the UK, 0.7 percent for France, and 1 percent for Germany. For Canada and Mexico, the overstay rate for FY2015 was 1.18 percent and 1.45 percent of the expected departures, respectively, through air and sea ports of entry. A wall would likely increase the number of people overstaying their visas.[10]

A recent paper has looked at the rise and fall of the numbers of low-skilled immigrants to the United States.[11] The authors note that after the "epochal" wave of unskilled immigrants from the 1970s to the 2000s, the numbers have slowed since the Great Recession. The number of undocumented immigrants has declined in absolute terms, while the overall population of low-skilled foreign workers has remained stable. The authors found that the immigration wave of the late twentieth century was enabled to a substantial extent by the rapid growth of the labor supply in Latin America and the Caribbean relative to the United States. Because labor-supply growth in migrant-sending nations is slowing and will continue to slow, the demographic push for U.S. immigration is abating.

The authors also suggest that the weakening of these migration pressures that began in the early 2000s may have been masked by the temporary labor-demand boost provided by the U.S. housing boom. The resulting post-2007 slowdown in low-skilled immigration, the authors find, is of a magnitude consistent with a decrease in the wage gap between high-skilled and low-skilled U.S. labor of 6 to 9 percentage points. If, as predicted by demographic forces, low-skilled immigration continues to decline in future decades, U.S. firms, especially those located in U.S.-Mexico border states and in the immigrant-intensive industries of agriculture and construction, eating and drinking establishments, and nondurable manufacturing, "are likely to face pressure to alter their production techniques in a manner that replaces low-skilled labor with other factors of production" (Hanson, Liu, and McIntosh 2017, 44).

Places with the fewest immigrants push back hardest against immigration.[12] In the 2016 presidential election, Donald Trump carried twenty-six of the thirty states where the share of residents born abroad is the smallest, according to the five-year (2011–15) estimates from the Census Bureau's American Community Survey. Native-born residents account for 91 percent of the population in states Trump won versus 81 percent in states he lost.

A poll released by Ipsos Mori in the UK that was conducted June 11–14, 2016, just three days before the Brexit vote, found that more than 46 percent thought that EU immigration had been good rather than bad for the economy.[13] There are stark differences between those who intended to vote to Leave and those who intended to vote to Remain regarding their views on immigration. Sixty-five percent of Leave supporters said immigration had been bad for Britain as a whole, and just 19 percent said the opposite. Remain voters had mirror-image attitudes, with 62 percent saying immigration had been good for the country and just 20 percent saying it had been bad.

Strikingly, people aged 18–34 were twice as likely as those over 55 to think EU immigration had been good for Britain (50 percent compared with 25 percent). Remain supporters were twice as positive as Leave voters on whether Britain had benefited from EU immigration economically with seven in ten saying the effect on the economy had been good, compared to 28 percent of Leave voters.

A survey by Opinium found that among people 18–24, reducing numbers coming into the UK was last among twenty-two priorities with the availability of jobs, protection of human rights, and well-funded public services their main concerns. When asked to rate Brexit priorities on a scale of 0 to 10, reducing immigration from the EU scored just 5.85 among 18- to 34-year-olds, below the need to share arts and culture between EU countries (6.34, in twenty-first place) and reducing poverty (6.21, nineteenth place).[14] A survey by Ipsos Mori found that people in the UK over the period 2015–

16 viewed the impact of immigration more positively but still wanted the overall number of immigrants to be reduced.[15]

A recent study examined data from the thirty-fourth British Social Attitudes Survey (BSAS) and found that when asked, "Do you think the number of immigrants to Britain nowadays should be [increased a lot, increased a little, remain the same as it is, reduced a little, or reduced a lot]?" 56 percent of respondents said "reduced a lot" and an additional 21 percent said "reduced a little."[16] But nearly three-quarters of those surveyed in the BSAS who were worried about immigration voted Leave, versus 36 percent who did not identify this as a concern. Roger Harding, head of the National Centre for Social Research, which examined the BSAS data, noted, "For leave voters, the vote was particularly about immigration and the social consequences of it."[17]

One of the very striking things about the Brexit referendum was the distinction between the stock and flow elements of immigration. London, with a high immigrant stock, voted to remain, but Boston, with a low stock but high recent flow, voted to leave. Immigrants voted against Brexit. Immigrants voted against Trump. We can only speculate about the reasons for this, but two suggest themselves: the fear/shock of the new and the pressure on public services, particularly during a period of austerity.

Views on Immigration in the Rest of the World

The 2013 International Social Survey Programme (ISSP) asked respondents across numerous countries about their views on crime rates among immigrant populations (table 9.1). The proportion of respondents who agreed or agreed strongly that immigrants increase crime rates are reported in the first column. The proportion was the lowest in the United States (20%). The second column reports on whether respondents felt immigration was good for the economy; the United States is highest at 52 percent versus 31 percent in the UK, 33 percent in France, and 48 percent in Germany. A high proportion of U.S. respondents are also supportive of free trade (54%). Column 3 shows that respondents in the UK are twice as likely to report that immigrants take away jobs from the native born than in the other three countries. Column 4 shows respondents are broadly split on the merits of free trade in all four countries, with the biggest support in the UK.

In addition to immigration, people around the world are also concerned about terrorism coming from abroad. For the last several decades Gallup has

Table 9.1. ISSP 2013 Views on Immigration: Percentage Who Agree or Agree Strongly

	(1)	(2)	(3)	(4)
France	42	33	28	45
Germany	48	48	22	46
United Kingdom	45	31	52	63
United States	20	52	35	54

(1) Immigrants increase crime rates. (2) Immigrants are generally good for the economy. (3) Immigrants take jobs away from people who were born in our country. (4) Free trade leads to better products becoming available.
Source: http://www.issp.org/menu-top/home/.

asked people around the world the following question: "How worried are you that you or someone in your family will become a victim of terrorism—very worried, somewhat worried, not too worried or not worried at all?" In December 2015, after the deadly attacks in Paris, the proportion saying "very worried" was 19 percent, which was the highest since September 2001.[18] Americans also reported in December 2015 that terrorism was the top issue facing the United States—Gallup found that 16 percent identified terrorism as the most important problem. By October 2016 Americans' views of the most important problem had shifted to the economy (17%), dissatisfaction with government (12%), and race relations (10%), with terrorism in ninth place (5%).[19]

Respondents in the Eurobarometer Survey series conducted by the European Commission were asked to identify the two most important problems in their country. A dozen or so options were available; table 9.2 plots the three most important: immigration, terrorism, and unemployment. In a previous paper (Blanchflower et al. 2014), my colleagues and I found that unemployment was the most important concern expressed by respondents across EU countries, but this has changed with the influx of refugees into Germany and terror attacks in France and Belgium. The table plots data drawn from three Eurobarometers, for November 2013, 2016, and 2017. Immigration was the most important in Germany (45%) in 2016, but the fear had dissipated somewhat by 2017 as it had in the UK. The fear of terrorism picked up sharply in all four countries between 2013 and 2017. Unemployment remained the most important problem in 2017 in Italy and France but less so than it was in 2013.

Table 9.3 reports the evidence from the 2002–14 European Social Surveys of answers to the question, "Is immigration bad or good for the econ-

Table 9.2. "What Do You Think Are the Two Most Important Issues Facing [Our Country] at the Moment?"

	Germany	France	Italy	UK
Immigration				
2013	16%	12%	8%	32%
2016	45%	19%	41%	28%
2017	42%	17%	32%	23%
Terrorism				
2013	2%	1%	1%	5%
2016	27%	31%	7%	14%
2017	20%	32%	12%	24%
Unemployment				
2013	19%	59%	56%	36%
2016	8%	49%	46%	17%
2017	6%	40%	43%	11%

Source: Eurobarometers #80.1 (November 2013); #86.2 (November 2016); and #88.3 (November 2017). https://www.gesis.org/eurobarometer-data-service/home/.

Table 9.3. Immigration Bad or Good for Country's Economy

	UK	Germany	France	Italy
2002	5.12	2.92	3.50	4.12
2008	3.05	4.12	2.99	—
2012	3.73	5.78	3.13	2.66
2014	4.70	6.20	2.94	—

Bad for the economy = 1; Good for the economy = 10.
Source: European Social Surveys, 2002–14, weighted.

omy?" on a scale of 1 to 10. Over the course of the surveys an increasing number of people in Germany said that immigration was good for the economy, while in the UK, France, and Italy, the trend was in the opposite direction, with a low point in 2008.

In an interesting new paper Moriconi, Peri, and Turati (2018) explore the relationship between immigration and European elections between 2007 and 2016 in twelve countries using data from the European Social Surveys. They develop an index of "nationalistic" attitudes of political parties to measure the shift in preferences among voters when confronted with influxes of skilled and unskilled immigrants. Unsurprisingly they find that highly educated native voters are less nationalistic in their attitudes toward immigrants than the less-educated natives. Consequently, they find that larger inflows of highly educated immigrants dampen nationalistic sentiments, while larger inflows of less-educated immigrants heighten them. Their analysis shows strong nationalistic sentiments in regional pockets in the United Kingdom, Ireland, France, Germany, Demark, Sweden, Norway, and, especially, Italy. They conclude that immigration policies, producing more balanced inflows of less- and highly skilled migrants, would shift political preferences away from nationalist voting. These policies, they suggest, would not reduce immigration but rebalance it, allowing the pro-growth impact of immigrants.

On November 14, 2016, a UK polling company, Ipsos Mori, conducted an online survey of adults under the age of 65 in twenty-five countries called "What worries the world." When asked, "Which topics do you find the most worrying in your country?" British respondents said, in order: immigration control (38%); health care (34%); poverty and social inequality (30%); rise of extremism (25%); terrorism (24%); and unemployment (20%). Out of the twenty-five countries Germany is most concerned about extremism, with 28 percent citing this as a worry versus 25 percent in Britain, 21 percent in France, and 11 percent in the United States.

According to the Pew Research Center's report "Europe's Growing Muslim Population," published in November 2017, in 2010 in the EU there were 495.3 million non-Muslims, which fell to 495.1 million in 2016, whereas the number of Muslims rose from 19.5 to 25.8 million. The biggest increases over this period were in Germany (+1.7 million), the UK (+1.1 million), France (+1 million), and Italy (+700,000). Smaller European countries also had numerically smaller but significant increases. The population share of Muslims in many EU countries has risen sharply over these years. The table below lists changes in the percentage of Muslims in the population from 2010 to 2016 from the Pew report.[20]

	2016	2010
Sweden	8.1	4.6
France	8.8	7.5
UK	6.3	4.7
Belgium	7.6	6.0
Germany	6.1	4.1
Netherlands	7.1	6.0
Austria	6.9	5.4
Italy	4.8	3.6

The rise in the Muslim share of the population is especially notable in Sweden and to a lesser extent in the UK, Austria, and Germany.

In the same report, Pew found that in countries with more asylum seekers
from Iraq and Syria, the public's perception of the threat they pose is relatively low.[21] The table below reports the extent to which respondents in the
2017 Pew Global Attitudes Survey believe large numbers of refugees from
countries such as Iraq and Syria represent a major, minor, or no threat to
their country. In addition I report counts of asylum applications from Iraqis
and Syrians between 2010 and 2016. In some European countries that have
attracted large numbers of refugees from Iraq and Syria, such as Germany,
public levels of concern about these refugees are relatively low. Meanwhile,
in Italy, where there are fewer refugees from Iraq and Syria, a much higher
share of the public says they pose a "major threat."

	Major threat (%)	Minor threat (%)	Not a threat (%)	#	Per 10,000 residents
Italy	65	23	7	7,000	1
Spain	42	23	33	10,000	2
France	39	41	20	18,000	3
UK	36	36	24	17,000	3
Netherlands	31	44	25	41,000	24
Germany	28	49	22	457,000	56
Sweden	22	48	30	138,000	139

To know them is to love them.

Immigration in the UK, Walking About, and the Maide Leisg

The United Kingdom was traditionally a net exporter of people until the
mid-1980s, when it became a net importer of people. About 70 percent of
the population increase between the 2001 and 2011 censuses, for example,
was due to foreign-born immigration.

The UK now has the fifth-largest immigrant population in the world, at
8.5 million, doubling from 1990 to 2015.[22] About 13 percent of the UK's
population is foreign born versus 14 percent in the United States, while a
third of the UK's immigrants are from the EU. In 2015 about 4.9 million

people born in the UK, including me, were living in other countries, the ten largest in the world. Only 25 percent of the UK's emigrant population lives in the EU.

There are many similarities between the flow of illegal immigrants especially from Mexico to the United States and the flow of legal workers from Eastern Europe to the UK since 2004. A major issue in the UK has been the rapid rise in the number of East Europeans who arrived in the last decade or so. In May 2004, eight Accession countries (A8)—the Czech Republic, Estonia, Hungary, Latvia, Lithuania, Poland, Slovenia, and Slovak Republic—were admitted to the EU, along with tiny Malta and Cyprus (AC-10). On January 1, 2007, Bulgaria and Romania (A2) also joined the EU. All of these countries entered a seven-year period of adjustment where residents would not have full rights to live and work in the rest of the EU. The UK Labour government decided to give the A8 rights to work in 2004, while the A2 were able to enter and work immediately upon accession in 2014. After seven years the doors opened fully for families and nonworkers to come. With the gates flung open, millions walked through. Lots of people in the UK were not pleased.

It is fair to say that the numbers of East Europeans, and especially Poles, that came far exceeded expectations. A report for the UK Home Office in 2003 had forecast that "net immigration from the AC-10 to the UK after the current enlargement of the EU will be relatively small, at between 5,000 and 13,000 immigrants per year up to 2010."[23] This was principally because of the low migration rates of the past. Another one the experts got wrong.

The UK Department of Work and Pensions reports the number of people who registered for a National Insurance Number (NINO), which is equivalent to a Social Security number in the United States for both the A8 and the A2.[24] Starting from 2004 Q1 through 2018 Q3, 2.7 million individuals from the A8 had registered. There have been a further 900,000 registrations from Bulgaria and Romania registering between 2014 Q1 and 2018 Q3. The 2003 Home Office report seriously underestimated the size of the flow.

Part of the reason for the massive flow of immigrants into the UK was that no other major country such as Germany or France opened its borders; in addition, many of the highly educated Poles spoke English, which made the UK especially attractive. Statistics Poland (2016) reported, based on a survey conducted in 2011–12, that English is the most popular foreign language among those in the 16–65 age group, spoken at various levels of competence by over a third of adult Poles (37%). In contrast, in the United States, according to the Census Bureau, the percentage of the nation's population age 5 and older that speaks a language other than English at home was 21.6 percent in 2016.[25]

The problem for the authorities is that they had no means of knowing how many of these East Europeans, who are mostly Poles, were living and working in the UK at any one time. The UK Passenger Survey counts people at arrivals halls but doesn't count them in departure halls. It asks them if they plan to stay in the UK for at least a year. Many of the East Europeans are coming, at least initially, for short spells.[26] In a single year, they often make multiple visits of varying durations. I recall Mervyn King one time at a meeting stressing how many people had come to the UK because of the number of flights from Warsaw and buses that were arriving at Victoria coach station. I piped up that I was surprised at how many flights there also were to Warsaw from UK airports and how many buses from Victoria coach station. The East Europeans were more like commuters than migrants, given that they could come to the UK a number of times of differing durations in a single year. Hence, it is almost impossible to know how many of these commuters are in the UK at any one time.

Return migration in the UK is not a new phenomenon. Dustmann and Weiss (2007) explored this issue empirically before the influx from Eastern Europe using data from the LFS from 1992 to 2004. The authors found that, taking the population of immigrants who were still in the country one year after arrival as the base, about 40 percent of all men and 55 percent of all women had left Britain five years later. Their data suggest that return migration is particularly pronounced for the group of immigrants from the EU, the Americas, and Australia/New Zealand; it was much less pronounced for immigrants from the Indian Subcontinent and from Africa.

The phenomenon of returning is not unique to the Poles in the UK. LaLonde and Topel (1997) found that 4.8 million of the 15.7 million immigrants to the United States who arrived between 1907 and 1957 had departed by the latter year. Chiswick and Hatton (2003) pointed out that return migration exceeded immigration to the United States during the 1930s.

I have another piece of evidence on the economics of walking about as it relates to immigration from a visit I made to a Scottish hotel. The owner told me that they were having a terrible time hiring Scots in their Scottish-themed hotels. In consequence, he had hired lots of Poles, who worked hard and looked great in kilts. He also told me an amusing story that may or may not be true. He said that now many of the records in the Scottish Highland Games were held by very large Poles who didn't look that great in kilts. They had solved the problem that the record books were full of names like Kaczkowski and Macherzynski. He had seen the WWF on TV and had come up with a fiendish plan. Andrzej Macherzynski was renamed McTavish, Jacenty Kaczkowski was called David Bell, and so on. Brilliant! Those competing in the Scottish hammer throw, the sheaf toss, the Maide Leisg (look it up!), and the caber toss especially were instructed to stay mum throughout or they would give the game away. Hopefully it was true!

I also gathered from a variety of factory visits when I was on the MPC that employers hugely valued their East European workers: they were never late, would work on weekends and until the job was done, were enthusiastic, and were highly productive. Employers liked their East European workers because of the enhanced flexibility they brought.

Helen Lawton and I (2010) looked at data from several Eurobarometers (2004–7) as well as the 2005 Work Orientation module of the ISSP to examine the attitudes of residents of these A8 countries. Eastern Europeans reported that they were unhappy with their lives and the country they lived in, they were dissatisfied with their jobs, and they experienced difficulties finding a good new job or keeping their existing job. Relatively high proportions expressed a desire to move abroad. We concluded that the UK is an attractive place for Eastern Europeans to live and work. We argued that "rather than dissipate, flows of Eastern European workers to the UK could remain strong well into the future" (2010, 181). That was a good call.

The proportion of the population that is foreign born has risen significantly in all of the main OECD countries. The data below for 2000 are taken from the OECD's "International Migration Outlook, 2016" (table 1.14) and for 2017 from the "International Migration Outlook, 2018," which show the change in the proportion of the population that was foreign born in 2017 compared with 2000, ranked from lowest to highest by the 2017 share (data are only available for 2015 for Japan). Japan has the lowest proportion and the Australasian countries, the highest. In all of these major countries the proportion rose, and it more than doubled in Italy, Spain, and Ireland.

	2017	2000		2017	2000
Japan	1.8	1.3	Germany	15.5	12.5
Italy	10.2	3.9	Sweden	18.0	11.3
Netherlands	12.5	10.2	Ireland	17.0	8.6
France	12.6	10.3	Austria	19.0	10.5
Spain	13.0	4.8	Canada	20.3	17.4
United States	13.5	10.7	New Zealand	23.2	17.4
United Kingdom	14.2	7.9	Australia	28.1	23.1

With so many workers leaving Poland, that generated a labor shortage and hence a rise in immigration there, too, to fill the gaps, mostly from Ukraine. Recent data from the central statistics office for Poland (Główny Urząd Statystyczny) on foreign work visas issued in 2017 show the number of work permits for foreigners in Poland grew in 2017, with more than 235,600 issued.[27] This is a near doubling (84%) from 2016, and a 258% increase from 2015. Ukrainians in 2017 received 81.7% of all work visas issued in Poland.

The (Small) Impact of Immigration on Jobs and Wages: Fact versus Opinion

There are widespread concerns among the public that immigrants impact wages and jobs. The academic literature says otherwise. A recent major study by the National Academies of Sciences, Engineering, and Medicine (2017) found that when measured over a period of more than ten years, the impact of immigration on the wages of natives overall is very small. Prior immigrants—who are often the closest substitutes for new immigrants—are most likely to experience wage impacts, followed by native-born high school dropouts, who share job qualifications similar to those of the large share of low-skilled workers among immigrants to the United States.

The study concluded that the literature on employment impacts finds little evidence that immigration significantly affects the overall employment levels of native-born workers. However, they noted, recent research shows that immigration reduces the number of hours worked by native teens (but not their employment rate). Moreover, as with wage impacts, there is some evidence that recent immigrants reduce the employment rate of prior immigrants, suggesting a higher degree of substitutability between new and prior immigrants than between new immigrants and natives.

The study also reported that immigrants influence the rate of innovation in the economy, which, they argued, potentially affects long-run economic growth (2017, 268). Immigrants, it seems, are more innovative than natives; more specifically, high-skilled immigrants raise the rate of patenting per capita, which is likely to boost productivity and per capita economic growth. Immigrants appear to innovate more than natives not because of greater inherent ability but due to their concentration in science and engineering fields.

The OECD (2016a) has rightly argued that there is a certain disconnect between the results of empirical research that studies the impact of immigration at the national level and the publicly perceived impact. Where the former generally find little impact in key areas such as the labor market, the infrastructure, or the public purse—be it positive or negative—in many countries, the public in general assume a negative impact.

As Jonathan Portes notes (2017), the consensus in the economic literature is that negative impacts of migration for native workers are, if they exist at all, relatively small and short-lived. Studies have generally failed to find any significant association between migration flows and changes in employment or unemployment for natives. Since 2014, Portes points out, the continued buoyant performance of the UK labor market has further reinforced this consensus. Rapid falls in unemployment have been combined with sustained high levels of immigration.

The OECD (2016b) further examined the literature on both wages and employment and provides a useful summary of the immigration impacts across countries. The impact on natives' wages from a 1-percentage-point rise in the immigrant share of the labor force tends to be insignificant, while some studies find small effects (both negative and positive, depending on the study). A review of 18 comparable empirical studies found that with a 1-percentage-point increase in the proportion of immigrants in the work-force, local wages fall just 0.12 percent.[28] The OECD notes that since migrants often only constitute a relatively small part of the population, this would imply an almost negligible fall in wages.

The OECD (2016b) notes that once again most studies tend to find no or only a small negative impact on the employment rate: "The majority of empirical studies on the labour market impact of migration look at the aggregate or average local impact, rather than on concrete case studies. Most of these studies find no effect of immigration on local wages nor on employment, while a minority find a small effect, either negative or positive. This is due to a number of reasons. First, migrants' skills often complement those of the native-born. Second, some native-born residents move up the occupational ladder in response to new foreign-born arrivals. Third, some previous residents move to other areas in reaction to new inflows. Fourth, any local impact is likely to be diluted by adjustment processes, for example changes in the industrial composition and production technologies as well as capital flows" (109).[29]

A recent meta-analysis updated the list of papers estimating the effect of immigration on wages.[30] Of the 28 countries and studies reviewed, 13 find no significant effect, 7 find a small positive effect, and 8 find a small negative effect. A similar meta-analysis for employment has shown that a 1-percentage-point increase in the share of immigrants has an almost negligible impact on native employment, reducing it by 0.024 percent.[31] Overall, only about half of studies found a downward effect on wages or employment that is statistically significant at the 10 percent level.

A report by Wadsworth and colleagues (2016) from the Centre for Economic Performance at the London School of Economics revealed the impact of EU immigration in the UK prior to Brexit. Their main findings were that EU immigrants are more educated, younger, more likely to be working, and less likely to claim benefits than the UK born. About 44 percent have some form of higher education compared with only 23 percent of the UK born. About a third of EU immigrants live in London.

Areas of the UK with large increases in EU immigration did not suffer greater declines in the number of available jobs or in the wages of UK-born workers. The big falls in wages after 2008 are due to the global financial crisis and a weak economic recovery, not immigration. Changes in wages and joblessness for less-educated UK-born workers show little correlation with changes in EU immigration. EU immigrants pay more in taxes than they take out in welfare and the use of public services. They therefore help reduce the budget deficit.

A 2015 analysis looked at the impact of migration on economic growth for twenty-two OECD countries between 1986 and 2006.[32] The results showed a positive impact of migrants' human capital on GDP per capita; in addition, a permanent increase in migration flows has a positive effect on productivity growth. It seems highly likely that Brexit and the end of free movement will result in a large decrease in immigration flows from European Economic Area countries to the UK.[33]

It also seems that the presence of a larger number of immigrants lowers prices. Immigrant nannies lower the price of childcare. One of the members of the MPC that I was on had a Latvian "ironer" to iron his clothes. Food prices in the UK are lower because of the presence of Poles, and in Los Angeles and in many other U.S. cities lawn services, house-cleaning services, and car washes are less expensive because of the presence of illegal immigrants.

Saul Lach (2007) examined the behavior of prices following the unexpected arrival of a large number of immigrants from the former Soviet Union (FSU) to Israel in 1990. He used store-level price data on 915 consumer price index products to show that the increase in aggregate demand prompted by the arrival of the FSU immigrants significantly reduced prices during 1990. Lach found that a 1-percentage-point increase in the ratio of immigrants to natives in a city decreased prices by 0.5 percentage points on average. Natives like lower prices.

Public perception of crime in the United States often doesn't align with the data. Opinion surveys regularly find Americans believe the crime rate is up. In twenty-three Gallup surveys conducted since 1989 a majority always said there was more crime in the United States compared with the year before. In every year since 2005 over 60 percent said there was more crime than a year earlier.[34] In a Pew Research Center survey in late 2016, 57 percent of registered voters said they thought the crime rate had worsened since 2008, 27 percent said it was the same, and 15 percent said it had improved, even though violent and property crime had fallen by double digits.[35] Interestingly, there is no indication in the data that respondents see any change in the likelihood of them personally experiencing crime.

According to Gallup there has been little change at all over time in the percentage of people in the United States who frequently or occasionally worry about their home being burglarized when they are not at home (44 percent in 2004 versus 41 percent in 2014–17).[36] Over these years there was a big decline in the proportion thinking they would be a victim of terrorism, down from 41 percent in 2001–4; 37 percent in 2005–8; 31 percent in 2009–13; and 30 percent in 2004–17. In an Ipsos Mori Public Perceptions poll taken in the fall of 2017, around eight in ten Americans thought the murder rate had risen (52%) since 2000 or was about the same (26%).[37] The rate has declined by 11 percent. Americans think one in three people in U.S.

jails and prisons was born in a foreign country. In fact, only one in twenty is an immigrant.

Perhaps surprisingly, a majority of the studies in the United States have found lower crime rates among immigrants than among non-immigrants, and that higher concentrations of immigrants are associated with lower crime rates. Some research even suggests that increases in immigration may partly explain the reduction in the U.S. crime rate. Wadsworth (2010), for example, found that cities with the largest increases in immigration between 1990 and 2000 experienced the largest decreases in homicide and robbery during the same time period.

A study by Ewing and colleagues (2015) at the American Immigration Council noted that while the illegal immigrant population in the United States more than tripled between 1990 and 2013 to more than 11.2 million, "FBI data indicate that the violent crime rate declined 48%—which included falling rates of aggravated assault, robbery, rape, and murder. Likewise, the property crime rate fell 41%, including declining rates of motor vehicle theft, larceny/robbery, and burglary." They also found from an analysis of data from the 2010 American Community Survey that roughly 1.6 percent of immigrant men aged 18–39 were incarcerated, compared to 3.3 percent of the native born.

Views on Immigration: Nations Divided

According to Ford and Goodwin, the left-behinds in the UK are strongly opposed to political and social developments they see as threatening sovereignty, continuity, and identity.

> Anxieties about immigration and its effects, demands for reductions in the number of immigrants, and the belief that immigration poses a serious problem to the nation are all expressed most strongly by the left behind coalition of older, less skilled and white workers.

They went on.

> Already disillusioned by the economic shifts that left them lagging behind other groups in society, these voters now feel their concerns about immigration and threats to national identity have been ignored or stigmatized as expressions of prejudice by an established political

class that appears more sensitive to protecting migrant newcomers and ethnic minorities than listening to the concerns of economically struggling white Britons. (2014, 126)

Ford and Goodwin's comments seem to apply equally well to the left-behinds in other countries such as the United States, France, and Austria.

Most U.S. voters view immigrants positively, but most Trump voters don't.[38] Overall the United States is supportive of immigration and that support if anything has increased slightly over time. Gallup has regularly asked, "Thinking now about immigrants, that is, people who come from other countries to live here in the United States: In your view, should immigration be kept at its present level, increased or decreased?" In its June 2018 poll, 29 percent (50%) said decreased, 39 percent (32%) said stay at the present level, and 28 percent (14%) said increased; the numbers in parentheses are those from a survey taken in July 2009. Similarly, when asked in these surveys, "On the whole, do you think immigration is a good thing or a bad thing for this country today?" in June 2018, 75 percent said immigration was a "good thing" versus 57 percent in July 2011.[39] So opinion is moving in favor of immigration in the United States.

One of the starkest divides in the United States between Trump and Clinton voters was their attitude toward immigration. A Pew poll taken between August 9 and 16, 2016, asked respondents for their views on undocumented immigrants.[40] Here Republican is defined to include Republican leaning, with the same holding true for Democrats, and I report below the percentage who answered yes to the following questions about immigrants and immigration.

	Republican	Democrat
Mostly fill jobs U.S. citizens do not want?	63	79
As hard-working as U.S. citizens?	65	87
No more likely than U.S. citizens to commit serious crime?	52	80
Should the U.S. build a wall along entire Mexican border?	63	14

According to a Pew Research Center survey conducted just before Election Day on October 25–November 8, about eight in ten Trump supporters who cast ballots or were planning to (79%) said illegal immigration was a "very big" problem in the United States.[41] (Twenty percent of Clinton voters responded affirmatively to the same question.) Even more Trump supporters (86%) said the immigration situation in the United States had "gotten worse" since 2008. In the same Pew survey, voters were asked whether they thought particular issues were a "very big problem" in the United States. The chart below lists the percentages of those who responded affirmatively.

	Clinton supporters	Trump supporters
Illegal immigration	20	79
Terrorism	42	74
Job opportunities for working-class Americans	45	63
Crime	38	55
Job opportunities for all Americans	43	58
Conditions of roads, bridges, infrastructure	46	36
Affordability of a college education	66	38
Racism	53	21
Gap between rich and poor	72	33
Gun violence	73	31
Climate change	66	14

A CBS News poll taken in March 2018 asked registered voters, "Do you favor or oppose building a wall along the U.S.-Mexico border to try to stop illegal immigration?" Overall, 60 percent opposed and 38 percent favored. Republicans favored 77 to 20, while Democrats opposed 10 to 88, with independents opposing 36 to 61.[42]

A Pew poll finds that overall most Americans think immigrants strengthen the country and have a positive view of the contributions of immigrants to the country.[43] About two-thirds (65%) say that immigrants "strengthen the country with their hard work and talents," while 26 percent say that immigrants are a burden because they take jobs, housing, and health care away from native-born Americans. Positive views of immigrants, Pew found, have continued to increase in recent years. Attitudes today are the reverse of what they were in 1994. At that time, 63 percent said immigrants did more to burden the country, while just 31 percent said they did more to strengthen the country. As recently as 2011, about as many said immigrants burdened

(44%) as strengthened (45%) the country. Majorities of those across levels of educational attainment take a positive view of immigrants' contributions to the country. However, views are the most positive among those with the highest levels of education. For example, four-fifths of postgraduates say immigrants strengthen the country, compared with three-fifths of those with no college experience. Adults ages 18–29 overwhelmingly say immigrants do more to strengthen than burden the country. Views also are broadly positive among those ages 30–49. Views among those 50 and older also tilt positive but by smaller margins.

A 2017 PRRI Report found that fears of immigration and cultural displacement were more powerful factors than economic concerns in explaining why white working-class voters went for Trump. Cultural anxiety mattered more than economic anxiety. This was based on surveys conducted before and after the 2016 election. Cox and coauthors (2017) found that nearly two-thirds of respondents thought that American culture and the American way of life had deteriorated since the 1950s. White working-class voters who said they felt "like a stranger in their own land" and believed that the United States needs protecting against foreign influence—the culturally displaced—were 3.5 times more likely to vote for Trump. White working-class voters who favored deporting immigrants living in the country illegally were 3.3 times more likely to have voted for Trump. More than six in ten thought the growing number of immigrants in America threatened American culture. For many of the left-behinds, this was a culture war.

The American National Election Studies (ANES) pre- and post-election survey of over 4,000 respondents found that racial attitudes toward blacks and immigration were the key factors associated with support for Trump in 2016.[44] The results indicate a probability of Trump support higher than 60 percent for an otherwise typical white voter who scores at the highest levels on either the anti-black racial resentment or the anti-black influence animosity scale McElwee and McDaniel constructed. This compares to a less than 30 percent chance for a typical white voter with below-average scores on either of the two measures of anti-black attitudes. The effect of immigration attitudes for white people was even stronger than anti-black attitudes. The results predict an approximately 80 percent probability of voting for Trump for an otherwise average white person with the most anti-immigrant attitudes, compared to less than 20 percent for a white person with the most pro-immigrant attitudes.

In the spring of 2018 President Trump introduced a zero-tolerance immigration policy that resulted in over 2,000 children being separated from their parents. After huge public outcry the program was reversed, not least because the majority of Americans were against the separations.[45] However, Republicans were more likely to support the policy. A Quinnipiac poll found that 66 percent of U.S. voters opposed taking the kids. In contrast, 55 percent of Republicans voters supported separating children from their immigrant parents. Ipsos and YouGov with the *Economist* found comparable results.[46]

Interestingly, at the same time a larger share of people at any point since 2001 said immigration is good for the nation. According to a Gallup poll taken in the first two weeks in June 2018, 75 percent of Americans said immigration in general is good, compared with 65 percent of Republicans.[47] Support for reining in immigration is now at its lowest level in more than half a century. A Pew Research poll taken in June 2018 found that immigration in the United States had emerged as the most important problem facing the nation.[48] In January 2017 immigration was cited less often as being an important problem facing the nation than health care, the economy, unemployment, race relations, and then president-elect Donald J. Trump.

In Las Vegas in June 2018 President Trump said about immigration, "I like the issue for [the] election." He went on. "Our issue is strong borders, no crime. Their issue is open borders, get MS-13 all over our country. . . . We need people to come in, but they have to be people that love this country, can love our country, and can really help us to make America great again."[49]

Being mean to immigrants has consequences; they leave. Donato Paolo Mancini and Jason Douglas in the *Wall Street Journal* have reported on an exodus of European workers from the UK, especially in the health-care field.[50] They filed an FOI request with the UK's General Medical Council and obtained data showing the number of specialized doctors with non-UK EU citizenship has reached an eight-year low of 10,487 in 2018, down from a peak of over 12,000 in 2014. The article also reported that widespread knowledge of English, the easy mutual recognition of qualifications, relatively good salaries, and world-class research had acted as magnets for doctors. But now, as a Brexit threatens, top doctors are quitting. They reported that the National Health Service had a personnel shortage just shy of 110,000 in the first six months of 2018, 11,500 of which were doctor positions. Down we all go.

Recessions and long periods of semi-slump have consequences, and there will inevitably be scapegoats. Perceptions and reality on the impact of immigration remain far apart across the political spectrum. Pity the poor immigrant these days, legal or illegal.

CHAPTER 10

Disastrous Cries for Help

On every major issue affecting this country, the people are right, and the governing elite are wrong.

—DONALD TRUMP[1]

The populist movements around the world are a direct result of the inadequate response by the elites to the Great Recession. They were cries for help. This is not unique to the UK or the United States; these are the first manifestations of the failures of the elites to notice what was happening outside the big cities. Living standards in the UK haven't risen for years and many good jobs have disappeared. We still seem to be in the long, dragging conditions of semi-slump. What we have seen is a silent, largely peaceful revolution: a silent riot in the United States, France, Italy, and elsewhere. I had expected that, as in previous recessions, there would be trouble on the streets, but that hasn't happened until recently. There were riots in the UK and Sweden in 2011 that were quickly snuffed out by the authorities. All of that changed in the autumn of 2018, with widespread protests in France against fuel taxes, which led to riots in Paris, which then spread to Belgium and the Netherlands.

There was a broad degree of commonality among those who voted for Trump, Brexit, and Frexit. The left-behinds had been put upon for too long. In the UK support for Brexit was high for those on low incomes and among the least educated. Three-quarters of those without qualifications versus a quarter with a postgraduate degree voted for Brexit. The young, minorities, and immigrants and those who lived in big cities voted against Brexit. The left-behinds voted for Trump, Brexit, and more.

Trump: He Can Create Change

According to a CNN exit poll, 51 percent of respondents who had a high school diploma or less or some college voted for Trump, compared with 44 percent of college graduates and 37 percent of those with a postgraduate degree.[2] Fifty-seven percent of whites versus 8 percent of blacks and 28 percent of Latinos voted for Trump. Thirty-six percent of those aged 18–29 and 41 percent of those aged 30–44 voted for Trump. In contrast, 52 percent of those 45 and above did. People living in the rural heartland voted for Trump. The less-educated, low-income, non-immigrant folks also voted for Frexit. The right-wing nationalist in France, Marine Le Pen, fared better in areas with a greater concentration of people without a high school degree.

> I voted for Donald Trump because he can create change for our country, economy, and world.
> —Erin Keefe, 22 years old, Manchester, N.H.[3]

After all the pain and suffering I documented in chapter 9 there was always going to be a backlash. The Clinton campaign clearly underestimated the hurt being felt by white non-Hispanics in the rust-belt states. It is no accident, in my view, that West Virginia, the unhappiest state, with the highest drug-poisoning death rate, was the state that showed the biggest increase in the Republican vote compared to the increase seen in the 2012 presidential election. Ohio was close behind.

Monessen, Pennsylvania, is a faded steel town of 7,500 people about thirty miles south of Pittsburgh. Trump visited there in June 2016. Monessen's population has dropped from 18,000 in 1960 to 7,500 in 2015, and the city's major steel mill closed in the 1980s. The city has 700 registered Republicans, but Trump won by 1,221 votes. Mayor Lou Mavrakis in an interview with *PRI's The World*'s Jason Margolis said, "What does our community look like? It looks like Beirut. If ISIS were to come here, they would keep on going because they'd say somebody already bombed us. And that's the way all the communities look that had steel mines up and down the Mon Valley."[4]

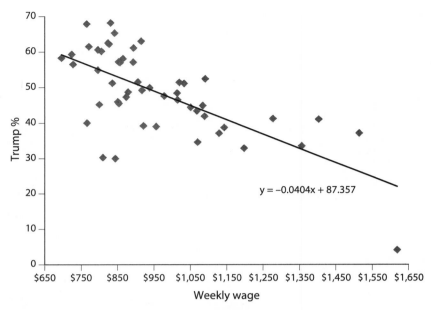

Figure 10.1. Trump % of vote by state and QCEW weekly wage.

In an earlier interview with Margolis, Mayor Mavrakis said that he knew that Trump couldn't bring back the steel mills but hoped he might be able to revive manufacturing. In the same interview long-time Democrat Billy Hans, Margolis reported, had already made up his mind: "I like Trump." The 58-year-old building contractor had never voted for a Republican for president, but he thought Trump could bring some jobs back to the area. "It's not going to be easy, but I think he can bring some back. He's got to get companies to invest."[5]

John Golomb, 65, a retired steelworker and a lifelong Democrat, explained why he voted for Donald Trump. "We want our jobs back," said Mr. Golomb, who lives in Monessen. He worked for thirty-five years in mills with 2,400-degree blast furnaces that made steel used to lay railroads and build cars. But the biggest mill shut three decades ago, and Monessen has been slowly dying ever since. "They forgot us. We're hoping he keeps some percentage of the promises of bringing coal and iron back to this country."[6]

Figure 10.1 shows that the Trump vote is negatively correlated with average weekly wages. I mapped onto the state voting data the Quarterly

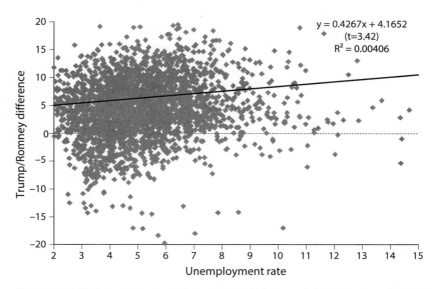

Figure 10.2. Difference between Trump-Romney share and the 2016 unemployment rate.

Census of Employment Wages (QCEW) for 2015 from the BLS. The best-fit line slopes downward. States with lower wages were more likely to vote Trump.

Figure 10.2 plots the Trump-Romney difference in the unemployment rate. The higher the unemployment rate the higher the difference. Places that were hurting voted for Trump. I also found that the Trump-Romney difference was positively correlated with the heavy drinking rate and obesity rates, and negatively correlated with life-expectancy rates. By state the Trump vote is positively correlated with the suicide rate and the incidence of bad mental health. Places that were hurting the most voted for Trump. I report below that disadvantaged communities, on a host of measures, in the UK went for Brexit and in France for Le Pen.

Nate Silver (2016) took a list of all 981 U.S. counties with 50,000 or more people based on data from the American Community Survey, and sorted it by the share of the population age 25 and over that had completed at least a four-year college degree. He found that Hillary Clinton improved on President Obama's 2012 performance in 48 of the country's 50 most well-educated counties. And on average, she improved on Obama's margin of victory in these countries by almost 9 percentage points, even though Obama had done well in them to begin with. The list includes major cities, like San Francisco, and counties that host college towns, like Washtenaw, Michigan, where the University of Michigan is located.

Silver then looked at the 50 least-educated counties. Clinton lost ground relative to Obama in 47 of the 50 counties—she did an average of 11 percentage points worse, in fact. Silver notes that these are the places that won Donald Trump the presidency, especially given that a fair number of them are in swing states such as Ohio and North Carolina. Trump improved on Mitt Romney's margin by more than 30 points in Ashtabula County, Ohio, for example, an industrial county along Lake Erie that hadn't voted Republican since 1984.

And this is also a reasonably diverse list of counties. While some of them are poor, a few others—such as Bullitt County, Kentucky, and Terrebonne Parish, Louisiana—have average incomes. There's also some racial diversity on the list: Starr County, Texas, is 96 percent Hispanic, for example, and Clinton underperformed Obama there (although she still won it by a large margin). Edgecombe County, North Carolina, is 57 percent black and saw a shift toward Trump.

Silver argues that there are several competing hypotheses that are compatible with this evidence, some of which will be favored by conservatives and some by liberals:

- Education levels may be a proxy for cultural hegemony. Academia, the news media, and the arts and entertainment sectors are increasingly dominated by people with a liberal, multicultural worldview, and jobs in these sectors also almost always require college degrees. Trump's campaign may have represented a backlash against these cultural elites.
- Educational attainment may be a better indicator of long-term economic well-being than household incomes. Unionized jobs in the auto industry often pay reasonably well, even if they don't require college degrees, for instance, but they're also potentially at risk of being shipped overseas or automated.
- Education levels probably have some relationship with racial resentment, although the causality isn't clear. The act of having at-

tended college itself may be important, insofar as colleges and universities are often more diverse places than students' hometowns.

- Education levels have strong relationships with media-consumption habits, which may have been instrumental in deciding people's votes, especially given the overall decline in trust in the news media.
- Trump's approach to the campaign—relying on emotional appeals while glossing over policy details—may have resonated more among people with lower education levels as compared with Clinton's "wonkier and more cerebral" approach.

White, less-educated, low-income people over the age of 45 at the individual level are the key characteristics. Where they lived matters too. The poorer the county the higher the probability they voted for Trump. These are precisely the characteristics of the people that I documented were in pain in the previous chapter.

But the empty promises keep on coming.

Brexit: We've Been Neglected So Long

At the time of this writing, three weeks before the March 29, 2019, deadline for Brexit, nobody has the faintest idea what form Brexit might take, or when, or even if, it will happen at all. There is still no credible deal that the UK parliament will accept, and a second vote seems possible.

A new study has examined subjective well-being around the time of the June 2016 Brexit vote and found short-lived impacts on well-being.[7] Elation on the part of the Leavers was roughly canceled out by the huge disappointment on the part of the Remainers, but each of these effects was short-lived. The authors found that those reporting a preference for leaving the EU were less satisfied with life pre-referendum. At the individual level, the referendum outcome produced a windfall satisfaction gain among Leavers compared to Remainers that lasted for only three months, a well-being effect of the same size as around 20 percent of annual incomes. The initial positive subjective well-being effect of the Brexit vote, the authors found, was particularly pronounced for male and older respondents who reported a preference for leaving the EU. However, adaptation to the Brexit result was short-lived, both for those who preferred continued EU membership and for those who did not. The Brexit vote did not have a permanent impact on well-being.

In 1937 George Orwell published *The Road to Wigan Pier*, which documented the hardships in the West Midlands, Lancashire, and Yorkshire. Wigan is an old coal and manufacturing town in Lancashire, which has traditionally returned a Labour Party candidate for the last hundred years. It is hurting again. Wigan no longer has any coal mines.

Andrew Higgins in the *New York Times* reported on his interviews with a Wigan resident, Colin Hewlett, age 61, shortly after the Brexit vote. Hewlett said, "I don't think a lot will change. But we have to give it a chance." Life, he said, has "gone to the dogs. I don't like people telling us what to do from miles away." In a period of three years, Mr. Hewlett explained, his take-home pay had crashed from more than $665 a week to just $318. Worse, he added, is that his previously secure full-time employment contract had morphed into a "zero-hours contract," under which his employer decides how much he works and how much it pays him depending on what it needs on any particular day. "It is basically slave labor," Mr. Hewlett said. He complained that an influx of eager workers from Eastern Europe meant that employers now had no incentive to offer a fixed contract or more than the minimum wage for menial work.[8] In the EU referendum, Wigan voted to leave by a 64 to 36 percent margin.

The surprise is there have been so few riots. Major riots did break out in England in 2011, which spread fast around the country. The authorities acted swiftly, and they have not been repeated. There were also smaller incidents in Sweden in 2010 and 2013. In the United States, they have been small, localized mostly in black inner-city neighborhoods in response to shootings of young black men by police.

There have been no riots in Austria, Italy, or the Netherlands as far as I can tell. In 2011, rioting broke out in England between August 6 and 11 in several London boroughs and spread quickly to several cities and towns across England. It involved looting, arson, and deployment of large numbers of police and resulted in the death of five people. Disturbances began on August 6 after a protest in the London borough of Tottenham, following the death of a local man who was shot by police on August 4. Several violent clashes with police ensued, along with the destruction of police vehicles, a double-decker bus, and many homes and businesses. Rioting spread to at least ten other London boroughs and then on to the English towns of Birmingham, Coventry, Leicester, Derby, Wolverhampton, Nottingham, West Bromwich, Bristol, Liverpool, Manchester, and Salford. More than 3,000 arrests were made, and more than 1,000 people were issued criminal charges for various offenses related to the riots. An estimated £200 million worth of property damage was incurred. The authorities came down hard on protestors and there have been no subsequent riots. The contagion was stopped, at least for a while.

But rioting has recently broken out in France and has spread to Belgium and the Netherlands. Anti-government *gilet jaune* (yellow vest) demonstrations over rising fuel taxes turned violent in Paris on four successive weekends in November and December 2018 and sent shock waves around the world. Stores were looted, masked men burned barricades, dozens of luxury cars were burned, buildings were set on fire, and anti-Macron graffiti was smeared on the Arc de Triomphe.[9] At the time of writing there are further planned demonstrations. In Brussels, several hundred protesters gathered at the beginning of December. Police barricaded off the district where the European Union buildings are located and prevented traffic circling in the area. Clashes were reported and 70 arrests were reported. In the Netherlands, about 100 protesters gathered in a peaceful demonstration outside the Dutch parliament in The Hague and at least two protesters were detained in central Amsterdam.[10] I recall speaking with someone from the ILO who told me that the big surprise in the period since 2008 was how few riots there had been. That seems to be changing fast. Riots are a function of hopelessness. Kim Willsher, the *Guardian*'s Paris correspondent, reported that one young male *gilet jaune* from the Auvergne in central France told her, "We're here for many reasons but basically because we're fed up. Everyone's fed up."[11] In response President Macron announced "concrete measures" from January 1, including increasing the minimum wage by €100 (£90) a month. Overtime would be exempt from tax and social charges, and a planned tax on pensions under €2,000 a month would be canceled.[12] All employers "who can" were asked to give workers a tax-free bonus at the end of the year. Maybe too little too late; only time will tell.

On June 23, 2016, the British people went to the polls to vote in the EU referendum. They were asked a simple question: "Should the United Kingdom remain a member of the European Union or leave the European Union?" Data from Google Trends show that the number of searches for "what is the EU" and "what is Brexit" started climbing across Britain late into the night on June 23, the day of the vote. The question "what is the EU?" spiked in popularity across all parts of the UK, in this order: Northern Ireland, Wales, England, Scotland.[13]

After the Brexit vote Faisal Islam, a reporter for Sky TV, went to Sunderland, home to a large Nissan car plant, to talk to voters. At the Colliery Tavern, he talked with the landlord, John Snaith, who was a Leave voter. Snaith said it was a protest. "Voters voted because we've been neglected so long. They thought this is a chance for them to hear our voice."[14] After the Brexit vote Nissan threatened to close the factory in case of a no-deal.

Wales voted overwhelmingly for Brexit. Seventeen of Wales's 22 local authorities voted Leave. Torfaen voted nearly 60 percent to 40 percent to leave the EU. My friend Aditya Chakrabortty from the *Guardian* visited Torfaen after the Brexit vote and noted how bad things were. "On a typical weekday, the indoor market is a desert. Those bits of the high street that aren't to let are betting parlours, vaping dens, and charity shops: the standard parade for hollowed-out towns across Britain. The reason isn't hard to fathom: the mines shut down decades back; the factories have pretty much disappeared. Those big employers still left aren't big employers anymore. One of the staff at BAE tells me that when he joined in 1982, it had 2,500 workers on its shopfloor; now, he reckons, it has 120. Swaths of Pontypool and the surrounding region of Torfaen now rank among the poorest in all of Britain. In one of the housing developments in Trevethin, 75% of all children under age four are raised in poverty."[15]

Boston, Lincolnshire, had the highest out vote in the UK. Immigration rose by 460 percent between 2004 and 2014, and immigrants are now 14 percent of the population. This was mostly due to East Europeans coming to work in low-paying jobs in the fields or in processing factories. James Pickard of the *Financial Times* interviewed Andrew Matson, procurement director of TH Clements, a supplier of vegetables. Matson warned that without East European migrants that make up half his seasonal workforce, he would have to pay higher wages, which would have to be passed on to supermarkets and ultimately to the consumer: "A pack of broccoli is 49p, five years ago it was 99p. You've not had deflation like that anywhere else. That'll have to change." Pickard also reported that a Lithuanian man asked why English people did not seem to like foreigners. "They complain about us. But why they not do the work?"[16]

Seaside towns that are in decline because of cheap air fares to the Mediterranean mostly voted for Brexit with two major exceptions, Brighton and

Hove—where I was born—which voted Remain. The main reason for their decline is that British tourists left for warmer climes when cheap flights became available. The Leave vote percentages were as follows: Blackpool (68%); Bournemouth (55%); Eastbourne (57%); Great Yarmouth (72%); Hastings (55%); Isle of Whyte (62%); Southend-on-Sea (58%); and Torbay (63%).

The Centre for Social Justice reported that, of the twenty neighborhoods across the UK with the highest levels of working-age people on out-of-work benefits, seven are in coastal towns. In one part of Rhyl, a seaside town in Wales, two-thirds of working-age people are dependent on out-of-work benefits. Coastal towns are among the most educationally deprived in the whole country. Some 41 percent of adults in Clacton have no qualifications, almost double the national average for England and Wales. Of the ten wards in England and Wales with the highest rates of teenage pregnancy, four are in seaside towns. The Blackpool local authority has the highest rate of children in care in the whole of England—150 per 10,000 people, which far exceeds the English average of 59.

The Centre for Social Justice (2016) examined in detail five coastal towns: Rhyl, Margate, Clacton-on-Sea, Blackpool, and Great Yarmouth. The proportion of working-age people on out-of-work benefits in the five towns ranged from 19 percent to 25 percent against a national figure of 11.5 percent. They concluded:

> Whilst each town has its own particular problems a recurring theme has been that of poverty attracting poverty. As employment has dried up so house prices have fallen and so less economically active people—such as single-parent families and pensioners—have moved in, seeking cheaper accommodation and living costs. Similarly, vulnerable people—such as children in care and ex-offenders—have been moved in as authorities take advantage of low-cost housing as large properties have been chopped into houses in multiple occupation. Parts of these towns have become dumping grounds, further depressing the desirability of such areas and so perpetuating the cycle.

Helen Pidd interviewed residents of Blackpool in the English North West, just north of Liverpool.[17] Four comments were particularly colorful.

Matthew Hodgkinson, a 19-year-old chef and trainee aerospace engineer, said he voted out for economic reasons: "It was because of the money we pay to stay in the EU, which I thought should stay in Britain. We could spend it on housing and healthcare—the NHS is close to collapsing."

Josie Crooks, a 19-year-old student and waitress, said she thought Brexit was worth the risk. "I wasn't sure which way to vote, even though I read a lot about it. In the end I thought: if we leave it's not going to be the end of the world. You've got to take the chance."

James Cross, a 39-year-old from Blackpool, argued, "Now that the result is in, the government should roll their sleeves up and make the best of it. They will have to rally around and get together. There's no point moaning. The powers that be will have to just get it sorted and crack on." There hasn't been much cracking on.

Sonia Chatterjee, 64, who has lived in Blackpool for forty years, said, "The EU has been good for us and we benefited from it but I just want our country back. We voted to go out. What's it got to do with them? We had a vote so why does parliament have to interfere? . . . I'm not fearful (Brexit won't happen) but I wouldn't put it past any of them—you never know what's going to happen with lawyers with politicians."[18]

After the Brexit vote, discontent was expressed by others in Blackpool who wanted leave to happen quickly. "I think they (the government) need to get a grip and get on with it," said retail manager Emma Jones, 40. "In June, we already voted to leave. There shouldn't be any laws or anything like that. We should just go ahead with it," said postman Dave Hudson, 41. "I don't think there are going to be any riots if it doesn't happen, but people will get impatient. For me it's got to be done proper, you can't just rush it."

The *New York Times* reported in August 2016 that there were great hopes in Blackpool that Brexit would turn the town around because of an increase in the number of Britons who were choosing not to vacation abroad because of the fall in the pound. "We don't care much for Europe here. We don't need it," the paper reported that James Martin said as he walked against the wind on the blustery seafront. "We're self-sufficient, pretty much."[19] Probably not.

Figure 10.3, following the work of Bell and Machin (2016), plots the Leave vote by county against the annual ASHE weekly earnings estimates.[20] It shows a strong negative slope, with the outlier to the far right, the City of London. Counties with higher pay were more likely to vote Remain. Counties with lower pay were more likely to vote Leave.

There are also significant positive relationships between voting to leave and the smoking rate (not reported), the obesity rate, and the suicide rate.

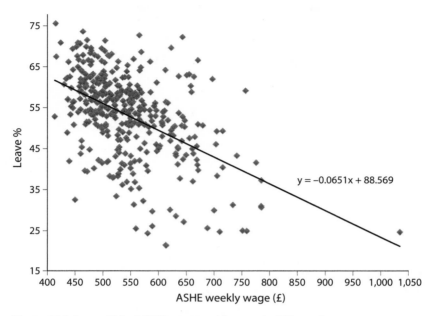

Figure 10.3. Leave % by ASHE gross weekly wage by UK county.

The poorer an area, the greater its overall dependence on welfare benefits. High dependency on welfare benefits in a county, just like a higher unemployment rate, raises the prospect an individual would vote to leave. The poorer the health in an area, the higher the likelihood of a Leave vote. Low-wage areas also voted for Leave.

Interestingly, where the Leave vote was highest by region, pay levels were lowest, as measured by the percent earning below two-thirds of the median wage and the percentage of workers earning less than the living wage. Data from the Social Mobility Commission (2016) and the Resolution Foundation show the East Midlands, West Midlands, Wales, and Yorkshire had the lowest pay levels, all of whom voted to Leave.

Sasha Becker, who was a colleague of mine at the University of Stirling and is now at the University of Warwick, also found that the 2016 Brexit referendum result is tightly correlated with previous election results for the UK Independence Party, as well as those of the extreme right-wing British National Party (Becker, Fetzer, and Novy 2016). Becker and his colleagues found that fundamental characteristics of the voting population were key drivers of the Vote Leave share, especially their age and education profiles, the historical importance of manufacturing employment, and low income and high unemployment. Migration was relevant only as it pertained to Eastern European countries, not older EU states or non-EU countries. The severity of fiscal cuts, which largely reflect weak fundamentals, they found, were also associated with Vote Leave. They also obtained similar findings at the much finer level of wards within cities.

Importantly, Becker and coauthors found areas with a strong tradition of manufacturing employment were more likely to vote Leave, as well as areas with relatively low pay and high unemployment. They also found supporting evidence that the growth rate of migrants from the twelve EU accession countries that joined the EU in 2004 and 2007 is linked to the Vote Leave share.

In addition, the quality of public service provision is systematically related to the Vote Leave share. Fiscal cuts in the context of the recent UK austerity program were strongly associated with a higher Vote Leave share. Alan Manning, a colleague of mine from LSE days, also examined Brexit votes by county and found that changes in the industrial structure of the area are important: falls in employment in heavy industry and the public sector between 1981 and 2011 are both related to a greater Leave vote (Langella and Manning 2016).

Kaufmann (2016) has argued that culture and personality, not material circumstances, separate Leave and Remain voters. He finds correlations between voting Leave and authoritarianism. He argues that among white British respondents, "there is almost no statistically significant difference in EU vote intention between rich and poor." By contrast, he notes, the probability of voting Brexit rises from around 20 percent for those most opposed to the death penalty to 70 percent for those most in favor. The link with authoritarian views may be right, but as I will show there are strong and statistically significant differences between rich and poor. The rich voted to Remain; the poor voted for Brexit.

Clarke and Whittaker (2016) found cultural and geographical factors play a key role in whether people voted for Leave or Remain; feelings of cohesion within the local area mattered. This looks like culture wars again. Goodwin and Heath (2016b) argue that income and poverty do seem to matter: "Groups of voters who have been pushed to the margins of our society, live on low incomes and lack the skills that are required to adapt and prosper amid a post-industrial and global economy, were more likely than others to endorse Brexit." They also found that the left-behind groups faced a "double whammy": "While they are being marginalised because of their lack of skills and educational qualifications this disadvantage is then being entrenched by a lack of opportunities within their local areas to get ahead and overcome their own disadvantage."

Ford and Goodwin have offered important insights about the intergenerational divide in views in the UK toward Europe and immigration. Their explanation resonates as it seems to explain the rise in populism elsewhere too.

> The voters of the 1950s and 1960s, most of whom grew up amidst economic depression and war, prized "material" values, like basic economic security and social stability. In sharp contrast, their children and grandchildren take such things for granted and, instead, focus on "post-material" values like liberty, human rights, and environmental protection. . . . Younger voters, who have grown up and prospered in a more mobile and interconnected world, tend to have weaker attachments to their nation of birth, a thinner and more instrumental sense of what national identity means, a greater openness to immigration, and a greater acceptance of ethnic diversity. (2014, 156)

The Left-Behinds Voted for Le Pen

In an intriguing essay, Christopher Caldwell suggests that for those cut off from France's new-economy citadels, the misfortunes are serious. He claims they're stuck economically. He points out that three years after finishing their studies, three-quarters of French university graduates are living on their own; by contrast, three-quarters of their contemporaries without university degrees still live with their parents.

Caldwell notes that the left-behinds are dying early. In January 2016, the national statistical institute INSEE announced that life expectancy had fallen for both sexes in France for the first time since World War II, and he suggests that the native French working class is driving the decline: "Unlike their parents in Cold War France, the excluded have lost faith in efforts to distribute society's goods more equitably."[21]

Another report found that countries with recent populist movements tend to have a combination of low trust in government and low expectations of their future lives.[22] Gallup terms those who lack confidence in their national government as "disaffected" and those who rate their lives on the same footing or worse in relation to their current lives as "discouraged." France and the UK rank in the top ten EU countries with the highest percentage of disaffected and discouraged residents.

Mark Lilla has argued that "economic stagnation, political stalemate, rising right-wing populism—this has been France's condition for a decade or more."[23] France had not been doing well, especially on the jobs front. In February 2017, the unemployment rate in France was 10 percent. For those aged 15–24 it was 23 percent. Long-term unemployment has risen from 35 percent of unemployment in 2009 to 44 percent in 2016. Underemployment rates in France are high. In 2015, 6.5 percent of all employment was made up of part-time workers who wanted full-time jobs. This compares with an average for the euro area of 4.6 percent and 5.6 percent in the UK.

Using two Eurobarometers, the regular surveys conducted by the European Commission, in 2010 and 2016, I have calculated whether respondents have had difficulties paying their bills most of the time, from time to time, or never. The percent saying most of the time in 2016 was especially high in France at 14 percent, up from 8 percent in 2010. In October 2016 respondents in the Eurobarometer #86.1 were asked if they thought the country was headed in the wrong or right direction. It is notable that 86 percent of respondents in France said the country was going in the wrong direction. This contrasts with 40 percent in the UK, 53 percent in western Germany, and 71 percent in Italy.

Given France's poor economic performance, especially in the old industrial areas, it is hardly surprising there has been a rise in right-wing populism there. Marine Le Pen came in second place in the polls leading into the first ballot on Sunday, April 23, 2017, just as her father did fifteen years earlier before losing in a landslide to Jacques Chirac. She developed a nationalist and protectionist program and pledged to leave the euro area and NATO. Le Pen had plans to lower the retirement age to 60, boost public services, raise welfare payments, and tax firms that hire foreigners.

I plot the Le Pen vote by department, similar to counties, against the unemployment rate in figure 10.4. It is clear from the trend lines that the first round of the Le Pen vote is positively correlated with the unemployment rate. I also find the Le Pen vote is negatively correlated with median income and positively correlated with the percentage of high school dropouts and the poverty rate. The Le Pen vote in the second round was also positively

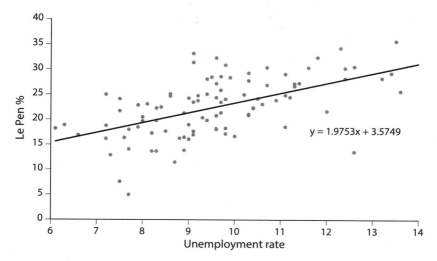

Figure 10.4. Le Pen first-round vote and the unemployment rate. *Note:* I am grateful to Leigh Thomas and Reuters for providing me with his data from the first round of voting.

correlated with the unemployment rate. This pattern repeats those observed earlier for Brexit and Trump. It's the same people.

As in the UK with Brexit and the United States with Trump, there was a major divide between the big cities and more rural areas, which have higher unemployment rates, higher levels of poverty, and poor provision of public services. In Paris, Bordeaux, Nantes, Rennes, and Lyon, Macron received more than 30 percent of the vote. In Hauts-de-France, which has a 12.1 percent unemployment rate, Le Pen received 31 percent of the vote. In Provence-Alpes-Côte d'Azur (11.4 percent unemployment rate), Le Pen received 28 percent of the vote.[24]

In the Pas-de-Calais, which has an unemployment rate of 13.3 percent, and which was long dependent on mining, primarily the coal mines near the town of Lens, Le Pen won 34 percent of the vote. Between 1975 and 1984, the region lost over 130,000 jobs and unemployment rose to 14 percent of the working population, well above the national average. In more recent years, the area has faced economic hardship as the mines closed, alongside a decline in the steel industry and major problems in the textile industry. The Front National won large parts of the deindustrialized north and east, as well as the south, while Macron took the west. He was strong in cosmopolitan cities, while Le Pen was strong in small towns and rural areas that felt abandoned. Le Pen took nine of the ten départements with France's highest unemployment rates.

What happened in France looks much like what happened in the UK and the United States. Less-educated whites living outside the big cities, who had been hurt by economic decline, falling real wages, unemployment, underemployment, and a lack of good jobs, voted for populism. Once again, they were against immigration, from outside the big cities, which have prospered, and the rule of the elites. This time right-wing populism lost. There isn't going to be a Frexit, but election winner Sebastian Kurz is president of Austria, and his party is in coalition with the far-right Freedom Party (FPO), suggesting that the French election may not be a turning point. This doesn't seem to be over yet.

Those who were left behind, who were not doing so well, turned toward populism around the world, which gave them hope. They had nowhere else to turn. The elites had left them behind. The commonality of those who voted for change was that they and their communities were not doing well.

And Then Quitaly, Maybe

The Brits narrowly and unexpectedly voted for Brexit, 52–48 percent. Americans elected Trump because of the vagaries of the electoral college, even though he obtained 3 million fewer votes than Hillary Clinton. Macron won in France, but Le Pen made a strong showing and reached the final round, which meant no Frexit. The majority of Brits polled now say they want to nationalize some of the "commanding heights" of the economy—water, electricity, and railways. The UK government recently had to nationalize the East Coast Railway, which had gone bankrupt.[25] It doesn't help that the UK has nine of the ten poorest regions in Europe.[26] Inner London is the richest region in Europe.

But this may not be the end of the rise of populism in Europe, as there have been populist uprisings in Italy, Slovenia, Hungary, and Austria. The pandemic isn't over. In May 2018 Italy struggled to form a government and was faced with a short-lived crisis that sent bond yields spiraling upward. On May 28, 2018, Italian president Sergio Mattarella blocked a bid by two populist parties, which are riding high in the opinion polls, the anti-establishment Five Star and the far-right anti-immigrant Northern League alliance, to form a government. While both are called "populist," they have conflicting policies, so it isn't surprising that their efforts to form a government ultimately failed. The Five Star Movement called for a universal basic income of $920 a month, implying a huge increase in government outlays. The Northern League has called for a flat tax rate of 15 percent and actions against refugees. It would also like to see heavy spending on infrastructure.

Both parties wish to roll back pension reforms and other plans aimed at boosting competitiveness. Both are strongly Eurosceptic and show little inclination to be bound by European Union rules and regulations. Both call for scrapping sanctions against Russia. There is likely to be a new set of elections where the main topic will probably be continued membership in the Euro. However, a recent Ipsos poll suggested only 29 percent of Italians supported quitting the Euro.[27] Italy has one of the lowest approval levels for membership of the single currency, but disapproval may not be the same as quitting. According to data from the October 2017 Eurobarometer, only 45 percent of Italians think the EU is a "good thing" for their country, compared with 64 percent across the Eurozone as a whole. QuItaly, as it is being called, or Itexit, probably won't happen.

On May 29, 2018, the *Financial Times* reported that Five Star leader Luigi di Maio called for a mass protest on June 2, a public holiday: "last night was the darkest in the history of Italian democracy."[28] The day before Tony Barber had argued in the same paper that Italy is home to the strongest antiestablishment parties in Europe and suggested that matters a lot as "events in Italy weigh more on the EU's destiny than events in the UK, which has been a semi-detached member of the bloc for most of the 45 years since its entry in 1973."[29]

Italian stock markets were down 2.5 percent on the news on May 28 and 29, 2018; stock and bond markets around the world were down, including in London, Paris, Frankfurt, Madrid, and Hong Kong, as well as on Wall Street. The Italian two-year yield at 2.5 percent was up 1.7 percentage points in a single day on May 29. Italian banks were hardest hit, with the country's largest financial institution, UniCredit, falling 5.6 percent. But lenders across Europe also sold off: Spain's Santander was down 5.4 percent; France's BNP Paribas dropped 4.5 percent; and Germany's Commerzbank fell 4 percent. The already struggling Deutsche Bank that is shedding jobs was down 4.6 percent. Some of Wall Street's biggest banks, including JPMorgan, Citigroup, Bank of America, and Morgan Stanley, were down 4 percent or more.

On May 31, 2018, Giuseppe Conte, a professor, was appointed prime minister with Matteo Salvini of the League and di Maio of Five Star as vice premiers. This avoided the possibility of new elections. Italian markets bounced back as investors judged that having a Five Star–League government was better than new elections with a slim majority. Both of the populist groups have said they will not push, for now, for Euro exit. A road sign proclaiming "Basta Euro" that stood outside the League party's headquarters was painted over at the end of May. As Gideon Rachman noted on June 4, 2018, in the *Financial Times*, there is likely lots of trouble brewing.

> Matteo Salvini, the League's leader and Italy's new interior minister, has promised to speed up deportations and detentions of up to 500,000 illegal immigrants—which could cause angst in Berlin, as well as potentially violating EU law. The League also wants a flat tax of 15 per cent on income. Five Star, its coalition partner, has argued for a universal basic income. Those policies together are a recipe for blowing up the EU's 3 per cent limit on national budget deficits. If the government in Rome ignores the EU's fiscal rules, the reaction from Brussels and Berlin will be harsh. When Italy then finds itself under pressure from the bond markets, the likes of Mr Varoufakis and Mr Savona will return to the argument that the EU elite is conspiring against the will of the people.[30]

On June 5, 2018, Bloomberg reported that Italian prime minister Giuseppe Conte pledged in his maiden speech that his government would push through measures ranging from a "citizen's income" for the poor to tax cuts and curbs on immigration, as he called for a stronger, fairer Europe.[31] Italian bonds extended their decline during his speech as he gave investors little indication that he would diverge from the Five Star–League program. Two-year securities led losses, with yields climbing by 16 basis points to 0.92 percent. Those on ten-year notes snapped four days of declines, rising 12 basis points to 2.65 percent. The roller coaster continues.

The Italian unemployment rate for May 2018 was 10.7 percent, down from 14.3 percent in November 2014. No wonder Italians are disgruntled.

There continue to be issues with the Italian budget. The new Italian government wants to spend more, including providing a minimum income for the unemployed, along with cutting taxes and scrapping extensions to the retirement age. The EU Commission and the IMF have both warned against Rome's stimulus plan.[32] The economic battle lines are being drawn in Italy as they have been in the UK over Brexit.

Why Right-Wing Populism?

Populism continues on its march through Europe. Hard-liner Janez Jansa has ridden a right-wing populist wave into power in Slovenia.[33] Slovenia looks like it is going to line up politically with Hungary, which reelected the right-wing populist Victor Orban as prime minister in April 2010, and Austria, where a far-right party has emerged as a strong political force. The young Sebastian Kurz of the right-leaning Austrian People's Party led his party to victory at just 31 years old and is Austria's youngest chancellor ever. Kurz is moving to the right on migration. Asylum seekers caught trying to cross the Mediterranean should be sent back, he says.[34]

I first met Vernon Bogdanor in early 2017 when we were both guests on *Daily Politics*, hosted by my old friend Andrew Neil, at the BBC's studios at Millbank opposite the Houses of Parliament. We started chatting about populism. He is the great expert on this populism stuff and I listened. He was also David Cameron's tutor at Oxford, who he said was one of his ablest students. A few days later he kindly sent me a few short essays that he called "squibs." I was especially taken by his definition of populism. Some say that a populist is merely a politician who proves unexpectedly popular. But perhaps we can try a more precise definition. The elite belong to the exam-passing classes. Most supporters of populist parties, he suggests, do not. We are both interested in the left-behinds who, he suggests, feel a strong sense of disenfranchisement and powerlessness, believing as they do that the political class makes its decisions without consulting their interests and looks down on them as "unreconstructed bigots." Fascism, he notes, is just a variant of right-wing populism.

A populist, Bogdanor suggests, is someone who believes that the traditional governing parties of moderate left and moderate right, which claim to oppose each other, in reality form a consensus, since they agree upon basic issues. In Britain, France, and the United States, for example, the main parties agreed on the benefits of immigration and the advantages of globalization. In Britain, the three major parties favored Britain's continued membership in the European Union. The people did not. In another of the squibs he argued that the real debate is not between left and right but between the people and the political class, the elite, which has its own interests in common, which are not those of the people. There surely is something in that suggestion.

The reason why there is right-wing and not left-wing populism, Bogdanor suggested to me, is that the populist reaction is nationalistic. The left continually underestimates the force of nationalism or patriotism, just as it did in the 1930s. Most working-class constituencies are deeply patriotic and conservative. One of the objections to Corbyn, the Labour Party leader in provincial England, Bogdanor suggested, is that he has been rude about the Queen! The left, he suggests, has been caught by identity politics. It has concentrated on the identity of minorities—whether subnational, ethnic, or sexual—and has neglected the identity of the majority, for example, the white English working class, which it regards as bigoted and racist. This can be compared, Bogdanor suggests, with Gordon Brown's comment in 2010 to a woman in Rochdale, whom he called a bigot.[35] Hence the expression of majority identity becomes politically illegitimate for the left. The left has succeeded in identifying itself with nationalism in Greece and Spain, which accounts, Bogdanor suggested, for its success there. There is a deep frustration with the left's obsession with political correctness and, more generally, with things that people don't see as relating to them.

In further communication with me Bogdanor suggested that contrary to what the Marxists believed, during a recession, class solidarity weakens but national solidarity increases. Whatever the economic benefits of immigration, it is resented for cultural reasons, as a threat to identity. People said that their communities had been altered out of all recognition and that they had not been consulted about it.

Half a decade ago, Bogdanor suggests, the ambitious would remain in their provincial towns to sustain the economy and take leadership positions. Now they go to elite universities and then work in big cities, leaving whole areas hollowed out. The Great Recession showed that they had made very unwise investments, that they were short-sighted, and that they were often unethical. Their high salaries were held to be a reward for risk-taking. But, when their risks went wrong, they were bailed out by the state. Private-sector gains and public-sector losses. They were incentive-driven capitalists when things went well but turned into socialists when things started going badly! Their victims had no such luxury. Bogdanor is right: one rule for the little people, another rule for the powerful—at least that is how the left-behinds feel.

In private communication with me, Matthew Goodwin, a professor of politics at the University of Kent, commented when I asked him why we have seen a burst of right-wing rather than left-wing populism that the issue "relates more to migration/actual demographic shifts and that the left has been outflanked on those issues, often by manipulative national populists. But also increasingly the left is now having its economic message met/diluted by national populists who are gradually becoming more protectionist (witness Le Pen attacking 'savage globalisation' or Sweden Democrats proposing labour market stress testing to protect 'native' workers)." Katsambekis (2017) suggests that populist radical-right parties all seem to favor a "strictly ethnic (even racial) understanding of the people, portrayed as a homogeneous organic community, opposing minorities (religious, ethnic, etc.) and expressing xenophobic, racist, or homophobic views. In this sense, such parties tend to be exclusionary and regressive, connecting the well-being of the 'native' people to the exclusion of alien 'others' and the restriction of the latter's rights and freedoms."

Judis (2016) argues that the populists roil the waters. They signal, he suggests, that the prevailing political ideology isn't working and needs repair and the standard worldview is breaking down. Judis further argues that if Trump were to demand an increase in guards along the Mexican border, that would not open up a gulf between the people and the elite. But promising a wall that the Mexican government will pay for—or the total cessation of immigration—does establish a frontier. Right-wing populists, he suggests, champion the people against an elite that they accuse of coddling a third group, which can consist of immigrants, Islamists, or African American militants. Trump voters, Judis says, invariably praised his self-financing, which was seen as making him independent of lobbyists, which was an important part of his appeal. Rich was OK.

Eatwell and Goodwin have explained the allure of populism succinctly: "Those with fewer qualifications and more traditionalist values are more alarmed about how their societies are changing: they fear the eventual destruction of their community and identity, they believe that both they and their group are losing out, and distrust their increasingly distant representatives. National populists spoke to these voters, albeit in ways that many dislike. For the first time in years their supporters now feel they have an agency in the debate" (2018, 275).

It's the Elites, Mate

Müller argues persuasively that a necessary but not sufficient condition of populism is to be critical of elites. In addition, he suggests, populists are always anti-pluralist, claiming they and they alone represent the people. Populist protest parties, he argues, cancel themselves out once they win an election as they can't protest against themselves in government but they can govern as populists, which he suggests goes against the conventional wisdom. Müller explains that any failures of populist movements can still be blamed on elites acting behind the scenes. Populism distorts the democratic process (2016, 4), but he suggests it may be useful in making clear that parts of the population really are unrepresented.

Tom Nichols, who used to work in the Government Department at Dartmouth, writes that the United States is now a country obsessed by the worship of its own ignorance (2017, ix). Trump, he says, won because "he connected with a particular kind of voter who believes that knowing about things like America's nuclear deterrent is just so much pointy-headed claptrap. Worse, voters not only didn't care that Trump is ignorant or wrong, they likely were unable to recognize his ignorance or errors" (2017, 212). Americans, he argues, "have reached a point where ignorance, especially of anything related to public policy, is an actual virtue" (2017, x). Trump, Nichols argues, sought power during the 2016 election "by mobilizing the angriest and most ignorant in the electorate" (2017, 215). Oh dear.

These were battles against the establishment. As left-wing columnist and author Owen Jones noted, "The illusion of every era is that it is permanent. Opponents who seem laughably irrelevant and fragmented can enjoy sudden reversals of fortunes. The fashionable common sense of today can become the discredited nonsense of yesterday and with surprising speed" (2014, 314).

The concern may not be about what Trump achieves; it seems that sticking it to the opposition is really what it is about. Charlie Sykes, a former talk-show host in Wisconsin, has argued that much of the conservative news media is now less pro-Trump than it is anti-anti-Trump. The distinction, Sykes argues, is important, "because anti-anti-Trumpism has become the new safe space for the right. Here is how it works," he suggests. "Rather than defend President Trump's specific actions, his conservative champions change the subject to (1) the biased 'fake news' media, (2) over-the-top liberals, (3) hypocrites on the left, (4) anyone else victimizing Mr. Trump or his supporters, and (5) whataboutism, as in 'What about Obama?' and 'What about Clinton?' "[36]

This all reminds me of the famous 1973 column by humorist Art Buchwald in relation to Watergate. It contained thirty-six responses for loyal Nixonites who were under attack that he argued they should cut out and carry in their pockets.[37] It starts out as follows.

1. Everyone does it.
2. What about Chappaquiddick?
3. A President can't keep track of everything his staff does.
4. The press is blowing the whole thing up.
5. Whatever Nixon did was for national security.
6. The Democrats are sore because they lost the election.
7. Are you going to believe a rat like John Dean or the president of the United States?
8. Wait till all the facts come out.
9. What about Chappaquiddick?
10. If you impeach Nixon you get Agnew (you didn't).
19. What about Chappaquiddick?
32. What about Chappaquiddick?

Press coverage of Trump has been unremittingly negative. In a study that obtained much attention in the right-wing press, Trump's coverage during his first 100 days set a new standard for negativity.[38] Of news reports with a clear tone, negative reports outpaced positive ones by 80 percent to 20 percent. Patterson concludes that "the fact that Trump has received more negative coverage than his predecessor is hardly surprising. The early days of his presidency have been marked by far more missteps and miss-hits, often self-inflicted, than any presidency in memory, perhaps ever. . . . Never in the nation's history has the country had a president with so little fidelity to the facts, so little appreciation for the dignity of the presidential office, and so little understanding of the underpinnings of democracy" (2016, 15).

Coal and Talc Jobs Are Not Coming Back, and Neither Are Dilapidated British Seaside Towns; Coal Remains Inaccessible because of Underground Flooding

It is hard to see what can be done to bring back jobs to rust-belt states like Michigan, Pennsylvania, and Ohio as Trump promised. Raising the world price of steel, coal, or talc is a non-starter. Even if there is a giant fiscal stimulus, why would firms not move production to, say, South Carolina, which has a private-sector unionization rate of 1.1 percent or Georgia at 2.7 percent or Texas at 2.5 percent when private-sector unionization rates in the rust belt are much higher (e.g., Michigan, 11.1%)? Technological change may still mean that capital is cheaper than labor, so it's more machines and robots rather than lots of new jobs for the unskilled. A rising tide can lift all boats of course.

In 1914, 181,000 miners were employed in the anthracite mines of northeastern Pennsylvania. On January 22, 1959, the Knox Coal Company's mine in Luzerne County, under the Susquehanna River, in the vicinity of Port Griffith, a small town, midway between Wilkes-Barre and Scranton, collapsed and the mighty Susquehanna River poured into the mines, flooding them throughout the interconnected underground system. Shortly after the flooding of the Knox Mine, two of the area's largest coal companies announced a full withdrawal from the anthracite business. Other companies whose mines lay some distance from the Knox disaster continued to operate on a much smaller scale into the early 1970s. The only anthracite production that still occurs in the area is large-scale surface mining of shallow old works.

Luzerne County's website suggests that even though the anthracite resource remaining in the ground is substantial, the complex geologic structure, steep terrain, and inefficient early mining of the thicker and more accessible blocks of coal "now preclude the use of modern mechanized equipment underground." In addition, "Billions of tons of anthracite are still in the ground but remain inaccessible because of underground flooding."[39] Longazel (2016) notes that in the years before 1980 there were consistently more than forty thousand manufacturing jobs in Luzerne County. By 1990 the number had dropped to about twenty-five thousand and by 2016 the number was fewer than twenty thousand.

U.S. coal production is in precipitous decline. In 2015, U.S. coal production, consumption, and employment fell by more than 10 percent. Between

2014 and 2015 the number of mines in Kentucky fell from 252 to 210 and the number of employees fell 13.8 percent. In West Virginia, the number of mines was down from 191 to 151 while the number of employees was down 14 percent. Pennsylvania saw mine numbers dropping from 222 to 195 with employee numbers down 14 percent. Virginia mine numbers dropped from 69 to 65 with employee numbers down 12 percent. According to the BLS, in June 1985, 178,000 people were employed in coal mining. This number was 50,000 in January 2017. By contrast, renewable energy—including wind, solar, and biofuels—now accounts for more than 650,000 U.S. jobs.[40] According to the Employment Situation Report published by the BLS in February 2019, the number of coal-mining jobs in January 2019 was up 1,800 to 52,700 from 50,900 a year earlier.

Donald Trump held a rally in Luzerne County to raise local hopes that things might change. He told a crowd at Wilkes-Barre, the seat of Luzerne County, on October 10, 2016, "Oh, we're going to make Pennsylvania so rich again, your jobs are coming back. We're going to be ending illegal immigration. We're going to stop the jobs from pouring out of our country."[41]

Justin Emershaw voted for Trump. After hearing Clinton's negative remarks during the campaign about coal, he said Trump struck a nerve with the coal industry when he talked about reopening mines. "The industry is really hurting," said Emershaw, who works for Coal Contractors Inc. in Hazleton, in Luzerne County. "We need somebody who's really going to make a change with it."[42] However, David Victor, an energy expert at the University of California–San Diego, observed a few days after the election, "I suspect there is no fuel for which the Trump victory will be more irrelevant than for coal."[43] The town of Hazleton saw the size of its Latino population rise from 4 percent in 2000 to 38 percent in 2006. In 2006, it passed an ordinance called the Illegal Immigration Relief Act (IIRF) that made it illegal for landlords to rent to undocumented immigrants and threatened fines for employers who hired them (Longazel 2016).[44] The ordinance was challenged in court and was declared illegal.

In 2016, 5,644 Democrats in Luzerne County changed their registration to Republican. Luzerne County flipped from voting for Obama by 5 points in 2012 to voting for Trump by 20 points.

There were unsuccessful interventions in other sectors too. Donald Trump offered $800 million in tax breaks to stop a Carrier Corporation furnace factory in Indiana from closing, keeping 800 production jobs from going to

Mexico. Despite that the company still plans to shift 1,300 jobs to Mexico. He also warned another Indiana company, Rexnord, about its plans to move its factory south of the border.[45] On December 2, 2016, Trump tweeted, "Rexnord of Indiana is moving to Mexico and rather viciously firing all of its 300 workers. This is happening all over our country. No more!"

Two months later Rexnord was still planning on moving to Mexico. Andrew Tangel reports that workers have been packing up machines while their replacements, visiting from Mexico, learn to do their jobs. Machinist Tim Mathis, who had worked at Rexnord for twelve years, said, "That's a real kick in the ass to be asked to train your replacement. To train the man that's going to eat your bread." Gary Canter, a machinist at Rexnord for eight years, said, "It just puzzles me to think that they have to [reduce costs] by dumping us out. It's very un-American." Tangel reported that Canter had voted for Trump and remained hopeful the president would ultimately boost manu-facturing, creating new jobs for his colleagues elsewhere even if the Rexnord plant isn't spared. "We gave this man a chance because it wasn't a typical politician that's done nothing for us."[46]

The false claims go on. President Trump had made claims at a Pennsyl-vania rally in August 2018 that "U.S. Steel is opening up seven plants." Fox News reported that "the Pittsburgh-based company has made no such an-nouncement."[47] Steel jobs are not coming back.

Obama won Trumbull County, Ohio, by 23 points but Trump won it by 6, not least on the promise of bringing manufacturing jobs back to Ohio. On November 26, 2018, General Motors announced that it would be closing five plants in the United States and cutting around fourteen thousand jobs. One of the plants is the Lordstown plant in Trumbull County, which had been there for fifty years; others are to be closed in Maryland and Michi-gan. Part of the problem was that the facility produced the Chevy Cruze, a more fuel-efficient vehicle, but sales fell because of lower fuel prices. General Motors also cited Trump's tariffs on steel and aluminum as raising costs. In June GM lowered its profit outlook for the year because it said tariffs were driving up production costs, raising prices even on domestic steel. Rising interest rates were also raising costs. The move follows job reductions by Ford.[48] Car jobs are not coming back.

Coal has almost entirely died in the UK. Most of the old coal-mining towns voted for Brexit. Coal production in the UK in the 1960s was around 177 million tonnes and the industry employed half a million miners. Output fell to 114 million tonnes by the mid-1970s and 300,000 workers. The

National Union of Miners (NUM) had a bitter fight with Prime Minister Margaret Thatcher, which resulted in a yearlong national strike in 1984–85, by which time output was at 133 million tonnes and 180,000 workers. Pit closures continued through the 1990s with only 21 million tonnes mined with 13,000 workers.

From 2000 to 2010 the coal industry contracted further, with output falling to 10 million tonnes. Kellingly, the UK's last deep mine, was closed in 2015. In 1982, the NUM had 170,000 members. By 2015 the number of members had fallen to 100.[49] In 1984 Yorkshire had 56 collieries. Today there are none. The coal mines in Yorkshire were concentrated in a few towns. For example, Barnsley had eleven pits in 1984; Doncaster had nine; Rotherham had ten; and Wakefield had fifteen. Each of these towns voted Brexit by large majorities—Barnsley (68%), Doncaster (69%), Rotherham (68%), and Wakefield (66%) against 52 percent nationally.

The problem with coal that is distinctive is that it is geographically concentrated. When coal jobs go, house prices plummet, and people can't just move out because they can't sell. Wales voting for Brexit is an obvious example. The same isn't true for taxi drivers, who will potentially be replaced by driverless cars as the concentration of economic activity in small towns isn't the same. They are not all located in a narrow Welsh valley like the Rhondda.

Wakefield, once a major coal town where 10,000 Poles live, is home to various Polish beauty parlors and hairdressers, estate agents, off licenses, dentists and doctors, and a string of Polish delis. Aneta Duchniak, who two years earlier opened the first Polish restaurant in Wakefield, wondered after Brexit if she would have many British customers: "They said, 'We want to support you, it's nothing against you, it's against Brussels controlling us.' Lots of my regulars voted to leave. One of them even told me she has a Polish cleaner. Roger, who comes in all the time for a cup of tea, voted out and he says he worked with lots of Polish people when he was a miner."[50] I recall watching an edition of BBC's *Question Time* from Wakefield where it was clear that there was a great deal of resentment in the air. Members of the audience objected to being thought of as "stupid," and one woman complained that "people are making out as if we are uneducated, that we didn't know what we were doing and they need to stop doing that." Another said, "I feel like we were treated by certain people, as this lady said, that we're uneducated stupid northerners, we're all racist up here, and we don't know what we're doing."[51]

St. Lawrence County, New York, on the U.S.-Canadian border, is the birthplace of my boss, Dartmouth president Phil Hanlon, who explained to me that talc mining was extremely important there when he was growing up. Apparently, the quality was high, but advances in technology meant that the quality of lower-grade talc found abroad could be improved and was a lot cheaper, with bad effect. Lower world prices wiped out the talc industry in St. Lawrence and the last mine closed in 2008. It hasn't helped that there have been concerns about the health risks of talc with courts awarding several multimillion-dollar payouts.[52] These lawsuits relate not just to its harmful impacts on users (causing ovarian cancer) but also to the miners who caught mesothelioma from breathing in the dust. In 2018 Johnson & Johnson and a company that supplied it with talc from mines in Vermont were ordered to pay a combined $117 million in damages after a jury found their popular baby powder product contained asbestos that caused cancer.[53]

The U.S. Geological Survey reported that talc production in millions of metric tons was 1,270 in 1990; 511 in 2009; and 550 in 2017.[54] In 2012 St. Lawrence County voted 57 percent Obama and 41 percent Romney. In 2016 St. Lawrence voted 51 percent Trump and 42 percent Clinton. Hope springs eternal, but talc mining sure as heck is not coming back.

After Arizona passed a series of tough anti-immigration laws, Bob Davis in the *Wall Street Journal* reported that Rob Knorr couldn't find enough Mexican field hands to pick his jalapeño peppers. He sharply reduced his acreage and invested $2 million developing a machine to remove pepper stems. His goal was to cut the number of laborers he needed by 90 percent and to hire higher-paid U.S. machinists instead. Mr. Knorr, Davis reports, said he was willing to pay $20 an hour to operators of harvesters and other machines, compared with about $13 an hour for field hands. He says he can hire skilled machinists at community colleges, so he can rely less on migrant labor. "I can find skilled labor in the U.S.," he says. "I don't have to go to bed and worry about whether harvesting crews will show up."[55] Technology remains an issue.

What about Chappaquiddick?

The concern especially in the United States and the UK is that nothing much is going to change and there will be widespread disappointment. Rioting in Paris may yet spread. The question, then, is who will be blamed. The media, the Democrats, the deep state, weak establishment Republicans, and Never-Trumpers are all on the menu. Already the guns are out for the Mueller investigation. More bloody excuses. The possibility, though, has arisen from the meeting of the G7 in Quebec, Canada, that Make America Great Again (MAGA) may end up being America Alone.[56] Trump's proposal to bring Russia back to the G7 didn't go down well. India, a nuclear power, has an economy 50 percent larger than Russia's, and what about China? There has been no pull-back from Crimea, which is why Russia was kicked out of the G7 in the first place. Trump eventually refused to sign the joint communiqué.

The summits with NATO and G7 were nothing short of disastrous. Nothing of substance came out of the meeting with Kim Jong-un in Singapore or with Putin in Helsinki. Trump is fully embroiled in a number of legal issues including the Mueller probe into Russian collusion. There have been multiple indictments including several from Trump's campaign. There are also a number of lawsuits involving the emoluments clause in the Constitution in relation to the Trump Hotel in Washington, D.C., as well as lawsuits relating to payoffs to two women with whom Trump allegedly had extramarital affairs. Plus, his fixer, Michael Cohen, and others are cooperating with special prosecutor Robert Mueller. Trump isn't going to have much time to spend fixing the plight of his core voters now that the Democrats have taken control of the House (as of January 2019) and subpoenas may start to fly.

The pain and suffering that I have documented have come about as communities have fractured and decent-paying jobs for the less educated have disappeared across advanced countries. Right-wing populist politicians told the left-behinds that they would do lots of deals and all would be well. They are not cracking on with Brexit, coal and steel jobs are not showing up, and tourists are not rushing back to English seaside towns. Tax cuts for the rich and a few dregs for the poor and there lurks the possibility of cuts to Social Security, Medicare, and Medicaid. Maybe a big infrastructure bill will do the trick? Time will tell, but sadly, nobody had a plan and they still don't. Delivering is harder than making promises.

What about Chappaquiddick?

PART III

What to Do?

CHAPTER 11

Full Employment

After he made a speech to the National Bureau of Economic Research in Cambridge, Massachusetts, in July 2018 Governor Mark Carney asked me what I thought the NAIRU (Non-Accelerating Inflation Rate of Unemployment), which is the technical name for full employment, was. I replied: "I know the MPC thinks it is around 4.5 percent but I think it is likely closer to 2.5 percent." The evidence seems to be that in the United States and the UK the NAIRU was likely around 4.5 percent before the Great Recession and 2.5 percent after it. The recession of 2008 and 2009 was a major structural break that policymakers still do not seem to accept or understand. The Great Recession has changed everything.

As I noted at the beginning of the book, and as it should be well clear by now, this book is about jobs, decent jobs that pay well, and the lack of them. The big issue is how to bring back the good, well-paying jobs. An obvious way is to let the economy run hot. Workers would become increasingly scarce, which is something that hasn't happened for years. That way wage growth would rise sharply, at rates comparable to those observed in the years before 2008, perhaps 4 percent or even 5 percent. That would make workers feel good and encourage many to join the labor force, including many of those who have been left behind for so long. That might well take the wind out of the sails of populism.

One of the first things I learned in my Economics A-level class in 1968 was that full employment didn't mean everyone had a job. Far from it. A dynamic capitalist economy, I was taught, was always changing, with firms being born and others dying. Workers move between firms and even set up their own business, and hence sometimes it was necessary for them to have, hopefully short, spells of unemployment. Some of those businesses succeed, but most fail. If unemployment gets too low wages would have to rise as the only way to get workers would be to pinch them from other firms, since there is no available pool of labor to dip into. I recall being taught that the full-employment rate of unemployment was 3 percent.

A big question is, how low can unemployment go? William Beveridge ([1944] 1960) tells the story in the prologue to his book that he described 3 percent in his original report as a "conservative rather than unduly hopeful aim for the average unemployment rate of the future under conditions of full-employment." When Keynes saw this number, he wrote to Beveridge to say that he saw no harm in aiming for 3 percent but that he would be surprised if it could go so low in practice. In the prologue Beveridge notes that in fact in the twelve years from 1948 through 1959 the unemployment rate surprised to the low side with no wage explosion and averaged 1.55%. Here are the UK numbers: 1948–50 = 1.5%; 1951 = 1.2%; 1952 = 2%; 1953 = 1.6%; 1954 = 1.3%; 1955 = 1.1%; 1956 = 1.2%; 1957 = 1.4%; 1958 = 2.1%; and 1959 = 2.2%. I see no reason we couldn't go as low again and get downside surprises to the unemployment rate globally.

It doesn't appear from the data we have that there was a wage explosion over those years. We have data available from the Bank of England on real consumption wages over this period. This is based on what they call the preferred earnings and CPI series (1900 = 100). In 1948 the index number was 143.97, which rose to 170.74 in 1959, which means real earnings rose by 18.6 percent over this eleven-year period. Such a rise in real wages would be welcomed around the world.

In the United States the unemployment rate was 2.5 percent in May and June 1953. From January 1960 through August 1975, the Japanese unemployment rate was never above 2 percent and in the latest data for April 2018 is 2.5 percent. Over the entire period of January 1955 through April 2018, Japanese unemployment averaged 2.7 percent versus 5.95 percent in the United States. Maybe this is the future for the United States and the UK? I see no reason why the U.S. and UK unemployment rates couldn't get close to 2.5 percent again. Japan has seen no nominal wage growth in nearly three decades and real wages are down 11 percent and may well be the precedent.

My contention, then, is that there is really no good reason why the unemployment rate could not go below 3 percent in the United States, the UK, and Germany again and maybe even to 2 percent. That is what happened, to the surprise of both Beveridge and Keynes, in the UK between 1948 and 1959, so why not again? The (failed) economic models say you shouldn't do this because this would push up inflation, but it hasn't even when unemployment rates dropped from 6 to 5 to 4 percent.

But that is what the inflation hawks said when the unemployment rate was at 6.5 percent and falling and nothing happened on the way down below 4.5 percent. I wouldn't be surprised if the same happens if the unemployment rate is allowed to drop from 4.5 to 2.5 percent; there will be little wage pressure and no inflation, so why not try it again? All three countries have nominal wage growth in 2019 of about 2.5–3 percent and much below pre-recession levels at comparably low unemployment rates. Let's give it a shot.

The puzzle for central bankers, who are trying to drive inflation down by raising rates as in the case of the Fed in the United States or threatening to do so in the case of the Bank of England, is that the models keep telling them there is about to be lots of price and wage inflation. Their problem is there isn't any such inflation. These models are primarily driven by what happened in the 1970s, when unions were powerful fifty years ago, after the Paris riots of May 1968.[1] The economists who play with their silly little out-of-date models simply can't figure out why there is no inflation. So, they are trying to drive the unemployment rate up.

Now is the time to realize there has been a structural break and the best thing to do is to look to the 1950s and try to get the unemployment rate down. The unemployment rate was 2.7 percent in 1952 in the United States. Such low rates in my view are not infeasible. That would give workers' wages a huge fillip. It is time to stop running Western economies on empty. The elites have argued we shouldn't and can't do this, but why believe them? They have been wrong at every turn. Yes, we can.

In reality, the high level of labor market slack and the weakness of workers' bargaining power are keeping pay and price inflation down. Full employment is a long way off. If it was anywhere close wage growth would be back to pre-recession levels of 4 percent or even higher. Workers are not standing by waiting for high-wage offers to roll in. A wage norm near 3 percent is operating. If and when an economy approaches full employment we will see wage growth rising to 4 percent or so. Until it does, it is a good indicator the economy is not close to full employment. I do expect wage growth will start to kick up gradually as the economy moves to the left of the flat part of the wage curve. It hasn't gotten there yet. It may not do so until the unemployment rate goes below 3 percent or even 2 percent or lower principally because of the large amount of underemployment, which is still well above prerecession levels. Underemployment pushes wages down; unemployment does not seem to these days.

Wages are the dog that hasn't barked around the world. There is no sign that is set to change any time soon. Woof, woof. All hands to the pump. It's time to prime that pump to change all that. Workers will see decent job opportunities opening in front of their very eyes. Three percent unemployment here we come, or maybe even 2 percent. Let the good times roll. I don't see any better choice.

Tivvy Junction

Moving closer to full employment would obviously boost the availability of good jobs, meaning, high-paying jobs. As labor becomes less readily available, firms have to bid workers away from other firms. They have to increase wages for menial jobs to such a degree that many who are outside the labor force want to take them. Working in a fast-food restaurant for seven bucks an hour would be very different from receiving twenty an hour. My own experience with this was that in 1975, the UK labor market was humming with an unemployment rate of below 5 percent. I went to work in Tiverton "Tivvy" Junction in Devon building the M5 motorway for the construction firm Tarmac, which became Carillion and failed in early 2018. Labor was in short supply in the 1970s, so I was hired as a "chain-boy" who worked for the surveyors marking out the lines where the bulldozers would have to cut. That job was previously paid youth rates, but I got full laborers' rates as the market was so tight. That was a good job, meaning it paid well. A rising tide lifts all boats: Richard Freeman taught me that those who do worst in the slump do best in the boom.

"Good jobs" basically just means high-paying jobs, with benefits and retirement plans. There are lots of them when the economy is at full employment. Chain-boys don't take laborers' jobs at laborers' rates during recessions. In 2017 many people found that their skills were being underutilized; at full employment that would not be the case. Workers who weren't using their skills fully could move up the job pyramid as the demand for workers took off. At full employment workers are able to start climbing the occupational ladder once again.

Policymakers are worried about what would happen to inflation if the unemployment rate continued to drop. That concern is driven by fears about what happened in the 1970s and 1980s, but that was then and this is now. Why believe them? They are precisely the people who have been saying for the last decade that wage growth was going to take off and the productivity puzzle was solved and next year there would be four rate rises followed by four the next year and four the next. None of that happened, so why trust them on inflation? I don't. In any case we know that a 1-percentage-point rise in the unemployment rate is five times worse, in terms of well-being, than a 1-percentage-point rise in inflation. Unemployment hurts (Blanchflower et al. 2014).

Wage inflation in the UK, the United States, and Germany has hardly moved at all in the last five years as the unemployment rate dropped from 6.5 to 5.5 percent, to 4.5 percent, and then to 4 percent. At the same time wage growth went from 2 percent to 2.8 percent. My central thesis is that a drop from 4.5 to 2.5 percent, and perhaps even lower, will have similar minimal impacts. Workers now have little bargaining power, and trade unions are weaker than they have been in many a moon, plus we are in a global marketplace, to a much greater extent than in the past, where firms can move production where they please. The Great Recession exacerbated these factors as it scared workers senseless.

The NAIRU Has Fallen

In New Hampshire, where I have lived for the past twenty-eight years, the monthly unemployment rate has been under 3 percent since the beginning of 2016. It is currently 2.5 percent (December 2018). A friend of mine who is a large employer in the Upper Valley near where I work told me, "From my limited perspective, there is no wage pressure out there, even with our low local unemployment." The EWA generally doesn't lie.

The fix is for central bankers and fiscal authorities to keep their feet on the stimulus gas pedal.[2] Paul Krugman argued in the *New York Times* that it is obvious that structural explanations of unemployment are wrong. He noted that anti-structuralists or demand siders tried to point out that if the structural story were true, there should be a lot of upward pressure on the wages of those workers who did have the right skills; in fact, nobody was seeing much in the way of wage gains. He goes on to argue that adequate stimulus would have sorted out many of the labor market problems we have observed. Krugman suggests, "There was also the problem Keynesian economics always faces: it just doesn't sound serious enough to Serious People. The idea that mass unemployment is fundamentally just a problem of inadequate demand . . . and that it is easily solved by spending more, sounds too easy."[3] It is time to spend more to get the economy buzzing. As Larry Summers has said, we should wait to see the whites of the eyes of inflation. I would extend that to wait to see any evidence of wage inflation of 4 percent.

The fall in the homeownership rate in the United States and the UK is an important factor behind my claim that the equilibrium unemployment rate can come down by a lot. This will increase mobility. In the UK, the arrival of several million workers from the ten Accession countries since 2004 has made the labor market perform more efficiently, largely unconstrained by the housing market. This has also contributed to a fall in the equilibrium unemployment rate as these workers are free to move about the country.

In addition, the low levels of unionization around the world and the spread of globalization have decreased workers' bargaining power as has the rise of monopsony power. Workers are fearful that their employer will move to Mexico or subcontract their work to India. In the UK workers are concerned that if they ask for significant pay increases thousands more Poles will enter the country and take their jobs away. A given unemployment rate is now associated with less wage pressure than it was in the past. This means that full employment in advanced countries—the natural rate of unemployment or NAIRU—is likely much lower than it was in the past.

Nobel Economics Laureate Ned Phelps concurs. Workers have been shaken by the Great Recession, he argues. Unemployment can surprise on the low side before wages start to rise back to the 4 percent or so they were growing at pre-recession. As Phelps says,

> For me, a compelling hypothesis is that workers, shaken by the 2008 financial crisis and the deep recession that resulted, *have grown afraid* to demand promotions or to search for better-paying employers—despite the ease of finding work in the recently tight labor market. A corollary hypothesis is that employers, disturbed by the extremely slow growth of productivity, especially in the past ten years, have grown leery of granting pay raises—despite the return of demand to pre-crisis proportions. . . . As the return of a strong dollar by early 2015 threatened to inundate American markets with

imports, firms became scared to supply more output at the same price. Or else they supplied the same output as before at reduced prices. And they refused to raise employees' wages. In short, more competition created "super-employment"—low unemployment and low inflation.[4]

That looks right.

Eddie Lazear, chairman of George W. Bush's Council of Economic Advisers, and J. R. Spletzer argued in 2012 that structural changes had not obviously occurred in the U.S. labor market that would prevent low unemployment rates from returning. Their view is that the patterns observed during the recession were primarily cyclical. That is my view too.

> The question is important because central banks may be able to reduce unemployment that is cyclic in nature, but not that which is structural. An analysis of labor market data suggests that there are no structural changes that can explain movements in unemployment rates over recent years. Neither industrial nor demographic shifts nor a mismatch of skills with job vacancies is behind the increased rates of unemployment. Although mismatch increased during the recession, it retreated at the same rate. The patterns observed are consistent with unemployment being caused by cyclic phenomena that are more pronounced during the current recession than in prior recessions. (Lazear and Spletzer 2012)

In his 1968 address to the American Economic Association, Milton Friedman famously argued that the natural rate of unemployment can be expected to depend upon the degree of labor mobility in the economy.[5] The functioning of the labor market will thus be shaped not just by long-studied factors such as the generosity of unemployment benefits and the strength of trade unions but also by the nature, and inherent flexibility and dynamism, of the housing market.

Friedman also made clear that the natural rate of unemployment is not unchanging: "I do not mean to suggest that it is immutable and unchangeable. On the contrary, many of the market characteristics that determine its level are man-made and policy-made" (1968, 9). Friedman goes on to argue, for example, that the strength of union power and the size of the minimum wage make the natural rate higher; their declines in recent years thus make the natural rate lower. He emphasized that improvements in labor exchanges, in availability of information about job vacancies and labor supply, all of which have been enhanced by the Internet, tend to lower the natural rate. That, I contend, is what has happened. The natural rate of unemployment in advanced countries has fallen sharply since the Great Recession.

Janet Yellen in a speech in September 2017 raised the possibility that, indeed, the natural rate has fallen and perhaps by a lot:

> Some key assumptions underlying the baseline outlook could be wrong in ways that imply that inflation will remain low for longer than currently projected. For example, labor market conditions may not be as tight as they appear to be, and thus they may exert less upward pressure on inflation than anticipated.
>
> The unemployment rate consistent with long-run price stability at any time is not known with certainty; we can only estimate it. The median of the longer-run unemployment rate projections submitted by FOMC participants last week is around 4-1/2 percent. But the long-run sustainable unemployment rate can drift over time because of demographic changes and other factors, some of which can be difficult to quantify—or even identify—in real time. For these and other reasons, the statistical precision of such estimates is limited, and the actual value of the sustainable rate could well be noticeably lower than currently projected.[6]

At the press conference following the FOMC rate increase decision on March 21, 2018, the new Fed chairman Jay Powell in response to a reporter's question as to whether he was satisfied by the current pace of wage growth said the following:

> As the market is tightened, as labor markets have tightened, and we hear reports of labor shortages that we see that, you know, groups of unemployed are diminishing, and the unemployment rate is going down, we haven't seen, you know, higher wages, wages going up more. And I would—I think I've been surprised by that, and I think others have as well. In terms of what's the right level, I don't think I have a view on what the right level of wages is, but I think we will know that the labor market is getting tight when we do see a more meaningful upward move in wages.[7]

Even in 2018, ten years in, they really don't have much of a clue as to what is going on in the labor market. At a speech at an ECB forum in June 2018, Jay Powell argued as follows:

Wage growth has been moderate, consistent with low productivity growth but also an indication that the labor market is not excessively tight. . . . What would be the consequences for inflation if unemployment were to run well below the natural rate for an extended period? The flat Phillips curve suggests that the implications for inflation might not be large, although a very tight labor market could lead to larger, nonlinear effects.

That wage explosion is really just around the corner. Actually, it isn't. Research from the Fed confirms that. Babb and Deitmeister find in their work that a noticeably higher inflation rate is only likely to emerge "once unemployment falls well below its current level" (2017, 16).

Staiger, Stock, and Watson examined the precision of estimates of the natural rate of unemployment. They note that the NAIRU "is commonly taken to be the rate of unemployment at which inflation remains constant. Unfortunately, the NAIRU is not directly observable. . . . The task of measuring the NAIRU is further complicated by the general recognition that, plausibly, the NAIRU has changed over the post-war period, perhaps as a consequence of changes in labor markets" (1997a, 195). They further note that "a wide range of values of the NAIRU are consistent with the empirical evidence" (1997a, 237) and, crucially, that the trigger point—when wages and prices start to rise—is poorly estimated. For example, they estimate a NAIRU for the United States of 6.2 percent in 1990 with a 95 percent confidence interval of 5.1 to 7.7 percent. In a different publication the same authors argue that the tightest of the 95 percent confidence intervals for 1994 in the United States is 4.8 to 6.6 percent. They conclude that "it is difficult to estimate the level of unemployment at which the curve predicts is constant rate of inflation" (1997b, 47). Doug Staiger is in the next office to me and is almost always right.

Standing By

It is my contention that the natural rate of unemployment in most advanced countries is well below 3 percent. Employment rates and participation rates can rise, and unemployment rates can fall and by a lot. Globalization has weakened workers' bargaining power. Migrant flows have put downward pressure on wages and greased the wheels of the labor market as their presence has increased mobility. The decline in the homeownership rate, which slows job creation and increases unemployment, has helped mobility and lowered the natural rate as has the influx of highly mobile migrants. The Great Recession exposed underlying weaknesses and exposed the possibility to the populace of catastrophic declines in house prices and pension pots. The balance between capital and labor shifted once again toward capital. Workers are frightened in a way that they weren't pre-recession. Hence the natural rate has fallen, and that is why there has been no spurt in wage growth as the unemployment rate fell from 10 to 8 percent; from 8 to 6 percent; and from 6 to 4 percent.

As William Beveridge noted in 1944, "full employment means that unemployment is reduced to short intervals of standing by, with the certainty that very soon one will be wanted in one's old job again or will be wanted in a new job that is within one's powers. . . . It means that the jobs are at fair wages, of such a kind, and so located that the unemployed men can reasonably be expected to take them: it means, by consequence, that the normal lag between losing one job and finding another will be short" ([1944] 1960, 18). We are a long way from that and we need to get there. I am standing by.

Beveridge also noted that "full employment means having more vacancies for workers than there are workers seeking vacancies," but "it does not mean having no unemployment at all" ([1944] 1960, 1).

It is my thesis in this book that there is no reason why unemployment couldn't surprise again on how low it can go. Full employment in advanced countries such as the United Kingdom and the United States is likely well below 3 percent. Already it is down to 3.3 percent in Germany in October 2018 without any obvious wage surge and seems set to go lower. It is 2.3 percent in Japan and nominal wages haven't grown in years. In December 2018 the lowest unemployment rate was 2.4 percent in Iowa with no obvious signs of a wage explosion. It was below 3 percent in nine other states: Hawaii (2.5%), New Hampshire (2.5%), Idaho (2.6%), North Dakota (2.7%), Vermont (2.7%), Minnesota (2.8%), Nebraska (2.8%), Virginia (2.8%), and South Dakota (2.9%). Thirty-two states had rates under 4 percent. Alaska had the highest rate at 6.3 percent.

Policymakers Have Endlessly Cried Wolf over Wage Growth

Policymakers in the UK have long been expecting wage growth to accelerate. For example, in the opening statement at the February 2018 press conference for the Bank of England's Inflation Report, Governor Mark Carney argued as follows: "The firming of shorter-term measures of wage growth in recent quarters, and a range of survey indicators that suggests pay growth will rise further in response to the tightening labour market, give increasing confidence that growth in wages and unit labour costs will pick up to target-consistent rates."[8]

Twelve months earlier, Governor Carney at the February 2017 press conference had argued, "Following a long period of consistently overestimating wage growth, the MPC has updated its view of the natural rate of unemployment. Specifically, the MPC now judges that the rate of unemployment the economy can achieve while being consistent with sustainable rates of wage growth to be around 4.5%, down from around 5% previously."[9]

The February 2018 Inflation Report reduced the MPC's estimate of the natural rate once again to 4.25 percent: "Based on a range of evidence, the MPC judges that the long-term equilibrium unemployment rate is around 4.25%, a little lower than judged a year ago and broadly in line with the current headline rate of unemployment."[10]

On February 21, 2018, the Bank of England's chief economist, Andy Haldane (wrongly, I argued at the time), continued the hopeful theme that wages were set to rocket: "The long-awaited—and we have been waiting for a long time—pickup in wages is starting to take root. We get intelligence from our agents that would suggest that wage settlements this year were going to pick up, perhaps to a number with a three in front of it, rather than a two in front of it."[11] He repeated that claim again in a subsequent speech later in 2018, but still not much action on the wage-growth front.[12]

They never give up. External MPC member Silvana Tenreyro seems to not care much about data at all but assumes wages are going to pick up anyway: "Many commentators have recently argued that the Phillips curve is no longer apparent in the data. . . . My view is that these fears are largely misplaced. . . . Successful monetary policy will make the Phillips curve harder to identify in the data. . . . I am unconvinced by reports of the death of the Phillips curve, so I expect this to translate into a pickup in domestic cost pressures."[13] I see no ships.

There had been a small pickup in settlements in 2018 reported by pay experts XpertHR. For 2018 they found that the median raise was 2.5 percent. This follows a seven-year stretch where pay awards were worth close to 2 percent. But by March 2019 XpertHR was reporting that employers were predicting that pay awards in 2019 would be at the same level as in 2018, at 2.5 percent in both services and manufacturing, driven by Brexit uncertainty. The Bank of England's agents in a special survey also found a pickup in 2018. The question is whether this is the start of a new constant at 2.5 percent as appears to have begun in the United States or the start of something bigger. This is pretty thin gruel to vote for rate rises on.

Flat Bits

Another way of looking at wage dynamics is through the Phillips curve, which Bill Phillips in his 1958 *Economica* article plotted as wage changes against the unemployment rate. The title of the article tells it all: "The Relation between Unemployment and the Rate of Change of Money Wage Rates in the United Kingdom, 1861–1957." Figure 11.1A plots U.S. monthly annual private-sector hourly wage growth for private-sector production and non-supervisory workers (PNSW) against the unemployment rate for the pre-recession period from January 1998 to December 2007. I also include the equation of the linear best-fit line, which is +7.3348 – .809 * unemployment rate. Plugging in an unemployment rate of 3.9%, as observed in April 2000, and in July 2018, for example, predicts wage growth of 7.3348 – (.809 * 3.8) = 4.3%.

Figure 11.1B plots U.S. monthly private-sector hourly annualized wage growth for PNSW against the underemployment rate U7 for the recovery period from January 2011 to October 2018. The best-fit line now is 3.4564 – .2885 * unemployment rate. Plugging in the current U7 underemployment rate of 2.9%, as observed in May 2018, predicts wage growth of 3.4564 – (0.2885 * 2.9) = 2.6%. If we plug in the lowest observed U7 rate of 2.3% observed in six separate months in 2000 we still only get wage growth of 2.8%, not anywhere close to 4%. As the U.S. economy approached full employment we would expect to see wage growth pick up faster than that.[14]

Ewald Nowotny, who sits on the Governing Council at the European Central Bank, put it punchily: "There's a big international discussion about why wages react so slowly to downward changes in the unemployment rate—

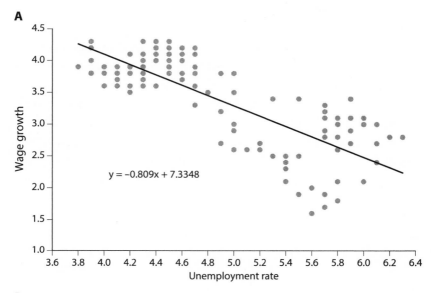

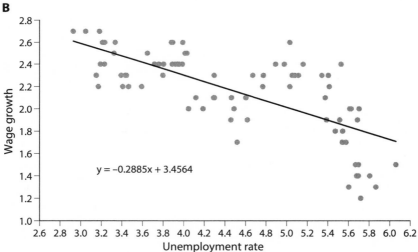

Figure 11.1. (A) U.S. hourly wage Phillips curve of production and non-supervisory workers, January 1998–December 2007. (B) U.S. hourly wage Phillips curve of production and non-supervisory workers, January 2011–October 2018. *Source:* BLS.

this is the famous Phillips curve problem. We had just recently a meeting at the Bank for International Settlements where Bill Dudley, the central-bank governor of New York, said that in the U.S. the Phillips curve now is 'flat as Kansas.' "[15] That is a bit of an exaggeration, but the Phillips curve is clearly flatter than it was post-recession compared with pre-recession.

In a recent speech external MPC member Gertjan Vlieghe argued that a credible Phillips curve still exists in the UK. His main evidence was a plot of wage changes against the unemployment rate, such as in the period 2001 through 2018. David Bell and I (2018b) argued this covered up major structural shifts as it does for the United States. Since 2008 the underemployment rate replaces the unemployment rate as the main measure of labor market slack.[16] Figure 11.2A covers Vlieghe's time period from January 2001 to May 2018 using data on total pay growth using single-month data. There is a downward-sloping Phillips curve for the entire period with a best-fit line with the equation of $y = -.7168x + 7.1158$. At the current unemployment rate U3 in May 2018 of 4.2% this predicts wage growth of $y = (-.7168 * 4) + 7.1158 = 4.2\%$ versus the actual of 2.5%. It may be credible, but it isn't much use for forecasting.

Figure 11.2B is for September 2014 to May 2018 and illustrates where the same wage-growth data are plotted against the U7 underemployment rate (part-time wants full-time/employment). The line of best fit is $y = +2.8374 - .1176 *$ unemployment rate. That predicts that wage growth at the most recent underemployment rate of 2.8% for August 2018 would be $y = +2.8374 - (.1176 * 2.8) = 2.5\%$. Using the lowest level of the underemployment rate of 1.9% that occurred in December 2004 predicts wage growth of only 2.6%. This seems the most appropriate way to model the post-recession Phillips curve given that the unemployment rate doesn't explain wages post-2008 whereas the underemployment rate does. The UK Phillips curve has flattened.

So, it looks awfully like the Phillips curve is shallower in the United States and the UK and likely elsewhere too. In a paper with my Dartmouth colleague Andy Levin (Blanchflower and Levin 2014), who was previously economic advisor to Janet Yellen and Ben Bernanke, we examined the impact of inactivity and underemployment on wages in the United States. The FOMC in our view underestimated the scale of slack in the labor market as did the MPC in the UK for broadly similar reasons. Both wrongly focused on the

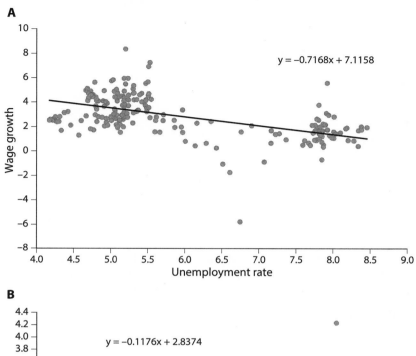

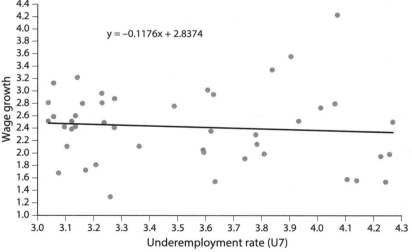

Figure 11.2. (A) UK AWE total pay single-month Phillips curve and the unemployment rate (U3), January 2001–May 2018. (B) UK AWE total pay single month and the under-employment rate (U7), September 2014–May 2018.

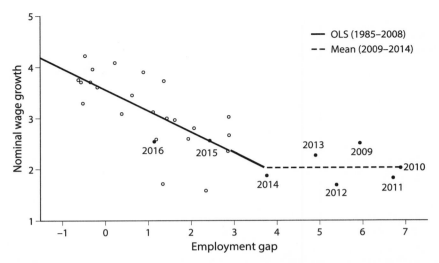

Figure 11.3. The wage curve. This figure shows the relationship between the annual average employment gap (expressed as a percent of the CBO's assessment of the potential labor force) and the twelve-month percent change in average hourly earnings of production and non-supervisory workers for each calendar year since 1985, with a label for each observation from 2009 to 2016. *Source:* Blanchflower and Levin 2014.

unemployment rate as the measure of slack. This was fine prior to 2008, but as I have shown in earlier chapters, this was not fine subsequently.

Figure 11.3 presents our interpretation of the relationship between nominal wage growth and the true unemployment rate (including underemployment and nonparticipation). I suspect that the wage curve is relatively flat at elevated levels of labor market slack, that is, a decline in slack does not generate any significant wage pressures, when the level of slack remains large. As noted above, our benchmark analysis indicates that the true unemployment rate is currently around 7 percent—a notable decline from its peak of more than 10 percent but still well above its longer-run normal level of around 5 percent. Thus, the shape of the wage curve can explain why nominal wage growth has remained stagnant at around 2 percent over the past few years even as the employment gap has diminished substantially. Moreover, our interpretation suggests that nominal wages will not begin to accelerate until labor market slack diminishes substantially further and the true unemployment rate approaches its longer-run normal level of around 5 percent.

The average hourly earnings of production and non-supervisory workers decelerated sharply during the recession and then remained at a plateau of around 2 percent despite the strengthening job market. This pattern Andy and I noted was consistent with other evidence of downward nominal wage rigidity, which essentially flattens out the "wage curve" at high levels of labor market slack. Moreover, our analysis indicated that nominal wage growth would pick up noticeably once the employment gap diminished further, and that's exactly what's been observed more recently.

The technical explanation of the employment gap is in fact the sum of three specific components. First, the unemployment gap is the deviation of the conventional unemployment rate labeled U3 by the BLS from professional forecasters' consensus projections of its longer-run normal rate (as reported in semi-annual Blue-Chip surveys). Second, the participation gap is the deviation (in percentage points) of the actual size of the labor force from CBO assessments of the potential labor force; this shortfall corresponds to the notion of "hidden unemployment" (that is, people who are not actively searching but who would rejoin the workforce if the job market were stronger). Third, the underemployment gap takes the BLS measure of people working part-time for economic reasons (expressed as a fraction of the potential labor force) as a deviation from its 1994–2007 average and then converts this deviation into full-time equivalent (FTE) jobs.

Indeed, for the year 2015, the average employment gap was about 2.5 percent of the potential labor force, while nominal earnings increased 2.6 percent. As shown in figure 11.3, that outcome is precisely in line with the implications of the wage curve fitted to the previous data from 1984 through 2014. The estimate for 2016 was below what the fitted wage curve would suggest. The U.S. economy is a long way from full employment and that is why so many are hurting. Trump called it right.

Learning from the Past

It seems to me we should learn from the lessons of the past. The puzzle for central bankers, who are trying to drive inflation down and increase unemployment by raising rates as in the case of the Fed in the United States or threatening to do so in the case of the Bank of England, is that the models keep telling them there is about to be lots of price and wage inflation. Their problem is there isn't any. They have wrongly concluded full employment is close by.

Central banks have been using models that are primarily driven by what happened in the 1970s, and the economists who play with them simply can't

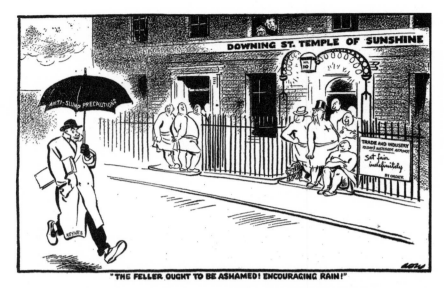

Figure 11.4. "The feller ought to be ashamed! Encouraging rain!" This is a famous cartoon by David Low printed in the UK *Evening Standard* on January 5, 1938, depicting the residences of the UK prime minister at #10 Downing Street and of the Chancellor of the Exchequer at #11. As background, the Treasury view was that fiscal policy had no effect on the total amount of economic activity and unemployment, even during times of economic recession. This view was most famously advanced in the 1930s by the staff of the British Chancellor of the Exchequer. In 2010 the UK Chancellor George Osborne implemented huge public spending cuts that he argued would result in an expansionary fiscal contraction but resulted in the slowest peacetime recovery in three hundred years since the South Sea Bubble. Depicted in the cartoon are John Maynard Keynes, Prime Minister Neville Chamberlain, Chancellor of the Exchequer Viscount John Allsebrook Simon, and the fictional character Colonel Blimp. The Treasury officials wrapped in towels at the Downing Street "Temple of Sunshine" next to a sign that the weather is "set fair indefinitely" are saying the feller ought to be ashamed for encouraging rain. Keynes is holding up an umbrella with the words "anti-slump precautions" on it. Top left the storm clouds are gathering. I showed the cartoon to Ben Bernanke when I met with him in his office at the Fed. *Source:* Copyright © David Low / Solo Syndication.

figure out why there is no inflation. So they are trying to drive the unemployment rate up because they just know inflation is about to take off even though it hasn't for years. Things are different nowadays.

Once economies reach full employment workers will be standing by as in the past, waiting for decent job offers. That is not happening now. The elites have kept saying inflation is set to explode but they have been wrong so many times, why believe them now? The problem is both price inflation and wage inflation are too low, not too high. Past remedies have failed. Now is the time for a big rethink.

One way to get toward full employment would be, as Larry Summers suggests (2018), to raise the 2 percent inflation target that exists around the world, in the United States, Canada, and the UK, for example, to something higher. Other possibilities include price-level or nominal GDP targets, as set out by Wessel (2018), but these amount to much the same thing, currently, as they would keep rates lower for longer. Summers argues that the Fed's logic in setting the target at 2 percent involves trading off what are seen as the costs of inflation and the benefits of avoiding deflation. In the last decade, he rightly points out, the costs of deflation have increased: "If deflation risks look considerably greater than they did in the 1990s and the costs of inflation look about the same, it follows that whatever inflation target was appropriate then is too low today" (2018, 2). With a higher inflation target the Fed would likely not be raising rates in 2018. Summers believes the current framework is "singularly brittle" and suggests that there is no evidence that the costs of running 3 percent rather than 2 percent inflation are especially large. I agree. The current framework has severe consequences for ordinary folk.

The fix is to get the unemployment rate in advanced countries down to levels not seen since the 1940s and 1950s; this can plausibly be done. Full employment is nowhere near the 4.5 percent or so that policymakers including at the Fed, the U.S. central bank, and the MPC in the UK seem to believe. That would be running an economy on a full tank. If we were anywhere close to full employment so many people wouldn't be hurting and hating, and wages would start to rise again. My experience at universities is that fights in departments occur when there is a lack of resources. The NAIRU pre-2008 was likely around 4.5 percent and in my view has now dropped to around an unemployment rate of 2.5 percent.[17]

Everyone wants a good, well-paying job. That is most likely to be delivered when workers are standing by for job offers at full employment. It is unclear where that point is exactly, but it is clear at the time of writing at the end of 2018 that we are not there yet.

CHAPTER 12

Put the Pedal to the Metal

The weakness of wage growth has continued to be a surprise to policymakers. At a press conference following the rate increase decision at the FOMC meeting on June 13, 2018, Fed chairman Jay Powell said, "We had anticipated, and many people have anticipated that wages—that in a world where we're hearing lots and lots about labor shortages—everywhere we go now, we hear about labor shortages, but where is the wage reaction? So, it's a bit of a puzzle. I wouldn't say it's a mystery, but it's a bit of a puzzle. And one of the things is, you will see pretty much people who want to get jobs—not everybody—but people who want to get jobs, many of them will be able to get jobs. You will see wages go up."[1]

Hope springs eternal. The projections from the September 2018 meeting showed that the FOMC members thought that the long-run value for unemployment, its natural rate, is in the range of 4.0–4.6 percent.[2] With the unemployment rate at 3.7 percent there surely, according to the FOMC, should have been roaring wage pressure, and fear of a wage explosion is one of the main reasons the Fed raised rates. The fact that there is little sign of wage growth picking up is neither a puzzle nor a mystery. The FOMC appears to have underestimated the amount of labor market slack.

Policymakers at the start of 2019 seem just as out of touch with what is going on outside the big cities as they were as the Great Recession was nearing. Too few of them have much idea that the NAIRU has likely fallen and or know why wage growth isn't skyrocketing. I recall having the same discussions at the MPC in June 2008. The FOMC raised rates based on no data. As I showed in chapter 5, the puzzle is largely solved; elevated levels of underemployment continue to push down on wages. Turning points are hard to call. Downside risks abound.

I went to talk to the *Guardian* editorial board and when we were done they presented me with the original of the cartoon in figure 12.1 that appeared on December 11, 2008. A "leaving do" is a farewell party, which I didn't have when I left the Bank of England. I voted to cut rates at every meeting from October 2007 through my last meeting in May 2008. Mervyn King was glad to see the back of me.

The economics of walking about suggests that economies are ticking along, although at a relatively slow pace. The United States looks to be the best of them. The concern is that a trade war may slow global trade. The introduction of tariffs in the Smoot-Hawley Tariff Act in the 1930s led to retaliation and disastrous consequences. Some progress has been made between Canada, the United States, and Mexico in the signing of the USMCA, which updates NAFTA. Progress was also apparently made at the G20 summit in Argentina when Trump and Xi agreed to a trade war ceasefire with a deal to suspend new trade tariffs. Trump will leave tariffs on $200 billion worth of Chinese imports at 10 percent at the beginning of the new year, agreeing to not raise them to 25 percent "at this time," the White House said in a statement. "China will agree to purchase a not yet agreed upon, but very substantial, amount of agricultural, energy, industrial, and other product from the United States to reduce the trade imbalance between our two countries," it said. "China has agreed to start purchasing agricultural product from our farmers immediately."[3] At the start of 2019 trade discussions between the United States and China were continuing.

The *New York Times* has reported that even the White House's own analysis from the President's Council of Economic Advisers has found that tariffs will hurt growth, as officials continue to insist otherwise![4] You couldn't make this up. Then Larry Kudlow, Donald Trump's chief economic advisor, accused Canadian prime minister Justin Trudeau of undermining the United States and its allies with comments he made at the G7 summit. Peter Navarro, a trade advisor to President Donald Trump, said, "There's a special place in hell for any foreign leader that engages in bad faith diplomacy with President Donald J. Trump and then tries to stab him in the back on the way out the door." Analogously, in February 2019 European Council President Donald Tusk warned of a "special place in hell" for those who pushed for Brexit "without even a sketch of a plan."[5]

Figure 12.1. "David Blanchflower to step down from Bank of England next year." This cartoon by the famous British political/economic cartoonist Kipper Williams appeared in the *Guardian* on December 11, 2008, just after I announced I would not be looking to renew my three-year term. For the uninitiated a "leaving do" is British slang for a farewell party. In the end I voted to cut rates at every meeting from October 2007 through March 2009, mostly alone, and after that, once the bank rate hit 0.5 percent, I voted for asset purchases in April and May 2009 of £125 billion, so I was the cutter in chief! I did not have a leaving do; I was offered one but declined. I wanted to get out of there as soon as I could. Prime Minister Gordon Brown rang me later and apologized for appointing me "to that awful job." *Source:* Kipper Williams, *The Guardian*, December 11, 2008.

Trump imposed tariffs such that every foreign company that sends steel and aluminum to the United States, including Canadian firms, would be forced to pay a 25 percent tariff on steel and a 10 percent tariff on aluminum.[6] Canada and other allies such as the UK apparently are national security threats to the United States. Then Trump imposed tariffs on $34 billion worth of Chinese goods, prompting a swift response from the Chinese and kicked off an unpredictable trade war. Farmers have been complaining that they are being hurt irreparably by the imposition of tariffs in retaliation for the tariffs being imposed on China and our allies. More than half of America's soybean exports go to China. The Trump administration is now proposing to employ $12 billion in emergency funds from the Department of Agriculture to subsidize losses of U.S. farmers resulting from the imposition of retaliatory tariffs, specifically on soybeans, pork, sorghum, corn, wheat, cotton, and dairy products, just to name a few. The administration is employing the Depression-era facility called the Commodity Credit Corporation (CCC), which was established to fund payments to farmers as part of a three-part program that includes direct assistance, the purchase of surplus agricultural products, and trade promotion of agricultural products.[7] U.S. exports of soybean to China were down 98 percent in 2018.[8]

Tariffs have already hurt Harley-Davidson's earnings; tariffs are expected to cost them $45–55 million in 2018. General Motors says commodity inflation pushed their costs up $300 million in its latest quarter from a year ago. Whirlpool says its costs will rise about $350 million in 2018. Coca-Cola hiked up prices in response to an increase in costs from freight to the metal used in Coke cans. Ford estimates that the tariffs will cost an estimated $500–600 million in 2018.[9] Oh, what a mess. Trade wars loom.

Some of the boost to the economy from the tax cuts implemented by the GOP will likely be negated by the slowing of the economy from the new tariffs. How much remains unclear. It is notable that the tax cuts are widely unpopular, which is why Republicans did not run on them in the November 2018 midterm elections. A poll from Monmouth University found 34 percent of adults approve of the tax cut now, a slide from January when adults were about evenly split between approving and disapproving.[10] In June 2018 in a POLITICO/Morning Consult poll, 37 percent of registered voters said they supported the tax-cut law, down from 44 percent in an April poll.[11]

U.S. GDP growth for 2018 Q2 came in at a frisky 4.1 percent annualized versus an upwardly revised 2.2 percent in Q1. Newt Gingrich argued that

President Trump "has once again achieved the impossible."[12] Trump claimed that "Americans are enjoying the best economy ever." Josh Boak and Christopher Rugaber from the AP noted that was not true: "His boast of record achievements on the economy and jobs ignores the Roaring Twenties, the war-time boom in the 1940s, the 1990s expansion and other times when unemployment was lower than now, economic growth was higher than now, or brisk productivity made the U.S. the world's economic powerhouse."[13]

The advance estimate data release for GDP growth in 2018 Q3 was published on October 29, 2018, just before the midterm elections on November 6, and it was good, but lower at 3.5 percent annualized rate. The U.S. economy is expected to slow from here. In its January 2019 World Economic Outlook Update the IMF estimated growth of 2.9 percent in 2018 and forecast 2.5 percent in 2019 and 1.8 percent in 2020.

Turning back now to the UK, Brexit has consistently ranked at or near the top of the list of the risks identified in the Deloitte survey of UK chief financial officers. In the Bank of England's own quarterly Decision Makers' Panel, around 40 percent of firms consistently identify Brexit as a major source of uncertainty, with less than 20 percent viewing it as unimportant. The MPC has called Brexit the biggest downside risk to the UK economy.

Support for Brexit appears to be hemorrhaging in the UK. A poll taken by Sky Data in July 2018 found that fully two-thirds of the public—including a majority of Leave voters—think the outcome of Brexit negotiations will be bad for Britain.[14] Most people would like to see a referendum asking for voters to choose between the deal suggested by the government, no deal, and remaining in the EU. Seventy-eight percent of respondents said they thought the government was doing a bad job negotiating Brexit. Thirty-one percent said they thought Brexit would be good for them personally compared with 42 percent saying it would be bad. Fifty-two percent said it would be bad for the economy while 35 percent said it would be good. Reports that the government is stockpiling food and medicines in case of a no-deal Brexit likely haven't helped. The *Washington Post* reported on the difficulty British farmers are having finding British applicants to pick crops—out of 10,000 applicants, two were British.[15]

I was on Bloomberg TV on November 27, 2018, with Bloomberg's Stephanie Flanders talking about the release that was expected any time from the Bank of England on its evaluation of the economic consequences of an abrupt Brexit. While we were live the news of the analysis came over the wires. It was shocking, showing that in the worst-case, "disorderly" apocalyptic scenario the bank expected that output would fall around 8 percent, the unemployment rate would rise to 7.5 percent, and house prices would drop 30 percent by the end of 2023.[16] In addition, under the disorderly scenario, the pound would fall 25 percent and be close to dollar parity, inflation would rise because of the reduction in supply, and net migration would decline to around minus 100,000. In response the bank argued that the MPC would respond by raising the bank rate from the current 0.75 percent to 5.5 percent.

My immediate reaction was, "When they talk about a huge drop in output and the Bank of England is going to raise rates to 5 percent MPC members will be thinking about a huge drop in output, which might well not be an argument to raise rates."[17] That would make matters much worse for ordinary people. I would be voting for rate cuts in those circumstances. Even Paul Krugman tweeted that the analysis made no sense: "I'm anti-Brexit, and have no doubt that it will make Britain poorer. And the BoE could be right about the magnitude. But they've really gone pretty far out on a limb here."

The Brexiters soon turned on Governor Carney. Jacob Rees-Mogg said that Carney, whom he had dubbed the "high priest of project fear," was a "second-tier Canadian politician" who "failed" to get a job at home. Carney spent the next few days trying to defend the Bank of England's independence. I have some sympathy with ex-MPC member Andrew Sentance's view that "the Bank of England is undermining its credibility and independence by giving such prominence to these extreme scenarios and forecasts." Too much belief in models and too little common sense. Another disaster for the Bank of England. A week is a long time in economics.

The latest polling in the United States on the direction the country is going is summarized by Real Clear Politics (RCP).[18] At the beginning of February 2019 RCP reported that the average of the last twelve polls showed that 33.5 percent of Americans said the country was headed in the right direction versus 58.8 percent opposed. A Eurobarometer survey asked respondents in EU countries in November 2017 whether they thought their country was going in the right direction, the wrong direction, or neither. The proportion saying in the right direction was as reported in figure 12.2. Over two-thirds of respondents are supportive in Portugal, while Greece (20.1%), Croatia (8.9%), Italy (10.7%), and Spain (15.8%) are least likely to report that way (May 2018 unemployment rates are in parentheses). Only a quarter in the UK thought positively about the economy at the end of 2017.

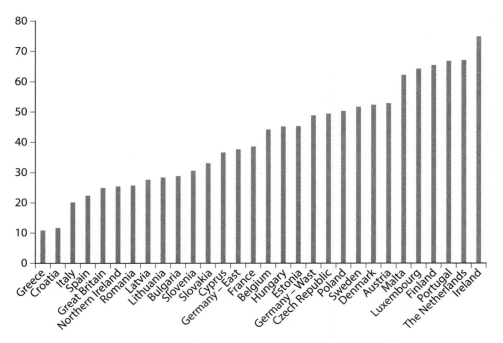

Figure 12.2. Percent saying the country is going in the right direction, EU28, 2017.

The question is, how far away is a recession? George Magnus pointed out that the current expansion in the United States, from the last trough in activity in June 2009, has now overtaken the expansion from February 1961 to December 1969 to be the second longest ever.[19] Assuming it keeps going until June 2019, which it may not, it will become the longest recovery ever, overtaking the 120-month expansion from 1991 to 2001. The average length of the twelve expansions since 1945, Magnus notes, has been 58.4 months and in the three cycles since 1991 the average was 95 months. The prospect of the economy slowing before the November 2020 presidential election, in my view, is likely better than 60/40: recoveries do not go on forever.[20] U.S. recoveries usually end because the Federal Reserve raises rates too soon, as they have continued to do in 2018.

We need to ask ourselves what now, given that central banks have fewer arrows in their economic quivers than they had when the Great Recession hit? In 2008 interest rates were around 5 percent and there was room to cut them to zero and even below. Right now central banks do not have that much room to maneuver. Congress is unlikely to act swiftly in the face of any downturn, and similarly in the UK, which is preoccupied with Brexit. The risks look to be to the downside. The left-behinds look set to continue to be left behind. Nobody has apologized for messing up.

Don't Let Things Drift

Tom Clark and Anthony Heath (2014) in their impressive and fascinating book documented who had been hurt and how by the Great Recession. The modern world, they argue, has been hit by an economic tornado that was not quite 1933; there has been no General Strike and no Jarrow March.[21] The fifty Brexit supporters marching from Sunderland to London in 2019, led by Nigel Farage, who left after a few miles, don't count. The book's theme is that the deep societal problems laid bare by the recession—problems of anxiety and isolation—were always more structural than cyclical. A rich country, they argue, should be perfectly able to endure getting a bit poorer during a passing downturn. The UK, they suggest, and I agree, didn't run into all the dislocation they uncovered because the crisis suddenly created frailty in downtrodden communities. It simply exposed underlying problems with deep roots in the long decades before, when inequality had run out of control. Clark and Heath also note that what happened post-recession had deep roots in the past, which has broad applicability across advanced countries: "It would be going too far to claim that all the real damage was done before the recession and was merely revealed by the downturn: we have seen that the purely recessionary surge in unemployment had profound and unhappy consequences for well-being. But the wider mood of anxiety that defines those hard times undoubtedly has deeper roots" (2014, 221–22).

As I noted in my review of their book, its theme is that "the deep societal problems laid bare by the recession—problems of anxiety and isolation—were always more structural than cyclical. A rich country, they argue, should be perfectly able to endure getting a bit poorer, during a passing downturn. The UK, they argue, and I agree, didn't run into all the dislocation they uncovered because the crisis suddenly created frailty in downtrodden communities. It simply exposed underlying problems with deep roots in the long decades before, when inequality had run out of control" (2015a, 579). Flickers of "depressionary social psychology," Clark and Heath argue, applied in the 1930s when cigarettes and cinema tickets were about the only goods with rising sales. They noted that during the Great Recession Britons developed a taste for more sugary and fattier foods. Shoppers switched to supermarket brands, drinking less in the pub and cooking with leftovers, doing more home cooking, more mending of clothes instead of buying new ones, and growing their own vegetables. Clark and Heath also provided evidence that people substituted processed foods for fruit and vegetables, resulting in a decrease in the nutritional quality of calories consumed.[22]

Clark and Heath (2014) warn that we should not underestimate the damage that hard times can do because there can be an enduring cost to letting things drift. Jobs, they argue, are at the heart of resolving hard times. These are harsh times, indeed. But they didn't have to be.

Le Pen, Brexit, and Trump provided alternative narratives for those who were left behind by economic change. They were told it wasn't their fault. These were the people who were bypassed by the march of progress, globalization, and technology. The elites told them they were ignorant, racist bigots. They needed to get with the program and to get with gay marriage and affirmative action and Black Lives Matter. Arguments in the United States over LGBTQ bathrooms were the last straw. Everyone in their town thought Hillary Clinton was a crook.

It was the fault of immigrants, job-killing regulations, Muslims, trade deals, TPP, NAFTA, and the EPA. The mainstream media, what Rush Limbaugh calls the "drive-by media," and their fake news were culpable. It was the European Union's, China's, and Mexico's fault and especially it was immigrants who were rapists, robbers, thugs, and different. Building the wall was a great way of sticking it in the face of Hillary and her liberal entourage. It was about sovereignty in the UK, taking back power from Europe, but mostly it was about blaming everyone else for the hurt that was deep inside. Making America Great Again meant bringing back high-paying union jobs to coal and steel towns. Trump supporters hadn't been abroad and had no inclination to change that. Most had no idea where Paris was even if they were told it wasn't Paris, Texas.

The left-behinds resented being thought of as stupid. Populism was a way out. It meant they could shift the blame. They love it that Trump irritates the left. They dislike outsiders. They hate it that the left, according to Bill O'Reilly and Fox News, has been trying to abolish Christmas and make everyone say "happy holidays." Political correctness is anathema to rural America. Trump told them that Obama was a Kenyan-born Muslim and an illegitimate black president, and they believed him and many still do. They believe in creationism and never went to the Harvard Natural History Museum, which in the entrance says if you believe in creationism don't enter. They built their own $100 million replica of Noah's ark in Kentucky instead.[23] Trump gave flyover America a chance to get their own back on the exam-taking classes. That made them feel better. This was deeply cultural.

Refugees who might turn into terrorists at the drop of a hat represented a growing threat, even though the chances of an American being killed by a terrorist over the last decade were lower than being hit by a falling piano. It also turned out that the probability of being killed by a refugee terrorist was less than that of being killed by a shark, an asteroid, an earthquake, or a tornado; choking on food; or being stung by hornets, wasps, or bees.[24]

Brexit meant bringing back prosperity to declining coal, steel, and seaside towns. Boris Johnson, who became UK foreign secretary and recently resigned over Theresa May's Chequers Brexit plan, complained about EU laws that determined the power of vacuum cleaners and what shape bananas had to be; he said such policies were "crazy."[25] Sovereignty meant that you could have any shape banana you want. Brexit was about holding your head up and not being beholden to others. Many yearn for the days of empire and long-lost glories.

I keep asking myself how Trump and the Brexiters could promise so much with so little chance of delivering. There was no chance on God's green earth that a wall was going to be built along the entire southern border. There was even less chance that Mexico was going to pay a dime toward it. As Eugene Robinson noted, "The idea of a 2,000-mile, 30-foot-high, 'big, beautiful' wall along the entire border was always more of a revenge fantasy than an actual proposal."[26] Republican congressmen and senators representing districts along the border oppose the wall. Representative Will Hurd (R-Texas), whose district includes 820 miles along the Mexican border, actively opposes its construction.

There was no way Donald Trump was going to pay off the debt in four or was it eight years? There was zero chance they were ever going to "lock her up." I was struck by the details of an ABC/*Washington Post* poll taken on April 17–20, 2017, that asked: "Do you (regret supporting Trump) or do you (think that supporting Trump was the right thing to do) in that election?" Only 2 percent said they regretted supporting Trump. Seventy-seven percent of Republicans said that Trump is in touch with the concerns of most people in the United States today; 65 percent of Republican voters said that he had done better than they expected in his first 100 days; and 80 percent said he had "done a great deal."[27] Trump was right when he said he could walk down Fifth Avenue and shoot someone and wouldn't lose support. He changed the narrative.

I realized on reading this survey that it didn't matter to his supporters if Trump was unable to create lots of jobs or build a wall. It didn't matter that he didn't have a plan to beat ISIS. The swamp wasn't going to drain and wouldn't go away readily but DJT was on the job. All would be forgiven as it was clear he had tried but it was all the fault of the Democrats, the drive-by media, and the elites. There are plenty of excuses. It doesn't matter that Trump hadn't managed to pass any of the ten pieces of legislation he had promised he would pass in his first one hundred days. This was all about not feeling stupid. Now there were plenty of people to blame—the left-wing fake media and the demonstrators who were all paid by George Soros despite there being no evidence to support such a contention.

In July 2018 nearly nine out of ten Republicans supported Trump. In a new article Montagnes, Peskowita, and McCrain (forthcoming) argue that people who identify as Republican may stop doing so if they disapprove of Trump. There seems to be some evidence in support of this thesis. There has been a decline of around 4 percentage points in GOP identification since the 2016 election in various polls from 28–29 percent of voters identifying as Republican to 25–26 percent.

Polling from NBC/Marris in July 2018 indicated that three key battleground states are worried about Trump's prospects of reelection in 2020. In Michigan, which Trump won by 11,000 votes, 36 percent of voters approve of Trump's job performance while 54 percent disapprove. In Wisconsin, which Trump won by 23,000 votes, 3 percent approve with 52 percent disapproving. In Minnesota, which Trump narrowly lost by 1.5 percentage points, his rating is 3 percent for, 51 percent against.[28]

It didn't matter that there was no £350 million a week to distribute to the NHS as the Brexiters claimed. The fact that the post-Brexit economy wasn't working well was the fault of the "Remoaners." It was the unreasonable behavior of the rest of the EU, especially Spain, which wanted to take Gibraltar if Brexit happened, just as the Argentinians—the Argies—tried to snatch the Falklands.[29] Ex-leader of the Tory Party Lord Michael Howard suggested that Prime Minister May should send out an armada: "Thirty-five years ago, this week, another woman prime minister sent a taskforce halfway across the world to defend the freedom of another small group of British people against another Spanish-speaking country, and I'm absolutely certain that our current prime minister will show the same resolve in standing by the people of Gibraltar." And Defence Secretary Sir Michael Fallon said the UK was prepared to go "all the way" to keep the Rock out of Spain's clutches.[30] Good Lord.

A YouGov poll taken in the UK on January 16, 2019, asked, "If there were a referendum today on whether or not the UK should remain a member of the EU, how would you vote?" Fifty-six percent said remain, 44 percent said leave. They were also asked, "Thinking about Brexit, would you now support or oppose a public vote on Britain's future relationship with the rest of the European Union?" Fifty-six percent supported and 43 percent opposed.

We Were Never All in This Together

On October 6, 2009, then Shadow Chancellor of the Exchequer George Osborne gave a speech to the Tory Party Conference outlining what austerity would look like. Seven months later he was chancellor and the cuts began. His broken promises still haunt me. Seven times in that speech he claimed, "We are all in this together": "I want my children to think that our generation paid off its debts, valued its savers, rewarded responsibility, invested in their future. And because I want it for my children, I want it for your children too. I want it for everyone's children. Because we are all in this together."[31] We weren't by a long shot.

At his 2010 spending review Chancellor Osborne insisted that those with the broadest shoulders should bear the greatest burden. The combined impact of direct tax and cash transfer changes was mostly regressive, moving income from poorer households to those who were better-off. After 2010–11, real spending on pensioners rose, for example, but it fell for children.

On April 19, 2017, George Osborne, the architect of austerity, accepted the job as editor of the *Evening Standard* and announced he would not stand as an MP in the June 2017 election. My friend, the always excellent Polly Toynbee, made clear what his legacy is:

Even as he said "all in it together" he cast the cruelest cuts on those with least. He set about denigrating disabled people as no other Tory government had done before, sending out stories of cheats running marathons to cover blatant, knowing cruelty. . . . Devious, malevolent and apparently indifferent to the consequences for millions of lives, Osborne has deliberately laid waste to the social security system. But far worse, he has demolished trust in it, undermining the idea that the state should support the weak, subsidize low-earners in housing they can afford or care for the sick. The fabric could be restored by future governments of good will but rebuilding lost public trust will be far harder.[32]

"All in it together" was a con.

The deep underlying causes of helplessness and hopelessness have not been addressed. Isolated people in fractured communities are susceptible to messages of hope. It is clear, though, as Case and Deaton (2017b) argue, that Americans are dying deaths of despair. They conclude that "the story is rooted in the labor market." In private communication Angus Deaton told me, "We didn't originally think so, but it really does look like the deteriorating labor market is the key, or at least one of them." Austerity along with attempts to balance budgets and cut entitlements in a recession made matters worse.

Trust and the Spreading of Hate

It is clear that trust, particularly in institutions, is waning, and there is a special distrust of elites.

Recall, of course, that the harshness of the Treaty of Versailles imposed on Germany after World War I led to a right-wing populist uprising that brought Hitler to power. In *The Economic Consequences of the Peace*, Keynes warned in 1920 of the consequences of the hardship that was being imposed.

Economic privation proceeds by easy stages, and so long as men suffer it patiently the outside world cares very little. Physical efficiency and resistance to disease slowly diminish, but life proceeds somehow, until the limit of human endurance is reached at last and counsels of despair and madness stir the sufferers from the lethargy which precedes the crisis. The man shakes himself, and the bonds of custom are loosed. The power of ideas is sovereign, and he listens to whatever instruction of hope, illusion, or revenge is carried to them in the air. . . . But who can say how much is endurable, or in what direction men will seek at last to escape from their misfortunes? (1920, 250–51)

As Robert Putnam in his insightful book *Bowling Alone* revealed, there has been "a steady withering of America's community bonds." The more integrated we are with our communities, Putnam noted, the less likely we are to experience colds, heart attacks, strokes, cancer, depression, and premature death of all sorts (2000, 327).

Social cohesion matters for health. Socially isolated people are more likely to smoke, drink, overeat, and engage in other health-damaging behaviors. As a rough rule of thumb, Putnam notes, if you belong to no groups but decide to join one, you cut your risk of dying over the next year in half (2000, 331). Social support, Putnam notes, also lessens depression.

Beginning in the late 1960s, Putnam and his coauthors write in *Better Together*, Americans began to "join less, trust less, give less, vote less and schmooze less" (2003, 4). They go on to note that the more neighbors who know one another by name, the fewer crimes a neighborhood as a whole will suffer. A child born in a state whose residents volunteer, vote, and spend time with friends is less likely to be born underweight, less likely to drop out of school, and less likely to kill or be killed than the same child—no richer or poorer—born in another state whose residents do not (2003, 269). Social ties bind. Putnam notes that the longer a kid lives in a bad neighborhood the worse the effects (2015, 217). We need to restore trust.

The European Social Survey shows that there has been a big decline in the UK in the proportion of people who meet socially with friends, relatives, or work colleagues at least once a week. This is down from 71 percent in 2002 to 61 percent in 2014.[33] In both the UK and the United States what Clark and Heath (2014) call the "gradual evolution of disadvantage" has taken place; the weak were hit more than the strong. In part as a matter of choice, politicians imposed austerity that hurt those at the bottom of the income distribution. I really can't see any other purpose; shrinking the state would inevitably hurt the poor. As I said in my review of their book in 2015, "The worst crisis in our lives is far from over; the concern is that things are soon going to get worse. These are certainly unusual times and harsh times. Something is deeply wrong. People are struggling to make ends meet. Politicians are making it harder for them. The discourse must change" (2015a, 582).

A cohesive society is one where citizens have confidence in others and public institutions. Today, trust is on the slide. Trust may affect economic performance, and policies can affect trust and well-being.[34] In the 1972 U.S. General Social Survey (GSS) around half of respondents said that "most people can be trusted." By 2016 only a third concurred. The OECD's "Society at a Glance" (OECD 2016) reports on trust in others by country. About 36 percent of interviewees expressed interpersonal trust. In Nordic countries over 60 percent of interviewees trust each other compared to less than 13 percent in Chile, Mexico, and Turkey. The UK and the United States are in the middle of the pack, with Germany higher and France lower.

An AP-GfK poll conducted in October 2013 found that Americans are suspicious of each other in everyday encounters.[35] Less than one-third expressed a lot of trust in clerks who swipe their credit cards, drivers on the road, or people they meet when traveling. Pew found that 19 percent of Millennials say most people can be trusted, compared with 31 percent of Gen Xers, 37 percent of Silents, and 40 percent of Boomers.[36] Just half of Americans (52%) say they trust all or most of their neighbors, while a similar share (48%) say they trust some or none of their neighbors, according to a 2016 Pew Research Center survey. Americans today are less likely to spend social evenings with their neighbors than in the past. In 1974, 61 percent of Americans said they would spend a social evening with someone in their neighborhood at least once a month, while 39 percent said they would do so less than once a month or not at all, according to the GSS. In 2014, fewer than half (46%) said they spend social evenings with their neighbors at least monthly, compared with 54 percent who do not.[37]

Trust in U.S. institutions slumped during Trump's first year in office.[38] According to the 2018 Edelman Trust Barometer, trust in the United States has suffered the largest-ever-recorded drop in the survey's history among the general population. Trust among the general population fell nine points to 43 percent, placing it in the lower quarter of the 28-country Trust Index. Trust among the informed public in the United States imploded, plunging 23 points to 45 percent, making it now the lowest of the 28 countries surveyed, below Russia and South Africa. The collapse of trust in the United States is driven by a staggering lack of faith in government, which fell 14 points to 33 percent among the general population, and 30 points to 33 percent among the informed public. The remaining institutions of business, media, and NGOs also experienced declines of 10 to 20 points. Richard Edelman, president and CEO of Edelman, said, "The root cause of this fall is the lack of objective facts and rational discourse."[39]

The finding of a decline in trust within the United States follows a report by Gallup that showed median approval of U.S. leadership across 134 countries fell from 48 to 30 percent in 2017.[40] Big losses of 10 percentage points or more occurred in 65 countries, including many U.S. allies. Portugal, Belgium, Norway, and Canada led the worldwide declines with approval dropping by at least 40 percentage points. In the UK only 33 percent approved of the performance of the leadership of the United States; the comparable values in other countries were 25 percent in France, 22 percent in Germany, and 20 percent in Canada.

In a Eurobarometer survey taken in November 2017, respondents were asked, "We would like to ask you a question about how much trust you have in certain institutions—national government and the European Union. For each of the following institutions, please tell me if you tend to trust it or tend not to trust it?" The results by country are set out in figure 12.3A for the two years (2007 and 2017) for views on trust of national government, ranked by 2017 levels, which show big falls in Greece, Spain, and France and rises elsewhere, including Portugal and Hungary. Figure 12.3B does the same for trust of the European Union; there are big falls in most countries. In the UK trust in the EU was low in both years, while Northern Ireland shows a fall from 2007 to 2017.

In another report published by the Joseph Rowntree Foundation, Dunatchik and coauthors found (2016) that 61 percent of people in the UK living on low incomes didn't trust politicians to tell the truth versus 50 percent of the higher-income group. When asked if "public officials don't much care about what people like me think," 39 percent of the low-income group said they "strongly agree" versus 19 percent of the high-income group. In response to the question "People like me don't have any say in what the government does," 38 percent of the low-income group strongly agreed versus 22 percent of the high-income group. As *Guardian* columnist Rafael Behr has noted: "Britain is strangled by barbed-wire fences of class, region, wealth, faith, age, the urban, the rural, Leavers and Remainers."[41]

In its 2017 Global Attitudes Survey, Pew asked respondents in thirty-eight countries, developed and developing, about their well-being and their

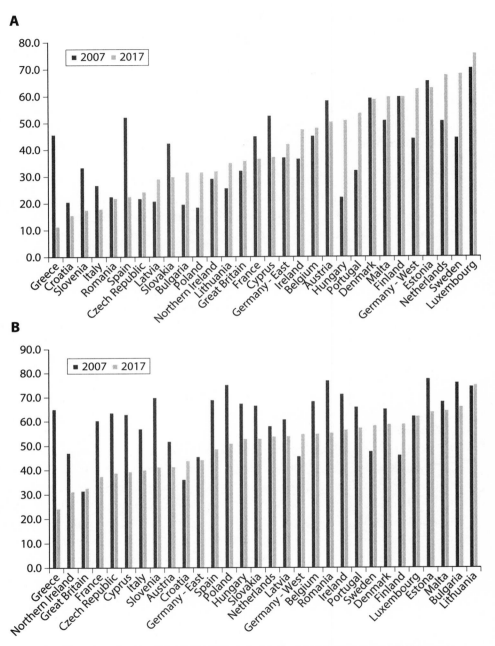

Figure 12.3. (A) Percentage of those who trust their national government. (B) Percentage of those who trust the European Union.

trust in their government.[42] The data are available for download. I am particularly interested in the responses to three questions:

> Question #1: "In general, would you say life in (survey country) today is better, worse, or about the same as it was fifty years ago for people like you?"
>
> Question #2: "When children today in (survey country) grow up, do you think they will be better off or worse off financially than their parents—better off; worse off; or the same?"
>
> Question #3: "How much do you trust the national government to do what is right for (survey country)—a lot, somewhat, not much, or not at all?"

Below I report the percentages saying "better" to question #1; "better off" to question #2; and "not much" or "not at all" to question #3, with respondents who said "don't know" or who refused to answer excluded from the calculations, for twelve advanced countries.

	Question #1	Question #2	Question #3
	(% life "better")	(% children "better off")	(% trust government "not much" or "not at all")
Australia	53	25	51
Canada	58	25	32
France	34	9	79
Germany	68	38	30
Greece	28	21	87
Italy	24	25	74
Japan	68	20	41
Netherlands	67	36	29
Spain	63	25	82
Sweden	66	45	33
United Kingdom	49	25	50
United States	43	38	48

It is apparent that in countries that were hit hard by the recession, for example, France, Greece, and Italy especially, more than two-thirds say that people "like you" are no better-off in 2017 than they were in 1967. More than half said that in the UK and the United States. The majority of respondents in every country don't believe that children will be as well off as their parents. Perhaps not surprisingly, trust in government is low when people are hurting and many have lost hope for the future of their kids.

It takes time to change the culture and rebuild communities. Putnam, Feldstein, and Cohen (2003) are right that we are better together. Now is the moment to try to rebuild our social capital. It is time to stop the breaking apart. Putnam (2015, 228) notes that it took several decades for economic malaise to undermine family structures. It will take decades to reconstruct them. Heckman and coauthors (2009), for example, have noted that investments in early childhood education convey high rates of return of 7–10 percent. It is hard to see what arguments there are against it.

In private communication, the always brilliant and insightful Robert Putnam told me, "The long-term crisis of the older manufacturing communities has undermined community morale and fractured old assumptions about self-worth. . . . These are people deeply anxious and angry about the decay of their communities not just upset that they personally lost their job. . . . Isolated people (isolated older white less educated guys, especially) in socially isolated or fragmented communities are much more vulnerable to Trumpism."

Going forward we are going to have to build ties that bind. Trust has to be rebuilt. Hate has to go. As a first step something has to be done about inequality and the overall sense of unfairness that is in the air. Too many people have been left behind. Little has changed, and these problems are going to persist going forward especially as Trump and Brexit fail to deliver on their promises. A storm of fury may well be on the horizon. I see little sign that any of this is going to change any time soon or that anything will be done to right these wrongs.

The lies need to be challenged. The BBC's Emily Maitlis distilled the challenge when she demolished Sean Spicer, the former White House press secretary, with a simple description of the lies he told about the crowds on the mall at Donald Trump's inauguration: "You joked about it when you presented the Emmy awards. But it wasn't a joke. It was the start of the most corrosive culture. You played with the truth. You led us down a dangerous path. You have corrupted discourse for the entire world by going along with these lies."[43] Richard Wolfe is right. The lies need to stop.[44] The guilty plea of Michael Cohen where he implicated the president in campaign finance illegalities and the conviction of Paul Manafort on the same day, August 21, 2018, look like important turning points. The Democrats have gained chairmanships of vital House committees and consequently subpoena power. It doesn't look, from thirty thousand feet, that peace and harmony are about to break out.

Green Eggs and Ham: Pitchforks to the Ready

Thorstein Veblen in his 1899 book *The Theory of the Leisure Class* made it very clear that the rich care about what he called conspicuous consumption. Conspicuous consumption means spending money on luxury goods and services to display economic power. The poor notice. Sir Philip Green bought British Home Stores (BHS), which I remember from my childhood as a rather rundown department store, in 2000 for £200 million. It didn't perform well, and he sold it for £1 and eventually it closed with the loss of 11,000 jobs. Despite the deficit of £571 million in the BHS pension scheme, Green and his family collected £586 million in dividends, rental payments, and interest on loans during their fifteen-year ownership. In 2016, he bought his third yacht, named *Lionheart*, for £100 million. The people surely notice the fat cats. And still nobody has taken his knighthood away, although there was a vote in the House of Commons recently to do just that; they did eventually strip Fred Goodwin, of RBS "fame," of his in 2012.[45] Ordinary people are aware that different rules appear to apply to them. The man (or woman) on the Clapham omnibus just doesn't understand. Nor should he.

I recall listening to billionaire John Cauldwell, who is the cofounder of mobile phone UK retailer Phone 4U, being interviewed on BBC *HARDtalk* on April 2, 2015 (downloadable from iTunes), about his motivations to get rich. He said he was motivated to make enough money to take care of his family; it was about financial security. Then it became about wealth and he wanted to get higher on the *Times* rich list. That lasted for three or four years. Then he thought about fulfilling the two parts of his childhood mission, which were to be wealthy and to be philanthropic. Phone 4U was worth £1.5 billion when he sold it in 2006 because he worried, rightly, there was a UK recession coming. "It's nice to be a winner," he said. It took him eight months to sell his first twenty-six phones. At one time he was, and he may well still be, the highest income tax payer in the UK. He was concerned, though, about the poor. "You cannot have a society where the rich are so stunningly rich, unbelievably rich and the poor are starving on the street. You can't have that," Cauldwell argued. When pushed, he agreed with the memo that Nick Hanauer, venture capitalist and billionaire, wrote to "My fellow zillionaires."

> If we don't do something to fix the glaring inequities in this economy, the pitchforks are going to come for us. No society can sustain this kind of rising inequality. In fact, there is no example in human history where wealth accumulated like this and the pitchforks didn't eventually come out. You show me a highly unequal society, and I will show you a police state. Or an uprising. There are no counterexamples. None. It's not if, it's when.[46]

Today Cauldwell is a major philanthropist. This again is very personal. He is a major contributor to the Great Ormond Street children's hospital in London that saved the life of my youngest daughter when she was a baby. Their motto is "the child first and always." Close to home. Bless him.

Great Ormond Street had, perhaps, an even more famous donor, J. M. Barrie. Although he and his wife were childless, Barrie loved children and had supported Great Ormond Street Hospital for many years. In 1929 Barrie was approached to sit on a committee to help buy some land so that the hospital could build a much-needed new wing. Barrie declined to serve on the committee but said that he "hoped to find another way to help." Two months later, the hospital board was stunned to learn that Sir James had handed over all his rights to Peter Pan. At a Guildhall dinner later that year Barrie, as host, claimed that Peter Pan had been a patient in Great Ormond Street Hospital and that "it was he who put me up to the little thing I did for the hospital."

On April 12, 2012, the Dartmouth Medical School changed its name to the Audrey and Theodore Geisel School of Medicine. Theodore Geisel was a Dartmouth graduate of the class of 1925. During his time as a student at Dartmouth he adopted a pen name, "Dr. Seuss." My kids grew up reading *The Cat in the Hat* and *Green Eggs and Ham* and *One Fish Two Fish Red Fish Blue Fish* and other such wonders. I even met a lady once in Hanover at a dinner party who knew Geisel and when she was a kid went with her parents to buy his new book in the Dartmouth bookstore and saw she was one of the characters. Gobsmacked apparently.

It is traditional for Dartmouth freshmen returning from their trips in the New Hampshire wilderness to stay overnight at our Moosilauke Ravine Lodge in the White Mountains and to be served green eggs and ham for breakfast in honor of Dr. Seuss. Nice. The Geisels, the most important phi-lanthropists in Dartmouth's history, were generous donors to the school during Theodore Geisel's lifetime and made significant provision for the college in their estate plans, reflecting the wealth generated by the beloved stories of Dr. Seuss (over 3.5 million hardback books sold in 2015 alone).[47] Dartmouth now has the Geisel School of Medicine.

Forbes reported that Theodore Geisel is the eighth-highest-earning de-ceased celebrity with earnings of $16 million in 2017 after Prince (7), Tom Petty (6), Bob Marley (5), Elvis Presley (4), Charles Schulz (3), Arnold Palmer (2), and Michael Jackson (1).[48] Where are the other great, living philanthropists besides Bill and Melinda Gates, Mark Zuckerberg, and War-ren Buffett? And now John Cauldwell.

Pitchforks to the ready. Relative things matter. The left-behinds who struggled noticed the elites were doing fine. Piketty, Saez, and Zucman (2017) argued that "an economy that fails to deliver growth for half of its population for an entire generation is bound to generate discontent with the status quo and a rejection of establishment politics." In a new international study called "Risks That Matter" the OECD (2019) found that in the twenty-one countries they studied, on average two-thirds of respondents picked "yes" or "definitely yes" when asked, "Should the government tax the rich more than they currently do, in order to support the poor?" In the United States 63 percent said "yes" or "definitely yes" compared with 62 percent in France, 69 percent in Canada, 73 percent in Italy, and 77 percent in Germany.

It would make sense to encourage philanthropy. It's time to do something about income and wealth inequality. Doing something about the cumulative disadvantage we are observing is in the rich's interests as Cauldwell realized. The haves need to help the have-nots and the left-behinds as they did in years gone by. The question is, how?

It Is Time to Put the Pedal to the Metal and Get the Job Market Humming Again

Now is the time to be all in this together. First, *we need to get to full employ-ment* and fast, wherever that is. It is time to keep priming the pumps. That would raise wages and lift spirits markedly.

Pulling back as the Fed did by raising rates was an error. There is nothing in the data that suggests they should do this. The world is different post-

2008, and most policymakers still haven't realized that and are living in the past when unions were powerful and there was no Internet; no iPhones; no iPads; no Netflix; and little or no globalization.

My son lives in Texas near an Amazon facility. He was in a swimming pool with his buddies one Saturday afternoon and ordered an inflatable pong table, as one does. (Don't ask, it's a beer-drinking game.) He called me up and said, "Dad, I love America. Guess how long it took for it to be delivered? Forty-five minutes." The world has changed, although maybe not for the better. The inflatable table lasted a couple of hours before it burst.

There is still a lot of slack in the U.S. labor market, which is why wage growth is well below what it was in the past at equivalent rates. The same applies in other countries including the UK and Germany, which also have unemployment rates below 5 percent. We need to encourage people to work by boosting labor demand and labor supply will follow. Inflation is a problem of a bygone age.

Beveridge showed it is possible for unemployment to surprise and go really low without bad consequences. That would ensure workers are stand-ing by waiting for job offers. There is nothing to fear except fear itself. That would push up wages and get the economy humming again. Once that has been achieved we can move on to address other problems. It is unclear when that would be but, as the saying goes, "I don't know how to define pornog-raphy but when I see it I will know." This will especially help people at the low end.

Having the economy cranking, and on fire, which hasn't happened in our lifetimes, with firms searching for workers, would allow those who have been pushed lower down the occupational pyramid to make better use of their skills. Young people with degrees who were forced to take jobs done previ-ously by those with high school education could move to graduate-level jobs. It would allow the underemployed to get more hours. It would allow workers to move from part-time jobs they were pushed into to full-time jobs, which would increase their happiness. It would allow the unemployed to get jobs and increase their happiness and that of everyone else. It would make being out of the labor force less attractive as the alternative of holding a job that paid more. This would be great for workers. Hard to see what is stopping it.

The move to defined contribution plans from defined benefit plans hurt workers in a recession. The value of their savings fell, hence many put off retiring. If they had been receiving defined benefit plans their payments would have been protected. Folks with defined contribution plans have no reason to retire; there is no compulsory retirement age for faculty, who are on defined contribution plans where I work. I have no intention of retiring any time soon. I still like my students!

To do this would require further monetary and fiscal stimuli. It would mean that central banks such as the Fed would have to stop raising rates and possibly turn them negative, although it is yet to be established that that is even feasible. This could well mean more quantitative easing. The idea that the ECB should stop doing quantitative easing when the unemployment rates in the Eurozone are high and underemployment remains high makes no sense. Japan is the precedent.

Central bankers have focused like a laser beam on nonexistent inflation, which was a story of the 1970s when unions were stronger. We know that even if inflation gets to 5 percent or so it isn't hard to stop it from going higher by raising rates. The problem is what to do in deflationary periods such as we saw post-recession. Shiller (1997) shows that people tend to dislike unemployment more than inflation. In work with David Bell and coauthors (Blanchflower et al. 2014), we showed that a 1-percentage-point rise in unemployment lowered well-being five times more than the equivalent rise in inflation. Joblessness hurts.

Moving to full employment would *boost wages*, which is its main point, and hence boost living standards. In the UK on March 9, 2017, the Institute for Fiscal Studies (IFS) estimated that median earnings will be no higher in 2022 than they were in 2007, before the financial crisis. Paul Johnson, the IFS's director, said that almost a decade on the prospects for income and earnings growth remained weak: "what really matters to people is what is happening to their incomes. Income and earnings growth over the next few years still look like being weak. On current forecasts, average earnings will be no higher in 2022 than they were in 2007. Fifteen years without a pay rise. I'm rather lost for superlatives. This is completely unprecedented."[49]

Second, an obvious way to boost labor demand is to *increase infrastructure spending in the United States and the UK*, which would create jobs although it is not obvious for whom and where. The big hang-up with the size of the debt makes no sense as every nation has both assets and liabilities. Plus, in 2018 and beyond money can be borrowed very cheaply. It matters mostly what the debt is used for, rather than its size. We also know that countries with high debt-to-GDP ratios can grow and the 90 percent rule has been debunked by Thomas Herndon. Consumption bad, investment good. There are many worthwhile projects that can be started, not least roads and bridges and public transportation. It is time to get commuting times down which, if it does nothing else, would increase happiness. It would also raise GDP of course.

The United States' crumbling infrastructure needs to get fixed, but the talk of a big infrastructure package has disappeared from the political radar screen. It is time for a new, New Deal. It's time to put America back to work. The unemployment rate of construction workers in the United States is still relatively high, at 5.4 percent. Private construction spending only returned to its pre-recession levels in 2014 and is up only 5.9 percent in nominal terms since its pre-recession high in February 2006.[50] Public construction in April 2018 was at broadly the same level it was at its pre-recession peak in November 2007. So, there is capacity for a construction burst to make up for the bust. An infrastructure plan may well be something the Democrat-controlled House and Donald Trump could agree upon in 2019.

Construction contracts can emphasize job creation. The federal government can move some of its own operations to deprived areas and set up enterprise zones to make it cheap for firms to move there. It makes sense to provide workers with incentives to work. A further issue is to provide incentives for firms to use labor over capital. The reason that technology has replaced jobs is that it has a relatively low price. It is time to give firms incentives to hire and train workers, to invest in human capital, rather than in machines. The practicalities of how you could do this are not simple. One way that has been found that is labor intensive is to encourage refurbishment of old properties rather than build new, which is more capital intensive.

Third, it is time to do something about *changing attitudes* and making them more positive. Blinder and Richards (2016) found that preferences for reduced migration in the UK have been softening in recent years. Grigorieff, Roth, and Ubfal (2016) conducted a set of experiments that suggest intriguing possibilities. First, they used a large representative cross-country experiment to show that when people are told the share of immigrants in their country, they become less likely to state that there are too many of them. Then, they conducted two online experiments in the United States, where they provided half of the participants with five statistics about immigration before evaluating their attitude toward immigrants with self-reported and behavioral measures.

This more comprehensive intervention improves people's attitude toward existing immigrants, although it does not change people's policy preferences regarding immigration. Republicans become more willing to increase legal immigration after receiving the information treatment. Finally, they measured the same self-reported policy preferences, attitudes, and beliefs in a four-week follow-up, and they show that the treatment effects persist. Specifically, these results suggest that targeting individuals with the most negative views on immigration would be the most effective way of changing people's attitudes toward immigrants.

The thirty-fourth British Social Attitudes Survey published in 2016 found that attitudes toward austerity were changing. After seven years of government austerity, public opinion showed signs of moving back in favor of wanting more tax and spend and greater redistribution of income. For the first time since the financial crash of 2007–8, more people (48%) wanted taxation increased to allow greater spending than wanted tax and spend levels to stay as they were (44%). More people (42%) agreed than disagreed (28%) that government should redistribute income from the better-off to those who are less well off. Shortly before the financial crisis fewer people supported redistribution than opposed it (34% and 38%, respectively, in 2006). The survey also found that attitudes toward benefit recipients were starting to soften and people particularly favored prioritizing spending on disabled people.

However, while these represent notable changes as compared with recent years, they still only represent a partial move back to an earlier mood. The 48 percent of people who now want more taxation and spending is greater than a joint-record low of 32 percent in 2010 but still lower than the rates of 63 percent in 1998 and 65 percent in 1991. People's top priorities for more spending remain as they have always been: health and education. Around 8 in 10 think the government should spend more or much more on health care (83%); 7 in 10 on education (71%); and 6 in 10 on the police (57%). Over time the proportion in the British Social Attitudes Surveys who say most dole claimants are "fiddling" has dropped from 35 percent in 2014 to 22 percent in 2016—its lowest level since the question was first asked on the survey in 1986. They also found the proportion of people (21%) that agree that most social security claimants do not deserve help is at a record low, down from 32 percent in 2014. It seems people are less supportive of austerity than they were. There is hope.

Fourth, it is time to *subsidize childcare* for working moms and dads. This could be done by making childcare costs fully tax deductible, which would encourage work, or states could offer subsidies. My friend who owns a child-care center would be delighted!

Fifth, mobility in the United States has halved in half a century. So, *measures to help people move* would make sense, especially from the states that are struggling. My kids moved to Texas, South Carolina, and Massachusetts to find work once they graduated from college because that is where the jobs are. Countries that have low mobility like Spain and Greece have high un-employment rates. Help needs to be given to young people to move out of their parents' basements and strike out on their own. Doing so would likely involve helping young people deal with their staggeringly high levels of student debt. Making student loans fully tax deductible would make a lot of sense. Encouraging mobility would be a start; tax subsidies for moving make sense.

By December 2017 the UK, over the preceding year, was the slowest-growing country in the EU. In part, the decline in net migration was because of the fall in the pound, which lowered the relative attractiveness of working in the UK, and the slowing economy as a result of the Leave vote meant there were fewer opportunities. In addition, the UK has become a less welcoming place. "These changes suggest that Brexit is likely to be a factor in people's decision to move to or from the UK," said Nicola White from the Office for National Statistics.[51] Research by Portes and Forte (2017) suggested that as a result of Brexit continued lower net migration from the EU over the com-ing years will be negative for GDP per capita.

It is time to encourage migration, especially for young people so they can move out of their parents' basements. States are already trying their own schemes. The state of Vermont recently announced a plan to encourage free-lancers to move to the state and offered a subsidy of $10,000.[52]

Sixth, another obvious possibility is to use the tax code to reduce income and wealth inequality. It would make sense that it would encourage work, so raising the threshold below which you pay tax would help. Another obvi-ous possibility would be to lower tax rates on those who make less than the median income. It would also make sense to remove the cap on social secu-rity, which makes no sense. Contributions should just rise as a fixed or even a rising proportion of income. It would make sense for a millionaire to pay at least the same proportion as his or her secretary and for a billionaire to pay a higher proportion than a millionaire. I am a great believer in providing incentives to work. It is inappropriate to subsidize indolence.

Finally, it is time to look at ways of encouraging and giving incentives for work to those at the bottom. There has also been talk of Universal Basic Income (UBI) whereby the federal government would provide each adult below a certain income level with a specific amount of money each year. It acts as a negative income tax. In a new Gallup poll taken in February 2018 an astonishing 48 percent of Americans support this idea. Alexandria Ocasio-Cortez won a surprise primary election in New York and called for a universal jobs guarantee, under which the federal government would provide a job for every American. This has support from Bernie Sanders. Senator Cory Booker (D-NJ) has introduced legislation that would see a three-year pilot project set up to guarantee jobs in fifteen regions of high unemployment. Among the bill's co-sponsors is Senator Kirsten Gillibrand (D-NY), who tweeted in support of the policy in April. The premise, as Laura Paddison notes, is that everyone should be entitled to a good job, one that pays at least $15 an hour and comes with health and other benefits.[53] These would potentially improve the lot of ordinary working folk, but unless there is a major move to the left these plans have little chance of being implemented.

We will have to wait until 2019 to find out whether Finland's UBI experiment worked.[54] Personally I would pilot studies to work out whether they are cost-effective. There may be better ways to lift living standards at the low end. Nobel Economics Laureate Jim Heckman and Jeff Smith (2000) examined the Job Training Partnership Act, which was a well-meaning attempt to help disadvantaged youths, and found that it had a negative impact on the earnings of disadvantaged males and zero impact on the earnings of disadvantaged females, and the program was closed. We need to invest in programs that work rather than waste money on programs that don't. That would likely mean lots of testing and piloting programs. What is generally clear is that what works in one place, say, Cleveland, may not work in Denver. Fifteen dollars an hour is very different in New York City than it is in New Orleans. I was always told that the federal minimum wage didn't bind north of the Mason-Dixon line. North of that line, including in New Hampshire, McDonald's sets the wage.

When I was first employed as a young lecturer in London the trade union had been fighting for a "part-timers charter" for lecturers who worked up to thirty hours a week. The union managed to negotiate that these additional rights would be given to every lecturer who worked more than sixteen hours a week, which the majority did. The next day after the agreement was signed the employer cut everyone's hours to below sixteen. The following day the agreement was scrapped.

What if Brexit and Trump Don't Deliver?

A big question is, what happens if Brexit and Trump don't deliver? So much has been promised and disappointment is in the air.

Will the pandemic spread, as the flu pandemic did in World War I, or will it be slowed by macroeconomic failure or boosted by macro success? What if Macron can't turn the French economy around as Hollande, Sarkozy, and Mitterrand were unable to do? What happens if the American, French, and British economies slow? Maybe the riots will no longer be silent? Le Pen isn't going away. Will the move to right-wing populism expand into other EU countries? Will the markets turn on Jeremy Corbyn if he becomes prime minister? A YouGov poll of 3,380 UK adults on June 7, 2018, found that 46 percent of respondents said that they expected Brexit to go badly and it has; 27 percent said they thought it would go well and it hasn't.[55]

Brexit negotiations are going badly, and there is growing talk of a second referendum after 700,000 demonstrated peacefully in London. In the period since the Brexit vote in 2016 the UK has slipped from being the fastest-growing country in the EU to the slowest. A forecast by the EU Commission at the end of 2018 was for the UK and Italy to be the slowest-growing countries in the EU28 in 2019. The EU forecast was 1.7 percent in 2017; 1.3 percent in 2018; and 1.2 percent in 2019 and 2020.[56] The official forecaster in the UK Office for Budget Responsibility had broadly similar weak GDP forecasts for these four years: 1.75, 1.3, 1.6, and 1.4 percent.[57]

On December 4, 2018, the UK government lost three votes in the House of Commons that held it in contempt of Parliament for not releasing the full legal briefings it had received on Brexit.[58] In a second blow the European Court of Justice ruled on December 10, 2018, that the UK can unilaterally revoke Article 50, arguing that a member state "cannot be forced to leave the European Union against its will." Later the same day, in what the *Financial Times* called a "humiliating setback," Prime Minister May canceled the Brexit vote, which she was inevitably going to lose.[59] The pound fell sharply on the news to an eighteen-month low of $1.2559, down 1 percent, and even more against the euro, to €1.1061, down 1.36 percent on the day. Yields on gilts also fell and the UK-focused FTSE 250 was down 2 percent on the day.

Once the vote on Brexit was pulled by the government, a sufficient number of Tory Brexiters opposed to the deal wrote to Sir Graham Brady, the chairman of the 1922 Committee, to trigger a vote of no confidence against Theresa May. In a last-ditch attempt to win, Number 10 Downing Street suggested that May would stand down before the next election. I was watching CNN the morning of the confidence vote, which went live to *Prime Minister's Questions* from the House of Commons for a good twenty minutes. At the end anchor Alisyn Camerota described what we had all been watching as "something out of Monty Python," which seems to be how the world now sees the Brexit debacle. May won the vote narrowly, but her position has been weakened, and it remains unclear if she will survive through the end of 2019, as there is no chance her Brexit plan can become law. The next day the prime minister went back to the EU Commission to try to get further concessions and, as expected, came home empty-handed. It was unclear why, after two and a half years of negotiating, she thought she could get more in an evening. The *Sun's* colorful headline on her return was "EU Leaders Tell PM to Get Stuffed." After two failed attempts to get May's deal through Parliament, less than two weeks before the UK was meant to leave the EU at the end of March 2019, Speaker John Bercow announced that he would not allow a third vote on the withdrawal agreement without substantial changes. Bercow's decision was based on an official parliamentary rule book that was first published by Thomas Erskine May in 1844 that says you can't keep voting on the same bill hoping you will get a different result. Brexit is going to be delayed. Chaos reigns.

The OECD in its forecast from November 2018 has GDP growth in the UK at 1.3 percent in 2018; 1.4 percent in 2019; and 1.1 percent in 2020. Its forecasts for Germany (1.9%, 1.8%, and 1.6%) and Italy (1.0%, 0.9%, and 0.9%) look optimistic as there are signs both are headed to recession in early 2019. According to the U.S. Census Bureau the median sales price of new homes sold in the United States fell in October 2018 to $309,700, down 3.1 percent from a year earlier and the lowest since February 2017. The Great Recession started in the U.S. housing market.

The problem is that the many populist promises were just pie in the sky and totally impractical. The Brexiters appear to have had no plan at all on what Brexit would look like. During the French Revolution, eventually the wine ran out. It was never going to be possible in France for Marine Le Pen to lower the retirement age to 60; the markets wouldn't allow it. The beautiful wall was never going to be built and Mexico was never going to pay for it. The GOP had no plans ready for repealing and replacing Obamacare as they didn't think Trump was going to win. Now the Tory party in the UK is fighting with itself like ferrets in a sack over soft or hard or no Brexit. The fact that the government has admitted that it is stockpiling food and medicines in case of a no-deal Brexit in 2019 doesn't augur well for the future, or indeed for support of such an action among the electorate.

The big rise in bank stocks after Macron won in the first round of the French presidential election gave a hint of what would have happened if Le Pen and Mélenchon were going to be fighting out the second round. Le Pen offered broadly popular programs to help her core voters. Early retirement at age 60 was obviously unaffordable as people live longer. This is an indicator of the scale of what could happen in UK markets if there is a disorderly Brexit disaster. It would likely result in a cataclysmic global fall in markets.[60] It gives an indicator of what would have happened if Le Pen had won.

The markets would have inevitably responded badly and dropped sharply. As Clinton advisor James Carville famously said, "I used to think that if there was reincarnation, I wanted to come back as the president or the pope or as a .400 baseball hitter. But now I would like to come back as the bond market. You can intimidate everybody." He also coined the phrase, "It's the economy, stupid." Thankfully markets stop politicians from doing dumb stuff.

Boosting growth is especially helpful for those at the bottom. The problem, though, is how exactly will that help West Virginia, Kentucky, Ohio, Michigan, Wisconsin, and Pennsylvania? How will it help the left-behinds in Wakefield, Blackpool, Toledo, or the Pas de Calais? Coal isn't coming back. Steel and talc aren't going to return, and the tourists aren't going to return to English seaside towns, so something else needs to. The march of technology continues. Trump has declared, "We are taking care of our miners," despite absolutely no evidence to support such a claim. The tariffs have hurt Trump's core supporters, hence the need for a $12 billion bailout that has not gone down well with the GOP. Senator Ron Johnson (R-WI), whom I met once and had a perfectly sensible conversation with, declared, "This is becoming more and more a soviet-type economy here."[61]

Capital is cheap relative to the price of labor. So, changing the relative price of labor can help raise the demand for good jobs. This can be done by providing incentives for firms to hire people rather than invest in capital. That is the change in the tax code that is needed. It would make sense to lower the relative price of labor. Tax reform that gives incentives for individuals to work also makes sense; earned income tax credits seem to work. Reforms need to be business friendly, because workers benefit generally from a firm's increased ability to pay. But they see no necessity to pay. That needs to change, and firms must be given incentives to share their profits with workers. It may take shaming them into it, but that's ok. Financial incentives work.

The tax code can swing into action here to reward work for those at the low end. One way would be to provide large earned income tax credits. The idea is to reward work. Plus raising the tax threshold at the bottom can help. For many who don't pay taxes, a negative income tax would help to lift their earnings. The tax code should be used to lower after-tax inequality. Lowering inequality seems a good idea. As Levitsky and Ziblatt have noted, though, "Adopting policies to address social and economic inequality is, of course, politically difficult—in part because of the polarization (and resulting gridlock) such policies seek to address" (2018, 229).

All hands to the pump. It's time to take a chance. Borrow to invest, especially in people in the country's future. The New Deal worked. Spending trillions on rebuilding America's crumbling infrastructure is a really good idea. There seems to be no chance that is going to happen, but it should. Austerity needs to become a long-ago nightmare.

The concern may be that in the long run it will not be possible to Make America Great Again for the less educated. Settlers arrived in the United States and obtained vast amounts of wealth. There were economic rents to be shared, and less-educated Americans obtained living standards for themselves that were simply not replicated by similar workers in Europe and beyond. The onset of global competition may mean that world has gone forever. It may not be possible to lift the living standards of Trump supporters back to where they were half a century ago. The UK and France will not be able to restore empire and share the spoils of monopoly power as they did a century ago.

There was never going to be lots of money after Brexit to fund the NHS. In June 2018 Prime Minister May once again was talking about using a Brexit dividend to fund the NHS although there is none. No post-Brexit paradise. No deal with the EU that doesn't allow for free movement of capital, services, goods, and people. You can't eat sovereignty. No repeal of

Obamacare. No draining of the swamp. No return of steel or coal jobs. No wall. Dreamland. Your Social Security, Medicare, and Medicaid were never safe, and the middle class was never going to get big tax cuts. The lobbyists were always going to ensure the tax cuts mostly went to business and rich donors. There has been no action on guns even after all the school shootings, even when the vast majority of Americans supported such moves. Trump promised there would be, but the NRA stopped all that. Inequality is going to rise, not fall, despite what was promised on the campaign trail. Wages haven't risen much and show little sign of getting going. The blame game has already begun.

William Beveridge, once again, in *Full Employment in a Free Society*, argued that full employment "means having always more vacant jobs than unemployed men, not slightly fewer jobs. It means that the jobs are at fair wages, of such a kind and so located that the unemployed men can reasonably be expected to take them" ([1944] 1960, 18). The same applies to unemployed women these days too. Fair wages for all would be good.

We were never all in this together and it is time we were. We are better together. People are hurting. The worry is that policymakers have not learned from their mistakes, but now they have little firepower to deal with the onset of the next economic crisis. The whole world wants a good job. Gizza job.

APPENDIX

Table A.1. U.S. Economic Indicators, January 2006–April 2008

	(1)	(2)	(3)	(4)	(5)	(6)	(7)	(8)	(9)	(10)	(11)	(12)
Jan-06	10.4	14.7	2292	2224	106.8	91.2	27.0	0.6	3.3	2.3	3.2	3.1
Feb-06	8.4	13.8	2125	2129	102.7	86.7	27.4	0.6	3.5	2.6	3.3	3.2
Mar-06	7.2	12.3	1965	2097	107.5	88.9	28.3	0.6	3.6	3.1	3.3	3.2
Apr-06	4.0	11.2	1821	1987	109.8	87.4	29.4	0.6	4.0	1.9	3.0	2.8
May-06	5.3	10.0	1944	1918	104.7	79.1	29.1	0.5	3.8	1.4	3.5	2.4
Jun-06	0.1	8.6	1819	1879	105.4	84.9	28.0	0.4	4.0	0.8	2.5	2.4
Jul-06	1.0	7.2	1746	1774	107.0	84.7	28.6	0.3	4.0	0.8	2.5	1.9
Aug-06	−2.2	5.7	1646	1731	100.2	82.0	24.5	0.3	4.0	1.0	2.6	5.0
Sep-06	−1.8	4.3	1721	1654	105.9	85.4	26.2	0.4	4.2	0.8	3.0	3.1
Oct-06	−4.4	3.0	1470	1560	105.1	93.6	25.6	0.4	4.0	0.5	3.4	3.6
Nov-06	−3.4	1.8	1565	1527	105.3	92.1	25.7	0.3	4.2	0.0	3.3	3.2
Dec-06	−0.2	0.7	1629	1628	110.0	91.7	27.6	0.3	4.3	0.4	3.3	2.9
Jan-07	−3.0	−0.1	1403	1566	110.2	96.9	29.6	0.4	4.2	0.9	3.4	3.0
Feb-07	−1.0	−0.8	1487	1541	111.2	91.3	27.8	0.3	4.1	1.7	3.2	3.3
Mar-07	−0.1	−1.3	1491	1569	108.2	88.4	30.3	0.3	4.2	1.5	3.0	3.7
Apr-07	−1.2	−2.1	1485	1457	106.3	87.1	29.0	0.2	3.8	1.5	3.0	3.1
May-07	−2.5	−2.8	1440	1520	108.5	88.3	29.1	0.2	4.1	1.4	2.9	3.2
Jun-07	−0.1	−3.4	1468	1413	105.3	85.3	27.6	0.2	4.1	1.2	2.9	3.0
Jul-07	−0.7	−3.8	1371	1389	111.9	90.4	30.0	0.3	4.1	1.3	2.5	3.6
Aug-07	0.2	−4.3	1347	1322	105.6	83.4	27.5	0.2	4.0	0.6	3.2	4.0
Sep-07	−4.7	−4.9	1182	1261	99.5	83.4	25.6	0.2	4.1	0.9	3.2	3.4
Oct-07	−5.6	−6.1	1274	1170	95.2	80.9	24.1	0.2	3.8	0.7	2.7	2.7
Nov-07	−3.9	−7.7	1178	1162	87.8	76.1	23.3	0.2	3.8	1.3	2.8	2.0
Dec-07	−6.6	−9.0	1000	1080	90.6	75.5	23.6	0.2	3.7	0.9	2.2	1.8
Jan-08	−5.3	−10.7	1071	1061	87.3	78.4	23.8	0.1	3.7	0.8	1.9	1.4
Feb-08	−8.2	1065	984	76.4	70.8	21.5	0.0	3.7	−0.1	1.7	1.3	
Mar-08		947	927	64.5	69.5	18.8	−0.2	3.6				
Apr-08			62.6									

(1) Median house prices of existing one-family homes, including condos, National Association of Realtors % oya
(2) Twenty-city house-price index—S & P / Case-Shiller % oya
(3) Housing starts—Census Bureau. Annualized level, thousands of units
(4) Permits to build—Census Bureau. Annualized level, thousands of units
(5) Consumer confidence—Conference Board Index
(6) Consumer confidence—Reuters / University of Michigan Index
(7) Consumer confidence—Conference Board % saying jobs are plentiful
(8) Private nonfarm payrolls—Bureau of Labor Statistics % change, three months on previous three months
(9) Private average hourly earnings—Bureau of Labour Statistics % oya
(10) Nominal retail sales—Census Bureau % change, three months on previous three months
(11) Real consumption—Bureau of Economic Analysis % oya
(12) Real personal disposable income—Bureau of Economic Analysis % oya
All data are seasonally adjusted except columns 1 and 2.

Table A.2. UK Economic Conditions, May 2004–March 2008

	(a) UK housing				
	(1) Halifax house-price index	(2) Nationwide house-price index	(3) HBF price balance	(4) RICS sales to stock ratio	(5) Loan approvals '000s
2007Q2	2.3	2.1	5	0.41	337
2007Q3	0.8	1.2	−1	0.38	318
2007Q4	−0.9	0.6	−22	0.33	242
2008Q1	−1.0	−1.7		0.27	
Aug-07	0.3	0.5	6	0.38	106
Sep-07	−0.6	0.5	−9	0.38	100
Oct-07	−0.7	1.1	−10	0.35	88
Nov-07	−1.3	−1.0	−24	0.33	81
Dec-07	1.4	−0.4	−33	0.30	72
Jan-08	0.0	−0.4	−41	0.29	74
Feb-08	−0.4	−0.5	−47	0.26	73
Mar-08	−2.5	−0.6		0.25	

	(b) UK consumer confidence			
	(6) Nationwide consumer confidence	(7) GfK balance	(8) GfK future economic situation	(9) GfK major purchases
May-04	100	−2	−14	12
Sep-04	106	−7	−14	5
Jan-05	110	1	−10	11
Jan-06	94	−3	−15	10
Sep-06	92	−7	−21	9
Dec-06	84	−8	−19	2
Mar-07	88	−8	−10	2
Apr-07	90	−6	−18	4
May-07	99	−2	−10	4
Jun-07	95	−3	−10	7
Jul-07	96	−6	−13	−5
Aug-07	94	−4	−15	3
Sep-07	99	−7	−19	−2
Oct-07	98	−8	−17	−2
Nov-07	86	−10	−21	−3
Dec-07	85	−14	−26	−8
Jan-08	81	−13	−26	−20
Feb-08	78	−17	−29	−21
Mar-08	77	−19	−32	−21
Series average	96	−7	−8	8

Table A.2. (*continued*)

	(c) Labor market surveys	
	(10) REC demand for staff	(11) CIPS/NTC
28-Feb-05	54.5	50.1
31-Mar-05	55.0	52.2
30-Apr-05	55.9	51.9
31-May-05	56.3	50.7
30-Jun-05	55.4	50.8
31-Jul-05	54.7	51.3
31-Aug-05	55.1	51.0
30-Sep-05	53.8	50.9
31-Oct-05	54.7	51.0
30-Nov-05	55.4	50.3
31-Dec-05	55.9	51.2
31-Jan-06	54.3	50.9
28-Feb-06	52.3	51.0
31-Mar-06	54.6	51.5
30-Apr-06	55.2	52.4
31-May-06	57.4	52.5
30-Jun-06	57.0	53.4
31-Jul-06	59.1	53.1
31-Aug-06	58.2	52.1
30-Sep-06	56.8	53.3
31-Oct-06	59.3	53.2
30-Nov-06	61.2	53.6
31-Dec-06	61.8	54.3
31-Jan-07	60.8	53.8
28-Feb-07	59.0	54.0
31-Mar-07	62.3	53.3
30-Apr-07	60.5	52.5
31-May-07	59.4	53.7
30-Jun-07	63.2	53.9
31-Jul-07	64.1	53.4
31-Aug-07	60.1	53.8
30-Sep-07	60.2	52.5
31-Oct-07	57.4	53.0
30-Nov-07	53.7	51.9
31-Dec-07	50.7	52.1
31-Jan-08	51.4	51.4
29-Feb-08	49.0	51.3

ACKNOWLEDGMENTS

I thank Orley Ashenfelter, David Bell, Mark Blyth, Vernon Bogdanor, Alex Bryson, Liam Delaney, Bob Hart, Doug Irwin, Geraint Johnes, Andy Levin, Andrew Oswald, John Pencavel, Adam Posen, Robert Putnam, Jon Skinner, and Doug Staiger. I am indebted to my editor, Joe Jackson, whose hard work has made the book so much more readable and better. I am especially grateful to my wife, Carol, for putting up with me talking about economics all the time.

DEDICATION

I first coined the phrase "the economics of walking about" in a lecture I gave in 2007 at Queen Mary College (QMC) in honor of my PhD supervisor, Professor Bernard Corry (Blanchflower 2007). As I said in my lecture, "Bernard was my mentor, friend, and inspiration and I miss him greatly. I guess he was the first one to really have believed in me and I think he would have been amused that one of his boys now has an office on Threadneedle Street." Bernard died at age seventy on January 10, 2001.

Bernard's compatriot in arms at Queen Mary was my other supervisor, Professor Maurice, the Lord Peston, of Mile End (as in the tube station next to QMC). Maurice died at age 85 on April 23, 2016, and I wrote his obituary for the Royal Economic Society. I wrote this: "He was a truly delightful friend and mentor and a fine, eclectic economist. Maurice was also a proud Arsenal fan."

In 1999 I wrote a paper in honor of the two of them (Blanchflower 1999). In it I said, "I first started work as a graduate student at Queen Mary College in 1983 after being persuaded to go there by Bernard Corry, who was the external examiner of my master's thesis at University College, Cardiff. He told me that (a) working on the wage impact of trade unions was a great topic; (b) there was nowhere else as wonderful as QMC to do this work; and (c) he would give me a full ESRC scholarship and lots of teaching to pay the bills. Probably because I was young(ish) and inexperienced at the time I believed him on all counts and I went! I eventually finished my PhD in a record, 21 months, with lots of input from both Maurice and Bernard."

This book is dedicated to the two of them, Bernard and Maurice. I hope they would like it. Their sons Robert Peston, the TV personality, and Dan Corry, the economist, assured me they would. That's alright, then. In 2009

Queen Mary awarded me an honorary DSc, which was kind and brought back many happy memories. Sadly, Maurice was too ill to come to the ceremony.

They taught me to do economics with a conscience.

NOTES

Chapter 1. What the Whole World Wants Is a Good Job

1. Yosser Hughes was a character in a 1980s BBC sitcom, *The Boys from the Black-stuff.* Yosser lost his job and his wife, struggled to keep his kids, and was driven to the edge of sanity in his unsuccessful quest to find another job, any job. People will do almost anything to get a decent job.

2. http://www.gallup.com/corporate/212381/who-we-are.aspx.

3. http://news.gallup.com/poll/189068/bls-unemployment-seasonally-adjusted .aspx.aspx.

4. I was once asked to speak at a conference on "the labor process," which the organizers told me I was a renowned expert in. I had no idea what it was but was relieved to discover it was the study of work!

5. Or "ready for the knacker's yard."

6. Galbraith once asked at the bookshop at the old LaGuardia terminal in New York if they carried *The Great Crash, 1929* by J. K. Galbraith. The lady behind the counter told him it was "not a book you can sell in an airport."

7. http://www.nber.org/cycles/recessions.html.

8. At the time of writing the Fed held $4.2 trillion in assets while the ECB held $5.4 trillion and the Bank of Japan $4 trillion. See "Global Economic Briefing: Central Bank Balance Sheets," Yardeni Research, August 25, 2018, www.yardeni .com.

9. F. B. Ahmad, L. M. Rossen, M. R. Spencer, M. Warner, and P. Sutton, "Provisional Drug Overdose Death Counts," National Center for Health Statistics, 2018.

10. Margot Sanger-Katz, "Bleak New Estimates in Drug Epidemic: A Record 72,000 Overdose Deaths in 2017," *New York Times*, August 15, 2018.

11. https://ec.europa.eu/info/business-economy-euro/indicators-statistics /economic-databases/business-and-consumer-surveys/download-business-and -consumer-survey-data/time-series_en.

12. See also Pedro Nicolaci da Costa, "There's a Worrying Disconnect between How

Fed Officials Look at the Economy and the Way Workers Experience It," *Business Insider*, May 23, 2018.

Chapter 2. Unemployment and Its Consequences

1. Glenn Kessler, "Donald Trump Still Does Not Understand the Unemployment Rate," *Washington Post*, December 12, 2016.

2. Louis Jacobson, "Donald Trump Says U.S. Has 93 Million People 'Out of Work,' but That's Way Too High," Politifact.com, August 31, 2015.

3. The Bureau of Labor Statistics of the U.S. Department of Labor is the principal federal agency responsible for measuring labor market activity, working conditions, and price changes in the economy.

4. Alana Semuels, "It's Not about the Economy," *Atlantic*, December 27, 2016.

5. Chris Isadore, "Jack Welch Questions Jobs Numbers," CNN Money, October 5, 2012.

6. Al Weaver, "Don Blankenship Dismisses Trump: 'We Still Expect to Win,'" *Washington Examiner*, May 7, 2018.

7. Larry Mishel, "The Outrageous Attack on the BLS," EPI blog, October 5, 2012, https://www.epi.org/blog/outrageous-attack-bls/.

8. https://stats.oecd.org/glossary/detail.asp?ID=2791.

9. Kathryn Vasel, "Wanted: 1,000 New Delta Flight Attendants," CNN Money, October 23, 2017.

10. Melody Simmons, "Thousands Wait to Apply for 1,200 New Amazon Jobs in Baltimore," *Baltimore Business Journal*, August 2, 2017.

11. Aaron Weiner, "Applications Pour in for D.C. Walmart Jobs," *Washington City Paper*, October 14, 2013.

12. The BLS also produces an estimate of (non-farm) employment based on an establishment survey. In April 2018 the estimate was 148,230,000. The numbers from the individual surveys are larger because they have a more expansive scope than the establishment survey and include self-employed workers whose businesses are unincorporated, unpaid family workers, agricultural workers, and private household workers, who are excluded by the establishment survey.

13. See Hyclak, Johnes, and Thornton 2017, 76.

14. I should note personal connections in that Sir David Metcalf was my PhD thesis external examiner and I replaced Sir Steve Nickell on the MPC.

15. Quoted in Harrison Jacobs, "The Revenge of the 'Oxy Electorate' Helped Fuel Trump's Election Upset," *Business Insider*, November 23, 2016.

16. Kathleen Frydl, "The Oxy Electorate: A Scourge of Addiction and Death Siloed in Fly-over Country," www.medium.com, November 16, 2016.

17. Mark Muro and Sifan Liu, "Another Clinton-Trump Divide: High Output America vs. Low Output America," Brookings, November 29, 2016.

18. Nicholas Eberstadt, "Our Miserable 21st Century," *Commentary*, February 15, 2017.

19. Blanchflower and Oswald 1999.

20. Office for National Statistics, "Personal Well-Being in the UK: January to December 2017," May 17, 2018, https://www.ons.gov.uk/peoplepopulationand community/wellbeing/bulletins/measuringnationalwellbeing/januarytodecem ber2017.

21. "The Five Giants," in *Beveridge at 70* (London: Fabian Society, 2012).

22. Stephen Armstrong, "Want, Disease, Ignorance, Squalor and Idleness: Are Beveridge's Five Evils Back?" *Guardian*, October 10, 2017; Armstrong 2017.

23. Armstrong, "Want, Disease, Ignorance, Squalor and Idleness"; Armstrong 2017.

24. Rowena Mason, "Corbyn Urges Benefits Rethink and End to 55p-a-Minute Helpline Rate," *Guardian*, October 11, 2017.

25. Joe Vesey-Byrne, "A Tory Cabinet Minister's Defence of the 55p per Minute Universal Credit Helpline Is Horrendous," *Independent*, October 12, 2017; Mike Sivier, "Theresa May and the 55p-per-Minute Miscalculation," *Vox Political*, October 12, 2017.

26. Office for National Statistics, "Contracts That Do Not Guarantee a Minimum Number of Hours: April 2018," April 23, 2018, https://www.ons.gov.uk /employmentandlabourmarket/peopleinwork/earningsandworkinghours /articles/contractsthatdonotguaranteeaminimumnumberofhours/april2018.

27. United Nations Human Rights, Office of the High Commissioner, "UN Poverty Expert Says UK Policies Inflict Unnecessary Misery," November 16, 2018, https://www.ohchr.org/EN/NewsEvents/Pages/DisplayNews.aspx?NewsID= 23884&LangID=E.

28. Chris Kirkham, "Percentage of Young Americans Living with Parents Rises to 75-Year High," *Wall Street Journal*, December 21, 2016.

29. Isabelle Fraser, "The Rise of Generation Rent: Number of Young Homeowners Halved in the Last 20 Years," *Telegraph*, December 22, 2016.

30. According to the BLS, in January 2017 there were 1,137,000 individuals who had been continuously unemployed for 52 weeks and over or 14 percent of the unemployed, down from 1,446,000 (17.4%) a year earlier. It reached a record high of 31.9 percent in 2011 Q2. Karen Kosanovich and E. T. Sherman, "Trends in Long Term Unemployment," Spotlight on Statistics, BLS, March 2015, https://www.bls.gov/spotlight/2015/long-term-unemployment/home .htm.

31. See Winkelmann and Winkelmann 1998; Clark and Oswald 1994; Frey and Stutzer 2002; and Ahn, García, and Jimeno 2004.

32. Linn, Sandifer, and Stein 1985; Frese and Mohr 1987; Jackson and Warr 1987;

Banks and Jackson 1982; Darity and Goldsmith 1996; Goldsmith, Veum, and Darity 1996; Brenner and Mooney 1983.

33. Goldsmith, Veum, and Darity 1996.

34. Moser et al. 1987.

35. Martikainen and Valkonen 1996.

36. Voss et al. 2004.

37. See Platt 1984; Pritchard 1992; Blakely, Collings, and Atkinson 2003; Hamermesh and Soss 1974; Daly, Wilson, and Johnson 2008; and Barr et al. 2012.

38. Beale and Nethercott 1987; Iverson and Sabroe 1988; Mattiasson et al. 1990.

39. Arcaya et al. 2014; Falba et al. 2005; Hammarstrom and Janlert 1994.

40. Wang and Morin 2009.

41. Ellwood 1982.

42. Gregg and Tominey 2005.

43. Thornberry and Christensen 1984; Raphael and Winter-Ebmer 2001; Fougere, Kramarz, and Pouget 2006; Freeman 1999.

44. Fougere, Kramarz, and Pouget 2006.

45. Raphael and Winter-Ebmer 2001; Ihlanfeldt 2007. See CEA 2016 for a helpful summary of employment, wage and education policies, and crime reduction, from which these references are obtained.

46. Grogger 1998; Doyle, Ahmed, and Horn 1999.

47. Falk and Zweimüller 2005; Carmichael and Ward 2000, 2001.

Chapter 3. Wage Growth and the Lack of It

1. Patrick Gillespie, "American Businesses Can't Find Workers," CNN Money, January 17, 2018.

2. Jennifer Levitz, "Perks for Plumbers: Hawaiian Vacations, Craft Beer and 'a Lot of Zen': The Tight Job Market Has Forced Plumbing Companies to Offer Silicon Valley–Style Benefits to Keep the Talent Happy," *Wall Street Journal*, May 23, 2018.

3. Bureau of Labor Statistics, "Occupational Employment and Wages—May 2017," https://www.bls.gov/news.release/pdf/ocwage.pdf.

4. Board of Governors of the Federal Reserve System, "The Beige Book," https://www.federalreserve.gov/monetarypolicy/files/BeigeBook_20181024.pdf.

5. The production and non-supervisory employee groups vary by industry. In service-providing industries, the data are collected for those who are not owners or who are not primarily employed to direct, supervise, or plan the work of others. In goods-producing industries, the data are collected for production employees in mining and logging and in manufacturing, and for construction employees in construction. Production and construction employees include working supervisors and group leaders who may be "in charge" of some em-

ployees but whose supervisory functions are only incidental to their regular work. The production employee/construction employee categories in goods-producing industries exclude employees not directly involved in production, such as managers, sales, and accounting personnel.

6. Each month the Current Employment Statistics (CES) program surveys approximately 146,000 businesses and government agencies, representing approximately 623,000 individual work sites, to provide detailed industry data on employment, hours, and earnings of workers on non-farm payrolls.

7. For details of the National Compensation Survey from which the ECI is collected, see https://www.bls.gov/opub/hom/pdf/homch8.pdf.

8. Haroon Siddique, "A Million NHS Workers Agree to a Pay Rise Worth 6.5% over Three Years," *Guardian*, June 8, 2018.

9. https://www.ons.gov.uk/employmentandlabourmarket/peopleinwork /earningsandworkinghours/adhocs/009221annualsurveyofhoursandearningsas hemeanregionaltimeseries1997to2018.

10. Quévat and Vignolles 2018.

11. Bourbeau and Fields 2017.

12. Statistics New Zealand, http://www.stats.govt.nz/browse_for_stats/income-and -work/employment_and_unemployment/labour-market-statistics-information -releases.aspx.

13. Australian Bureau of Statistics, "Labour Market Statistics, March 2017 Quarter," May 3, 2017.

14. Statistics Netherlands, https://opendata.cbs.nl/statline/#/CBS/en/dataset /82838eng/table?ts=1542313897166.

15. Michelle Lam, "Japan's Wage Puzzle Still Unsolved," *TS Lombard Daily Note*, January 17, 2017.

16. http://www.mhlw.go.jp/english/database/db-l/29/2911pe/2911pe.html.

17. U.S. Census Bureau, "Income and Poverty in the United States: 2015," September 2016, https://www.census.gov/library/publications/2016/demo/p60 -256.html.

18. Clarke et al. 2017.

19. Corlett 2016.

20. Blanchflower 2004, 2015b.

21. Office for National Statistics, "Measuring National Well-Being: Life in the UK: 2016," table 7.1, September 22, 2016.

22. Office for National Statistics, "Household Disposable Income and Inequality," UK reference tables.

23. The employment annual growth rates were simply taken from the ONS labor market release a01mar2018.xls, table 1. We used the data for January–March for Q1; April–June for Q2; July–September for Q3; and October–December

for Q4. Output per worker was obtained from Office for National Statistics, "Time Series: Output per Worker: Whole Economy SA: Index 2016 = 100, UK," https://www.ons.gov.uk/employmentandlabourmarket/peopleinwork /labourproductivity/timeseries/a4ym/prdy.

24. Office for National Statistics, "International Comparisons of UK Productivity (ICP), Final Estimates, 2015," Statistical Bulletin, April 5, 2017.

25. Silvana Tenreyro, "The Fall in Productivity Growth: Causes and Implications" (Peston Lecture, Queen Mary University of London, January 15, 2018).

26. Rates were 2015 Q3 0.4%; 2015 Q4 −0.1%; 2016 Q1 0.3%; 2016 Q2 −0.5%; 2016 Q3 0.4%; 2016 Q4 0.9%; 2017 Q1 0.8%; 2017 Q2 0.8%; 2017 Q3 0.9%.

27. The 16+ employment rate in the United States in January 2008 was 62.9% versus 60.4% in January 2018. In contrast in the UK they were 60.4% and 60.9%, respectively, on these dates. BLS (www.bls.gov) and ONS (ONS.ac.uk) (Table a01oct2008.xls).

28. According to www.unionstats.gsu.edu, private-sector unionization rates in the United States in 2017 were 6.5%, down from 10.3% since 1995, versus, according to the ONS, 13.4% in the UK, down from 21.4% in 1995. https:// www.gov.uk/government/uploads/system/uploads/attachment_data/file /616966/trade-union-membership-statistical-bulletin-2016-rev.pdf.

29. Mark Carney, "Prospects for the UK Labour Market," September 6, 2014, https://www.bis.org/review/r140910a.pdf, p. 6.

30. Larry Elliott, "Interest Rates Will Stay Low for 20 Years, Says Bank of England Expert," *Guardian*, August 9, 2018.

31. Andrew G. Haldane, "Pay Power," October 10, 2018, https://www.bis.org /review/r181011f.pdf, p. 13; Chris Giles, "BoE Deputy Governor Warns on 'False Dawn' for Wages," *Financial Times*, October 17, 2018.

32. "Minutes of the Federal Open Market Committee July 26–27, 2016," https:// www.federalreserve.gov/monetarypolicy/files/fomcminutes20160727.pdf, p. 9.

33. "Minutes of the Federal Open Market Committee January 30–31, 2018," https://www.federalreserve.gov/monetarypolicy/files/fomcminutes20180131 .pdf, p. 15.

34. Federal Reserve Press Release, January 30, 2019, https://www.federalreserve .gov/monetarypolicy/files/monetary20190130a1.pdf.

35. Kumar and Orrenius 2015; Dent et al. 2014; Aaronson and Jordan 2014; Smith 2014; Higgins 2014.

36. https://www.workplaceoptions.com/workplaceoptionsoctober2013survey2 -worklife/.

37. As noted by Isabel V. Sawhill and Christopher Pulliam, "Money Alone Doesn't

Buy Happiness, Work Does," Brookings, November 5, 2018, https://www
.brookings.edu/blog/up-front/2018/11/05/money-alone-doesnt-buy-happiness
-work-does/.

38. Ibid.; http://www.pewglobal.org/2014/10/09/emerging-and-developing
-economies-much-more-optimistic-than-rich-countries-about-the-future
/inequality-05/.

39. Board of Governors of the Federal Reserve System, "Report on the Economic
Well-Being of U.S. Households in 2017," May 2018, https://www.federalreserve
.gov/publications/files/2017-report-economic-well-being-us-households
-201805.pdf.

40. Pedro Nicolaci da Costa, "There's a Worrying Disconnect between How Fed
Officials Look at the Economy and the Way Workers Experience It," *Business
Insider*, May 23, 2018.

41. "Minutes of the Federal Open Market Committee May 1–2, 2018," https://
www.federalreserve.gov/monetarypolicy/files/fomcminutes20180502.pdf, p. 7.

42. Record of Meeting, Community Advisory Council and the Board of Governors,
Friday, May 4, 2018, https://www.federalreserve.gov/aboutthefed/files/cac
-20180504.pdf, p. 10.

43. Ibid., 13.

44. The data and documentation for the Eurobarometer Surveys are available here:
https://www.gesis.org/eurobarometer-data-service/survey-series/standard
-special-eb/.

45. McGuinnity and Russell 2013; Bossert and D'Ambrosio 2016.

46. Smith, Stillman, and Craig 2013.

47. Reeves, McKee, and Stuckler 2014.

48. Rohde et al. 2016.

49. Kalil 2013.

Chapter 4. The Semi-Slump and the Housing Market

1. "The NBER's Business Cycle Dating Committee," http://www.nber.org/cycles
/recessions.html.

2. David Blanchflower, "And Next for Britain, the Semi-Slump," *Guardian*, July
14, 2009.

3. David Blanchflower, "After the Crash: The Semi-Slump We're in," *Guardian*,
November 8, 2011.

4. Editorial, "The Economy: Politicians and the Semi-Slump," *Guardian*, September 10, 2009.

5. Lord Robert Skidelsky, "Economy: Budget Statement—Motion to Take Note
Part of the Debate—in the House of Lords at 5:43 p.m. on 13th November
2018," https://www.theyworkforyou.com/lords/?id=2018-11-13b.1828.0.

6. https://data.oecd.org/gdp/quarterly-gdp.htm.

7. Claire Jones, "Jens Weidmann Links EU Migration to Pay Pressure in Germany," *Financial Times*, January 19, 2018.

8. David Blanchflower and Elias Papaioannou, "A Different Financial Disease Means the UK Needs a Different Treatment," *Daily Telegraph*, June 8, 2010.

9. Oswald 1996, 1997, 1999.

10. U.S. Census Bureau, "Americans Moving at Historically Low Rates, Census Bureau Reports," November 16, 2016, http://census.gov/newsroom/press-releases/2016/cb16-189.html.

11. Smith, Rosen, and Fallis 1988; Hammnett 1991; Rohe and Stewart 1996; Henley 1998.

12. Blanchflower and Oswald 2013.

13. Ibid., table 9.

14. Svenja Gudell, "Q4 2016 Negative Equity Report: Improvement Continues, but at a Much Slower Rate," www.Zillow.com, March 7, 2017.

15. These are the latest data from Zillow.

16. http://ec.europa.eu/eurostat/statistics-explained/index.php/Housing_statistics.

17. Hipple 2015.

18. Krueger 2017, table 1, shows a rise in the participation rate of women age 25–34 from 2007–2017 (first half), from 74.4% to 75.3% but not for 35–44 (75.5% to 74.8%) or 45–54 (76% to 74.4%).

19. Ben Casselman, "Why Some Scars from the Recession May Never Vanish," *New York Times*, October 5, 2017.

20. Michael Saunders, "The Labour Market" (Speech given at the Resolution Foundation, January 13, 2017, Bank of England).

21. https://www.census.gov/hhes/school/data/cps/historical/index.html.

22. https://www.census.gov/data-tools/demo/idb/informationGateway.php.

23. Holzer 2007.

24. Schmitt and Warner 2010.

25. Blanchflower 2000, 2004, 2015b.

26. The only other OECD country to see an increase in the self-employment rate in recent years was the Netherlands, which has seen a rise every year since 2000: 2000 = 11.2%; 2005 = 12.4%; 2008 = 13.2%; 2010 = 15%; and 2013 = 15.9%.

27. Blanchflower 2015a.

28. Office for National Statistics, "Self-employed Workers in the UK, 2014," August 20, 2014, Department for Work and Pensions, Family Resource Survey, http://www.ons.gov.uk/ons/dcp171776_374941.pdf; Office for National Statistics, "Trends in Self-employment in the UK," February 7, 2018, https://www.ons.gov.uk/employmentandlabourmarket/peopleinwork/employmentand employeetypes/articles/trendsinselfemploymentintheuk/2018-02-07.

29. Office for National Statistics, "Contracts That Do Not Guarantee a Minimum Number of Hours," April 2018, https://www.ons.gov.uk/employmentand labourmarket/peopleinwork/earningsandworkinghours/articles/contractsthat donotguaranteeaminimumnumberofhours/april2018.

30. Estimates of earnings used in the calculations refer to gross earnings of full-time wage and salaried workers. However, this definition may vary slightly from one country to another. Further information on the national data sources and earnings concepts used in the calculations can be found at www.oecd.org/employ ment/outlook.

31. https://data.oecd.org/inequality/income-inequality.htm.

32. My thanks to Deutsche Bank chief economist Torsten Slok for providing me with these data.

33. Office for National Statistics, "Household Disposable Income and Inequality in the UK: Financial Year Ending 2016," January 10, 2017, https://www.ons .gov.uk/peoplepopulationandcommunity/personalandhouseholdfinances /incomeandwealth/bulletins/householddisposableincomeandinequality /financialyearending2016.

34. Ibid.

35. "Union Membership and Coverage Database from the CPS," www.Unionstats .com; "Trade Union Statistics, 2017," https://www.gov.uk/government/statistics /trade-union-statistics-2017.

36. Card, Lemieux, and Riddell 2004.

37. Blanchflower and Bryson 2003, 2004a, 2004b, 2010.

38. Blanchflower and Slaughter 1999.

39. McBride (2001) does a similar test.

40. Hollander 2001; Ferrer-i-Carbonell 2005; Johansson-Stenman, Carlsson, and Daruvala 2002; Senik 2004.

41. Clark and Oswald 1996.

42. Clark, Frijters, and Shields 2008.

43. Alesina, Di Tella, and MacCulloch 2004.

44. Ifcher, Zarghamee, and Graham 2016.

45. Berg and Veenhoven 2010.

46. Krueger 2012.

47. Chetty et al. 2014.

48. Neal Gabler, "The Secret Shame of Middle Class Americans," *Atlantic*, May 2016.

Chapter 5. Underemployment

1. "Did We Take Low Interest Rates for Granted?" editorial, *New York Times*, January 6, 2017.

2. "Minutes of the Federal Open Market Committee December 13–14, 2016,"

https://www.federalreserve.gov/monetarypolicy/files/fomcminutes20161214
.pdf, p. 8.

3. https://www.ecb.europa.eu/pub/economic-bulletin/html/eb201604.en.html
#IDofChapter1_2.

4. Ignazio Visco, "For the Times They Are A-Changin' . . ." (Speech at the London
School of Economics, November 11, 2015).

5. Dennis Lockhart, "A Potentially Momentous Year for Policy," January 12, 2015,
https://www.frbatlanta.org/news/speeches/2015/150112-lockhart.

6. See also Pencavel 2018.

7. Brechling 1965; Ball and St. Cyr 1966; Hart and Sharot 1978.

8. See Ashenfelter, Farber, and Ransom 2010 and Manning 2003.

9. Kahn 2010.

10. Valletta, Bengali, and van der List 2015.

11. J. Larrimore, A. Durante, K. Kreiss, E. Merry, C. Park, and C. Sahm, "Shedding
Light on Our Economic and Financial Lives," FEDS Notes, May 22, 2018.

12. Eurostat, "Underemployment and Potential Additional Labour Force Statistics,"
https://ec.europa.eu/eurostat/statistics-explained/index.php/Underemployment
_and_potential_additional_labour_force_statistics#Underemployed_part-time
_workers.

13. Bell and Blanchflower, forthcoming, 2018a, 2018b, 2014, 2013, 2011.

14. With the UKLFS, full-time or part-time status is self-defined. Analysis of the
2006 data suggests that 90% of those who describe themselves as part-timers
worked 5–32 hours per week, while 90% of those who describe themselves as
full-timers worked 34–60 hours per week (Walling and Clancy 2010).

15. There is an issue with holes in the data the ONS provides for the UK to the
EULFS so we make use of the original data from the UKLFS. They do not
provide data on those who want fewer hours but only those who want more,
which means we cannot use these data to calculate our index.

16. The A8 is the Czech Republic, Estonia, Hungary, Latvia, Lithuania, Poland,
Slovenia, and the Slovak Republic. The A2 is Bulgaria and Romania.

17. Department for Work and Pensions, "National Insurance Number Allocations
to Adult Overseas Nationals to December 2017," February 22, 2018, https://
www.gov.uk/government/statistics/national-insurance-number-allocations-to
-adult-overseas-nationals-to-december-2017.

18. https://data.oecd.org/unemp/harmonised-unemployment-rate-hur.htm.

19. See Bell and Blanchflower 2018b.

20. http://stats.oecd.org/index.aspx?queryid=36324#.

21. Hong et al. (2018) make use of a slightly different concept of involuntary part-
time employment than we do. David Bell and I use the Eurostat definition.
Hong et al. make use of the OECD definition of involuntary part-time, which
produces different estimates.

22. Austria, Belgium, Cyprus, Denmark, Estonia, Finland, France, Germany, Greece, Iceland, Ireland, Lithuania, Luxembourg, Malta, Portugal, Spain, Sweden, Switzerland, and the UK. We mapped on some additional unemployment rates that were missing from the master file for Cyprus, Lithuania, and Malta. See Bell and Blanchflower 2018b.

23. U3 = Total unemployed, as a percent of the civilian labor force (official unemployment rate)—3.9%

    U4 = Total unemployed plus discouraged workers, as a percent of the civilian labor force plus discouraged workers—4.2%

    U5 = Total unemployed, plus discouraged workers, plus all other persons marginally attached to the labor force, as a percent of the civilian labor force plus all persons marginally attached to the labor force—4.8%

    U6 = Total unemployed, plus all persons marginally attached to the labor force, plus total employed part-time for economic reasons, as a percent of the civilian labor force plus all persons marginally attached to the labor force—7.5%

    The numbers are the latest seasonally adjusted data at the time of writing (July 2018). Persons marginally attached to the labor force are those who currently are neither working nor looking for work but indicate that they want and are available for a job and have looked for work sometime in the previous twelve months. Discouraged workers, a subset of the marginally attached, have given a job-market-related reason for not currently looking for work. Persons employed part-time for economic reasons are those who want and are available for full-time work but have had to settle for a part-time schedule. https://www.bls .gov/news.release/empsit.t15.htm.

24. Philippa Dunn pointed out to us that the BLS's original broad labor market utilization measure was called U7 as outlined in Shiskin (1976) and Sorrentino (1993, 1995). U6 was defined differently from 1976 to 1993 as total full-time job seekers, plus half of the part-time job seekers, plus half of the total number of persons working part-time for economic reasons, as a percent of the civilian labor force, less half of the part-time labor force. U7 then added discouraged workers in the denominator and numerator. The definitions were changed to those described in the appendix as a result of the redesign of the CPS in January 1994. The new modified set of alternative indicators U1–U6, dropping U7, were described in Bregger and Haugen 1995. In 1994 the old U7 was 10.2% and the new U6 was 10.9%.

Chapter 6. Something Horrible Happened

1. Sir Nick, as he was at the time, told me that the first time he had ever heard of subprime mortgages was from me!

2. In the end I crossed the Atlantic every three weeks for six years. I just remember

being exhausted all the time and my golf game collapsed and my handicap doubled!

3. "Minutes of the Federal Open Market Committee September 16, 2008," https://www.federalreserve.gov/monetarypolicy/files/FOMC20080916meeting .pdf, p. 72.

4. Ibid., 3.

5. Ashley Seager and Larry Elliott, "UK Rate Cut Vital to Avoid Slump, Says MPC Member," *Guardian*, January 28, 2008.

6. "Minutes of the Federal Open Market Committee March 18, 2008," https://www.federalreserve.gov/monetarypolicy/files/fomcminutes20080318.pdf.

7. Testimony to Treasury Select Committee, September 11, 2008, http://www .publications.parliament.uk/pa/cm200708/cmselect/cmtreasy/1033/8091107 .htm. See also David G. Blanchflower, "Sir Mervyn King Missed the Big One Despite Plenty of Wake-up Calls," *Independent*, May 14, 2012.

8. Larry Kudlow, "Kudlow 101: There Ain't No Recession," *National Review*, December 7, 2007.

9. Employment Situation, December 2007, BLS.

10. Megan Keller, "Kudlow: 'Recession Is So Far in the Distance I Can't See It,'" *The Hill*, November 20, 2018.

11. "Lessons of the Fall," *Economist*, October 18, 2007.

12. Treasury Select Committee, "The Run on the Rock, Volume 1," January 24, 2008, The Stationery Office, London, https://publications.parliament .uk/pa/cm200708/cmselect/cmtreasy/56/56i.pdf.

13. "Rush on Northern Rock Continues," BBC News, September 15, 2007.

14. Graham Wearden, "Santander to Buy A&L for £1.3bn," *Guardian*, July 2008.

15. Harry Wallop, "Bradford & Bingley: A History of How and When It All Went Wrong," *Telegraph*, September 28, 2008.

16. "Lessons of the Fall."

17. Martin Wolf, "Osborne Has Now Been Proved Wrong on Austerity," *Financial Times*, September 26, 2013.

18. Sumeet Desai and Matt Falloon, "Bank's Blanchflower Says Big Rate Cuts Needed," Reuters, August 28, 2008.

19. MPC Minutes, September 3 and 4, 2008, https://www.bankofengland.co.uk /minutes/2008/monetary-policy-committee-september-2008.

20. David Blanchflower, "Pity the Lost Generation," *New Statesman*, September 24, 2009.

21. Mark Carney, "The Spectre of Monetarism" (Roscoe Lecture, Liverpool John Moores University, December 5, 2016).

22. Quoted in Susan Page, "10 Years Later We May Not Be Ready for Another Fiscal Crisis," *USA Today*, July 18, 2018.

23. Nassim Nicholas Taleb, he of Black Swan fame, has argued that what we have

seen is a rebellion against the inner circle of policymakers who are telling us (1) what to do, (2) what to eat, (3) how to speak, (4) how to think, and (5) whom to vote for. He calls them the Intellectual Yet Idiot (IYI). See "The Intellectual Yet Idiot," Medium.com, September 16, 2016. He says, colorfully, the IYI has been wrong, historically, on "Stalinism, Maoism, GMOs, Iraq, Libya, Syria, lobotomies, urban planning, low carbohydrate diets, gym machines, behaviorism, transfats, Freudianism, portfolio theory, linear regression, Gaussianism, Salafism, dynamic stochastic equilibrium modeling, housing projects, selfish gene, election forecasting models, Bernie Madoff (pre-blowup) and p-values. But he is convinced that his current position is right." He doesn't mean me of course!

24. Letter to the Queen from the British Academy signed by 33 economists including 9 members, ex- and future, of the MPC and civil servants: http://www.feed -charity.org/user/image/besley-hennessy2009a.pdf.

25. Charlie Bean, "Measuring Recession and Recovery: An Economic Perspective" (Speech at RSS Statistics User Forum Conference, October 27, 2010).

26. Blanchflower 2013.

27. A. L. Sussman, "Q & A: Paul Romer on 'Mathiness' and the State of Economics," *Wall Street Journal*, August 17, 2015.

28. Wolfgang Münchau, "A Warning for the Losers of the Liberal Elite: If You Make the Same Mistakes in the Battles of 2017, Populists Will Win Everywhere," *Financial Times*, January 15, 2017.

29. Narayana Kocherlakota, "Economic Forecasting Is Still Broken," Bloomberg Opinion, May 19, 2017.

30. Ibid.

31. Office for Budget Responsibility, "Forecast Evaluation Report, October 2017," https://obr.uk/fer/forecast-evaluation-report-october-2017/, p. 6.

32. Ibid., 7.

33. Business Leader, "Brexit Wasn't a 'Michael Fish Moment': But Economics Does Need to Change," *Guardian*, January 8, 2017.

34. David Miles, "Andy Haldane Is Wrong: There Is No Crisis in Economics. Brexit Forecast Failures Tell Us Nothing New," *Financial Times*, January 11, 2017.

35. Chari and Kehoe 2006.

36. Russ Roberts, "What Do Economists Actually Know?" Newco Shift, March 2, 2017, https://shift.newco.co/what-do-economists-know-199bf5793ae6 #.7gy2oul7n.

37. Adam Ozimek, "The Value of Empirical Economics," *Economy.com*, March 8, 2017, https://www.economy.com/dismal/analysis/datapoints/294247/The -Value-of-Empirical-Economics/.

38. Noah Smith, "Anti-empiricism Is Not Humility," http://noahpinionblog .blogspot.com, March 10, 2017.

39. John Cochrane, "Russ Roberts on Economic Humility," *Grumpy Economist*, March 3, 2017, http://johnhcochrane.blogspot.com/2017/03/russ-roberts-on -economic-humility.html.

40. Robert Shiller, "Richard Thaler Is a Controversial Nobel Prize Winner—but a Deserving One," *Guardian*, October 11, 2017. Six percent of all Nobels have been awarded, says Shiller, to people who can be classified as behavioral economists including Richard Thaler (2017), Bob Shiller (2013), George Akerlof (2001), Robert Fogel (1993), Daniel Kahneman (2002), and Elinor Ostrom (2009).

41. Stephen Nickell, "Household Debt, House Prices and Consumption Growth" (Speech given at Bloomberg in London, September 14, 2004).

42. Charles Bean, speech given at the Colchester Town Partnership Annual Dinner, Moot Hall, Colchester, November 25, 2004, https://www.bankofengland .co.uk/-/media/boe/files/speech/2004/colechester-town-partnership-annual -dinner.

43. Ryan Cooper, "The Biggest Policy Mistake of the Last Decade," *The Week*, August 14, 2018.

44. The 2015 numbers are taken from the OBR's March 2017 forecast.

45. "Budget 2011: Chancellor George Osborne's Speech in Full," *Daily Telegraph*, March 23, 2011, https://www.telegraph.co.uk/finance/budget/8401022/Budget -2011-Chancellor-George-Osbornes-speech-in-full.html.

46. David Blanchflower and Robert Skidelsky, "Cable's Attempt to Claim Keynes Is Well Argued—but Unconvincing," *New Statesman*, January 27, 2011.

47. Joe Stiglitz, "When It Comes to the Economy, Britain Has a Choice: May's 80s Rerun or Corbyn's Bold Rethink," *Prospect Magazine*, October 9, 2017.

48. Martin Wolf, "How Austerity Has Failed," *New York Review of Books*, July 11, 2011.

49. George Osborne, "A New Economic Model," https://conservative-speeches.sayit .mysociety.org/speech/601526.

50. The result was ultimately published as Herndon, Ash, and Pollin 2014.

51. Simon Wren-Lewis, "The Biggest Economic Policy Mistake of the Last Decade, and It Had Nothing to Do with Academic Economists," Mainly Macro Blog, August 21, 2018.

52. P. De Grauwe, "Cherished Myths Fall Victim to Economic Reality," *Financial Times*, July 22, 2008.

53. Mervyn King, "The Inflation Target Ten Years On" (Speech at the London School of Economics, November 2002).

54. Robert Skidelsky, "We Forgot Everything Keynes Taught Us," *Washington Post*, October 13, 2008.

55. Wolfgang Münchau, "The Elite's Marie Antoinette Moment: Right Response

Is to Focus on the Financial Sector and Inequality," *Financial Times*, November 27, 2016.

56. Simon Wren-Lewis, "Miles on Haldane on Economics in Crisis," Mainly Macro Blog, January 13, 2017.

57. Skidelsky 2009. Robert sent me an early copy of his book. He was much amused to find out, though, that on the day it arrived my Bernese Mountain dog, Monty, shredded the book to pieces and I had to buy another one. Sadly, he never did that to any other book.

58. I first met Larry Summers (who was the youngest full professor at Harvard ever, and a star) in the 1980s when he used to come to the unemployment seminar at the London School of Economics. I chatted with him once over dinner in Hawaii after a seminar and he told me I should do public service in the UK. I took his advice as one mostly should. At a press conference I did once hear him apologize to the people of South Korea for a comment he had made.

59. Paul Krugman, "The State of Macro Is Sad (Wonkish)," *New York Times*, August 12, 2016.

60. Ben Riley-Smith and Michael Wilkinson, "Michael Gove Compares Experts Warning against Brexit to Nazis Who Smeared Albert Einstein's Work as He Threatens to Quit David Cameron's Cabinet," *Telegraph*, June 21, 2016. In a tweet to me Gove even claimed I was "mugged by reality." The UK economy quickly thereafter went from the fastest growing in the G7 to the slowest.

Chapter 7. Sniffing the Air and Spotting the Great Recession

1. Lempert explains that the man on the Clapham omnibus is the "judicially constructed image of a sane, sober but not extraordinarily gifted person who never takes unreasonable chances, and does nothing extraordinary, but does everything that is ordinary, to perfection" (2003, 3).

2. David Blanchflower, "Recent Developments in the UK Economy: The Economics of Walking About" (Bernard Corry Memorial Lecture, Queen Mary College, University of London, May 30, 2007).

3. Blanchflower, Oswald, and Garrett 1990; Blanchflower, Oswald, and Sanfey 1996.

4. Sorrentino 1981. The data for the UK are for 1961 and 1971 rather than 1960 and 1970 (for the United States).

5. Fujihara et al. 2017.

6. "2008 Plastic Surgery Statistics," American Society of Plastic Surgeons, https://www.plasticsurgery.org/news/plastic-surgery-statistics?sub=2008+Plastic+Surgery+Statistics.

7. Tamar Lewin, "The Hemline Index, Updated," *New York Times*, October 19, 2008.

8. I am grateful to Mike McKee for providing me with Richard Yamarone's data from the Bloomberg terminal.

9. Griff Witte, "As Brexit Approaches, Signs of a Gathering Economic Storm for Britain," *Washington Post*, December 13, 2016.

10. Zlata Rodionova, "Brexit Hits Pink Wafer Maker Rivington Biscuits as It Goes into Administration Cutting 100 Jobs," *Independent*, December 15, 2016.

11. Jill Treanor, "JP Morgan to Move Hundreds of Jobs out of the UK Due to Brexit," *Guardian*, May 3, 2017.

12. Amelia Heathman, "Which Companies Could Leave the UK Because of Brexit?" Verdict.co.uk, August 2, 2017.

13. Sarah Gordon and Jim Pickard, "More UK Businesses Join Airbus Lead on Hard Brexit Warning," *Financial Times*, June 21, 2018.

14. Patrick Greenfield, "Airbus Plans UK Job Cuts amid Fears of Hard Brexit Impact," *Guardian*, June 19, 2018.

15. Aditya Chakrabortty, "Airbus Has Delivered a Body Blow to Brexit Britain: It Won't Be the Last," *Guardian*, June 22, 2018.

16. Peter Campbell, "Jaguar Land Rover Says Hard Brexit Will Cost It £1.2bn a Year," *Financial Times*, July 4, 2018.

17. Ibid.

18. https://money.cnn.com/interactive/news/economy/brexit-jobs-tracker/.

19. Leo Lewis, "Japanese Drugmaker Moves European HQ from London over Brexit," *Financial Times*, March 11, 2019.

20. Ian Ayres, "Man vs. Machine—Grape Expectations: The Price of Wine," *Financial Times*, September 1, 2007.

21. I even had a hat made for them saying "Myth and Measurement" to go with our "Wage Curve" hats.

22. Kolev and Hogarth 2010.

23. Ghent and Kudlyack 2010.

24. http://www.bankofengland.co.uk/publications/Pages/agentssummary/default .aspx.

25. I am grateful to Bill Lines from the Baltic Exchange for providing these data.

26. Mickey Fulp, "The 14-Year Record of the Baltic Dry Index," Kitco.com, January 12, 2017, www.kitco.com/commentaries/2016-12-21/The-14-Year-Record-of -the-Baltic-Dry-Index.html.

27. https://www.bloomberg.com/quote/BDIY:IND.

28. MPC Minutes, August 6 and 7, 2008, para. 34, https://www.bankofengland.co .uk/minutes/2008/monetary-policy-committee-august-2008.

29. Ibid., para. 41.

30. https://www.bankofengland.co.uk/-/media/boe/files/speech/2007/recent -developments-in-the-uk-economy-the-economics-of-walking-about; David Blanchflower, "Inflation, Expectations and Monetary Policy" (Speech given at

the Royal Society, George Street, Edinburgh, April 29, 2008), https://www
.bankofengland.co.uk/-/media/boe/files/speech/2008/inflation-expectations
-and-monetary-policy.

31. The FOMC's median GDP forecast was 2.7% in 2018, 2.4% in 2019, and 2%
in 2020. The OECD's "Economic Outlook, March 2018" forecast was for U.S.
GDP growth of 2.9% in 2018 and 2.8% in 2019. The World Bank's "Global
Economic Forecast 2018" (January) had 2.5% in 2018, 2.2% in 2019, and 2%
in 2020. The IMF's *World Economic Outlook* in April 2018 (IMF 2018) pro-
jected growth of 2.9% in 2018 and 2.7% in 2019.

32. Silvana Tenreyro, "Models in Macroeconmics" (Speech given at the University
of Surrey, June 4, 2018).

33. Jon Cunliffe, "The Phillips Curve: Lower, Flatter or in Hiding?" (Speech given
at the Oxford Economics Society, Bank of England, November 14, 2017).

34. Based on Eurostat news releases, November 2018, http://ec.europa.eu/eurostat
/news/news-releases.

35. Eurostat news release, "Annual Growth in Unit Labour Costs at 2.2% in Euro
Area," 143/2018, September 14, 2018.

36. Kate Allen and Adam Samson, "Markets Hit as ECB Officials Strike Upbeat
Note," *Financial Times*, June 6, 2018.

37. Peter Praet, "Monetary Policy in a Low Interest Rate Environment" (Speech
given to the Congress of Actuaries, June 6, 2018, Berlin), https://www.ecb
.europa.eu/pub/pdf/annex/ecb.sp180606_slides.en.pdf?0924e43dc5efe28f616f
666074bd791b.

38. Allen and Samson, "Markets Hit as ECB Officials Strike Upbeat Note."

39. Sabine Lautenschläger, "Monetary Policy—End of History?" (Speech at the
Center for Financial Studies Colloquium, Frankfurt, May 29, 2018).

40. "Monthly New Residential Construction, September 2018," Release Number:
CB18-158, October 17, 2018, https://www.census.gov/construction/nrc/pdf
/newresconst_201809.pdf.

41. Megan Davies, "Twelve Charts to Watch for Signs of the Next U.S. Downturn,"
Reuters, July 25, 2018.

42. Nic Fildes, "UK High Street Braces for More Store Closures," *Financial Times*,
May 20, 2018.

43. Office for National Statistics, "Making Ends Meet: Are Households Living
beyond Their Means?" July 26, 2018, https://www.ons.gov.uk/economy
/nationalaccounts/uksectoraccounts/articles/makingendsmeetarehouseholdsliv
ingbeyondtheirmeans/2018-07-26.

44. David Smith, "Why Jobs Are Booming When Growth Stays Weak," *Sunday
Times*, June 17, 2018.

45. Miles Johnson, "How Investors Failed to Spot Carillion's Mounting Problems,"
Financial Times, January 15, 2018.

46. Hallie Dietrick, "What You Need to Know about the Collapse of Carillion, a U.K. Construction Giant," *Fortune*, January 15, 2018.

47. Gill Plimmer, Cat Rutter Pooley, Jim Pickard, and Josephine Cumbo, "Recriminations Fly after Carillion Collapses," *Financial Times*, January 15, 2018.

48. Aditya Chakrabortty, "The Company That Runs Britain Is Near to Collapse: Watch and Worry," *Guardian*, January 12, 2018.

49. Julia Kollewe, "HS2 Contractor Carillion Investigated by FCA," *Guardian*, January 3, 2018.

50. Rob Davies, "Debt-Laden Four Seasons Health Care Suffers £27.5m Loss," *Guardian*, November 16, 2017; "Four Seasons Health Care Rescue Talks Suffer Setback," *Guardian*, January 11, 2018.

Chapter 8. The People Have Lost Their Pep

1. There is a bronze statue of Frost on the Dartmouth campus. On it is written, "Something there is that doesn't love a wall," the first line of the famous poem "Mending Wall." https://news.dartmouth.edu/news/2016/03/dartmouth-artists -take-inspiration-frost-statue.

2. https://www.ons.gov.uk/peoplepopulationandcommunity/wellbeing/datasets /headlineestimatesofpersonalwellbeing.

3. Plesh, Adams, and Gansky 2012.

4. Kennedy et al. 2014.

5. Freburger et al. 2009.

6. Palmer et al. 2000; Harkness et al. 2005.

7. Leino, Berg, and Puska 1994; Heistaro et al. 1998.

8. Huppe, Muller, and Raspe 2007.

9. Christopher Ingraham, "Not Only Are Americans Becoming Less Happy— We're Experiencing More Pain Too," *Washington Post*, December 6, 2017.

10. Pratt and Brody 2014a.

11. Mojtabai and Olfson 2014.

12. NHS Digital 2016.

13. NHS Digital 2017.

14. For example, the incidence of depression was 0.6% in 1997; 1.5% in 2005; 1.6% in 2010; 1.9% in 2012; 2.4% in 2014; 2.9% in 2016; and 3.6% in 2018.

15. Exceptions are interesting essays by Kuhn, Lalive, and Zweimüller (2009) and Ludwig, Marcotte, and Norberg (2009). For a recent discussion, see the work by Katolik and Oswald (2017), who discuss research on the impact of advertising on antidepressant consumption, the link between antidepressants and the midlife crisis, and evidence on how antidepressants are connected to crime, suicide, and financial hardship.

16. Askitas and Zimmermann 2015.

17. Walburn et al. 2009.
18. Gouin and Kiecolt-Glaser 2011.
19. Marucha, Kiecolt-Glaser, and Favagehi 1998.
20. Kopp et al. 2003.
21. De Wit et al. 2010.
22. https://stateofobesity.org/rates/.
23. 1. West Virginia; 2. Mississippi; 3. Alabama; 4. Arkansas; 5. Louisiana; 6. Tennessee; 7. Kentucky; 8. Texas; 9. Oklahoma; 10. Indiana.
24. http://www.oecd.org/health/obesity-update.htm.
25. Albania; Argentina; Australia; Azerbaijan; Belarus; Belgium; Bosnia; Brazil; Brunei; Bulgaria; Cambodia; Canada; Chile; China; Colombia; Costa Rica; Croatia; Czech Republic; Denmark; Dominican Republic; Ecuador; El Salvador; Estonia; Finland; France; Germany; Greece; Honduras; Hungary; Iceland; Iraq; Ireland; Israel; Italy; Japan; Kyrgyzstan; Laos; Latvia; Lithuania; Luxembourg; Macedonia; Malta; Mexico; Myanmar; Netherlands; Nicaragua; Nigeria; Norway; Paraguay; Peru; Philippines; Poland; Portugal; Puerto Rico; Romania; Russia; Serbia; Singapore; Slovakia; South Africa; South Korea; Spain; Sweden; Switzerland; Tanzania; Turkey; the UK; Ukraine; Uruguay; the United States; Uzbekistan; and Zimbabwe. Blanchflower 2009; Blanchflower and Oswald 2017.
26. The U-shape is confirmed by other studies (Deaton 2008; Stone et al. 2010; Van Landeghem 2012; Wunder et al. 2013; Schwandt 2016). Gazioglu and Tansel (2006) found that job satisfaction in the UK was U-shaped according to age. It even turns out that there is evidence of a midlife crisis in apes (Weiss et al. 2012). Glenn (2009) argued that it was appropriate to only look at patterns without controls; we disagreed (Blanchflower and Oswald 2009).
27. I estimated OLS regressions in every case containing only an age and age-squared terms pooled across countries.

    "How satisfied with life as a whole?" = $-.0423$ Age + $.00038$ Age^2 (min = 56).

    "How satisfied with the state of the economy as a whole?" = $-.03955$ Age + $.00036$ Age^2 (min = 55).

    "How satisfied with the national government?" = $-.0584$ Age + $.00058$ Age^2 (min = 50).

    "How satisfied with the way democracy works in country?" = $-.0522$ Age + $.00047$ Age^2 (min = 55).

    "How satisfied with state of education nowadays?" = $-.0425$ Age + $.00039$ Age^2 (min = 54).

    "How satisfied with state of health services in country nowadays?" = $-.0852$ Age + $.00081$ Age^2 (min = 52).

28. Life satisfaction = $-.0196$ Age $-.00018$ Age^2 (min = 56).

National economy = –.0131 Age – .00015 Age^2 (min = 44).

Employment in country = –.0089 Age – .00009 Age^2 (min = 50).

Financial situation = –.0133 Age – .00012 Age^2 (min = 51).

Public services = –.0149 Age – .00015 Age^2 (min = 48).

29. Stone, Schneidera, and Brodericka 2017.
30. Steptoe, Deaton, and Stone 2015, fig. 3.
31. Ibid., fig. 2.
32. Stone et al. 2010.
33. Anderson, Russell, and Schumm 1983; Orbuch et al. 1996.
34. For the technically minded this is obtained by taking the variable *hapmar*, reversing the coding, and regressing it on age and age-squared—the resulting equation is happiness of marriage = 2.809163 – .0098172 Age (t = 7.9) + .0001041 Age^2 (t = 8.4). The minimum of 47 is obtained by differentiating with respect to age, setting to zero, and solving. The answer is similar if I include 72 single year of age dummies; the smallest was the dummy for age 49.
35. https://www.americashealthrankings.org/explore/2015-annual-report/measure /MentalHealth/state/ALL.
36. Bohnert et al. 2011.
37. Kanny et al. 2015.
38. "Deaths: Final Data for 2014," National Vital Statistics Reports, June 30, 2016.
39. See *American Association of Suicidology—Facts & Statistics*, https://www .suicidology.org/resources/facts-statistics; and Curtin, Warner, and Hedegaard 2015.
40. Curtin, Warner, and Hedegaard 2016.
41. Oswald and Tohamy 2017.
42. "Suicide among Veterans and Other Americans, 2001–2014," Department of Veterans Affairs, Office of Suicide Prevention, August 3, 2016.
43. Platt, Micciolo, and Tansella 1992.
44. Kao et al. 2014.
45. Pierce and Schott 2016.
46. Jonathan Auerbach and Andrew Gelman, "Stop Saying White Mortality Is Rising," *Slate*, March 28, 2017.
47. Malcolm Harris, "The Death of the White Working Class Has Been Greatly Exaggerated," *Pacific Standard*, March 28, 2017.
48. Noah Smith, "The Blogs vs. Case-Deaton," Noahpinion, Wednesday, March 29, 2017, http://noahpinionblog.blogspot.ie/2017/03/the-blogs-vs-case-deaton .html.
49. Paul Overberg, "The Divide between America's Prosperous Cities and Struggling Small Towns—in 20 Charts," *Wall Street Journal*, December 29, 2017.
50. An unintentional injury is one that was unplanned. Unintentional injuries can

be defined as events in which the injury occurs in a short period of time and the harmful outcome was not sought. Or the outcome was the result of one of the forms of physical energy in the environment or normal body functions being blocked by external means, e.g., drowning. The most common unintentional injuries result from motor vehicle crashes, falls, fires and burns, drowning, poisonings, and aspirations.

51. MacKenzie et al. 2006.
52. Mack, Jones, and Ballesteros 2017.
53. Peterson et al. 2018; Murphy et al. 2018; Hedegaard, Miniño, and Warner 2018.
54. Kochanek et al. 2017; Murphy et al. 2017.

Chapter 9. Somebody Has to Be Blamed

1. Laura Bush, "Separating Children from Their Parents at the Border 'Breaks My Heart,'" *Washington Post*, June 17, 2018.
2. Chris Reeves, "MSNBC Analysts: Trump Is Creating 'Concentration Camps' for Immigrant Children," Townhall.com, June 15, 2018.
3. Jenna Johnson, "Trump Calls for 'Total and Complete Shutdown of Muslims Entering the United States,'" *Washington Post*, December 7, 2015.
4. "Full Text: Donald Trump Announces a Presidential Bid," *Washington Post*, June 16, 2015.
5. Lewis and Peri 2014.
6. Pew Research Center, "U.S. Unauthorized Immigration Population Estimates," November 2016.
7. Jens Manuel Kronstad, Jeffrey S. Passel, and D'Vera Cohn, "5 Facts about Illegal Immigration in the US," November 3, 2016, http://www.pewresearch.org/fact -tank/2017/04/27/5-facts-about-illegal-immigration-in-the-u-s/.
8. Jeffrey S. Passel, D'Vera Cohn, and John Gramlich, "Number of U.S.-Born Babies with Unauthorized Immigrant Parents Has Fallen since 2007," Pew Research Center, FactTank, November 1, 2018.
9. "CBP Border Security Report: Fiscal Year 2017," December 5, 2017, U.S. Customs and Border Protection, https://www.cbp.gov/sites/default/files/assets /documents/2017-Dec/cbp-border-security-report-fy2017.pdf; Miriam Jordan, "U.S. Says Deportations Rose 2% in the Latest Year," *Wall Street Journal*, December 30, 2016.
10. U.S. Department of Homeland Security, "Entry/Exit Overstay Report Fiscal Year 2015," https://www.dhs.gov/sites/default/files/publications/FY%2015 %20DHS%20Entry%20and%20Exit%20Overstay%20Report.pdf.
11. Hanson, Liu, and McIntosh 2017.

12. Ronald Brownstein, "Places with the Fewest Immigrants Push Back Hardest against Immigration," CNN, August 22, 2017.

13. https://www.ipsos.com/sites/default/files/migrations/en-uk/files/Assets/Docs /Polls/EU%20immigration_FINAL%20SLIDES%2020.06.16%20V3.pdf.

14. Toby Helm, "Immigration Is Lowest Concern on Young Voters' Brexit List," *Guardian*, January 21, 2017.

15. "Shifting Grounds: Attitudes towards Immigration and Brexit," Ipsos Mori, October 17, 2017.

16. Blinder and Richards 2016.

17. May Bulman, "Brexit: People Voted to Leave EU Because They Feared Immigration, Major Survey Finds," *Independent*, June 28, 2017.

18. http://www.gallup.com/poll/4909/Terrorism-United-States.aspx.

19. Zac Auter, "Americans Continue to Cite the Economy as Top Problem," Gallup, October 14, 2016.

20. Pew Research Center, "Europe's Growing Muslim Population," https://www .researchgate.net/publication/322791924_Europe's_Growing_Muslim _Population_Muslims_are_projected_to_increase_as_a_share_of_Europe's _population_--_even_with_no_future_migration, November 29, 2017, p. 30.

21. Ibid., 24.

22. Phillip Connor and Jens Manuel Krogstad, "5 Facts about Migration and the UK," Pew Research Center, June 21, 2016.

23. Dustmann et al. 2003.

24. National Statistics Department for Work and Pensions, "National Insurance Number Allocations to Adult Overseas Nationals to June 2018," August 24, 2017, https://www.gov.uk/government/statistics/national-insurance-number -allocations-to-adult-overseas-nationals-to-june-2018.

25. U.S. Census Bureau, "New American Community Survey Statistics for Income, Poverty and Health Insurance Available for States and Local Areas," September 14, 2017, https://www.census.gov/newsroom/press-releases/2017/acs-single -year.html?CID=CBSM+ACS16.

26. Office for National Statistics, "Note on the Difference between National Insurance Number Registrations and the Estimate of Long-Term International Migration: 2016," May 2016, https://www.ons.gov.uk/peoplepopulationand community/populationandmigration/internationalmigration/articles/noteon thedifferencebetweennationalinsurancenumberregistrationsandtheestimateof longterminternationalmigration/2016.

27. Frey Lindsay, "Ukrainian Immigrants Give the Polish Government an Out on Refugees," *Forbes*, September 18, 2018.

28. Longhi, Nijkamp, and Poot 2005.

29. A very small impact on wages from immigration in the UK was also found by

Nickell and Saleheen (2015). In my first year at the Bank of England Jumana Saleheen worked for me as my research advisor.

30. Kerr and Kerr 2011.

31. Longhi, Nijkamp, and Poot 2005.

32. Boubtane, Dumont, and Rault 2015.

33. Forte and Portes 2017.

34. "Crime," www.gallup.com/poll/1603/crime.aspx.

35. John Gramlich, "Voters' Perceptions of Crime Continue to Conflict with Reality," Pew Research Center, FactTank, November 16, 2016.

36. Frank Newport, "Americans' Fear of Walking Alone Ties 52-Year Low," Gallup, November 2, 2017, https://news.gallup.com/poll/221183/americans-fear-walking-alone-ties-year-low.aspx.

37. "A Nation of Pessimists: Americans Don't Realize How Good Things Are. Results from Ipsos 'Perils of Perceptions' 2017 Survey," Ipsos Mori, December 6, 2017, https://www.ipsos.com/sites/default/files/ct/news/documents/2017-12/perils-of-perception-us-pr-12-6-2017.pdf .

38. Pamela Constable, "Most U.S. Voters View Immigrants Positively, but Most Trump Voters Don't," *Washington Post*, March 31, 2016.

39. https://news.gallup.com/poll/1660/immigration.aspx.

40. Pew Research Center, "On Immigration Policy, Partisan Differences but Also Some Common Ground," August 25, 2016; John Gramlich, "Trump Voters Want to Build the Wall, but Are More Divided on Other Immigration Questions," Pew Research Center, November 29, 2016; Jaya Padmanabhan, "What a Pew Poll Says about Our Views on Undocumented Immigrants," *San Francisco Examiner*, December 28, 2016.

41. Pew Research Center, "A Divided and Pessimistic Electorate," November 10, 2016, http://www.people-press.org/2016/11/10/a-divided-and-pessimistic-electorate/.

42. Jennifer De Pinto, Fred Backus, Kabir Khanna, and Anthony Salvanto, "Americans Continue to Oppose U.S.-Mexico Border Wall: CBS News Poll," CBS News, March 12, 2018.

43. Pew Research Center, "The Partisan Divide on Political Values Grows Even Wider," October 5, 2017.

44. Sean McElwee and Jason McDaniel, "Economic Anxiety Didn't Make People Vote for Trump, Racism Did," *Nation*, May 8, 2017; http://electionstudies.org/studypages/download/datacenter_all_NoData.php.

45. Niraj Chokshi, "75 Percent of Americans Say Immigration Is Good for Country, Poll Finds," *New York Times*, June 23, 2018.

46. "American Public Does Not See Celebrity Candidates as the Answer," Ipsos, June 15, 2018; YouGov for the *Economist*, poll, June 17–19, 2018.

47. Megan Brenan, "Record-High 75% of Americans Say Immigration Is a Good Thing," Gallup, June 21, 2018.

48. Pew Research Center, "Voters More Focused on Control of Congress—and the President—than in Past Midterms," June 20, 2018, http://www.people-press .org/2018/06/20/voters-more-focused-on-control-of-congress-and-the -president-than-in-past-midterms/.

49. Philip Rucker, "Trump, Stumping in Nevada, Makes Immigration a Central Midterms Issue for GOP," *Washington Post*, June 23, 2018.

50. Donato Paolo Mancini and Jason Douglas, "EU Doctors Quit Britain as Brexit Looms: An Exodus of Medical Specialists Is Putting New Strains on the U.K.'s National Health System," *Wall Street Journal*, December 2, 2018.

Chapter 10. Disastrous Cries for Help

1. "The only antidote to decades of ruinous rule by a small handful of elites is a bold infusion of popular will. On every major issue affecting this country, the people are right, and the governing elite are wrong." Donald J. Trump, *Wall Street Journal*, April 15, 2016.

2. http://www.cnn.com/election/results/exit-polls/national/president.

3. https://www.washingtonpost.com/graphics/opinions/trump-supporters-why -vote/.

4. Jason Margolis, "How Trump Won Over Pennsylvania's Steel-Town Democrats and Tennessee's Christians," *PRI's The World*, November 10, 2016, http://www .wuwm.com/post/how-trump-won-over-pennsylvanias-steel-town-democrats -and-tennessees-christians#stream/0.

5. Jason Margolis, "Trump's Anti-globalization Message Resonates in 'Forgotten' Pennsylvania Town," *PRI's The World*, July 20, 2016, https://www.pri.org/stories /2016-07-20/forgotten-world-trumps-anti-globalization-message-resonates -struggling.

6. Kris Maher, Valerie Bauerlein, and Jim Carlton, "Voter Anxiety That Fueled Trump's Victory Turns to Hope for Jobs," *Wall Street Journal*, January 19, 2017.

7. Powdthavee et al. 2017.

8. Andrew Higgins, "Wigan's Road to 'Brexit': Anger, Loss and Class Resentments," *New York Times*, July 5, 2016.

9. Harriet Agnew, "Macron Calls Emergency Meeting after Riots Leave France in Shock," *Financial Times*, December 2, 2018; Angelique Chrisafis, "Paris Rioting: French Government Considers State of Emergency over 'Gilets Jaunes' Protests," *Guardian*, December 2, 2018.

10. Noemie Bisserbe, Nick Kostov, and Stacy Meichtry, "Paris Protests Turn Violent Again Despite Heavy Security," *Wall Street Journal*, December 8, 2018.

11. Kim Willsher, "Paris under Siege as Gilets Jaunes Open 'Act IV': A Fourth Weekend of Protest," *Guardian*, December 8, 2018.

12. Kim Willsher, "Macron Bows to Protesters' Demands and Says: I Know I Have Hurt Some of You," *Guardian*, December 10, 2018.

13. A. Selyukh, "After Brexit Vote, Britain Asks Google: 'What Is the EU?'" NPR News, June 24, 2016.

14. F. Islam, "Post-Brexit Sunderland: 'If This Money Doesn't Go to the NHS, I Will Go Mad,'" *Guardian*, August 9, 2016.

15. A. Chakrabortty, "Just About Managing? In Towns Like Pontypool That's a Dream," *Guardian*, November 22, 2016.

16. James Pickard, "Welcome to the Most Pro-Brexit Town in Britain," *Financial Times*, February 2, 2017.

17. Helen Pidd, "Blackpool's Brexit Voters Revel in 'Giving the Metropolitan Elite a Kicking,'" *Guardian*, June 27, 2016; Chakrabortty, "Just About Managing?"

18. Elisabeth O'Leary, "'Get on with it': English Seaside Town Has Brexit Message for PM May," Reuters, November 8, 2016.

19. Steven Erlanger, "A Once-Declining British Resort Town Sees New Life, Post-Brexit," *New York Times*, August 21, 2016.

20. I am grateful to Oliver Heath for providing me with these county-level data.

21. Christopher Caldwell, "The French, Coming Apart," *City Journal*, Spring 2017.

22. Zapryanova and Christiansen 2017.

23. Mark Lilla, "France: Is There a Way Out?" *New York Review of Books*, March 10, 2016.

24. http://elections.interieur.gouv.fr/presidentielle-2017/; https://www.bdm.insee.fr/bdm2/choixCriteres?codeGroupe=712.

25. Sebastian Payne, "East Coast Collapse Gives a Boost to UK Rail Nationalisation," *Financial Times*, May 16, 2018.

26. In order: 1. West Wales; 2. Cornwall; 3. Durham and Tees Valley; 4 Lincolnshire; 5. South Yorkshire; 6. Shropshire and Staffordshire; 7. Lancashire; 8. Northern Ireland; and joint 10. East Yorkshire and North Lincolnshire. http://inequalitybriefing.org/graphics/briefing_43_UK_regions_poorest_North_Europe.pdf.

27. Chiara Albanese and Marco Bertacche, "Italians Still Want the Euro," June 5, 2018, https://www.bloomberg.com/news/articles/2018-06-05/euro-skeptics-won-the-election-but-italians-still-want-the-euro.

28. James Politi and Kate Allen, "Italian Market Turmoil Deepens as President Picks New Premier," *Financial Times*, May 29, 2018.

29. Tony Barber, "The Chiaroscuro of Italian Populism," *Financial Times*, May 28, 2018.

30. Gideon Rachman, "Italy, Democracy and the Euro Cage," *Financial Times*, June 4, 2018.

31. John Follain, Lorenzo Totaro, and Chiara Albanese, "Italy's Conte Promises Populist Agenda, Urges Strong Europe," Bloomberg, June 5, 2018.

32. Miles Johnson and Mehreen Khan, "Italy Remains Defiant over Government Budget Plans," *Financial Times*, November 13, 2018; Miles Johnson, "IMF Warns Italy That Budget Plans Risk Backfiring," *Financial Times*, November 13, 2018.

33. Barbara Surk, "Slovenia Elections Tilt Another European Country to the Right," *New York Times*, June 3, 2018.

34. Bojan Pancevski, "Austrian Leader's Blueprint for Europe's Establishment: Move to the Right," *Wall Street Journal*, May 25, 2018.

35. Polly Curtis, "How Gillian Duffy Nipped out for a Loaf—but Left Gordon Brown in a Right Jam," *Guardian*, April 29, 2010.

36. Charlie Sykes, "If Liberals Hate Him, Then Trump Must Be Doing Something Right," *New York Times*, May 12, 2017.

37. Art Buchwald, "What about Chappaquiddick?" *Los Angeles Times*, July 12, 1973.

38. http://insider.foxnews.com/2017/05/19/harvard-study-80-percent-trump-coverage-was-negative-during-first-hundred-days.

39. www.Luzernecounty.org.

40. Nadia Popovich, "Today's Energy Jobs Are in Solar, Not Coal," *New York Times*, April 25, 2017.

41. Laura McCrystal, "Trump and His Supporters, Defiant in Blue-Collar Pennsylvania," Philly.com, October 11, 2017.

42. Jan Murphy, "Luzerne Countians Voted for Trump, but Now 'He's Going to Need Our Prayers' More than Ever," PennLive.com, January 19, 2017.

43. Michelle Nijhuis, "Why Trump Can't Make Coal Great Again," *National Geographic*, March 28, 2017.

44. Chico Harlan reported that similar lawsuits were also filed in Farmers Branch, Texas; Valley Park, Missouri; Riverside, New Jersey; Escondido, California; and Fremont, Nebraska. All the lawsuits have been stopped by court rulings, settlements, or challenges with enforcement with several also having been ordered to pay the legal fees for the civil rights groups that brought suits. Chico Harlan, "In These Six American Towns, Laws Targeting 'the Illegals' Didn't Go as Planned," *Washington Post*, January 26, 2017.

45. Bob Tita and Andrew Tangel, "Trump Warns Another U.S. Company," *Wall Street Journal*, December 5, 2016.

46. Andrew Tangel, "Companies Plow Ahead with Moves to Mexico Despite Trump's Pressure," *Wall Street Journal*, February 8, 2017.

47. Hope Yen, "AP FACT CHECK: Trump Says US Steel Opening Mills: Not So," *Fox News*, August 2, 2018.

48. Philip Bump, "Trumbull County, Ohio, Shifted 30 Points to Vote Trump; That Didn't Save Its Car Plant," *Washington Post*, November 26, 2018; Neal E. Boudette, "G.M. to Idle Plants and Cut Thousands of Jobs as Sales Slow," *New York Times*, November 26, 2018; Neal E. Boudette, "Ford, an Automaker at a Crossroads, Seeks Cuts and Partners," *New York Times*, October 5, 2018.

49. Terry Macalister, Pamela Duncan, Cath Levett, Finbarr Sheehy, Paul Scruton, and Glenn Swann, "The Demise of UK Deep Coal Mining: Decades of Decline," *Guardian*, December 18, 2015.

50. Helen Pidd, "Britain's Poles: Hard Work, Yorkshire Accents and Life Post-Brexit Vote," *Guardian*, October 25, 2016.

51. Aletha Adu, "'We Northerners ARE Educated': Feisty Brexit Voters SLAP DOWN Remoaners on Question Time," *Express*, December 2, 2016.

52. Brian Kelly, "Balmat Mine Owner Loses $10.5m Asbestos Liability Case," *Watertown Daily Times*, February 12, 2015; CNBC, "Jury Awards More than $70 Million to Woman in Baby Powder Lawsuit," October 28, 2016.

53. Xander Landen, "Vermont Talc at Center of $117 Million Contaminated Baby Powder Case," *VTDigger*, April 16, 2018, https://vtdigger.org/2018/04/16/vermont-talc-center-117-million-contaminated-baby-powder-case/.

54. https://minerals.usgs.gov/minerals/pubs/commodities/talc/.

55. Bob Davis, "The Thorny Economics of Illegal Immigration," *Wall Street Journal*, February 6, 2016.

56. The Quebec meeting has been called the G6+1 rather than G7. David Leonhardt, "The G6+1," *New York Times*, June 8, 2018.

Chapter 11. Full Employment

1. Alissa J. Rubin, "May 1968: A Month of Revolution Pushed France into the Modern World," *New York Times*, May 5, 2018.

2. Krugman notes that one of his favorite quotes from Keynes comes from *Essays in Persuasion*, in which he tried to explain the nature of the Great Depression, which was still in its early stages, and declared that "we have magneto [alternator] trouble." The economic engine was as powerful as ever—but one crucial part was malfunctioning and needed to be fixed. That's about where we are now, Krugman says. The defective alternator is the financial system. We replaced the old, bank-centered system with a high-tech gizmo that was supposed to be more efficient—but it relied on fancy computer chips to function, and it turns out that there were some fatal errors in the programming. He concludes by asking, "Anybody know a good mechanic?" Paul Krugman, "Magneto Trouble," *New York Times*, March 10, 2008.

3. Paul Krugman, "Pessimism and Paralysis in the Aftermath of the Financial Crisis," *New York Times*, December 9, 2017.

4. Edmund S. Phelps, "Nothing Natural about the Natural Rate of Unemployment," *Project Syndicate*, November 2, 2017. Several years ago Ned Phelps and I were both hired by Bloomberg to go to their headquarters in New York and debate with Jean-Claude Trichet on whether the UK should join the Eurozone in front of an invited audience. Ned and I argued vehemently against. I do recall we won the debate on a show of hands!

5. Friedman explained what the natural rate of unemployment is and what determines it: "The 'natural rate of unemployment,' in other words, is the level that would be ground out by the Walrasian system of general equilibrium equations, provided there is imbedded in them the actual structural characteristics of the labor and commodity markets, including market imperfections, stochastic variability in demands and supplies, the cost of gathering information about job vacancies and labor availabilities, the costs of mobility, and so on" (1968, 8).

6. Janet L. Yellen, "Inflation, Uncertainty, and Monetary Policy" (Speech at "Prospects for Growth: Reassessing the Fundamentals," 59th Annual Meeting of the National Association for Business Economics, Cleveland, September 26, 2017).

7. Transcript of Chairman Powell's press conference, March 21, 2018, https://www.federalreserve.gov/mediacenter/files/FOMCpresconf20180321.pdf.

8. https://www.bankofengland.co.uk/-/media/boe/files/inflation-report/2018/february/opening-remarks-february-2018.pdf?la=en&hash=7DE6659ABAA226A7DFAE1A252F4CF0B50E43FB8F.

9. https://www.bankofengland.co.uk/-/media/boe/files/inflation-report/2017/opening-remarks-february-2017.pdf?la=en&hash=141A342DDF73DE7E8584CBE4BDBA4C323E484C5E.

10. Bank of England Inflation Report, February 2018, https://www.bankofengland.co.uk/-/media/boe/files/inflation-report/2018/february/inflation-report-february-2018.pdf?la=en&hash=555ED88EF574D368B81BF703480C1987EEBBA883, p. 20.

11. David Goodman, "Carney Says More BOE Rate Hikes Ahead, Stays Vague on Timing," Bloomberg, February 21, 2018.

12. Anurag Kotoky and Lucy Meakin, "BOE's Haldane Sees U.K. Wage Growth Starting to Strengthen," Bloomberg, October 10, 2018; Andy Haldane, "Growing, Fast and Slow" (Speech given at the University of East Anglia, February 17, 2015).

13. Silvana Tenreyro, "Models in Macroeconomics" (Speech given at Surrey University, June 4, 2018).

14. Larry Summers, "Only Raise US Rates When Whites of Inflation's Eyes Are Visible," *Financial Times*, February 8, 2015.

15. Quoted in Carolynn Look, "It's Hard to Lift Wages When Phillips Curve Is as Flat as Kansas," Bloomberg, November 3, 2017.

16. Gertjan Vlieghe, "From Asymmetry to Symmetry: Changing Risks to the Economic Outlook" (Speech given at the Confederation of British Industry, March 23, 2018).

17. Jim Poterba, president of the NBER, asked me what I thought the NAIRU was, pre-2008, which encouraged me to write this sentence! Doug Staiger once told me that macroeconomists just assumed it was a rolling average of past, current, and future unemployment rates, which does not allow the possibility that the NAIRU is a lot below current unemployment rates.

Chapter 12. Put the Pedal to the Metal

1. Transcript of Chairman Powell's Press Conference, June 13, 2018, https://www.federalreserve.gov/mediacenter/files/FOMCpresconf20180613.pdf. p. 12.

2. https://www.federalreserve.gov/monetarypolicy/files/fomcprojtabl20180926.pdf.

3. Roberta Rampton and Michael Martina, "U.S., China Agree on Trade War Ceasefire after Trump, Xi Summit," Reuters, December 1, 2018.

4. Tim Tankersley and Alan Rappeport, "White House Analysis Finds Tariffs Will Hurt Growth, as Officials Insist Otherwise," *New York Times*, June 7, 2018.

5. Eli Watkins, "Peter Navarro Says 'There's a Special Place in Hell' for Justin Trudeau," CNN, June 10, 2018.

6. Annie Lowery, "Trump's Smart Tariffs Don't Make Economic Sense," *Atlantic*, March 1, 2018.

7. Robert Eisenbeis, "Whack a Mole," Cumberland Advisers, July 26, 2018, Sarasota, Florida.

8. Adriana Belmonte, "The Incredible U.S.-to-China Soybean Nosedive, in One Chart," Yahoo Finance, November 17, 2018.

9. Andrew Edgecliffe-Johnson, "Cost Impact of Tariffs Laid Bare in Corporate Earnings," *Financial Times*, July 26, 2018.

10. Heather Long, " 'Not What We Expected': Trump's Tax Bill Is Losing Popularity," *Washington Post*, June 29, 2018.

11. Toby Eckert, "Poll: Support for GOP Tax Law Erodes," *Politico*, June 27, 2018.

12. Newt Gingrich, "Trump's GDP Achieves Mission Impossible (and Shocks His Critics)," Fox News, July 27, 2018, https://www.foxnews.com/opinion/newt-gingrich-trumps-gdp-achieves-mission-impossible-and-shocks-his-critics.

13. Josh Boak and Christopher Rugaber, "AP FACT CHECK: Trump Says Economy Best 'EVER': It's Not," AP, June 4, 2018.

14. Harry Carr, "Sky Data Poll: 78% Think the Government Is Doing a Bad Job on Brexit," *Sky News*, July 30, 2018.

15. William Booth and Karla Adam, "British Farmers Worry: Who Will Pick the Fruit after Brexit?" *Washington Post*, July 29, 2018.

16. Bank of England, "EU Withdrawal Scenarios and Monetary and Financial Stability: A Response to the House of Commons Treasury Committee," November 2018, https://www.bankofengland.co.uk/-/media/boe/files/report/2018/eu-withdrawal-scenarios-and-monetary-and-financial-stability.pdf?la=en&hash=B5F6EDCDF90DCC10286FC0BC599D94CAB8735DFB.

17. https://archive.org/details/BLOOMBERG_20181128_160000_Bloomberg_Markets_European_Close/start/2640/end/2700.

18. https://www.realclearpolitics.com/epolls/other/direction_of_country-902.html.

19. George Magnus, "The US Economy Is Doing Well—but Headwinds Are Building," *Prospect*, January 8, 2018.

20. Heather Long, "The U.S. Is on Track for the Longest Expansion Ever, but It's Coming at a Cost," *Washington Post*, April 18, 2018.

21. The Jarrow March of October 5–31, 1936, involved 200 men marching from Jarrow in northeast England to London, carrying a petition requesting help for their town following the closure in 1934 of its main employer, Palmer's shipyard.

22. See Griffith, O'Connell, and Smith 2013.

23. "Ark Encounter features a full-size Noah's Ark, built according to the dimensions given in the Bible. Spanning 510 feet long, 85 feet wide, and 51 feet high, this modern engineering marvel amazes visitors young and old. Ark Encounter is situated in beautiful Williamstown, Kentucky, halfway between Cincinnati and Lexington on I-75." https://arkencounter.com.

24. Dave Mosher and Skye Gould, "How Likely Are Foreign Terrorists to Kill Americans? The Odds May Surprise You," *Business Insider*, January 31, 2017.

25. Jon Henley, "Is the EU Really Dictating the Shape of Your Bananas?" *Guardian*, May 11, 2016.

26. Eugene Robinson, "Trump's Border-Wall Fantasy Is Crumbling," *Washington Post*, April 24, 2017.

27. http://apps.washingtonpost.com/g/page/politics/post-abc-poll-trump-popularity-through-nearly-100-days-as-president/2198/.

28. Mark Murray, "Polls: Trump Approval Sags in Trio of Midwest States," NBC News, July 25, 2018.

29. When the Scottish referendum took place, Spain opposed their independence because of what it would signal to Catalonia. Now Spain is supporting Scotland remaining in the EU.

30. Jason Groves, "PM 'Would Go to War over Rock': Leading Tories in Startling

Claim That May Is Ready to Defend Gibraltar Just Like Thatcher Did the Falklands," *Daily Mail*, April 2, 2017.

31. "In Full: George Osborne's Speech at the Tory Conference," *The Scotsman*, October 8, 2012, https://www.scotsman.com/news/politics/in-full-george-osborne-s-speech-at-the-tory-conference-1-2565552.

32. Polly Toynbee, "With a Whiff of Sulphur, George Osborne Was Gone—but for How Long?" *Guardian*, April 20, 2017.

33. Office for National Statistics, "Social Capital Indicators," May 2017, table 1.2.

34. Algan and Cahuc 2013.

35. http://surveys.ap.org/data/GfK/AP-GfK%20October%202013%20Poll%20Topline%20Final_TRUST.pdf.

36. Pew Research Center, "Millennials in Adulthood: Detached from Institutions, Networked with Friends," http://www.pewsocialtrends.org/2014/03/07/millennials-in-adulthood/, March 7, 2014.

37. George Gao, "Americans Divided on How Much They Trust Their Neighbors," Pew Research Center, FactTank, April 13, 2016, http://www.pewresearch.org/fact-tank/2016/04/13/americans-divided-on-how-much-they-trust-their-neighbors/.

38. Andrew Edgecliffe-Johnson and Shannon Bond, "Trust in US Institutions Slumps during Trump's First Year," *Financial Times*, January 21, 2018.

39. https://www.edelman.com/news-awards/2018-edelman-trust-barometer-reveals-record-breaking-drop-trust-in-the-us.

40. Julie Ray, "World's Approval of U.S. Leadership Drops to New Low," Gallup, January 18, 2018.

41. Rafael Behr, "Class, Race, Wealth: Britain Is a Nation Blighted by Divisions," *Guardian*, November 29, 2016.

42. www.pewglobal.org/datasets/2018/.

43. https://www.realclearpolitics.com/video/2018/08/02/bbc_host_to_sean_spicer_you_have_corrupted_discourse_in_the_entire_world_with_your_lies.html.

44. Richard Wolfe, "Trump and Brexit: How Can the US and UK Media Tackle a Culture of Lies?" *Guardian*, July 27, 2018.

45. A taxi driver in Edinburgh, where Goodwin lives in retirement, once told me that it was a common, coordinated practice in restaurants in Edinburgh whenever Fred the Shred, as he was known, ordered food for the kitchen and waitstaff to spit in it. Waiters can always spit in your soup. Ugh.

46. Nick Hanauer, "The Pitchforks Are Coming . . . For Us Plutocrats," http://www.politico.com/magazine/story/2014/06/the-pitchforks-,are-coming-for-us-plutocrats-108014, July/August 2014.

47. Diane Roback and Nasha Gilmore, "Facts & Figures 2015: For Children's Books, Popular Franchises Dominate," *Publishers Weekly*, March 22, 2016.

48. Zack O'Malley Greenburg, "The Top-Earning Dead Celebrities of 2017," *Forbes*, October 30, 2017.

49. Institute for Fiscal Studies, "Spring Budget 2017: IFS Director Paul Johnson's Opening Remarks," https://www.ifs.org.uk/uploads/budgets/budget2017 /budget2017_pj2.pdf.

50. U.S. Census Bureau, "Construction Spending," https://www.census.gov /construction/c30/historical_data.html.

51. Office for National Statistics, "Migration Statistics Quarterly Report: November 2017," https://www.ons.gov.uk/peoplepopulationandcommunity/population andmigration/internationalmigration/bulletins/migrationstatisticsquarterly report/november2017#statisticians-comment.

52. Emma Taggert, "Vermont Will Pay People Who Work from Home up to $10,000 to Move There," Mymodernmet.com, June 1, 2018.

53. Laura Paddison, "What Is a Federal Jobs Guarantee?" *Huffington Post*, July 6, 2018.

54. Antti Jauhiainen and Joona-Hermanni Mäkinen, "Universal Basic Income Didn't Fail in Finland, Finland Failed It," *New York Times*, May 2, 2018.

55. https://yougov.co.uk/opi/surveys/results?utm_source=Twitter&utm_medium =daily_questions&utm_campaign=question_1#/survey/ea30cfa2-6a2d-11e8 -b423-d74e00ea34be/question/75c67445-6a2e-11e8-9d33-9d5c8eb86689 /politics.

56. EU Commission, "Economic Forecast for the UK," Autumn 2018, https://ec .europa.eu/info/business-economy-euro/economic-performance-and-forecasts /economic-performance-country/united-kingdom/economic-forecast-united -kingdom_en.

57. Office for Budget Responsibility, Economic and Fiscal Outlook, October 2018, table 1.1.

58. Kylie MacLellan, "May's Government Loses Contempt Vote over Brexit Legal Advice," Reuters, December 4, 2018.

59. Laura Hughes, George Parker, and Cat Rutter Pooley, "May Aborts Planned Brexit Vote in Humiliating Setback," *Financial Times*, December 10, 2018.

60. David Blanchflower, "Two Big Brexit Themes, Pulling in Opposite Directions— Experts Debate the Data," *Guardian*, April 25, 2017.

61. Ramsey Touchberry, "Republican Senator Says Trump Is Creating 'Soviet Type of Economy' after Tariffs Create $12 Billion Aid Package," *Newsweek*, July 25, 2018.

REFERENCES

Aaronson, D., and A. Jordan. 2014. "Understanding the Relationship between Real Wage Growth and Labor Market Conditions." Chicago Fed Letter No. 327, October.

Aaronson, S., T. Cajner, B. Fallick, F. Galbis-Reig, C. Smith, and W. Wascher. 2014. "Labor Force Participation: Recent Developments and Future Prospects." *Brookings Papers on Economic Activity* (Fall): 197–275.

Abowd, J. M., K. L. McKinney, and N. L. Zhao. 2018. "Earnings Inequality and Mobility Trends in the United States: Nationally Representative Estimates from Longitudinally Linked Employer-Employee Data." *Journal of Labor Economics* 36 (S1): S183–S300.

Aguiar M., and E. Hurst. 2007. "Measuring Trends in Leisure: The Allocation of Time over Five Decades." *Quarterly Journal of Economics* 122 (3): 969–1006.

Ahn, N., J. R. García, and J. F. Jimeno. 2004. "The Impact of Unemployment on Individual Well-Being in the EU." Working Paper No. 29, European Network of Economic Policy Institutes.

Alesina, A. 2010. "Fiscal Adjustments: Lessons from Recent History." Paper prepared for the Ecofin meeting in Madrid, April 15.

Alesina, A., O. Barbiero, C. Favero, F. Giavazzi, and M. Paradisi. 2015. "Austerity in 2009–2013." NBER Working Paper #20827.

Alesina, A., R. Di Tella, and R. MacCulloch. 2004. "Inequality and Happiness: Are Europeans and Americans Different?" *Journal of Public Economics* 88 (9–10): 2009–42.

Algan, Y., and P. Cahuc. 2013. "Trust, Well-Being and Growth: New Evidence and Policy Implications." IZA Discussion Paper No. 7464, Bonn.

Amiti, M., and J. Konings. 2007. "Trade Liberalization, Intermediate Inputs, and Productivity: Evidence from Indonesia." *American Economic Review* 97 (5): 1611–38.

Anderson, S. A., C. S. Russell, and W. R. Schumm. 1983. "Perceived Marital Quality and Family Life-Cycle Categories: A Further Analysis." *Journal of Marriage and the Family* 45: 127–39.

Andrews, D., and A. C. Sánchez. 2011. "Drivers of Homeownership Rates in Selected OECD Countries." OECD Economics Department Working Paper No. 849. Paris: OECD Publishing.

Arcaya, M., M. M. Glymour, N. A. Christakis, I. Kawachi, and S. V. Subramanian. 2014. "Individual and Spousal Unemployment as Predictors of Smoking and Drinking Behavior." *Social Science and Medicine* 110 (June): 89–95.

Armstrong, S. 2017. *The New Poverty*. New York: Verso.

Ashenfelter, O. 2008. "Predicting the Quality and Prices of Bordeaux Wines." *Economic Journal* 118 (529): F174–F184.

———. 2017. "The Hedonic Approach to Vineyard Site Selection: Adaptation to Climate Change and Grape Growing in Emerging Markets." IZA Working Paper No. 10777, May.

Ashenfelter, O. C., H. Farber, and M. R. Ransom. 2010. "Labor Market Monopsony." *Journal of Labor Economics* 28 (2): 203–10.

Askitas, N., and K. F. Zimmermann. 2015. "Health and Well-Being in the Great Recession." *International Journal of Manpower* 36 (1): 26–47.

Assari, S., and M. M. Lankarani. 2016. "Depressive Symptoms Are Associated with More Hopelessness among White than Black Older Adults." *Frontiers in Public Health* 4 (May): 82.

Atlas, S. J., and J. Skinner. 2010. "Education and the Prevalence of Pain." In *Research Findings in the Economics of Aging*, ed. D. Wise, 145–66. Chicago: University of Chicago Press and NBER.

Autor, D. 2015. "Why Are There Still So Many Jobs? The History and Future of Workplace Automation." *Journal of Economic Perspectives* 29 (3): 3–30.

Azar, J., I. Marinescu, and M. I. Steinbaum. 2017. "Labor Market Concentration." NBER Working Paper #24147.

Babb, N. R., and A. K. Deitmeister. 2017. "Nonlinearities in the Phillips Curve for the United States: Evidence Using Metropolitan Data." Finance and Economics Discussion Series, Divisions of Research & Statistics and Monetary Affairs, Federal Reserve Board, Washington, DC.

Balestra, C., and R. Tonkin. 2018. "Inequalities in Household Wealth across OECD Countries: Evidence from the OECD Wealth Distribution Database." OECD Statistics Working Paper No. 88. Paris: OECD.

Ball, R. J., and E. B. A. St. Cyr. 1966. "Short-Term Employment Functions in British Manufacturing Industry." *Review of Economic Studies* 32 (3): 179–207.

Bank of England. 2008. *Inflation Report, August 2008*. London.

Banks, M. H., and P. R. Jackson. 1982. "Unemployment and the Risk of Minor Psychiatric Disorder in Young People: Cross-sectional and Longitudinal Evidence." *Psychological Medicine* 12: 789–98.

Barr, B., D. Taylor-Robinson, A. Scott-Samuel, M. McKee, and D. Stuckler. 2012.

"Suicides Associated with the 2008–10 Economic Recession in England: Time Trend Analysis." *British Medical Journal* 345: e5142.

Barry, J. M. 2009. *The Great Influenza: The Story of the Deadliest Pandemic in History.* New York: Penguin Books.

Beale, N., and S. Nethercott. 1987. "The Health of Industrial Employees Four Years after Compulsory Redundancy." *Journal of the Royal College of General Practitioners* 37: 390–94.

Bean, C. 1994. "European Unemployment: A Survey." *Journal of Economic Literature* 38 (3–4): 573–619.

Becker, S. O., T. Fetzer, and D. Novy. 2016. "Who Voted for Brexit? A Comprehensive District-Level Analysis." *Economic Policy* 32 (92): 601–50.

Belfield, C., R. Blundell, J. Cribb, A. Hood, R. Joyce, and A. N. Keiller. 2017. "Two Decades of Income Inequality in Britain: The Role of Wages, Household Earnings and Redistribution." *Economica* 84 (334): 157–79.

Bell, B. 2015. "Wage Stagnation and the Legacy Costs of Employment." *CentrePiece*, Centre for Economic Performance, London School of Economics, Autumn.

Bell, B., and S. Machin. 2016. "Brexit and Wage Inequality." In *Brexit Beckons: Thinking Ahead by Leading Economists*, ed. R. E. Baldwin, 111–14. London: CEPR Press.

Bell, D. N. F., and D. G. Blanchflower. 2011. "UK Underemployment in the Great Recession." *National Institute Economic Review* 215: R23–R33.

———. 2013. "Underemployment in the UK Revisited." *National Institute Economic Review* 224 (1): F8–F22.

———. 2014. "Labour Market Slack in the UK." *National Institute Economic Review* 229 (1): F4–F11.

———. 2018a. "Underemployment and the Lack of Wage Pressure in the UK." *National Institute Economic Review* 243 (1): R53–R61.

———. 2018b. "The Lack of Wage Growth and the Falling NAIRU." *National Institute Economic Review* 244 (2): R1–R16.

———. 2018c. "The Well-Being of the Overemployed and the Underemployed and the Rise in Depression in the UK." Originally NBER Working Paper #24840, July; forthcoming in the *Journal of Economic Behavior and Organization.*

———. Forthcoming. "Underemployment in the US and Europe." *Industrial and Labor Relations Review.*

Belot, M., and J. C. van Ours. 2001. "Unemployment and Labor Market Institutions: An Empirical Analysis." *Journal of the Japanese and International Economies* 15 (4): 403–18.

Benjamin, D. K., and L. A. Kochin. 1979. "Searching for an Explanation of Unemployment in Interwar Britain." *Journal of Political Economy* 87 (3): 441–78.

———. 1982. "Unemployment and Unemployment Benefits in Twentieth-Century Britain: A Reply to Our Critics." *Journal of Political Economy* 90 (2): 410–36.

Berg, M., and R. Veenhoven. 2010. "Income Inequality and Happiness in 119 Nations." In *Happiness and Social Policy in Europe*, ed. B. Greve, 174–94. Cheltenham: Edward Elgar.

Beugnot, J., G. Lacroix, and O. Charlot. 2014. "Homeownership and Labour Market Outcomes: Micro versus Macro Performances." IZA Discussion Paper No. 8599, October.

Beveridge, W. 1942. "Social Insurance and Allied Services." London: HMSO.

———. (1944) 1960. *Full Employment in a Free Society: A Report*. New York: Routledge.

Bewley, T. 2002. *Why Wages Don't Fall during a Recession*. Cambridge, MA: Harvard University Press.

Bhaskar, V., A. Manning, and T. To. 2002. "Oligopsony and Monopsonistic Competition in Labor Markets." *Journal of Economic Perspectives* 16 (2): 155–74.

Bianchi, S. M. 2010. *Family Change and Time Allocation in American Families*. New York: Alfred Sloan Foundation.

Bick, A., N. Fuchs-Schündeln, and D. Lagakos. 2018. "How Do Hours Worked Vary with Income? Cross-country Evidence and Implications." *American Economic Review* 108 (1): 170–99.

Blakely, T. A., S. C. D. Collings, and J. Atkinson. 2003. "Unemployment and Suicide: Evidence for a Causal Association?" *Journal of Epidemiology and Community Health* 57: 594–600.

Blanchard, O. 2009. "The State of Macro." *Annual Review of Economics* 1 (1): 209–28.

———. 2016. "Do DSGE Models Have a Future?" Policy Brief, Peterson Institute for International Economics. August.

Blanchard, O., and J. Wolfers. 2000. "The Role of Shocks and Institutions in the Rise of European Unemployment: The Aggregate Evidence." *Economic Journal* 110 (462): 1–33.

Blanchflower, D. G. 1991. "Fear, Unemployment and Pay Flexibility." *Economic Journal* 101 (406): 483–96.

———. 1999. "Changes over Time in Union Relative Wage Effects in Great Britain and the United States." In *Essays in Honour of Bernard Corry and Maurice Peston*, vol. 2, *The History and Practice of Economics*, ed. S. Daniel, P. Arestis, and J. Grahl, 3–32. Cheltenham: Edward Elgar.

———. 2000. "Self-employment in OECD Countries." *Labour Economics* 7 (September): 471–505.

———. 2004. "Self-employment: More May Not Be Better." *Swedish Economic Policy Review* 11 (2): 15–74.

———. 2007. "Recent Developments in the UK Economy: The Economics of Walking About." *Bank of England Quarterly Bulletin* 47 (2): 317–29.

———. 2008. "Inflation, Expectations and Monetary Policy." Speech at the Royal

Society, George Street, Edinburgh, April 29. In *Bank of England Quarterly Bulletin*, 229–38.

———. 2009. "International Evidence on Well-Being." In *Measuring Subjective Well-Being of Nations: National Accounts of Time-Use and Well-Being*, ed. A. B. Krueger, 155–226. Chicago: University of Chicago Press and NBER.

———. 2013. "Where Were You?" In *Leadership and Cooperation in Academia: Reflecting on the Roles and Responsibilities of University Faculty and Management*, ed. R. Sugden, J. R. Wilson, and M. Valania, 234–68. Cheltenham: Edward Elgar.

———. 2015a. "Hard Times Are Only Going to Get Harder." *British Journal of Sociology* 66 (3): 577–83.

———. 2015b. *Self-employment across Countries in the Great Recession of 2008–2014.* Amsterdam: Randstad.

Blanchflower, D. G., D. N. F. Bell, A. Montagnoli, and M. Moro. 2014. "The Happiness Tradeoff between Unemployment and Inflation." *Journal of Money Credit and Banking* (supplement) 46 (2): 117–41.

Blanchflower, D. G., and A. J. Bryson. 2003. "Changes over Time in Union Relative Wage Effects in the UK and the US Revisited." In *International Handbook of Trade Unions*, ed. J. T. Addison and C. Schnabel, 197–245. Cheltenham: Edward Elgar.

———. 2004a. "What Effects Do Unions Have on Wages Now and Would Freeman and Medoff Be Surprised?" *Journal of Labor Research* 25 (3): 383–414, and in *What Do Unions Do: The Evidence Twenty Years Later?*, ed. J. T. Bennett and B. E. Kaufman. London: Taylor and Francis.

———. 2004b. "Union Relative Wage Effects in the USA and the UK." *Proceedings of the Industrial Relations Research Association* (January 3–5): 133–40.

———. 2010. "The Wage Impact of Trade Unions in the UK Public and Private Sectors." *Economica* 77 (305): 92–109.

Blanchflower, D. G., and A. E. Clark. 2019. "Unhappiness and Family Finances: Evidence from One Million Europeans." NBER Working Paper #25597.

Blanchflower, D. G., R. Costa, and S. Machin. 2017. "The Return of Falling Real Wages." CEP Real Wages Update, March Paper #CEPRWU006, May.

Blanchflower, D. G., and H. Lawton. 2010. "The Impact of the Recent Expansion of the EU on the UK Labour Market." In *EU Labor Markets after Post-Enlargement Migration*, ed. M. Kahanec and K. F. Zimmermann, 181–215. New York: IZA and Springer.

Blanchflower, D. G., and A. J. Levin. 2014. "Labor Market Slack and Monetary Policy." NBER Working Paper #21094.

Blanchflower, D. G., and L. Lynch. 1994. "Training at Work: A Comparison of US and British Youths." In *Training and the Private Sector: International Comparisons*, ed. L. Lynch, 233–60. Chicago: University of Chicago Press and NBER.

Blanchflower, D. G., and A. J. Oswald. 1988. "Internal and External Influences upon

Pay Settlements: New Survey Evidence." *British Journal of Industrial Relations* 3: 363–70.

Blanchflower, D. G., and A. J. Oswald 1990. "The Wage Curve." *Scandinavian Journal of Economics* 92 (2): 215–35.

———. 1994. *The Wage Curve*. Cambridge, MA: MIT Press.

———. 1999. "Well-Being, Insecurity and the Decline of American Job Satisfaction." Working paper.

———. 2003. "Does Inequality Reduce Happiness? Evidence from the States of the USA from the 1970s to the 1990s." Mimeographed, Warwick University.

———. 2004a. "Well-Being over Time in Britain and the USA." *Journal of Public Economics* 88 (7–8): 1359–86.

———. 2004b. "Money, Sex and Happiness." *Scandinavian Journal of Economics* 106 (3): 393–415.

———. 2005. "The Wage Curve Reloaded." NBER Working Paper #11338.

———. 2008. "Is Well-Being U-Shaped over the Life Cycle?" *Social Science and Medicine* 66 (6): 1733–49.

———. 2009. "The U-Shape without Controls: A Response to Glenn." *Social Science and Medicine* 69 (4): 486–88.

———. 2011. "International Happiness: A New View on the Measure of Performance." *Academy of Management Perspectives* 25 (1): 6–22.

———. 2013. "Does High Home-ownership Impair the Labor Market?" NBER Working Paper #19079, May.

———. 2016. "Antidepressants and Age: A New Form of Evidence for U-Shaped Well-Being through Life." *Journal of Economic Behavior and Organization* 127: 46–58.

———. 2017. "Is There Modern Evidence for a Midlife Psychological Low? Two Approaches in Six Data Sets on 1.3 Million Citizens." Working paper.

———. Forthcoming. "Unhappiness and Pain in Modern America: A Review Essay, and Further Evidence, on Carol Graham's *Happiness for All?*" *Journal of Economic Literature*.

Blanchflower, D. G., A. J. Oswald, and M. D. Garrett. 1990. "Insider Power in Wage Determination." *Economica* 57: 143–70.

Blanchflower, D. G., A. J. Oswald, and P. Sanfey. 1996. "Wages, Profits and Rent Sharing." *Quarterly Journal of Economics* 111 (1): 227–51.

Blanchflower, D. G., A. J. Oswald, and S. Stewart-Brown. 2013. "Is Psychological Well-Being Linked to the Consumption of Fruit and Vegetables?" *Social Indicators Research* 114 (3): 785–801.

Blanchflower, D. G., A. J. Oswald, and B. Van Landeghem. 2009. "Imitative Obesity and Relative Utility." *Journal of the European Economic Association* 7 (2/3): 528–38.

Blanchflower, D. G., and A. Posen. 2014. "Wages and Labor Market Slack: Making the Dual Mandate Operation." Peterson Institute Working Paper No. 14-6, September.

Blanchflower, D. G., and C. Shadforth. 2009. "Fear, Unemployment and Migration." *Economic Journal* 119 (535): F136–F182.

Blanchflower, D. G., and M. Slaughter. 1999. "The Causes and Consequences of Changing Earnings Inequality: W(h)ither the Debate?" In *Growing Apart: The Causes and Consequences of Global Wage Inequality*, ed. A. Fishlow and K. Parker, 67–94. New York: Council on Foreign Relations Press.

Blau, F., and L. Kahn. 2013. "Female Labor Supply: Why Is the US Falling Behind?" *American Economic Review* 103 (3): 251–56.

Blicher, B., and R. L. Pryles. 2017. "Managing Endodontic Pain: The Evidence against Opioids." *Inside Dentistry* 13 (5): 53–58.

Blinder, S., and L. Richards. 2016. "UK Public Opinion toward Immigration: Overall Attitudes and Level of Concern." Migration Observatory, November 28.

Blundell, R., C. Crawford, and W. Jin. 2014. "What Can Wages and Employment Tell Us about the UK's Productivity Puzzle?" *Economic Journal* 124 (May): 307–407.

Blyth, M. 2013. "The Austerity Delusion: Why a Bad Idea Won Over the West." *Foreign Affairs* 92 (3): 41–56.

———. 2015. *Austerity: The History of a Dangerous Idea*. New York: Oxford University Press.

Board of Governors of the Federal Reserve. 2017. "Report on the Economic Well-Being of U.S. Households in 2016." Washington, DC.

Bohnert, A. S. B., M. Valenstein, M. J. Bair, MD, et al. 2011. "Association between Opioid Prescribing Patterns and Opioid Overdose-Related Deaths." *Journal of the American Medical Association* 305 (13): 1315–21.

Bond, T. N., and K. Lang. 2018. "The Sad Truth about Happiness Scales: Empirical Results—Data Appendix." NBER Working Paper #24853.

———. Forthcoming. "The Sad Truth about Happiness Scales: Empirical Results." *Journal of Political Economy*.

Borowczyk-Martins, D., and E. Lalé. 2016. "Employment Adjustment and Part-time Work: Lessons from the United States and the United Kingdom." IZA Working Paper No. 9847, March.

———. 2018. "The Welfare Effects of Involuntary Part-time Work." *Oxford Economic Papers* 70 (1): 183–205.

Bossert, W., and C. D'Ambrosio. 2016. "Economic Insecurity and Variations in Resources." Working Paper No. 422, Society for the Study of Income Inequality.

Boubtane, E., J. C. Dumont, and C. Rault. 2015. "Immigration and Economic Growth in the OECD Countries, 1986–2006." CESifo Working Paper Series No. 5392.

Bourbeau, E., and A. Fields. 2017. "Annual Review of the Labour Market, 2016." Statistics Canada, April 28.

Brechling, F. 1965. "The Relationship between Output and Employment in British Manufacturing Industries." *Review of Economic Studies* 32 (91): 187–216.

Bregger, J. E., and S. E. Haugen. 1995. "BLS Introduces New Range of Alternative Unemployment Measures." *Monthly Labor Review* 118 (10): 19–26.

Brenner, M. H., and A. Mooney. 1983. "Unemployment and Health in the Context of Economic Change." *Social Science and Medicine* 17 (16): 1125–38.

Broadberry, S. B., B. M. S. Campbell, A. Klein, M. Overton, and B. van Leeuwen. 2015. *British Economic Growth, 1270–1870*. Cambridge: Cambridge University Press.

Brown, G. 2010. *Beyond the Crash: Overcoming the First Crisis of Globalization*. New York: Free Press.

Bucknor, C., and A. Barber. 2016. "The Price We Pay: Economic Costs of Barriers to Employment for Former Prisoners and People Convicted of Felonies." CEPR Working Paper, June.

Cajner, T., D. Mawhirter, C. Nekarda, and D. Ratner. 2014. "Why Is Involuntary Part-time Work Elevated?" FEDS Notes, April 14.

Card, D. 1990. "The Impact of the Mariel Boatlift on the Miami Labor Market." *Industrial and Labor Relations Review* 43 (2): 245–57.

———. 2001. "The Effect of Unions on Wage Inequality in the U.S. Labor Market." *Industrial and Labor Relations Review* 54 (2): 296–315.

Card, D., A. R. Cardoso, J. Heining, and P. Kline. 2016. "Firms and Labor Market Inequality: Evidence and Some Theory." *Journal of Labor Economics* 36 (S1): S13–S70.

Card D., and S. DellaVigna. 2013. "Nine Facts about Top Journals in Economics." *Journal of Economic Literature* 51 (1): 144–61.

Card, D., and A. B. Krueger. 1995. *Myth and Measurement: The New Economics of the Minimum Wage*. Princeton: Princeton University Press.

Card, D., T. Lemieux, and C. Riddell. 2004. "Unions and Wage Inequality." *Journal of Labor Research* 25 (3): 519–62.

Carmichael, F., and R. Ward. 2000. "Youth Unemployment and Crime in the English Regions and Wales." *Applied Economics* 32 (5): 559–71.

———. 2001. "Male Unemployment and Crime in England and Wales." *Economics Letters* 73: 111–15.

Carpenter, C. S., B. Chandler, B. McClellan, and D. I. Rees. 2016. "Economic Conditions, Illicit Drug Use, and Substance Use Disorders in the United States." NBER Working Paper #22051, February.

Case, A., and A. Deaton. 2015. "Rising Morbidity and Mortality in Midlife among

White Non-Hispanic Americans in the 21st Century." *Proceedings of the National Academy of Sciences* 112 (49): 15078–83.

———. 2017a. "Suicide, Age, and Wellbeing: An Empirical Investigation." In *Insights in the Economics of Aging*, ed. D. A. Wise, 307–34. NBER Economics of Aging Series. Chicago: University of Chicago Press.

———. 2017b. "Mortality and Morbidity in the 21st Century." Brookings Papers, March 17.

Centre for Social Justice. 2016. "Turning the Tide: Social Justice in Five Seaside Towns." August. https://www.centreforsocialjustice.org.uk/core/wp-content/uploads/2016/08/Turning-the-Tide.pdf.

Chari, V. V., and P. Kehoe. 2006. "Modern Macroeconomics in Practice: How Theory Is Shaping Policy." *Journal of Economic Perspectives* 20 (4): 3–28.

Chartered Institute of Personnel and Development (CIPD). 2013. "Zero Hours Contracts." Research Report.

Chen, Z., and D. Meltzer. 2008. "Beefing Up with the Chans: Evidence for the Effects of Relative Income and Income Inequality on Health from the China Health and Nutrition Survey." *Social Science and Medicine* 66: 2206–17.

Cherlin, A. J. 2014. *Labor's Love Lost: The Rise and Fall of the Working-Class Family in America*. New York: Russell Sage Foundation.

Chetty, R., N. Hendren, and L. F. Katz. 2016. "The Effects of Exposure to Better Neighborhoods on Children: New Evidence from the Moving to Opportunity Experiment." *American Economic Review* 106 (4): 855–902.

Chetty, R., N. Hendren, P. Kline, and E. Saez. 2014. "Where Is the Land of Opportunity? The Geography of Intergenerational Mobility in the United States." *Quarterly Journal of Economics* 129 (4): 1553–1623.

Chevalier, C. M., and R. Lardeux. 2017. "Homeownership and Labor Market Outcomes: Disentangling Externality and Composition Effects." INSEE Working Paper.

Chida, Y., and A. Steptoe. 2008. "Positive Psychological Well-Being and Mortality: A Quantitative Review of Prospective Observational Studies." *Psychosomatic Medicine* 70: 741–56.

Chiswick, B. R., and T. J. Hatton. 2003. "International Migration and the Integration of Labour Markets." In *Globalization in Historical Perspective*, ed. M. D. Bordo, A. M. Taylor, and J. G. Williamson, 65–120. Chicago: University of Chicago Press.

Christakis, N. A., and J. H. Fowler. 2007. "The Spread of Obesity in a Large Social Network over 32 Years." *New England Journal of Medicine* 357: 370–79.

Cicero, T. J., M. S. Ellis, H. L. Surratt, and S. P. Kurtz. 2014. "The Changing Face of Heroin Use in the United States: A Retrospective Analysis of the Past 50 Years." *JAMA Psychiatry* 71: 821–26.

Clark, A. E., P. Frijters, and M. Shields. 2008. "Relative Income, Happiness and Utility: An Explanation for the Easterlin Paradox and Other Puzzles." *Journal of Economic Literature* 46 (1): 95–144.

Clark, A. E., and A. J. Oswald. 1994. "Unhappiness and Unemployment." *Economic Journal* 104 (424): 648–59.

———. 1996. "Satisfaction and Comparison Income." *Journal of Public Economics* 61 (3): 359–81.

Clark, T., and A. Heath. 2014. *Hard Times: The Divisive Toll of the Economic Slump.* New Haven: Yale University Press.

Clarke, S., A. Corlett, D. Finch, L. Gardiner, K. Henehan, D. Tomlinson, and M. Whittaker. 2017. "Are We Nearly There Yet? Spring Budget 2017 and the 15-Year Squeeze on Family and Public Finances." Resolution Foundation, March. https:// www.resolutionfoundation.org/app/uploads/2017/03/Spring-Budget-2017 -response.pdf.

Clarke, S., and M. Whittaker. 2016. "The Importance of Place: Explaining the Characteristics Underpinning the Brexit Vote across Different Parts of the UK." Resolution Foundation, July. https://www.resolutionfoundation.org/app/uploads /2016/07/Brexit-vote-v4.pdf.

Coase, R. H. 1992. "The Institutional Structure of Production." *American Economic Review* 82 (4): 713–19.

Colgan, J. D., and R. O. Keohane. 2017. "The Liberal Order Is Rigged." *Foreign Affairs* 96 (3): 36–44.

Collins, M. 1982. "Unemployment in Interwar Britain: Still Searching for an Explanation." *Journal of Political Economy* 90 (2): 369–79.

Corlett, A. 2016. "Spotlight: The Earnings of the Self-employed." RF Earnings Outlook, Quarterly Briefing Q2 2016, Resolution Foundation.

Council of Economic Advisers (CEA). 2016a. "The Long-Term Decline in Prime-Age Male Labor Force Participation." June.

———. 2016b. "Economic Perspectives on Incarceration and the Criminal Justice System." April.

Cox, D., R. Lienesch, and R. P. Jones. 2017. "Beyond Economics: Fears of Cultural Displacement Pushed the White Working Class to Trump." PRRI/The Atlantic Report, May 9.

Cross, R. 1982. "How Much Voluntary Unemployment in Interwar Britain?" *Journal of Political Economy* 90 (2): 380–85.

Curtin, S. C., M. Warner, and H. Hedegaard. 2015. "Suicide Rates for Females and Males by Race and Ethnicity: United States, 1999 and 2014." April, National Center for Health Statistics, CDC.

———. 2016. "Increase in Suicide in the United States, 1999–2014." NCHS Data Brief #241, April 2016.

Daly, M. C., A. J. Oswald, D. Wilson, and S. Wu. 2011. "Dark Contrasts: The Paradox of High Rates of Suicide in Happy Places." *Journal of Economic Behavior and Organization* 80 (3): 435–42.

Daly, M. C., D. J. Wilson, and N. J. Johnson. 2013. "Relative Status and Well-Being: Evidence from U.S. Suicide Deaths." *Review of Economics and Statistics* 95 (5): 1480–1500.

Danner, D. D., D. A. Snowdon, and W. V. Friesen. 2001. "Positive Emotions in Early Life and Longevity: Findings from the Nun Study." *Journal of Personality and Social Psychology* 80 (5): 804–13.

Darity, W. R., Jr., and A. H. Goldsmith. 1996. "Social Psychology, Unemployment and Macroeconomics." *Journal of Economic Perspectives* 10 (1): 121–40.

Darling, A. 2011. *Back from the Brink: 1000 Days at Number 11*. London: Atlantic Books.

Datta, N., G. Giupponi, and S. Machin. 2018. "Zero Hours Contracts and Labour Market Policy." Paper presented for the 68th Economic Policy Panel Meeting in Vienna, 4–5 October.

de Wit, L. M., F. S. Luppino, A. van Straten, and P. Cuijpers. 2010. "Obesity and Depression: A Meta-analysis of Community-Based Studies." *Psychiatry Research* 178 (2): 230–35.

Deaton, A. 2008. "Income, Health and Wellbeing around the World: Evidence from the Gallup World Poll." *Journal of Economic Perspectives* 22 (2): 53.

Deeg, D. J. H., and R. J. van Zonneveld. 1989. "Does Happiness Lengthen Life? The Prediction of Longevity in the Elderly." In *How Harmful Is Happiness? Consequences of Enjoying Life or Not*, ed. R. Veehoven, 29–43. Rotterdam: Universitaire Pers Rotterdam.

Delaney, L., et al. 2017a. "The Scarring Effect of Unemployment on Subjective Well-Being across Europe." Working paper.

———. 2017b. "Involuntary Part-time Employment and Mental Health: Evidence from Britain." Working paper.

Dent, R., S. Kapon, F. Karahan, B. W. Pugsley, and A. Şahin. 2014. "The Long-Term Unemployed and the Wages of New Hires." Federal Reserve Bank of New York Liberty Street Economics, November 19.

Department for Business. 2014. "The Impacts of Migration on UK Native Employment: An Analytical Review of the Evidence." Home Office Occasional Paper 109, March.

Diener, E., and M. Y. Chan. 2011. "Happy People Live Longer: Subjective Well-Being Contributes to Health and Longevity." *Applied Psychology: Health and Well-Being* 3: 1–43.

Diener, E., S. D. Pressman, J. Hunter, and D. Chase. 2017. "If, Why, and When Subjective Well-Being Influences Health, and Future Needed Research." *Applied Psychology: Health and Well-Being* 9 (2): 133–67.

Disney, R., and P. Simpson. 2017. "Police Workforce and Funding in England and Wales." IFS Briefing Note #208, May 15.

Doctor, J. N., and M. Menchine. 2017. "Tackling the Opioid Crisis with Compassion: New Ways to Reduce Use and Treatment." Brookings, March 20.

Doyle, J. M., E. Ahmed, and R. N. Horn. 1999. "The Effects of Labor Markets and Income Inequality on Crime: Evidence from Panel Data." *Southern Economic Journal* 65 (4): 717–38.

Duesenberry, J. S. 1949. *Income, Saving, and the Theory of Consumer Behavior*. Cambridge, MA: Harvard University Press.

Duflo, E. 2017. "The Economist as Plumber." NBER Working Paper #23213, March.

Dunatchik, A., M. Davies, J. Griggs, F. Hussain, and C. Jessop. 2016. "Social and Political Attitudes of People on Low Incomes." York: Joseph Rowntree Foundation.

Dustmann, C., M. Casanova, M. M. Fertig, I. Preston, and C. M. Schmidt. 2003. "The Impact of EU Enlargement on Migration Flows." Home Office Online Report 25/03. Research Development and Statistics Directorate, London.

Dustmann, C., and Y. Weiss. 2007. "Return Migration: Theory and Empirical Evidence from the UK." *British Journal of Industrial Relations* 45 (2): 236–56.

Easterlin, R. A. 1974. "Does Economic Growth Improve the Human Lot? Some Empirical Evidence." In *Nations and Households in Economic Growth: Essays in Honor of Moses Abramowitz*, ed. P. A. David and M. W. Reder, 89–125. New York: Academic Press.

Eatwell, R., and M. Goodwin. 2018. *National Populism: The Revolt against Liberal Democracy*. London: Pelican Books.

Eberstadt, N. 2016. *Men without Work: America's Invisible Crisis*. West Conshohocken, PA: Templeton Press.

Economic Innovation Group. 2018. *The 2017 Distressed Communities Index*. https://eig.org/wp-content/uploads/2017/09/2017-Distressed-Communities-Index.pdf.

Eichengreen, B. 2015. *Hall of Mirrors: The Great Depression, the Great Recession and the Uses—and Misuses—of History*. Oxford: Oxford University Press.

El-Arian, M. 2016. *The Only Game in Town: Central Banks, Instability, and Avoiding the Next Collapse*. New Haven: Yale University Press.

Ellwood, D. 1982. "Teenage Unemployment: Permanent Scars or Temporary Blemishes?" In *The Youth Labor Market Problem: Its Nature, Causes and Consequences*, ed. R. B. Freeman and D. A. Wise, 349–90. Chicago: University of Chicago Press.

Eurofound. 2017. "Estimating Labour Market Slack in the European Union." Publications Office of the European Union, Luxembourg.

Even, W. E., and D. A. Macpherson. 2016. "The Affordable Care Act and the Growth of Involuntary Part-time Employment." IZA Discussion Paper No. 9324.

Ewing, W. A., D. E. Martínez, and R. G. Rumbaut. 2015. "The Criminalization of

Immigration in the United States." Special Report, American Immigration Council, July.

Fairlie, R., and L. G. Kletzer. 2003. "The Long-Term Costs of Job Displacement among Young Workers." *Industrial and Labor Relations Review* 56 (4): 682–98.

Falba, T., H. Teng, J. L. Sindelar, and W. T. Gallo. 2005. "The Effect of Involuntary Job Loss on Smoking Intensity and Relapse." *Addiction* 100 (9): 1330–39.

Falk, A., and J. Zweimüller. 2005. "Unemployment and Right-Wing Extremist Crime." CEPR Discussion Paper No. 4997.

Feinstein, C. H. 1972. *National Income, Output and Expenditure of the United Kingdom, 1855–1965.* Cambridge: Cambridge University Press.

Feldman, D. C. 1996. "The Nature, Antecedents and Consequences of Underemployment." *Journal of Management* 22 (3): 385–407.

Feldstein, M. S. 1967. "Specification of the Labour Input in the Aggregate Production Function." *Review of Economic Studies* 34 (4): 375–86.

———. 2017. "Why Is Growth Better in the United States than in Other Industrial Countries?" NBER Working Paper #23221.

Ferrer-i-Carbonell, A. 2005. "Income and Wellbeing: An Empirical Analysis of the Comparison Income Effect." *Journal of Public Economics* 89: 997–1019.

Fetzer, T. 2018. "Did Austerity Cause Brexit?" Working Paper No. 381, Centre for Comparative Advantage in the Global Economy, Department of Economics, University of Warwick, July 22.

Fitzpatrick, S., G. Bramley, F. Sosenko, and J. Blenkinsopp. 2018. "Destitution in the UK 2018." York: Joseph Rowntree Foundation.

Foote, C., and R. Ryan. 2012. "Labor-Market Polarization over the Business Cycle, Public Policy." Discussion Paper No. 12-8, Federal Reserve Bank of Boston, December.

Ford, R., and M. Goodwin. 2014. *Revolt on the Right: Explaining Support for the Radical Right in Britain.* New York: Routledge.

Forte, G., and J. D. Portes. 2017. "Macroeconomic Determinants of International Migration to the UK." GLO Discussion Paper No. 69.

Fougere, D., F. Kramarz, and J. Pouget. 2006. "Youth Unemployment and Crime in France." CEPR Discussion Paper No. 5600.

Freburger, J. K., M. H. George, R. P. Agans, A. M. Jackman, J. D. Darter, A. S. Wallace, L. D. Castel, W. D. Kalsbeek, and T. S. Carey. 2009. "The Rising Prevalence of Chronic Low Back Pain." *Archives of Internal Medicine* 169 (3): 251–58.

Freeman, R. B. 1999. "The Economics of Crime." In *Handbook of Labor Economics*, vol. 3C, ed. O. C. Ashenfelter and D. Card, 3529–71. Amsterdam: Elsevier North Holland.

———. 2007. "Labor Market Institutions around the World." NBER Working Paper #13242.

Frese, M., and G. Mohr. 1987. "Prolonged Unemployment and Depression in Older Workers: A Longitudinal Study of Intervening Variables." *Social Science and Medicine* 25: 173–78.

Frey, B. S., and A. Stutzer. 2002. *Happiness and Economics: How the Economy and Institutions Affect Human Well-Being.* Princeton: Princeton University Press.

Friedman, M. 1953. *Essays in Positive Economics.* Chicago: University of Chicago Press.

———. 1968. "The Role of Monetary Policy." *American Economic Review* 58 (1): 1–17.

Friedman, M., A. Grawert, and J. Cullen. 2016. "Crime in 2016: Updated Analysis." Brennan Center for Justice, NYU School of Law. https://www.brennancenter.org/sites/default/files/analysis/Crime_in_2016_Updated_Analysis.pdf.

Fry, R. 2016. "For First Time in Modern Era, Living with Parents Edges Out Other Living Arrangements for 18- to 34-Year-Olds." Pew Research Center, May.

Fry, R., and A. Brown. 2016. "In a Recovering Market, Homeownership Rates Are Down Sharply for Blacks, Young Adults." Pew Research Center, December 15.

Fujihara, N., M. E. Lark, Y. Fujihara, and K. C. Chung. 2017. "The Effect of Economic Downturn on the Volume of Surgical Procedures: A Systematic Review." *International Journal of Surgery* 44 (August): 56–63.

Galbraith, J. K. 2009. *The Great Crash.* New York: Mariner Books, Houghton Mifflin.

Garcia, M. C., M. Faul, G. Massetti, C. Thomas, Y. Hong, U. E. Bauer, and M. F. Iademarco. 2017. "Reducing Potentially Excess Deaths from the Five Leading Causes of Death in the Rural United States." *Morbidity and Mortality Weekly Report* 66 (2): 1–7.

Garriga, C., B. J. Noeth, and D. Schlagenhauf. 2017. "Household Debt and the Great Recession." *Federal Reserve Bank of St. Louis Review* 99 (2): 183–205.

Gazioglu, S., and A. Tansel. 2006. "Job Satisfaction in Britain: Individual and Job-Related Factors." *Applied Economics* 38: 1163–71.

Ghent, A. C., and M. Kudlyack. 2010. "Recourse and Residential Mortgage Default: Theory and Evidence from U.S. States." Working Paper No. 09-10R, Federal Reserve Bank of Richmond.

Glauber, R. 2017. "Involuntary Part-time Employment: A Slow and Uneven Economic Recovery." Carsey Research National Issue Brief #116, University of New Hampshire, Spring.

Glenn, N. 2009. "Is the Apparent U-Shape of Well-Being over the Life Course a Result of Inappropriate Use of Control Variables? A Commentary on Blanchflower and Oswald." *Social Science and Medicine* 69 (4): 481–85.

Golden, L. 2016. "Still Falling Short on Hours and Pay: Part-time Work Becoming New Normal." Economic Policy Institute, December 5.

Golden, L., and T. Gebreselassie. 2007. "Overemployment Mismatches: The Preference for Fewer Work Hours." *Monthly Labor Review* 130 (4): 18–37.

Goldin, C. D., and L. F. Katz. 2007. "Long-Run Changes in the Wage Structure: Narrowing, Widening, Polarizing." *Brookings Papers of Economic Activity* 2: 135–65.

Goldman, N., D. Glei, and M. Weinstein. 2018. "Declining Mental Health among Disadvantaged Americans." *Proceedings of the National Academy of Sciences* 115 (25): 1–6.

Goldsmith, A. H., J. R. Veum, and W. Darity. 1996. "The Psychological Impact of Unemployment and Joblessness." *Journal of Socio-Economics* 25 (3): 333–58.

Goodwin, J. S., Y. Kuo, D. Brown, D. Juurlink, and M. Raji. 2018. "Association of Chronic Opioid Use with Presidential Voting Patterns in US Counties in 2016." *JAMA Network Open* 1 (2).

Goodwin, M., and O. Heath. 2016a. "The 2016 Referendum, Brexit and the Left Behind: An Aggregate-Level Analysis of the Result." *Political Quarterly* 87 (3): 323–32.

———. 2016b. "Brexit Vote Explained: Poverty, Low Skills and Lack of Opportunities." York: Joseph Rowntree Foundation.

Gouin, J. P., and J. K. Kiecolt-Glaser. 2011. "The Impact of Psychological Stress on Wound Healing: Methods and Mechanisms." *Immunology and Allergy Clinics of North America* 31 (1): 81–93.

Government Accountability Office (GAO). 2011. "Criminal Alien Statistics: Information on Incarcerations, Arrests and Costs." Report to Congressional Requestors, March.

Graham, C., and S. Pinto. 2016. "Unhappiness in America: Desperation in White Towns, Resilience and Diversity in the Cities." Brookings, September 29.

Graham, C., and J. R. Pozuelo. 2017. "Happiness, Stress, and Age: How the U-Curve Varies across People and Places." *Journal of Population Economics* 30 (1): 225–64.

Green, R., and P. H. Hendershott. 2001. "Home-ownership and Unemployment in the U.S." *Urban Studies* 38 (9): 1509–20.

Gregg, P. A., and E. Tominey. 2005. "The Wage Scar from Male Youth Unemployment." *Labour Economics* 12: 487–509.

Griffith, R., M. O'Connell, and K. Smith. 2013. "Food Expenditure and Nutritional Quality over the Great Recession." Institute for Fiscal Studies Briefing Note 143.

Grigorieff, A., C. Roth, and D. Ubfal. 2016. "Does Information Change Attitudes towards Immigrants? Representative Evidence from Survey Experiments." IZA Discussion Paper No. 10419, December.

Grogger, J. 1998. "Market Wages and Youth Crime." *Journal of Labor Economics* 16 (4): 756–91.

Hacker, J. S. 2008. *The Great Risk Shift: The New Economic Insecurity and the Decline of the American Dream.* Oxford: Oxford University Press.

Hacker, J. S., G. A. Huber, A. Nichols, P. Rehm, M. Schlesinger, R. Valletta, and S. Craig. 2014. "The Economic Security Index: A New Measure for Research and Policy Analysis." *Review of Income and Wealth* 60: S5–S32.

Haltiwanger, J. C., H. R. Hyatt, L. B. Kahn, and E. McEntarfer. 2018. "Cyclical Job Ladders by Firm Size and Firm Wage." *American Economic Journal: Macroeconomics* 10 (2): 52–85.

Hämäläinen, K., and P. Böckerman. 2004. "Regional Labour Market Dynamics, Housing, and Migration." *Journal of Regional Science* 44: 543–68.

Hamermesh, D. 2018. "Citations in Economics: Measurement, Uses and Impacts." *Journal of Economic Literature* 56 (1): 115–56.

Hamermesh, D. S., and N. M. Soss. 1974. "An Economic Theory of Suicide." *Journal of Political Economy* 82 (1): 83–98.

Hammarstrom, A., and U. Janlert. 1994. "Unemployment and Change of Tobacco Habits: A Study of Young People from 16 to 21 Years of Age." *Addiction* 89 (12): 1691–96.

Hammnett, C. 1991. "The Relationship between Residential Migration and Housing Tenure in London, 1971–81: A Longitudinal Analysis." *Environment and Planning A* 23 (8): 1147–62.

Hansen, K., and S. Machin. 2002. "Spatial Crime Patterns and the Introduction of the UK Minimum Wage." *Oxford Bulletin of Economics and Statistics* 64: 677–99.

Hanson, G., C. Liu, and C. McIntosh. 2017. "The Rise and Fall of U.S. Low-Skilled Immigration." NBER Working Paper #23753, August.

Harberger, A. 1993. "The Search for Relevance in Economics." *American Economic Review Papers and Proceedings* 83: 1–16.

Harkness, E. F., G. J. Macfarlane, A. J. Silman, and J. McBeth. 2005. "Is Musculoskeletal Pain More Common Now than 40 Years Ago? Two Population-Based Cross-Sectional Studies." *Rheumatology (Oxford)* 44 (7): 890–95.

Hart, R. A. 2017. "Hours vs. Employment in Response to Demand Shocks." Online blog/paper. IZA World of Labor #393, October.

Hart, R. A., and T. Sharot. 1978. "The Short-Run Demand for Workers and Hours: A Recursive Model." *Review of Economic Studies* 45 (2): 299–309.

Hazledine, T. 1981. "Employment Functions and the Demand for Labour in the Short-Run." In *The Economics of the Labour Market*, ed. Z. Hornstein, J. Grice, and A. Webb, 149–81. London: HMSO.

Heckman, J. J. 2007. "Comments on 'Are Protective Labour Market Institutions at the Root of Unemployment? A Critical Review of the Evidence,' by David Howell, Dean Baker, Andrew Glyn, and John Schmitt." *Capitalism and Society* 2 (1): Article 5, 15.

Heckman, J. J., S. H. Moon, R. Pinto, P. A. Savelyev, and A. Yavitz. 2009. "The Rate of Return to the High/Scope Perry Preschool Program." NBER Working Paper #15471.

Heckman, J. J., and J. Smith. 2000. "The Sensitivity of Experimental Impact Estimates (Evidence from the National JTPA Study)." In *Youth Employment and Joblessness in Advanced Countries*, ed. D. G. Blanchflower and R. B. Freeman, 331–56. Chicago: University of Chicago Press.

Hedegaard, H., S. C. Curtin, and M. Warner. 2018. "Suicide Mortality in the United States, 1999–2017." Centers for Disease Control and Prevention, NCHS Data Brief No. 330, November.

Hedegaard, H., A. M. Miniño, and M. Warner. 2018. "Drug Overdose Deaths in the United States, 1999–2017." Centers for Disease Control and Prevention. NCHS Data Brief No. 329, November.

Heistaro, S., E. Vartiainen, M. Heliovaara, and P. Puska. 1998. "Trends of Back Pain in Eastern Finland, 1972–1992, in Relation to Socioeconomic Status and Behavioral Risk Factors." *American Journal of Epidemiology* 148 (7): 671–82.

Helliwell, J. F., H. Huang, and S. Wang. 2019. "Changing World Happiness." In World Happiness Report 2019, ed. J. F. Helliwell, R. Layard, and J. D. Sachs.

Hemingway, H., and M. Marmot. 1999. "Psychosocial Factors in the Aetiology and Prognosis of Coronary Heart Disease: Systematic Review of Prospective Cohort Studies." *British Medical Journal* 318: 1460–67.

Henley, A. 1998. "Residential Mobility, Housing Equity and the Labour Market." *Economic Journal* 108 (447): 414–27.

Herndon, T., M. Ash, and R. Pollin. 2014. "Does High Public Debt Consistently Stifle Economic Growth? A Critique of Reinhart and Rogoff." *Cambridge Journal of Economics* 38 (2): 257–79.

Higgins, P. 2014. "Using State-Level Data to Estimate How Labor Market Slack Affects Wages." Federal Reserve Bank of Atlanta macroblog, April 17.

Hills, J. 2015. "The Coalition's Record on Cash Transfers, Poverty and Inequality, 2010–2015." STICERD Working Paper No. 11.

Hills, S., R. Thomas, and N. Dimsdale. 2010. "The UK Recession in Context: What Do Three Centuries of Data Tell Us?" *Bank of England Quarterly Bulletin* Q4: 277–91.

Hipple, S. F. 2015. "People Who Are Not in the Labor Force: Why Aren't They Working?" *Beyond the Numbers* 4 (15), U.S. Bureau of Labor Statistics, December.

Hirsch, B. T., M. M. Husain, and J. V. Winters. 2016. "Multiple Job-Holding, Local Labor Markets, and the Business Cycle." *IZA Journal of Labor Economics* 5 (4).

Hollander, H. 2001. "On the Validity of Utility Statements: Standard Theory versus Duesenberry's." *Journal of Economic Behavior and Organization* 45: 227–49.

Holzer, H. J. 2007. "Collateral Costs: The Effects of Incarceration on the Employment and Earnings of Young Workers." IZA Discussion Paper No. 3118.

Hong, G. H., Z. Kóczán, W. Lian, and M. Nabar. 2018. "More Slack than Meets the Eye? Recent Wage Dynamics in Advanced Economies." IMF Working Paper No. 18/50, IMF Research Department.

Howell, D., D. Baker, A. Glyn, and J. Schmitt. 2007. "Are Protective Labour Market Institutions at the Root of Unemployment? A Critical Review of the Evidence." *Capitalism and Society* 2 (1): 1–73.

Howell, R. T., M. L. Kern, and S. Lyubomirsky. 2007. "Health Benefits: Meta Analytically Determining the Impact of Well-Being on Objective Health Outcomes." *Health Psychology Review* 1 (1): 83–136.

Hsieh, C., and E. Moretti. 2018. "Housing Constraints and Spatial Misallocation." *American Economic Journal: Macroeconomics.* https://faculty.chicagobooth.edu /chang-tai.hsieh/research/growth.pdf.

Huppe, A., K. Muller, and H. Raspe. 2007. "Is the Occurrence of Back Pain in Germany Decreasing? Two Regional Postal Surveys, a Decade Apart." *European Journal of Public Health* 17 (3): 318–22.

Hyclak, T., G. Johnes, and R. Thornton. 2017. *Fundamentals of Labor Economics.* 2nd ed. Mason, OH: South-Western.

Ifcher, J., H. Zarghamee, and C. Graham. 2016. "Income Inequality and Well-Being in the U.S.: Evidence of Geographic-Scale- and Measure-Dependence." IZA Discussion Paper No. 10155.

Ihlanfeldt, Keith R. 2007. "Neighborhood Drug Crime and Young Males' Job Accessibility." *Review of Economics and Statistics* 89 (1): 151–64.

Institute of Medicine of the National Academy of Sciences. 2011. *Relieving Pain in America: A Blueprint for Transforming Prevention, Core, Education and Research.* Washington, DC: National Academies Press.

International Labour Organisation (ILO). 1995. "World Employment Report." Geneva: ILO.

International Monetary Fund (IMF). 2017. *World Economic Outlook.* Washington, DC.

———. 2018. *World Economic Outlook.* Washington, DC.

Irwin, D. A. 2017. "The False Promise of Protectionism: Why Trump's Trade Policy Could Backfire." *Foreign Affairs* 96 (3): 45–56.

Iverson, L., and S. Sabroe. 1988. "Participation in a Follow-up Study of Health among Unemployed and Employed People after a Company Closedown: Drop Outs and Selection Bias." *Journal of Epidemiology and Community Health* 42: 396–401.

Jackson, P., and P. Warr. 1987. "Mental Health of Unemployed Men in Different Parts of England and Wales." *British Medical Journal* 295: 525.

Jae, S., D. J. Price, F. Guvenen, and N. Bloom. 2015. "Firming Up Inequality." NBER Working Paper #21199.

Jeffery, M. M., W. M. Hooten, E. P. Hess, E. R. Meara, J. S. Ross, H. J. Henk, B. Borgundvaag, N. D. Shah, and M. F. Bellolio. 2017. "Opioid Prescribing for Opioid-Naive Patients in Emergency Departments and Other Settings: Characteristics of Prescriptions and Association with Long-Term Use." *Annals of Emergency Medicine* 71 (3): 326–36.

Johansson-Stenman, O., F. Carlsson, and D. Daruvala. 2002. "Measuring Future Grandparents' Preferences for Equality and Relative Standing." *Economic Journal* 112: 362–83.

Jones, O. 2014. *The Establishment: And How They Get Away With It*. London: Allen Lane.

Judis, J. B. 2016. *The Populist Explosion: How the Great Recession Transformed American and European Politics*. New York: Columbia Global Reports.

Kahn, L. B. 2010. "The Long-Term Labor Market Consequences of Graduating from College in a Bad Economy." *Labour Economics* 17: 303–16.

Kahneman, D., and A. B. Krueger. 2006. "Developments in the Measurement of Subjective Well-Being." *Journal of Economic Perspectives* 20: 3–24.

Kakutani, M. 2018. *The Death of Truth: Notes on Falsehood in the Age of Trump*. New York: Tim Duggan Books.

Kalil, A. 2013. "Effects of the Great Recession on Child Development." *Annals of the American Academy of Political and Social Science* 560: 232–50.

Kanny, D., R. D. Brewer, J. B. Mesnick, L. J. Paulozzi, T. S. Naimi, and H. Lu. 2015. "Vital Signs: Alcohol Poisoning Deaths—United States, 2010–2012." *Morbidity and Mortality Weekly Report* 63 (53): 1238–42.

Kao, L., S. Xirasagar, K. Chung, H. Lin, S. Liu, and S. Chung. 2014. "Weekly and Holiday-Related Patterns of Panic Attacks in Panic Disorder: A Population-Based Study." *PLoS One* 9 (7): e100913.

Katolik, A., and A. J. Oswald. 2017. "Antidepressants for Economists and Business-School Researchers: An Introduction and Review." Working paper, University of Warwick.

Katsambekis, G. 2017. "The Populist Surge in Post-Democratic Times: Theoretical and Political Challenges." *Political Quarterly* 88 (2): 202–10.

Katz, L. F., and A. B. Krueger. 2017. "The Role of Unemployment in the Rise in Alternative Work Arrangements." *American Economic Review* 107 (5): 388–92.

———. 2019. "Understanding Trends in Alternative Work Arrangements in the United States." NBER Working Paper #25425.

Kaufmann, E. 2016. "Brexit Voters: NOT the Left Behind." Fabian Society. June 24. http://fabians.org.uk/brexit-voters-not-the-left-behind/.

Kegler, S. R., D. M. Stone, and K. M. Holland. 2017. "Trends in Suicide by Level of Urbanization—United States, 1999–2015." *Morbidity and Mortality Weekly Report* 66: 270–73.

Kennedy, J., J. M. Roll, T. Schraudner, S. Murphy, and S. McPherson. 2014. "Prevalence of Persistent Pain in the U.S. Adult Population: New Data from the 2010 National Health Interview Survey." *Journal of Pain* 15 (10): 979–84.

Kerr, S. P., and W. R. Kerr. 2011. "Economic Impacts of Immigration: A Survey." *Finnish Economic Papers* 24 (1): 1–32.

Keynes, J. M. 1920. *The Economic Consequences of the Peace*. New York: Harcourt, Brace, and Howe. http://oll.libertyfund.org/titles/keynes-the-economic-consequences-of-the-peace.

———. 1931. "An Economic Analysis of Unemployment." In *Unemployment as a World Problem*, ed. Q. Wright and J. M. Keynes, 1–42. Chicago: University of Chicago Press.

Kiley, M. T. 2014. "An Evaluation of the Inflationary Pressure Associated with Short- and Long-term Unemployment." Working Paper No. 2014-28, Finance and Economics Discussion Series Divisions of Research & Statistics and Monetary Affairs Federal Reserve Board, Washington, DC.

Knapp, M., D. McDaid, E. Mossialos, and G. Thornicroft, eds. 2007. *Mental Health Policy and Practice across Europe*. Maidenhead: Open University Press and McGraw-Hill Education.

Knowlton, K. 2018. *Cattle Kingdom: The Hidden History of the Cowboy West*. Boston: Mariner Books.

Kochanek, K. D., S. L. Murphy, J. Xu, and E. Arias. 2017. "Mortality in the United States, 2016." NCHS Data Brief No. 293, December. https://www.cdc.gov/nchs/data/databriefs/db293.pdf.

Koivumaa-Honkanen, H., R. Honkanen, M. Koskenvuo, and J. Kaprio. 2003. "Self-Reported Happiness in Life and Suicide in Ensuing 20 Years." *Social Psychiatry Psychiatric Epidemiology* 38 (5): 244–48.

Kolev, G., and R. Hogarth. 2010. "Illusory Correlation in the Remuneration of Chief Executive Officers: It Pays to Play Golf, and Well." Working paper, Department of Economics and Business, Universitat Pompeu Fabra.

Kopp, M., H. Bonatti, C. Haller, G. Rumpold, W. Söllner, B. Holzner, H. Schweigkofler, F. Aigner, H. Hinterhuber, and V. Günther. 2003. "Life Satisfaction and Active Coping Style Are Important Predictors of Recovery from Surgery." *Journal of Psychosomatic Research* 55: 371–77.

Krueger, A. 2012. "The Rise and Consequences of Inequality." Center for American Progress, January 12.

———. 2015. "How Tight Is the Labor Market?" NBER Reporter No. 3, Martin Feldstein Lecture, NBER.

———. 2016. "Where Have All the Workers Gone?" Paper presented at conference at Federal Reserve Bank of Boston, October 4.

———. 2017. "Where Have All the Workers Gone? An Inquiry into the Decline of the U.S. Labor Force Participation Rate." *Brookings Papers on Economic Activity*, BPEA Conference Draft, September 7–8.

Krueger, A., J. Cramer, and D. Cho. 2014. "Are the Long-Term Unemployed on the Margins of the Labor Market?" *Brookings Papers* (Spring): 229–96.

Krueger, A. B., and A. Mas. 2004. "Strikes, Scabs, and Tread Separations: Labor Strife and the Production of Defective Bridgestone/Firestone Tires." *Journal of Political Economy* 112 (2): 253–89.

Krugman, P. 2018. "Good Enough for Government Work? Macroeconomics since the Crisis." *Oxford Review of Economic Policy* 34 (1–2): 156–68.

Kügler, A., U. Schönberg, and R. Schreiner. 2018. "Productivity Growth, Wage Growth and Unions." In *Price and Wage-setting in Advanced Economies*. Frankfurt am Main: European Central Bank.

Kuhn, A., R. Lalive, and J. Zweimuller. 2009. "The Public Health Costs of Job Loss." *Journal of Health Economics* 28 (6): 1099–1115.

Kumar, A., and P. Orrenius. 2015. "A Closer Look at the Phillips Curve Using State Level Data." Federal Reserve Bank of Dallas Working Paper No. 1409, May.

Lach, S. 2007. "Immigration and Prices." *Journal of Political Economy* 115 (4): 548–87.

Lalé, E. 2015. "Multiple Jobholding over the Past Two Decades." *Monthly Labor Review* 138 (4): 1–40.

LaLonde, R., and R. Topel. 1997. "Economic Impact of International Migration and the Economic Performance of Migrants." In *Handbook of Population and Family Economics*, ed. M. R. Rosenzweig and O. Stark, 799–850. Vol. 1. Part B. Amsterdam: Elsevier Science.

Langella, M., and A. Manning. 2016. "Who Voted Leave?" *Centrepiece* (Autumn).

Layard, R. 1982. "Youth Unemployment in Britain and the United States Compared." In *The Youth Labor Market Problem: Its Nature, Causes, and Consequences*, ed. R. B. Freeman and D. A. Wise, 499–542. Chicago: University of Chicago Press.

———. 1986. *How to Beat Unemployment*. Oxford: Oxford University Press.

Layard, R., and S. N. Nickell. 1987. "The Labour Market." In *The Performance of the British Economy*, ed. R. Dornbusch and R. Layard, 131–79. Oxford: Oxford University Press.

Layard, R., S. N. Nickell, and R. Jackman. 1991. *Unemployment: Macroeconomic Performance and the Labour Market*. New York: Oxford University Press.

Lazear, E. P., and J. R. Spletzer. 2012. "The United States Labor Market: Status Quo or a New Normal?" NBER Working Paper #18386.

Leino, P. I., M. A. Berg, and P. Puska. 1994. "Is Back Pain Increasing? Results from National Surveys in Finland during 1978/9–1992." *Scandinavian Journal of Rheumatology* 23 (5): 269–76.

Lempert, R. O. 2003. "Following the Man on the Clapham Omnibus: Social Science Evidence in Malpractice Litigation." Law and Economics Working Papers Archive: 2003–2009, University of Michigan Law School.

Leontief, W. 1971. "Theoretical Assumptions and Non-observed Facts." *American Economic Review* 61 (1): 1–7.

Levitsky, S., and D. Ziblatt. 2018. *How Democracies Die*. New York: Crown.

Lewis, E., and G. Peri. 2014. "Immigration and the Economy of Cities and Regions." NBER Working Paper #20428, August.

Lewis, H. G. 1957. "Hours of Work and Hours of Leisure." Paper presented at the Proceedings of the Ninth Annual Meeting of the Industrial Relations Research.

———. 1969. "Employer Interests in Employee Hours of Work." *Cuadernos de Economia* 6 (18): 38–54.

Lewis, R. A., N. H. Williams, A. J. Sutton, K. Burton, N. U. Din, H. E. Matar, M. Hendry, C. J. Philips, S. Nafees, D. Fitzsimons, I. Rickard, and C. Wilkinson. 2013. "Comparative Clinical Effectiveness of Management Strategies for Sciatica: Systematic Review and Network Meta-analyses." *Spine Journal* 15 (6): 1461–77.

Li, G., and B. McCully. 2016. "Is Underemployment Underestimated? Evidence from Panel Data." FEDS Notes, May 16.

Linn, M., R. Sandifer, and S. Stein. 1985. "Effects of Unemployment on Mental and Physical Health." *American Journal of Public Health* 75: 502–6.

Longazel, J. 2016. *Undocumented Fears: Immigration and the Politics of Divide and Conquer in Hazleton, Pennsylvania*. Philadelphia: Temple University Press.

Longhi, S., P. Nijkamp, and J. Poot. 2005. "A Meta-analytic Assessment of the Effect of Immigration on Wages." *Journal of Economic Surveys* 19 (3): 451–77.

Loopstra, R., and D. Lalor. 2017. "Financial Insecurity, Food Insecurity, and Disability: The Profile of People Receiving Emergency Food Assistance from the Trussell Trust Foodbank Network in Britain." Trussell Trust. https://trusselltrust.org/wp-content/uploads/sites/2/2017/06/OU_Report_final_01_08_online.pdf.

Lucas, R. E. 2003. "Macroeconomic Priorities." *American Economic Review* 93 (1): 1–14.

Ludwig, J., D. E. Marcotte, and K. Norberg. 2009. "Anti-depressants and Suicide." *Journal of Health Economics* 28 (3): 659–76.

Luppino, F. S., L. M. de Wit, P. V. Bouvy, T. Stijnen, P. Cuijpers, B. W. Penninx, and F. G. Zitman. 2010. "Overweight, Obesity, and Depression: A Systematic Review and Meta-analysis of Longitudinal Studies." *Archives of General Psychiatry* 67 (3): 220–29.

Luttmer, E. F. P. 2005. "Neighbors as Negatives: Relative Earnings and Well-Being." *Quarterly Journal of Economics* 120 (3): 963–1002.

Machin, S., and A. Manning. 1999. "The Causes and Consequences of Long-Term Unemployment in Europe." In *Handbook of Labor Economics*, vol. 3C, ed. O. C. Ashenfelter and D. Card, 3085–3139. Amsterdam: Elsevier North Holland.

Mack, K. A., C. M. Jones, and M. F. Ballesteros. 2017. "Illicit Drug Use, Illicit Drug Use Disorders, and Drug Overdose Deaths in Metropolitan and Nonmetropolitan Areas—United States." *Morbidity and Mortality Weekly Report* 66 (19): 1–12.

MacKenzie, E. J., F. P. Rivara, G. J. Jurkovich, et al. 2006. "A National Evaluation of the Effect of Trauma-Center Care on Mortality." *New England Journal of Medicine* 354: 366–78.

Mankiw, N. G. 2006. "The Macroeconomist as Scientist and Engineer." *Journal of Economic Perspectives* 20 (4): 29–46.

Manning, A. 2003. *Monopsony in Motion*. Princeton: Princeton University Press.

Martikainen, P., and T. Valkonen. 1996. "Excess Mortality of Unemployed Men and Women during a Period of Rapidly Increasing Unemployment." *Lancet* 348 (9032): 909–12.

Marucha, P. T., J. K. Kiecolt-Glaser, and M. Favagehi. 1998. "Mucosal Wound Healing Is Impaired by Examination Stress." *Psychosomatic Medicine* 60: 362–65.

Marx, K. 1867. *Das Kapital*. New York: Verlag von Otto Meisner.

Mattiasson, I., F. Lindgarde, J. A. Nilsson, and T. Theorell. 1990. "Threats of Unemployment and Cardiovascular Risk Factors: Longitudinal Study of Quality of Sleep and Serum Cholesterol Concentrations in Men Threatened with Redundancy." *British Medical Journal* 301: 461–66.

McBride, M. 2001. "Relative-Income Effects on Subjective Wellbeing in the Cross-section." *Journal of Economic Behavior and Organization* 45: 251–78.

McGuinnity, F., and H. Russell. 2013. "Work-Family Conflict and Economic Change." In *Economic Crisis, Quality of Work and Social Integration: The European Experience*, ed. D. Gallie, 246–64. Oxford: Oxford University Press.

Metcalf, D., S. J. Nickell, and N. Floros. 1982. "Still Searching for an Explanation of Unemployment in Interwar Britain." *Journal of Political Economy* 90 (2): 386–99.

Mishel, L. 2012. "Unions, Inequality, and Faltering Middle-Class Wages." Economic Policy Institute, August 29.

Mishel, L., and N. Sabadish. 2013. "CEO Pay in 2012 Was Extraordinarily High Relative to Typical Workers and Other High Earners." Economic Policy Institute, June 26.

Mojtabai, R., and M. Olfson. 2014. "National Trends in Long-Term Use of Antidepressant Medications: Results from the U.S. National Health and Nutrition Examination Survey." *Journal of Clinical Psychiatry* 75 (2): 169–77.

Montagnes, B. P., Z. Peskowita, and J. McCrain. Forthcoming. "Bounding Partisan Approval Rates under Endogenous Partisanship: Why High Presidential Partisan Approval May Not Be What It Seems." *Journal of Politics*.

Moore, P. A., and E. V. Hersh. 2013. "Combining Ibuprofen and Acetaminophen for Acute Pain Management after Third-Molar Extractions." *Journal of the American Dental Association* 144 (8): 898–908.

Moriconi, S., G. Peri, and R. Turati. 2018. "Skill of Immigrants and Vote of the Natives: Immigration and Nationalism in European Elections, 2007–16." NBER Working Paper #25077.

Moser, K. A., P. O. Goldblatt, A. J. Fox, and D. R. Jones. 1987. "Unemployment and Mortality: Comparison of the 1971 and 1981 Longitudinal Study Census Samples." *British Medical Journal* 1: 86–90.

Moy, E., M. C. Garcia, B. Bastian, L. M. Rossen, D. D. Ingram, M. Faul, G. M. Massetti, C. C. Thomas, Y. Hong, P. W. Yoon, and M. F. Iademarco. 2017. "Leading Causes of Death in Nonmetropolitan and Metropolitan Areas—United States, 1999–2014." *Morbidity and Mortality Weekly Report* 66 (1): 1–8.

Muhuri, P. K., J. C. Gfroerer, and M. C. Davies. 2013. "Associations of Nonmedical Pain Reliever Use and Initiation of Heroin Use in the United States." Rockville, MD: Substance Abuse and Mental Health Services Administration, Center for Behavioral Health Statistics and Quality.

Müller, J. W. 2016. *What Is Populism?* Philadelphia: University of Pennsylvania Press.

Murphy, S. L., J. Xu, K. D. Kochanek, and E. Arias. 2018. "Mortality in the United States, 2017." Center for Disease Control and Prevention, NCHS Data Brief No. 328, November. https://www.cdc.gov/nchs/products/databriefs/db328.htm.

Murphy, S. L., J. Q. Xu, K. D. Kochanek, S. C. Curtin, and E. Arias. 2017. "Deaths: Final Data for 2015." *National Vital Statistics Reports* 66 (6): 1–75.

Nahin, R. L. 2015. "Estimates of Pain Prevalence and Severity in Adults: United States, 2012." *Journal of Pain* 16 (8): 769–80.

National Academies of Sciences, Engineering, and Medicine. 2017. *The Economic and Fiscal Consequences of Immigration*. Washington, DC: National Academies Press.

NHS Digital. 2016. "Prescriptions Dispensed in the Community: Statistics for England, 2005–2015." https://digital.nhs.uk/data-and-information/publica tions/statistical/prescriptions-dispensed-in-the-community/prescriptions -dispensed-in-the-community-statistics-for-england-2005-2015.

———. 2017. "Prescriptions Dispensed in the Community: Statistics for England, 2006–2016." https://digital.nhs.uk/data-and-information/publications/statistical /prescriptions-dispensed-in-the-community/prescriptions-dispensed-in-the -community-statistics-for-england-2006-2016-pas.

Nichols, T. 2017. *The Death of Expertise: The Campaign against Established Knowledge and Why It Matters*. Oxford: Oxford University Press.

Nickell, S. J., and J. Saleheen. 2015. "The Impact of Immigration on Occupational Wages: Evidence from Britain." Bank of England Staff Working Paper No. 574.

Nijkamp, P., and J. Poot. 2005. "The Last Word on the Wage Curve?" *Journal of Economic Surveys* 19: 421–50.

Orbuch, T. L., J. S. House, R. P. Mero, and P. S. Webster. 1996. "Marital Quality over the Life Course." *Social Psychology Quarterly* 59: 162–71.

Organisation for Economic Co-operation and Development (OECD). 1994. "The OECD Jobs Study; Evidence and Explanations." Paris: OECD.

———. 2014. "OECD Economic Surveys: United States." Paris: OECD.

———. 2016a. "OECD Economic Surveys: United States Overview." June. Paris: OECD.

———. 2016b. "International Migration Outlook, 2016." Paris: OECD.

———. 2016c. "Society at a Glance." Paris: OECD.

———. 2017. "OECD Employment Outlook, 2017." Paris: OECD.

———. 2018a. "International Migration Outlook, 2018." Paris: OECD.

———. 2018b. "Economic Outlook, March 2018." Paris: OECD.

———. 2019. "Risks That Matter: Main Findings from the 2018 Risks That Matter Survey." Paris: OECD.

Ormerod, P. A., and G. D. N. Worswick. 1982. "Unemployment in Interwar Britain." *Journal of Political Economy* 90 (2): 400–409.

Orwell, G. 1937. *The Road to Wigan Pier*. London: Victor Gollancz.

Oswald, A. J. 1996. "A Conjecture on the Explanation for High Unemployment in the Industrialized Nations; Part 1." Working paper, Department of Economics, University of Warwick, November.

———. 1997. "The Missing Piece of the Unemployment Puzzle." Inaugural Lecture, Department of Economics, University of Warwick, November.

———. 1999. "The Housing Market and Europe's Unemployment: A Non-technical Paper." Warwick University, May.

Oswald, A. J., and N. Powdthavee. 2007. "Obesity, Unhappiness, and the Challenge of Affluence: Theory and Evidence." *Economic Journal* 117: F441–F454.

Oswald, A. J., and A. Tohamy. 2017. "Female Suicide and the Concept of the Midlife Crisis." IZA Discussion Paper No. 10759.

Palmer, K. T., K. Walsh, H. Bendall, C. Cooper, and D. Coggon. 2000. "Back Pain in Britain: Comparison of Two Prevalence Surveys at an Interval of 10 Years." *British Medical Journal* 320 (7249): 1577–78.

Parker K., and W. Wang. 2013. "Modern Parenthood: Roles of Moms and Dads as They Balance Work and Family." Pew Research Center.

Patterson, T. E. 2016. "News Coverage of Donald Trump's First 100 Days." Shorenstein Center on Media, Politics and Public Policy, Harvard Kennedy School.

Paul, K. I., and K. Moser. 2009. "Unemployment Impairs Mental Health: Meta-analyses." *Journal of Vocational Behavior* 74: 264–82.

Pencavel, J. 1986. "Labor Supply of Men: A Survey." In *Handbook of Labor Economics*, ed. O. Ashenfelter and D. Card, 3–102. Amsterdam: Elsevier North Holland.

————. 2016. "Whose Preferences Are Revealed in Hours of Work?" *Economic Inquiry* 54 (1): 9–24.

Pencavel, J. 2018. *Diminishing Returns at Work*. Oxford: Oxford University Press.

Pennycook, M., G. Cory, and V. Alakeson. 2013. "A Matter of Time: The Rise of Zero-Hours Contracts." London: Resolution Foundation.

Peston, M. H. 2006. "The 364 Were Correct." In *Were 364 Economists All Wrong?* ed. P. Booth. London: Institute of Economic Affairs.

Peterson, C., D. M. Stone, S. M. Marsh, P. K. Schumacher, H. M. Tiesman, W. L. McIntosh, C. N. Lokey, A. T. Trudeau, B. Bartholow, and F. Luo. 2018. "Suicide Rates by Major Occupational Group—17 States, 2012 and 2015." *Morbidity and Mortality Weekly Report* 67 (45): 1253–60.

Phillips, A. W. 1958. "The Relation between Unemployment and the Rate of Change of Money Wage Rates in the United Kingdom, 1861–1957." *Economica* 25 (100): 283–99.

Pierce, J. R., and P. K. Schott. 2016. "Trade Liberalization and Mortality: Evidence from U.S. Counties." Paper #2016-094. Finance and Economics Discussion Series, Divisions of Research & Statistics and Monetary Affairs, Federal Reserve Board, Washington, DC.

Pike, A., D. MacKinnon, M. Coombes, T. Champion, D. Bradley, A. Cumbers, L. Robson, and C. Wymer. 2016. "Uneven Growth: Tackling City Decline." York: Joseph Rowntree Foundation.

Piketty, T. 2014. *Capital in the Twenty-First Century*. Cambridge, MA: Belknap Press of Harvard University Press.

Piketty, T., E. Saez, and G. Zucman. 2017. "Economic Growth in the US: A Tale of Two Countries." Vox, March 29. https://voxeu.org/article/economic-growth-us-tale-two-countries.

————. 2018. "Distributional National Accounts; Methods and Estimates for the United States." *Quarterly Journal of Economics* 133 (2): 553–609.

Platt, S. 1984. "Unemployment and Suicidal Behaviour: A Review of the Literature." *Social Science and Medicine* 19 (2): 93–115.

Platt, S., R. Micciolo, and M. Tansella. 1992. "Suicide and Unemployment in Italy: Description, Analysis and Interpretation of Recent Trends." *Social Science and Medicine* 34: 1191–1201.

Plesh, O., S. H. Adams, and S. A. Gansky. 2012. "Racial/Ethnic and Gender Prevalences in Reported Common Pains in a National Sample." *Journal of Orofacial Pain* 25: 25–31.

Portes, J. D. 2017. "Written Evidence to Parliament." Home Affairs Committee.

Portes, J. D., and G. Forte. 2017. "The Economic Impact of Brexit-Induced Reductions in Migration." *Oxford Review of Economic Policy* 33 (S1): S31–S44.

Pouliakas, K. 2017. "Multiple Job-Holding: Career Pathway or Dire Straits?" *IZA World of Labor* 356 (May).

Powdthavee, P., A. C. Plagnol, P. Frijters, and A. E. Clark. 2017. "Who Got the Brexit Blues? Using a Quasi-Experiment to Show the Effect of Brexit on Subjective Wellbeing in the UK." IZA Working Paper No. 11206, December.

Pratt, L. A., and D. J. Brody. 2014a. "Depression in the U.S. Household Population, 2009–2012." NCHS Data Brief No. 172, December.

———. 2014b. "Depression and Obesity in the U.S. Adult Household Population, 2005–2010." NCHS Data Brief No. 167, October.

Pressman, S. D., and S. Cohen. 2005. "Does Positive Affect Influence Health?" *Psychological Bulletin* 131 (6): 925–71.

Pritchard, C. 1992. "Is There a Link between Suicide in Young Men and Unemployment? A Comparison of the UK with Other European Community Countries." *British Journal of Psychiatry* 160: 750–56.

Putnam, R. D. 2000. *Bowling Alone: The Collapse and Revival of American Community.* New York: Simon and Schuster.

———. 2015. *Our Kids: The American Dream in Crisis.* New York: Simon and Schuster.

Putnam, R. D., L. M. Feldstein, and D. Cohen. 2003. *Better Together: Restoring the American Community.* New York: Simon and Schuster.

Quévat, B., and B. Vignolles. 2018. "The Relationships between Inflation, Wages and Unemployment Have Not Disappeared: A Comparative Study of the French and American Economies." INSEE, Conjoncture in France, March.

Quinones, S. 2015. *Dreamland: The True Tale of America's Opiate Epidemic.* New York: Bloomsbury Press.

Raphael, S., and R. Winter-Ebmer. 2001. "Identifying the Effect of Unemployment on Crime." *Journal of Law and Economics* 44 (1): 259–83.

Rapley, J. 2017. *Twilight of the Money Gods: Economics as a Religion and How It All Went Wrong.* New York: Simon and Schuster.

Rees, A. 1989. *The Economics of Trade Unions.* 3rd ed. Chicago: University of Chicago Press.

Reeves, A. M., M. McKee, and D. Stuckler. 2014. "Economic Suicides in the Great Recession in Europe and North America." *British Journal of Psychiatry* 205: 246–47.

Reinhart, C. M., and K. S. Rogoff. 2009. "The Aftermath of Financial Crises." NBER Working Paper #14656.

———. 2010. "Growth in a Time of Debt." *American Economic Review* 100 (2): 573–78.

Reis, R. 2017. "Is Something Really Wrong with Macroeconomics?" *Oxford Review of Economic Policy* 34 (1–2): 132–55.

Rieder, T. N. 2017. "In Opioid Withdrawal, with No Help in Sight." *Health Affairs* 36 (1): 182–85.

Rinne, U., and K. F. Zimmermann. 2012. "Another Economic Miracle? The German Labor Market and the Great Recession." *IZA Journal of Labor Policy* 1: 3.

———. 2013. "Is Germany the North Star of Labor Market Policy?" *IMF Economic Review* 61: 702–29.

Rohde, N., K. K. Tang, L. Osberg, and D. S. P. Rao. 2016. "The Effect of Economic Insecurity on Mental Health: Recent Evidence from Australian Panel Data." *Social Science and Medicine* 151: 250–58.

Rohe, W., and L. Stewart. 1996. "Homeownership and Neighborhood Stability." *Housing Policy Debate* 7 (1): 173–84.

Romer, P. 2015. "Mathiness in the Theory of Economic Growth." *American Economic Review: Papers and Proceedings* 105 (5): 89–93.

Rosen, S. 1969. "On the Interindustry Wage and Hours Structure." *Journal of Political Economy* 77 (2): 249–73.

Rosenfeld, R. 2016. "Documenting and Explaining the 2015 Homicide Rise: Research Directions." National Institute of Justice, U.S. Department of Justice.

Rousseau, J. J. 1762. *The Social Contract*. Amsterdam: Chez Marc-Michel Ray.

Royal College of Paediatrics and Child Health. 2017. "Poverty and Child Health: Views from the Frontline." http://www.cpag.org.uk/sites/default/files/pdf%20RCPCH.pdf.

Rudd, R. A., P. Seth, F. David, and L. Scholl. 2016. "Increases in Drug and Opioid-Involved Overdose Deaths—United States, 2010–2015." *Morbidity and Mortality Weekly Report* 65: 1445–52.

Sacerdote, B. 2017. "Fifty Years of Growth in American Consumption, Income, and Wages." NBER Working Paper #23292.

Saez, E., and G. Zucman. 2016. "Wealth Inequality in the United States since 1913: Evidence from Capitalized Tax Income Data." *Quarterly Journal of Economics* 131 (2): 519–78.

Schaefer, D., and C. Singleton. 2017. "Real Wages and Hours in the Great Recession: Evidence from Firms and Their Entry-Level Jobs." CESIFO Working Paper No. 6766.

Schmitt, J., and K. Warner. 2010. "Ex-Offenders and the Labor Market." *Journal of Labor and Society* 14: 87–109.

Schnell, M., and J. Currie. 2017. "Addressing the Opioid Epidemic: Is There a Role for Physician Education?" NBER Working Paper #23645.

Schwandt, H. 2016. "Unmet Aspirations as an Explanation for the Age U-Shape in Wellbeing." *Journal of Economic Behavior and Organization* 122 (February): 75–87.

Schwarz, M. 2016. "The IMF and the Crises in Greece, Spain and Portugal." Independent Evaluation Office, IMF.

Senik, C. 2004. "When Information Dominates Comparison: A Panel Data Analysis

Using Russian Subjective Data." *Journal of Public Economics* 88 (9–10): 2099–2123.

Shah, A. J., C. J. Hayes, and B. C. Martin. 2017. "Characteristics of Initial Prescription Episodes and Likelihood of Long-Term Opioid Use—United States, 2006–2015." *Morbidity and Mortality Weekly Report* 66 (10): 265 –69. U.S. Department of Health and Human Services, Centers for Disease Control and Prevention.

Shank, S. 1986. "Preferred Hours of Work and Corresponding Earnings." *Monthly Labor Review* (November): 40–44.

Shiller, R. J. 1997. "Why Do People Dislike Inflation?" In *Reducing Inflation: Motivation and Strategy*, ed. C. Romer and D. H. Romer, 13–70. Chicago: University of Chicago Press.

Shin, H. S. 2009. "Reflections on Northern Rock: The Bank Run That Heralded the Global Financial Crisis." *Journal of Economic Perspectives* 23 (1): 101–11.

Shiskin, J. 1976. "Employment and Unemployment: The Doughnut and the Hole." *Monthly Labor Review* (February): 3–10.

Silver, N. 2016. "Education, Not Income, Predicted Who Would Vote for Trump." FiveThirtyeight.com, November 22.

Sinha, R. 2009. "Chronic Stress, Drug Use and Vulnerability to Addiction." *Annals of the New York Academy of Sciences* 1141 (October): 105–30.

Skidelsky, R. 2009. *Keynes: The Return of the Master*. London: Allen Lane.

Smith, C. L. 2014. "The Effect of Labor Slack on Wages: Evidence from State-Level Relationships." FEDS Notes, June 2.

Smith, H. L. 2017. *Don't Let My Past Be Your Future: A Call to Arms*. London: Constable.

Smith, L., K. Rosen, and G. Fallis. 1988. "Recent Developments in Economic Models of Housing Markets." *Journal of Economic Literature* 26: 29–64.

Smith, T. G., S. Stillman, and S. Craig. 2013. "The U.S. Obesity Epidemic: New Evidence from the Economic Security Index." Paper presented at the Agricultural and Applied Economics Annual Meeting, Washington, DC.

Social Mobility Commission. 2016. *State of the Nation 2016: Social Mobility in Great Britain*. November. London: Printed in the UK on behalf of the Controller of Her Majesty's Stationery Office.

———. 2017. *State of the Nation 2017: Social Mobility in Great Britain*. November. London: Printed in the UK on behalf of the Controller of Her Majesty's Stationery Office.

Solow, R. 2008. "Comments." *Journal of Economic Perspectives* 22 (1): 243–50.

Song, J., D. J. Price, F. Guvenen, N. Bloom, and T. von Wachter. Forthcoming. "Firming Up Inequality." *Quarterly Journal of Economics*.

Sorrentino, C. 1981. "Youth Unemployment: An International Perspective." *Monthly Labor Review* (July): 3–15.

Sorrentino, C. 1993. "International Comparisons of Unemployment Indicators." *Monthly Labor Review* 116 (3): 3–24.

———. 1995. "International Unemployment Indicators, 1983–93." *Monthly Labor Review* 118 (8): 31–50.

Staiger, D., J. Stock, and M. Watson. 1997a. "How Precise Are Estimates of the Natural Rate of Unemployment?" In *Reducing Inflation: Motivation and Strategy*, ed. C. D. Romer and D. H. Romer, 195–246. Chicago: University of Chicago Press and NBER.

———. 1997b. "The NAIRU, Unemployment and Monetary Policy." *Journal of Economic Perspectives* 11 (1): 33–49.

Stansbury, A. M., and L. H. Summers. 2017. "Productivity and Pay: Is the Link Broken?" NBER Working Paper #24165, December.

Statistics New Zealand. 2013. "Introducing New Measures of Underemployment." April. http://archive.stats.govt.nz/browse_for_stats/income-and-work/employ ment_and_unemployment/introducing-new-measures-underemployment.aspx.

Statistics Poland. 2016. *Human Capital in Poland in the Years 2012–2016*. Gdańsk: Główny Urząd Statystyczny Central Statistical Office.

Steptoe, A., A. Deaton, and A. Stone. 2015. "Subjective Wellbeing, Health, and Ageing." *Lancet* 385 (9968): 640–48.

Stiglitz, J. E. 2018. "Where Modern Macroeconomics Went Wrong." *Oxford Review of Economic Policy* 34 (1–2): 70–106.

Stone, A. A., S. Schneidera, and J. E. Brodericka. 2017. "Psychological Stress Declines Rapidly from Age 50 in the United States: Yet Another Well-Being Paradox." *Journal of Psychosomatic Research* 103: 22–28.

Stone, A. A., J. E. Schwartz, J. E. Broderick, and A. Deaton. 2010. "A Snapshot of the Age Distribution of Psychological Well-Being in the United States." *Proceedings of the National Academy of Sciences of the United States of America* 107: 9985–90.

Stuckler, D., and S. Basu. 2013. *The Body Economic: Eight Experiments in Economic Recovery, from Iceland to Greece*. New York: Basic Books.

Sum, A., and I. Khatiwada. 2010. "The Nation's Underemployed in the 'Great Recession' of 2007–09." *Monthly Labor Review* 133 (11): 3–15.

Summers, L. H. 1991. "The Scientific Illusion in Empirical Macroeconomics." *Scandinavian Journal of Economics* 93 (2): 129–48.

———. 2018. "Why the Fed Needs a New Monetary Policy." Report from the Hutchins Center on Fiscal and Monetary Policy, Brookings, June.

Taleb, N. N. 2007. *The Black Swan*. New York: Random House.

Tang, N. K., P. M. Salkovskis, A. Hodges, et al. 2008. "Effects of Mood on Pain Responses and Pain Tolerance: An Experimental Study in Chronic Back Pain Patients." *Pain* 138 (2): 392–401.

Teater, D. 2014. "Evidence for the Efficiency of Pain Medications." National Safety Council, Washington, DC. https://www.nsc.org/Portals/0/Documents /RxDrugOverdoseDocuments/Evidence-Efficacy-Pain-Medications.pdf.

Thaler, R. H. 2018. " From Cashews to Nudges: The Evolution of Behavioral Economics." *American Economic Review* 108 (6): 1265–87.

Thornberry, T., and R. Christensen. 1984. "Unemployment and Criminal Involvement: An Investigation of Reciprocal Causal Structures." *American Sociological Review* 56: 609–27.

Tomlinson, D. 2017. "You're Hired: Lessons for President Trump from a Comparison of Living Standards and Inequality in the US and the UK." Resolution Foundation, January.

Tsang, A., M. Von Korff, S. Lee, J. Alonso, E. Karam, M. C. Angermeyer, G. L. Borges, E. J. Bromet, K. Demytteneare, G. de Girolamo, R. de Graaf, O. Gureje, J. P. Lepine, J. M. Haro, D. Levinson, M. A. Oakley Browne, J. Posada-Villa, S. Seedat, and M. Watanabe. 2008. "Common Chronic Pain Conditions in Developed and Developing Countries: Gender and Age Differences and Comorbidity with Depression-Anxiety Disorders." *Journal of Pain* 9 (10): 883–91.

Tyson, C. J. 2008. "Cognitive Constraints, Contraction Consistency, and the Satisficing Criterion." *Journal of Economic Theory* 138 (1): 51–70.

UNICEF. 2017. *Building the Future: Children and the Sustainable Development Goals in Rich Countries.* Florence: United Nations Office of Research.

United States Conference of Mayors. 2017. *U.S. Metro Economies: Past and Future Employment Levels.* Washington, DC. http://www.usmayors.org/wp-content /uploads/2017/05/Metro-Economies-Past-and-Future-Employment-12.pdf.

Valletta, R. G., L. Bengali, and C. van der List. 2018. "Cyclical and Market Determinants of Involuntary Part-time Employment." FRBSF Working Paper 2015-19.

Van Baardwijk, M., and P. H. Franses. 2010. "The Hemline and the Economy: Is There Any Match?" Econometric Institute Report 2010-40. Econometric Institute, Erasmus School of Economics.

Van Landeghem, B. 2012. "A Test for the Convexity of Human Well-Being over the Life Cycle: Longitudinal Evidence from a 20-Year Panel." *Journal of Economic Behavior and Organization* 81: 571–82.

Vance, J. D. 2016. *The Hillbilly Elegy: A Memoir of a Family and Culture in Crisis.* New York: Harper Collins.

Vandoros, S., M. Avendano, and I. Kawachi. 2018. "The EU Referendum and Mental Health in the Short Term: A Natural Experiment Using Antidepressant Prescriptions in England." *Journal of Epidemiology and Community Health*, November 21.

Veblen, T. 1899. *The Theory of the Leisure Classes: An Economic Study of Institutions.* London: George Allen and Unwin.

Veliziotis, M., M. Matsaganis, and A. Karakitsios. 2015. "Involuntary Part-time Employment: Perspectives from Two European Labor Markets." Improve Discussion Paper 15/2, January.

Vespa, J. 2017. "The Changing Economics and Demographics of Young Adulthood: 1975–2016." Population Characteristics Current Population Reports, April.

Visser, J. 2016. "What Happened to Collective Bargaining during the Great Recession?" *IZA Journal of Labor Policy* 5 (9): 1–35.

Voss, M., L. Nylén, B. Floderus, F. Diderichsen, and P. D. Terry. 2004. "Unemployment and Early Cause-Specific Mortality: A Study Based on the Swedish Twin Registry." *American Journal of Public Health* 94 (12): 2155–61.

Wadsworth, J., S. Dhingra, G. Ottaviano, and J. Van Reenen. 2016. "Brexit and the Impact of Immigration on the UK." CEP Brexit Analysis No. 5, Centre for Economic Performance.

Wadsworth, T. 2010. "Is Immigration Responsible for the Crime Drop? An Assessment of the Influence of Immigration on Changes in Violent Crime between 1990 and 2000." *Social Science Quarterly* 91 (2): 531–55.

Walburn, J., et al. 2009. "Psychological Stress and Wound Healing in Humans: A Systematic Review and Meta-analysis." *Journal of Psychosomatic Research* 67 (3): 253–71.

Walling, A., and G. Clancy. 2010. "Underemployment in the UK Labour Market." *Economic and Labour Market Review* 4 (2): 15–24.

Wang, W., and R. Morin. 2009. "Home for the Holidays . . . and Every Other Day." Pew Research Center.

Weidner, J., and J. C. Williams. 2016. "Update of 'How Big Is the Output Gap?'" Federal Reserve Bank of San Francisco Economic Letter 2009-19. June 12.

Weiss, A., J. E. King, M. Inoue-Murayama, T. Matsuzawa, and A. J. Oswald. 2012. "Evidence for a Midlife Crisis in Great Apes Consistent with the U-Shape in Human Well-Being." *Proceedings of the National Academy of Sciences of the USA* 109 (49): 1–4.

Wessel, D. 2018. "Alternatives to the Fed's 2 Per Cent Inflation Target." Report from the Hutchins Center on Fiscal and Monetary Policy, Brookings, June.

Whang, W., L. D. Kubzansky, I. Kawachi, et al. 2009. "Depression and Risk of Sudden Cardiac Death and Coronary Heart Disease in Women: Results from the Nurses' Health Study." *Journal of the American College of Cardiology* 53 (11): 950–58.

White House. 2011. "Epidemic: Responding to America's Prescription Drug Abuse Crisis." Washington, DC. http://publications.iowa.gov/12965/1/NationalRx AbusePlan2011.pdf.

Wilkins, R., and M. Wooden. 2011. "Economic Consequences of Studying Under-employment." In *Underemployment: Psychological, Economic and Social Challenges*, ed. D. Maynard and D. C. Feldman, 13–34. New York: Springer.

Wilson, R. S., J. L. Bienias, et al. 2003. "Negative Affect and Mortality in Older Persons." *American Journal of Epidemiology* 158 (9): 827–35.

Winkelmann, L., and R. Winkelmann. 1998. "Why Are the Unemployed So Un-happy? Evidence from Panel Data." *Economica* 65 (257): 1–15.

Wolff, E. N. 2017. "Household Wealth Trends in the United States, 1962 to 2016: Has Middle Class Wealth Recovered?" NBER Working Paper #24085, November.

World Bank. 2018. "Global Economic Forecast 2018." January, Washington, DC.

Wren-Lewis, Simon. 2018. *The Lies We Were Told: Politics, Economics, Austerity and Brexit*. Bristol: Bristol University Press.

Wunder, C., A. Wiencierz, J. Schwarze, and H. Küchenhoff. 2013. "Well-Being over the Life Span: Semiparametric Evidence from British and German Longitudinal Data." *Review of Economics and Statistics* 95 (1): 154–67.

Yagan, D. 2017. "Employment Hysteresis from the Great Recession." NBER Working Paper #23844.

Yamarone, R. 2012. *The Trader's Guide to Key Economic Indicators*. New York: John Wiley.

———. 2017. *The Economic Indicator Handbook: How to Evaluate Economic Trends to Maximize Profits and Minimize Losses*. Hoboken, NJ: Bloomberg Press.

Yellen, J., and G. Akerlof. 2006. "Stabilization Policy: A Reconsideration." *Economic Inquiry* 44 (1): 1–22.

Zaninotto, P., J. Wardle, and A. Steptoe. 2016. "Sustained Enjoyment of Life and Mortality at Older Ages: Analysis of the English Longitudinal Study of Ageing." *British Medical Journal* 355: i6267.

Zapryanova, G., and A. Christiansen. 2017. "Hope, Trust Deficits May Help Fuel Populism." Gallup, April 7.

Zuckoff, M. 2005. *Ponzi's Schemes*. New York: Random House.

INDEX

Page numbers in *italics* refer to figures and tables.

Aaronson, Daniel, 96–97
Abbey National, 159
Abowd, John, 99
added workers, 19–20
Affordable Care Act (ACA), 126, 345
Afghanistan, 244
Africa, 24, 226, 252
Aguiar, Mark, 26
Airbus, 187–88
Akerlof, George, 165
Alabama, 227
Alaska, 193
alcohol abuse, 7, 24, 36, 221, 225, 229–31, 233, 235, 267
Alesina, Alberto, 175
Alliance & Leicester (A&L), 159
Allsebrook, John, *314*
Alston, Philip, 35
aluminum, 319
Amazon, 18
American Community Survey, 116, 245, 258
American Economic Association, 188–89
American Economic Review, 188–89
American International Group (AIG), 162, 188
American National Election Studies (ANES), 261
American Time Use Survey, 27, 101, 226
Andrews, Dan, 92

Annual Survey of Hours and Earnings (ASHE), 56–57
antidepressants, 36, 218, 220–24, 227, 229
Arizona, 3, 193
Armstrong, Stephen, 32–33, 35
Ashenfelter, Orley, 188–90
Assari, Shervin, 220
Auerbach, Jonathan, 234
austerity: backlash against, 341; Brexit vote linked to, 36–37, 172, 214, 276; failures of, 36, 79–80, 160, 166–67, 171–77, 214, 327–28; mental health compromised by, 32, 222, 232; public sector weakened by, 10, 246; rationale for, 80, 171, 175, 179; regressivity of, 113, 173–74, 276, 329
Australia, 60, 79, 81, 92, 134, 230, 231, 252
Austria: business and consumer confidence in, 77, 196; immigration to, 238, 250; inequality viewed in, 107; labor market protections in, 85; populism in, 259, 280, 283; recession in, 78; underemployment in, 136
automobile industry, 23, 188, 201, 268
automobile loans, 74
Azar, José, 125

Babb, Nathan R., 305
Bain, George, 182

Balestra, Carlotta, 110–11
Baltic Dry Index (BDI), 197
Bank of America, 188, 281
Bank of Canada, 160
Bank of England. *See* Monetary Policy
    Committee (MPC), Bank of England
Bank of Japan (BOJ), 4, 83, 160, 161
Barber, Alan, 102–3
Barber, Brendan, 56
Barber, Tony, 281
Barclays, 187, 188
Barrie, J. M., 336
Barry, John M., 212–13
Basu, Sanjay, 232
Beal, Inga, 188
Bean, Charles, 164, 170–71
Becker, Sasha, 275–76
behavioral economics, 1, 169
Behavioral Risk Factor Surveillance System
    (BRFSS), 227
Behr, Rafael, 331
Beige Book, 48, 52–54, 198
Belgium, 78, 92; business and consumer
    confidence in, 77, 196; civil unrest in,
    264, 271; declining trust in, 321; terror
    attacks in, 247; underemployment in,
    136; unemployment in, 41; wages in, 61,
    106
Bell, David N. F., 32, 68, 274, 339; non-
    wage compensation research by, 57; pub-
    lic health research by, 146, 222; under-
    employment research by, 118, 124–25,
    128, 137, 142, 144–46, 310
Belot, Michele, 90
Bengali, Leila, 126, 128
Benjamin, Daniel K., 21–22
Bernanke Ben, 151, 153, 162–63
Better Together (Putnam, Feldstein, and
    Cohen), 329, 334
Beveridge, William, 10–11, 28, 32, 298–99,
    306, 338, 348
Beveridge Report (1942), 10
Bewley, Truman, 191

Bhaskar, V., 124
Bhutan, 244
Bianchi, Suzanne M., 72
Black Death, 81
Blackrock, 188
Blair, Tony, 183
Blanchard, Olivier, 86, 168, 178
Blankenship, Don, 16
Blinder, Scott, 340
Blundell, Richard, 64–65
Blyth, Mark, 160, 171, 175
BNP Paribas, 281
Böckerman, Petri, 91
Boak, Josh, 320
Bogdanor, Vernon, 283–85
bonds, 209, 281
bonuses, 54, 69
Booker, Cory, 343
Boom-Bust Barometer, 208
Borowczyk-Martins, Daniel, 126–27
Bourdain, Anthony, 231
Bowling Alone (Putnam), 329
Bradford & Bingley (B&B), 159, 202
Brady, Graham, 345
Brexit, 9, 171, 271–72, 280, 323, 325; aus-
    terity linked to, 36–37, 172, 214, 276;
    fear and uncertainty surrounding, 179,
    186–87, 205, 209, 222, 262, 320–21,
    344; migration linked to, 7, 24, 241,
    245–46, 256–57, 276, 342, 346; opposi-
    tion to, 239, 264–65, 272–73, 345; sup-
    port for, 62, 113, 188, 191, 264, 269,
    272–76, 279, 290–91, 324, 326–27
Bridgestone/Firestone, 190–91
British Home Stores (BHS), 335
British National Party, 275
British Social Attitudes Survey (BSAS), 246,
    341
broadband access, 34
Brody, Debra J., 224
Brown, Gordon, 151, 164, 284, *318*
Brown, Willie, 182
Buchwald, Art, 287

Bucknor, Cherrie, 102–3
Buffett, Warren, 337
Bulgaria, 41, 93, 131, 133, 251
bulk shipping, 197
Bundesbank, 207
Bureau of Labor Statistics (BLS), 4, 15, 16, 51
Bush, George W., 303
Bush, Laura, 239
business confidence, 8
Business Cycle Dating Committee, 78, 142–43, 195
Byron Burger (restaurant chain), 209

Cajner, Tomaz, 125, 127
Caldwell, Christopher, 277
California, 3, 193, 201, 243
Calvetron Brands, 209
Cameron, David, 241, 283
Camerota, Alisyn, 345
Canada, 41, 154, 317; declining trust in, 321; drug and alcohol abuse in, 230, 231; Great Recession in, 78, 81; homeownership in, 92; immigration to, 244; inequality in, 111, 114; inflation targets in, 315; obesity in, 224; participation rate in, 94, 100; productivity in, 65; unemployment in, 40, 134; U.S. leadership condemned in, 321; wage stagnation in, 58
Canter, Gary, 290
Card, David, 113, 190, 191
Carney, Mark, 65, 163, 205, 297, 307, 321
Carpenter, Christopher S., 36
Carpetright, 209
Carrier Corporation, 289–90
Carrillion (construction firm), 209–10
Carville, James, 346
Case, Ann, 214, 219, 227, 229–31, 233–34, 328
Casselman, Ben, 96
Cauldwell, John, 335–37
Centers for Disease Control (CDC), 231, 235–36

Chakrabortty, Aditya, 179, 188, 272
Chamberlain, Neville, 314
Chan, Micaela Y., 220
Chatterjee, Sonia, 274
Cherlin, Andrew J., 233–34
Chetty, Raj, 87, 108
Chevalier, Charles-Marie, 92
Chida, Yoichi, 223
childcare, 24, 25, 72, 342
child poverty, 33
Chile, 61, 78, 116, 330
China, 24, 56, 94, 293, 317, 319
Chirac, Jacques, 278
Chiswick, Barry R., 252
Christensen, R. L., 44
Chubb, 188
Citigroup, 188, 281
Clark, Tom, 323–24, 329–30
Clarke, Stephen, 276
Clinton, Hillary, 15, 259, 280, 289, 292, 324; cerebrality of, 269; miscalculations by, 265; Obama over- and underperformed by, 267–68; support for, 24, 239, 260
coal mining, 23, 94, 173, 214, 270, 279, 288–91
Coase, Ronald, 169
Coca-Cola, 319
Cochrane, John, 169
Cohen, Don, 329, 334
Cohen, Michael, 293, 334–35
Cohen, Sheldon, 220
Colbert, Stephen, 175
Colgan, Jeff D., 115
Collins, Michael, 22
Commerzbank, 281
Commodity Credit Corporation (CCC), 319
Community Advisory Council (CAC), 76
commuting, 88, 90, 91, 340
Conference Board, 194–95, 210
confidence indices, 8, 194–95, 200, 202, 210

conspicuous consumption, 335

construction industry, 93, 203, 209–10, 214, 236, 245, 340, 360–61n5

consumer confidence, 8, 194–95, 200, 202, 210

consumer price index (CPI), 70, 71

Conte, Giuseppe, 282

continuing education, 73

Cooper, Ryan, 171–72

Corbyn, Jeremy, 284, 344

Corry, Bernard, 181

cosmetic surgery, 184

Costa, Rui, 62

Council of Economic Advisers (CEA), 26, 27, 45, 101, 102, 105

Council of Mortgage Lenders (CML), 202–3

Cox, Daniel, 261

Crawford, Claire, 64–65

creationism, 324–25

credit cards, 74, 75

Credit Suisse, 188

crime, 44–45, 240, 257–58

Croatia, 116, 134, 136, 321–22

Crooks, Josie, 274

Cross, James, 274

Cross, Rod, 22

Cunliffe, Jon, 67, 206

Current Employment Statistics (CES), 51

Current Population Survey, 17, 51, 118

Cyprus, 134, 136, 251

Czech Republic, 78, 133, 141, 189, 251

da Costa, Pedro Nicolaci, 8–9, 68, 75

Daly, Mary, 232–33

Darling, Alistair, 158–60

Datta, Nikhil, 104

Davies, Megan, 209

Davis, Bob, 292

Deaton, Angus, 214, 219, 227, 229–31, 233–34, 328

debt, 74, 108, 342

deflation, 204, 315, 339

De Grauwe, Paul, 176

Delaney, Liam, 43

Delta Air Lines, 17

demand curve, 2

Denmark, 78, 81, 92, 233; business and consumer confidence in, 196; immigration to, 249; inequality in, 106; underemployment in, 136

depression, psychological, 7, 32, 36, 43, 126, 146, 218, 220–24

Desai, Sumeet, 161

Detmeister, Alan K., 305

Deutsche Bank, 187, 188, 281

Diener, Ed, 220

di Maio, Luigi, 281, 282

disability, 21, 41, 95, 217, 341

discouraged workers, 19–20, 278, 367n23

Douglas, Jason, 261

Draghi, Mario, 184

drug and alcohol use, 7, 24, 27, 235; "deaths of despair" from, 229–30, 236; in United Kingdom, 218, 221–23, 229, 231; in United States, 36, 214, 216–18, 220, *221*, 224, 225, 227, *229*, 230–31, 236

Duchniak, Aneta, 291

Dudley, William, 310

Duesenberry, James, 115

Duflo, Esther, 177–78

Dunatchik, Allison, 331

Dunlop, John, 8, 182

Dunn, Philippa, 367n24

Dustmann, Christian, 252

Dutch East Indies, 81

dynamic stochastic general equilibrium (DSGE), 178

earned income tax credits, 347

East Coast Railway, 280

EasyJet, 188

Eatwell, Roger, 285–86

Eberstadt, Nicholas, 25, 26–27, 102

The Economic Consequences of the Peace (Keynes), 328–29

Economic Indicator Handbook (Yamarone), 185

Economic Policy Institute (EPI), 16

Economic Sentiment Index (ESI), 8, 195–96

economics of walking about (EWA), 8, 97, 180–89, 196, 199, 211, 252, 317

Edelman, Richard, 331

Edelman Trust Barometer, 330

Eichengreen, Barry, 174

El-Arian, Mohammed, 170

Elizabeth II, queen of England, 164

El Salvador, 244

Emershaw, Justin, 289

Employment Cost Index, 51

employment rate, 18–19, 20, 25, 97, *98–99*

Employment Situation Report, 4, 289

energy prices, 206

enterprise zones, 340

environmental regulations, 324

Equal Opportunity Project, 108

Estonia, 78, 134, 136, 251

Euro currency, 281

Eurobarometer Surveys, 225, 226, 247, 253, 321, 331, *332*

European Banking Authority, 188

European Central Bank (ECB), 4, 83, 120, 160–61, 207, 339

European Commission, 8, 29, 194–96, 283

European Court of Justice, 344

European Labor Force Surveys (EULFS), 118, 133, 134

European Medicines Agency, 188

European Social Survey (ESS), 107, 225–26, 247–48, 329

European Union (EU), 18, 194–95, 283; job insecurity in, 29–31

Eurostat, 130

Even, William E., 126

Ewing, Walter A., 258

exchange rates, 302–3, 342, 344–45

ex-offenders, 102–3

Expectations Index, 210

Falk, Armin, 45

Falkland Islands, 327

Fallon, Michael, 160, 327

Falloon, Matt, 161

family structure, 72

Federal Open Market Committee (FOMC), 67, 68–70, 97, 205, 310, 312

Federal Reserve Board, 7, 11, 48, 52, 160, 166–67; interest rates raised by, 83, 299, 313, 322, 337–38, 339

Feldman, Daniel C., 127

Feldstein, Lewis M., 329, 334

Feldstein, Martin S., 123

Fetzer, Thiemo, 36

Fildes, Nic, 209

financial sector, 84, 201, 203

Finland, 78, 106, 136, 196, 218, 233, 343

Fitzpatrick, Suzanne, 33

Five Star Movement, 7, 9, 280–81, 282

Flanders, Stephanie, 320–21

flexible work schedules, 54, 56, 100, 104. *See also* gig economy; part-time work; self-employment

Florida, 3, 86–87, 97, 102, 201, 243

Floros, Nicos, 22

flu pandemic (1918), 212–13, 344

food insecurity, 33, 36

food stamps, 129

Foote, Christopher L., 102

Ford, Robert, 258–59, 277

Ford Motor Company, 201, 319

Forte, Giuseppe, 342

Four Seasons Health Care, 210

Fox Quesada, Vicente, 242

Fox News, 324

France, 39, 74, 154, 330, 347; business and consumer confidence in, 196, 333–34; civil unrest in, 271; drug and alcohol abuse in, 231; governments mistrusted in, 331; Great Recession in, 78, 81, 85, 93; immigration to, 244, 246, 248, 249, 283; inequality in, 105–6, 111; inequality viewed in, 107, 116; job insecurity in, 28;

France (*cont.*)

physical and mental health in, 219–20, 223, 229, 230; obesity in, 224; populism in, 7, 259, 264, 265, 278–79; productivity in, 63, 65; quality of life perceptions in, 76–77, 215; terror attacks in, 247; underemployment in, 49, 136, 138, 278; unemployment in, 40, *41*, 93, 278; unionization in, 114; U.S. leadership condemned in, 321; wage growth in, 58, 207; young people's living arrangements in, 277

Franses, Philip Hans, 185

Freeman, Richard, 86

free trade, 24, 246

Friedman, Milton, 303–4

fringe benefits, 209

Front National, 7, 279

Frost, Robert, 213

Fry, Richard, 37

Frydl, Kathleen, 24

full employment, 6–7, 25, 94, 140, 145, 297–316; inaccurate forecasts of, 7, 11, 68, 69, 75, 313; wage growth linked to, 49

Full Employment in a Free Society (Beveridge), 25, 348

The Full Monty (film), 10

Galbraith, John Kenneth, 3, 165

Gallup, George, 1

Garcia, Macarena C., 235

Garriga, Carlos, 74, 111–12

Gates, Bill, 337

Gates, Melinda, 337

Geisel, Theodore, 336–37

Geithner, Timothy, 153

Gelman, Andrew, 234

General Motors, 201, 290, 319

Georgia (Asia), 244

Georgia (U.S), 288

Germany, 39, 74, 154, 215, 330; business and consumer confidence in, 76, 196,

278; drug and alcohol abuse in, 231; Great Recession in, 57, 78, 82, 85, 123; immigration to, 238, 239, 244, 246–50; inequality in, 106, 111; inequality viewed in, 116; inflation in, 301; job insecurity in, 28; physical and mental health in, 218–19, 220, 223, 226, 230; obesity in, 224; productivity in, 63, 65; real earnings in, 61; underemployment in, 130–31, 132, 136, 138; unemployment in, *40*, 41, 88, 141, 144, 216, 298–99, 306, 338; unionization in, 114; U.S. leadership condemned in, 321; wage growth in, 48, 57–58, 207

Gibraltar, 326–27

Gieve, John, 159

gig economy, 83, 103–5. *See also* flexible work schedules; part-time work; self-employment

Gillibrand, Kirsten, 343

Gingrich, Newt, 319–20

Glauber, Rebecca K., 128

Global Attitudes Survey, 74, 250, 331, 333

globalization, 56, 84, 141, 236, 283, 285, 306, 338

Goebbels, Joseph, 179

Golden, Lonnie, 127

Goldman, Noreen, 220–21

Goldman Sachs, 187, 188

Golomb, John, 266

Goodwin, Fred, 335

Goodwin, Matthew, 258–59, 276–77, 285–86

Gore, Al, 25

Gove, Michael, 179

Graham, Carol, 220, 226

Great Depression, 3, 5, 10, 79, 163, 174

The Great Influenza (Barry), 212

Great Recession, 23, 24, 178, 297; dating of, 78, 142–43, 195; drug abuse during, 36; epidemics likened to, 212–13; failure to predict, 9–10, 151–66, 198–205; foreclosures during, 91; in Germany, 78, 82,

85, 123; household debt during, 74; housing market during, 3, 32, 84, 91, 93, 193–94, 199–204, 216; inequality worsened by, 111–12, 284–85; job insecurity linked to, 28; long-term unemployment and, 41, 84, 99; overemployment during, 144–45; physical and emotional costs of, 216–23; underemployment during, 123, 129, 131–32, 134, 144–45; unemployment benefits during, 21, 201; in United Kingdom, 3, 26, 63, 78, 79–81, 84, 93, 123, 129, 132, 151–52, 154, 158–80, 195, 199–204; in United States, 3, 9, 41, 78–79, 81, 100, 111–12, 129, 154, 168, 195–96, 199–201, 204; wage stagnation linked to, 48, 64, 144, 301, 302, 306, 312–13

Greece, 38, 216; business and consumer confidence in, 76, 196, 321–22, 333–34; governments mistrusted in, 331; Great Recession in, 78, 81, 85; homeownership and unemployment in, 88, 213; left nationalism in, 284; underemployment in, 49, 128, 132, 136; unemployment in, 41, 49, 132, 134, 216, 342; wage stagnation in, 58

Green, Philip, 335
Green, Richard K., 89
Gregg, Judd, 88
Grigorieff, Alexis, 340–41
Guatemala, 244

Hacker, Jacob S., 74–75
Haldane, Andrew, 67, 167, 307
Haltiwanger, John C., 64
Hämäläinen, Kari, 91
Hanauer, Nick, 336
Hanlon, Phil, 292
Hans, Billy, 266
Hansen, Kristine, 44–45
Harberger, Arnold, 168
Harding, Roger, 246
Harley-Davidson, 201, 319

Harmonized Index of Consumer Prices (HICP), 206
Harris, Malcolm, 234
Hart, Robert A., 123–24
Hartz reforms (Germany), 57
Hatton, Timothy J., 252
Hawaii, 227, 306
Hayden, Michael, 239
Heath, Anthony, 323–24, 329–30
Heath, Oliver, 276–77
Heckman, James J., 86, 334, 343
Hemingway, Harry, 223
hemline index, 185
Hendershott, Patric H., 89
Hendren, Nathan, 87
Herndon, Thomas, 175, 340
heuristics, 8
Hewlett, Colin, 270
Higgins, Andrew, 270
Hillbilly Elegy (Vance), 21, 27
Hills, John, 113
Hirsch, Barry T., 140
Hitler, Adolf, 328
Hodgkinson, Matthew, 273–74
Holland, Kristin M., 231
Hollande, François, 344
homeownership, 39, 85, 86, 143; decline in, 302, 306; drawbacks of, 88–92, 94, 96; unemployment linked to, 85, 88–90, 145, 213, 302
Honduras, 244
Hong, Gee Hee, 141–42
Hoover, Herbert, 174
hours worked, 2, 26, 123, 132, 134. See also part-time work; underemployment
household debt, 74
House of Fraser, 209
housing market, 62, 170–71, 208–9; during Great Recession, 3, 32, 84, 91, 93, 193–94, 199–204, 216; immigration and, 244; indebtedness and, 74; land use regulations and, 91–92; living arrangements affected by, 38; mobility and, 86–88, 90–

housing market (*cont.*)
94, 117, 302, 303, 306; in Spain, 39, 84–
85, 92. *See also* homeownership;
mortgages
housing subsidies, 35, 129
Howard, Michael, 327–28
Howell, David, 86
Howell, Ryan T., 220
HSBC, 188
Hsieh, Chang-Tai, 91
Hudson, Dave, 274
Hume, David, 199
Hungary, 78, 116, 136, 251, 280, 283, 331
Hurd, Will, 325
Hurst, Erik, 26
Husain, Muhammad M., 140

Iceland, 78, 81, 133, 136
Idaho, 306
identity politics, 284
Illinois, 243
immigrants: Brexit vote linked to, 7, 24,
241, 245–46, 256–57, 276, 342; hostility
toward, 24, 214, 234–35, 238–63, 284,
324; return migration by, 252; Trump's
policy toward, 93, 239, 241–42, 262; in
United Kingdom, 24, 84, 86, 93, 131,
238, 239, 244–53, 255–57, 262, 272,
277, 302, 340, 342; wages and, 84, 254–
58, 306; young people's acceptance of,
277
incarceration rates, 72, 102–3
India, 56, 252, 293
Indiana, 289–90
inequality, 72, 105–15, 323
inflation, 23, 84, 120, 155, 204–8; in Canada, 58; fear of, 67, 176, 299, 314–15,
339; long-term unemployment and, 70;
low unemployment decoupled from, 11,
301. *See also* wage growth
Institute for Fiscal Studies (IFS), 339
interest rates, 150, 158, 173, 206, 281, 313,
321, 322, 337–38; as inflation-fighting

tool, 7, 11, 67, 83, 162, 205, 206, 299;
in Italy, 281, 282; negative, 83, 161, 339;
quantitative easing and, 160; recoveries
stalled by increases in, 83
International Labor Organization (ILO), 17,
18, 85
International Monetary Fund (IMF), 9,
121, 154, 205, 283, 345
International Social Survey Programme
(ISSP), 116, 218–19, 225, 246, 253
Iowa, 193, 306
involuntary part-timers (IPT), 118–21,
125–29, 132–33, 136–38, *139*. *See also*
part-time work; underemployment
Iraq, 239, 244, 250
Ireland, 77, 81, 136, 231; Great Recession
in, 78, 84, 93, 131–32, 134; immigration
to, 249, 253; underemployment in, 138
Irwin, Doug, 114
ISIS, 326
Islam, Faisal, 272
Israel, 61, 74, 79, 81, 116, 141, 257
Italy, 38, 154, 233; business and consumer
confidence in, 196, 321–22, 333–34;
drug and alcohol abuse in, 231; Great Recession in, 78, 81–82; homeownership in,
92; immigration to, 238, 248, 249, 250,
253; job insecurity in, 28; long-term unemployment in, *40*, 41; outlook for, 344;
physical and mental health in, 219–20,
223; populism in, 7, 9, 264, 280–83;
productivity in, 65; quality of life perceptions in, 76–77; unemployment in, 247,
282; underemployment in, 49, 132;
unionization in, 114; wage inequality in,
106

Jackman, Richard, 85
Jacques Vert, 209
Jaguar Land Rover (JLR), 188
Jamie's Italian (restaurant chain), 209
Jansa, Janez, 283
Japan, 154, 220, 339; Great Recession in,

78, 81; inequality viewed in, 116; obesity in, 224; participation rate in, 95; productivity in, 65; quantitative easing in, 4; unemployment in, *40*, 41, 134, 141, 306; wage stagnation in, 55, 60; work ethic in, 74

Jin, Wenchao, 64–65

"jingle mail," 193

job insecurity: job satisfaction diminished by, 28–29; survey data on, 29–31

Job Training Partnership Act (1982), 343

Johnes, Geraint, 240

Johnson, Boris, 192, 325

Johnson, Paul, 339

Johnson, Ron, 346

Johnson & Johnson, 292

Jones, Emma, 274

Jones, Owen, 286

Joseph Rowntree Foundation, 33

Journal of Political Economy, 22

JP Morgan Chase, 187, 188, 281

Judis, John B., 285

Julius, DeANne, 159

Kahn, Lisa, 49

Kahneman, Daniel, 90

Kakutani, Michiko, 179

Das Kapital (Marx), 6

Katsambekis, Giorgos, 285

Katz, Larry, 87, 104

Kaufmann, Eric, 276

Keefe, Kevin, 265

Kegler, Scott R., 231

Kentucky, 227, 268

Keohane, Robert O., 115

Keynes, John Maynard, 11, 176–77, 298–99, *314*, 328–29; "animal spirits: viewed by, 187, 194; austerity opposed by, 173; "semi-slump" feared by, 3, 79, 80, 212

Khatiwada, Ishwar, 128–29

Kiley, Michael T., 70

Kim Jong-un, 293

King, Mervyn, 56, 154, 176, 204, 252, 317

Knorr, Rob, 292

Knox Coal Company, 288

Kocherlakota, Narayana, 165–66

Kochin, Levis A., 21–22

Koivumaa-Honkanen, Heli-Tuulie, 233

Korea, 79

Krueger, Alan B., 104, 190; happiness research by, 90; long-term unemployment research by, 41, 70–71; minimum wage research by, 191; participation rate research by, 95, 101, 219

Krugman, Paul, 174, 178, 179, 193–94, 301–2, 321

Kudlow, Larry, 154–55, 317

Kügler, Alice, 57–58

Kurz, Sebastian, 280, 283

labor disputes, 190–91

labor economics, 2, 8, 19

labor force participation rate (LFPR). *See* participation rate

labor market concentration, 125

labor market slack, 55, 68–69, 97, *98–99*, 138; participation rates and, 94; underemployment as, 6, 25, 119, 122, 144–47, 310; understatement of, 15, 16, 206, 208, 316; wage stagnation linked to, 6, 25, 84, 338

Labour Force Survey (LFS), 31, 56, 203, 225, 252

Lach, Saul, 257

Lalé, Etienne, 126–27, 140

LaLonde, Robert J., 252

Lalor, Doireann, 34

Lam, Michelle, 60

Lankarani, Maryam Moghani, 220

Lardeux, Raphaël, 92

Larrimore, Jeff, 129

Latvia, 78, 131, 134, 251

Lauder, Leonard, 184

Lautenschläger, Sabine, 207–8

Lawton, Helen, 253

Layard, P. Richard G., 39, 71, 85, 183

Lazear, Edward, 303
League (Italy), 7, 9, 280–81, 282
Lehman Brothers, 80, 153, 162
leisure, 26–27, 72
Lempert, Richard O., 371n1
Leontief, Wassily, 164
Le Pen, Marine, 344; early retirement age promised by, 278, 346; opposition to, 242; as protectionist, 285; support for, 9, 24, 265, 278–80, 324
Levin, Andrew T., 310, 313
Levitsky, Steven, 347
Lewin, Tamar, 185
Lewis, H. Gregg, 122
life expectancy, 33, 43–44, 45, 100, 214, 236–37, 267, 277
Lilla, Mark, 278
Limbaugh, Rush, 324
lipstick index, 184
literacy, 34
Lithuania, 83, 131, 134, 136, 229, 251
Liu, Sifan, 24–25
Lloyds Bank, 162, 187, 188
Lockhart, Dennis, 121
Longazel, Jamie, 288
long-term unemployment (LTU), 21, 39–42, 69–71, 84, 99, 203
Loopstra, Rachel, 34
Louisiana, 268
Love, Andrew, 154
Lucas, Bob, 165
Luppino, Floriana S., 224
Luttmer, Erzo F. P., 115
Luttmer, Erzo G. J., 115
Luxembourg, 78, 92, 136
luxury purchases, 184–85

Macedonia, 41
Machin, Stephen, 44–45, 62, 274
Macmillan, Harold, 77
Macpherson, David A., 126
Macpherson, Nick, 151
Macron, Emmanuel, 271, 279–80, 344, 346

Magnus, George, 322
Maitlis, Emily, 334
Malta, 136, 251
Manafort, Paul, 335
Mancini, Donato Paolo, 261
Mankiw, N. Gregory, 177
Manning, Alan, 124, 276
manufacturing, 23, 93, 173, 201, 203, 214, 245, 276
Maplin (electronics retailer), 209
Margolis, Jason, 265–66
Mariel Boatlift (1980), 190
Markit, 194
Marks and Spencer, 209
Marmot, Michael, 223
marriage, 38, 44, 227
Martin, James, 274
Marx, Karl, 6
Mas, Alexandre, 190
Mathis, Tim, 290
Matson, Andrew, 272
Mattarella, Sergio, 280
Mavrakis, Lou, 265–66
May, Theresa, 187, 325, 326, 344, 345, 347
McCafferty, Ian, 66
McClellan, Chandler B., 36
McCrain, Joshua, 326
McDaniel, Jason, 261
McDonald's Corporation, 201
McElwee, Sean, 261
McFall, John, 159
Medicaid, 129, 217, 293
Medicare, 293
Mélenchon, Jean-Luc, 346
Men without Work (Eberstadt), 25
Metcalf, David, 21, 22
Mexico, 78, 238, 244, 251, 289–90, 330
Michigan, 23–24, 288, 326
midlife crisis, 224–29
Midlife in the U.S. Study (MIDUS), 221
Miles, David, 167–68
military spending, 5
minimum wage, 45, 191, 271, 303–4

Minnesota, 193, 306, 326

Mishel, Lawrence, 16, 109, 113

Mitterrand, François, 344

mobility, 32, 39, 72–73, 85, 108, 303; housing market and, 86–88, 90–94, 117, 302, 303, 306; immigration and, 306; inequality and, 116; tax incentives for, 342

Monetary Policy Committee (MPC), Bank of England, 29, 151; blundering by, 65–67, 68, 153–63, 166–67, 199, 204–6, 307, 310, 312; Brexit viewed by, 320; data gathered by, 194, 196, 197–98, 308; rate cuts by, 83, 150; rate hikes by, 11, 299, 313, 321

MoneyGram, 188

Monnat, Shannon, 24

monopsony, 124, 302

Montagnes, B. Pablo, 326

Montana, 193

Moretti, Enrico, 91

Morgan Stanley, 281

Moriconi, Simone, 248–49

mortgages, 74, 75, 92, 201–3; recourse vs. non-recourse, 193

Moser, Klaus, 43

Mothercare (retailer), 209

Mount Tambora, 81

Moving to Opportunity (MTO), 87

Moy, Ernest, 235

Moyer, Christopher, 18

Mueller, Robert, 293

Muhuri, Pradip K., 219

Müller, Jan-Werner, 286

Münchnau, Wolfgang, 165, 176

Muro, Mark, 24–25

Muslims, 239, 241–42, 249–50, 324

Myth and Measurement (Card and Krueger), 191

N. Brown (retailer), 209

NAFTA (North American Free Trade Agreement), 23, 114, 317, 324

Nahin, Richard L., 219

NAIRU (Non-Accelerating Rate of Unemployment), 94, 145, 297, 302, 304–5, 315, 316

National Bureau of Economic Research (NBER), 3, 17, 78, 142–43

National Health Service (NHS), 56, 261–62, 326, 347

National Rifle Association (NRA), 348

National Union of Miners (NUM), 291

NATO (North Atlantic Treaty Organization), 278, 293

Navarro, Peter, 317

Nebraska, 306

Neil, Andrew, 283

Nestle, 188

Netherlands, 41, 60, 219; business and consumer confidence in, 196; civil unrest in, 264, 271; Great Recession in, 78; homeownership in, 92; inequality viewed in, 107; self-employment in, 62, 364n26; underemployment in, 132, 136

Nevada, 3, 201, 232

New Deal, 5

New Hampshire, 232, 301, 306

New Jersey, 243

New Look (clothing retailer), 209

New Mexico, 231

New York City, 243

New Zealand, 58, 60, 78, 116, 134, 252

Next (clothing retailer), 209

Nichols, Tom, 286

Nickell, Stephen J., 22, 71, 85, 151, 170

NIMBY effect, 88, 90, 91

Noeth, Bryan J., 74

Nomura, 188

Non-Accelerating Inflation Rate of Unemployment (NAIRU), 94, 145, 297, 302, 304–5, 315, 316

North Carolina, 193, 268

North Dakota, 193, 232, 306

Northern Ireland, 34, 331

Northern League, 7, 9, 280–81, 282

Northern Rock, 158–59

Norway, 79, 106, 132, 133, 136, 249, 321
not in labor force (NILF) cohort. *See* out of
    labor force (OLF) cohort
Nowotny, Ewald, 308, 310
numeracy, 34

Obama, Barack, 15, 16, 24, 101, 267–68,
    292
obesity, 7, 77, 218, 223–24, 267, 274
Ocasio-Cortez, Alexandria, 343
Office for Budgetary Responsibility (OBR),
    166–67
Office for National Statistics (ONS), 31, 66,
    67
Ohio, 23, 24, 236, 265, 268, 288, 290
oil prices, 83
opioid abuse, 214, 221; deaths from, 7, 217,
    229, 236; economic decline linked to, 36;
    inefficacy of, 216–17; in rural areas, 231,
    235; voting behavior linked to, 24
Orban, Victor, 283
Oregon, 193
O'Reilly, Bill, 324
Organization for Economic Co-operation
    and Development (OECD), 18, 205,
    255–56, 330; inequality measured by,
    105, 110–11; long-term unemployment
    measured by, 40, 41; mobility measured
    by, 72–73; participation rates measured
    by, 94, 100; real earnings measured by,
    59, 60–61; wage growth measured by, 48,
    58, 59
Ormerod, Paul, 22
Orwell, George, 10, 46, 270
Osborne, George, 172, 175, *314*, 327–28
Oswald, Andrew J., 142, 182, 225; housing
    market research by, 88, 90–91, 94, 145;
    life satisfaction research by, 115, 218,
    225, 227, 229; unemployment research
    by, 71, 88
out of labor force (OLF) cohort, 16, 20, 21,
    41, 70, 95, 99; health conditions among,
    219; time use by, 26–27

outsourcing, 56
Overberg, Paul, 234
overemployment, 118, 121, 133, *135*, 140,
    146; during Great Recession, 144–45;
    wage gains linked to, 142
Ozimek, Adam, 169

Paddison, Laura, 343
paper industry, 23
Paris climate accord, 23
participation rate, 18–19, 20, 25–26, 39,
    69, 94–101, 305–6; inequality linked to,
    105
part-time employment, 6, 35, 49, 54, 69,
    206, 208; in academia, 343–44; indus-
    tries dependent on, 127; measurement of,
    118; wage penalty linked to, 128. *See also*
    flexible work schedules; gig economy;
    self-employment
part-time for economic reasons (PTFER)
    cohort, 118, 126, 129–32
part-timers who want full-time jobs
    (PTWFT), 118, 128, 129, 131–32
Patterson, Tom, 287
Paul, Karsten I., 43
Paulson, Henry, 163
Pecket, Elliott, 186–87
Peek, Liz, 16
Pencavel, John, 122, 123
Pennsylvania, 24, 236, 265, 288, 289
Pennycook, Matthew, 104
pensions, 32, 57, 62, 281, 338–39
Peri, Giovanni, 248–49
Personal Consumption Expenditures (PCE),
    72
Peskowitz, Zachary, 326
Peters, William, 213
Phelps, Ned, 302–3
Phillips, William, 308, *309*
Phillips curve, 208, 305, 307–11
Phone 4U, 335
Pickard, James, 272
Pidd, Helen, 273

Piketty, Thomas, 108, 109, 165, 337
Pinto, Sergio, 220
plastic surgery, 184
Poland, 81, 136; emigration from, 86, 93, 131, 251–54; Great Recession in, 79; underemployment in, 132; unemployment in, 134; wage growth in, 61
political correctness, 284, 324
Portes, Jonathan, 255, 342
Portugal, 38, 77, 78, 229; business and consumer confidence in, 196, 321; declining trust in, 321, 331; immigration to, 238; underemployment in, 136; unemployment in, 41, 132, 134
Posen, Adam, 70
Pouliakis, Konstantinos, 140
Powell, Jerome, 67–68, 304–5, 316
Pozuelo, Julia Ruiz, 226
Praet, Peter, 207
Pratt, Laura A., 224
Precis (clothing retailer), 209
Present Situation Index, 210
Pressman, Sarah D., 220
Prezzo (restaurant chain), 209
Prisoner Dilemma, 190
productivity, 63, 166–67; in housing-constrained cities, 91–92; immigration linked to, 255, 256; wage growth linked to, 64–65, 69, 84, 120, 121, 191, 302
progressive taxation, 342
protectionism, 114, 285
Protective Labor Market Institutions (PLMIs), 86
public schools, 72
Pulliam, Christopher, 74
Purchasing Manager Indices (PMIs), 194, 196, 205, 206
Putin, Vladimir, 293
Putnam, Robert, 329, 334

quantitative easing, 4, 62, 160, 162, 339
Quévat, Benjamin, 58
Quinones, Sam, 217

Rachman, Gideon, 282
Rapley, John, 165, 181, 193
Real Clear Politics (RCP), 321
recessions, 7, 191, 209
Rees, Daniel I., 36
Rees-Mogg, Jacob, 321
refugees, 7, 238, 241, 247, 250, 281, 325
Reinhart, Carmen, 3, 175
Reis, Ricardo, 178
rental housing, 34–35
rent controls, 85
replacement rate, 86
retirement age, 100, 278, 282–83, 339, 345, 346
return migration, 252
Rexnord Corporation, 290
Richards, Lindsay, 340
Rieder, Travis, 217
Rinne, Ulf, 57
Rivington Biscuits, 187
The Road to Wigan Pier (Orwell), 46, 270
Roberts, Russ, 169
Robinson, Eugene, 325
Rogoff, Kenneth, 3, 175
Romania, 93, 131, 251
Romney, Mitt, 24, 267, 268, 292
Rosen, Sherwin, 123
Rosengren, Eric, 153
Roth, Christopher, 340–41
Roubini, Nouriel, 152
Royal Bank of Scotland (RBS), 160, 162, 188, 335
RSA Insurance, 188
Rugaber, Christopher, 320
rules of thumb, 8
Russia, 281, 293, 330
Ryan, Richard W., 102
Ryanair, 188
Ryssdal, Kai, 67

S&P, 188
Sabadish, Natalie, 109
Sacerdote, Bruce, 71–72

Saez, Emmanuel, 108, 109–10, 337

Salvini, Matteo, 282

Sánchez, Aida Caldera, 92

Sanders, Bernie, 115, 343

Santander, 159, 281

Sarkozy, Nicolas, 344

Saunders, Michael, 100

savings, 75

Sawhill, Isabel V., 74

Schlagenhauf, Don, 74

Schwarz, Moises, 154

Seager, Ashley, 153–54

seasonal employment, 56

self-employment, 141; in Netherlands, 62, 364n26; primary vs. secondary, 140; in United Kingdom, 62, 83, 103–4, 140. *See also* flexible work schedules; gig economy; part-time work

Semuels, Alana, 16

Sentence, Andrew, 321

Shadforth, Chris, 29, 84

Shapiro, Leo, 185

Sharot, Tali, 123

Shaw, George Bernard, 240

Shiller, Robert, 169–70, 339

shortages, 2–3, 47

Silver, Nate, 267–69

single-parent households, 72

Skidelsky, Robert, 80, 173, 176

skills, 34; deterioration of, 42; middle-level, 102

Slichter, Sumner, 182

Slovak Republic, 41, 79, 133, 141, 251

Slovenia, 78, 116, 133, 251, 280, 283

Smiffys (dressmakers), 186–87

Smith, Harry Leslie, 37

Smith, Jeff, 343

Smith, Noah, 169, 234

Smith, Steve, 180

Smith, Vernon, 115–16

smoking, 27, 44, 45, 275

Smoot-Hawley Tariff Act (1930), 317

Snaith, John, 272

Social Security, 293, 342

Social Security Disability Insurance (SSDI), 217

Société Générale, 188

"Society at a Glance" (OECD), 330

Solow, Robert, 168, 182

Song, Jae, 109

Soros, George, 326

Sorrentino, Constance, 183

South Africa, 330

South Carolina, 288

South Dakota, 227

South Sea Bubble, 81

soybeans, 319

Spade, Kate, 231

Spain, 38, 154, 326–27; business and consumer confidence in, 196, 321–22; governments mistrusted in, 331; Great Recession in, 78, 84–85; housing in, 39, 84–85, 92; immigration to, 238, 253; inequality viewed in, 116; left nationalism in, 284; obesity in, 224; physical pain in, 219; quality of life perceptions in, 76–77; real earnings in, 61; underemployment in, 49, 131–32, 136; unemployment in, 88, 132, 134, 213, 342

Speth, Ralf, 188

Spicer, Sean, 334

Spletzer, J. R., 303

Staiger, Douglas, 305

Standard Chartered, 187, 188

Stansbury, Anna M., 65

Steele, Michael, 239

steel industry, 23, 319

Steptoe, Andrew, 223

Stevenson, Betsy, 16

Stiglitz, Joseph, 174, 178–79

Stock, James H., 305

stock market, 112; crashes of, 3, 4, 79, 185, 212

Stone, Deborah M., 231

stress, 7, 36, 185, 220, 223; in middle age, 218, 224, 226; unemployment and underemployment linked to, 41–43, 45, 126

Stuckler, David, 232

student debt, 74, 342

subprime mortgages, 193

Sudan, 244

suicide, 24, 36, 222; happiness paradox and, 232–33; job insecurity and unemployment linked to, 43–44, 45; in United Kingdom, 232, 274; in United States, 7, 214, 220–21, 225, 229–33, 236, 267

Sum, Andrew, 128–29

Summers, Lawrence H., 65, 96, 178, 302, 315

supply curve, 2, 64, 123, 124

Survey of Household Economics and Decision Making, 52

Svensson, Lars, 161

Sveriges Riksbank, 160, 161

Sweden, 78, 81, 83, 230, 233; business and consumer confidence in, 196; civil unrest in, 264, 270; immigration to, 238, 239, 249, 250, 285; inequality in, 106; inequality viewed in, 107; underemployment in, 131, 132, 136

Swiss National Bank, 160, 161

Switzerland, 61, 79, 83; homeownership and unemployment in, 85, 88; inequality viewed in, 107; underemployment in, 133, 136

Sykes, Charlie, 286–87

Syria, 7, 239, 250

talc mining, 292

Taleb, Nassim Nicholas, 199, 368–69n23

Tang, Nicole K. Y., 220

Tangel, Andrew, 290

Taylor, George, 185

tax cuts, 69, 205, 319

tax incentives, 104, 342, 346–47

Teater, Donald, 216

Tennessee, 227

Tenreyro, Silvana, 205–6, 307

terrorism, 238, 239, 241, 246–47, 249, 257

Texas, 243, 268, 288

Thaler, Richard, 8, 169

Thatcher, Margaret, 10, 21, 161, 172, 291

The Theory of the Leisure Class (Veblen), 335

Thornberry, Terence P., 44

To, Ted, 124

tobacco use, 27, 44, 45, 275

Tomlinson, Daniel, 101–2

Tonkin, Richard, 110–11

Topel, Robert H., 252

Toynbee, Polly, 327–28

Toys "R" Us, 209

Trans-Pacific Partnership (TPP), 23, 114, 324

Treasury bills, 208, 209

Treasury Select Committee (TSC), 159–60

Treatise of Human Nature (Hume), 199

Treaty of Versailles (1919), 328

Trudeau, Justin, 317

Trump, Donald, 4, 7, 180, 264, 280, 319–20; coal revival promised by, 289, 346; corrosive effects of, 330–31; Federal Reserve denounced by, 83; immigration policies of, 93, 239, 241–42, 262; manufacturing revival promised by, 290; overoptimistic forecasts by, 205; press coverage of, 287; support for, 23, 24–25, 215, 217, 224, 235, 237, 245, 259–61, 265–68, 279, 286–87, 292, 324–26; trade targeted by, 114, 115, 317, 319; unemployment rate viewed by, 15–16

Truss, Liz, 34

Tsang, Adley, 219–20

Turati, Riccardo, 248–49

Turkey, 79, 330

turnover, in workplace, 124

Ubfal, Diego, 340–41

UBS, 188

underemployment, 20, 32, 54–55, 59, 118–47, 206, 231, 278; behavior and, 126–29; evidence on, 129–32; as labor market underemployment (*cont.*)

slack, 6, 25, 119, 122, 144–47, 310; persistence of, 2, 49, 300; stress linked to, 41–43, 45, 126; unions' decline linked to, 141; U7 measurement of, 118, 119, 129, 136–37, 138, 143–44, 308, 310, *311*; wage growth and, 120–21, 124, 141–42, 145, 300, 312

unemployment, 2, 132, 195, 201, 214, 290, 342; in France, 40, *41*, 93, 278; in Germany, *40*, 41, 88, 141, 144, 216, 298–99, 306, 338; historical trends in, 5, *19, 55*; homeownership linked to, 85, 88–90, 145, 213, 302; inflation fears and, 299, 301; in Italy, 247, 282; long-term (LTU), 21, 39–42, 69–71, 84, 99, 203; measurement of, 5–6, 15–20, 40, 305; natural rate of, 94, 145, 297, 302, 304–5, 315, 316; overemphasis on, 16, 23, 25; psychological impact of, 10–11, 22–23, 28–33, 35–36, 41–43, 56; stress and suicide linked to, 44, 45, 126; underemployment decoupled from, 119–20, 122; in United Kingdom, 3–4, 6, 10–11, 21, 32–37, 41, 48, 49, 54–55, 84, 85, 130, 134, 137, 140–42, 144, 183–84, 209–10, 255, 273, 297–300, 310–12, 338; voting behavior linked to, 267; wages linked to, 4, 6. *See also* Non-Accelerating Inflation Rate of Unemployment (NAIRU)

unemployment benefits, 85, 303; during Great Recession, 21, 201; in United Kingdom, 20, 34

UNICEF, 33

UniCredit (Italy), 281

unionization, 6, 28, 89, 268, 299, 303, 339; decline of, 83, 113–14, 141, 301, 302; in Germany, 57; in southern United States, 288; in United Kingdom, 64

United Kingdom, 319; austerity in, 36, 113, 166, 172, 174, 175, 214, 276; bank run in, 158–59; child poverty in, 33; civil un-

rest in, 270–71; coal mining in, 270, 290–91; consumer confidence in, 194, 195–96, 322, 334; drug and alcohol abuse in, 218, 221–23, 229, 231; food insecurity in, 36; Great Recession in, 3, 26, 63, 78, 79–81, 84, 93, 123, 129, 132, 151–52, 154, 158–80, 195, 199–204; happiness and life satisfaction in, 145, 215, 218, 225, 226; high-skilled jobs in, 101; housing market in, 93, 145, 151–52, 159, 170, 202, 302; immigration to, 24, 84, 86, 93, 131, 238, 239, 244–53, 255–57, 262, 272, 277, 302, 340, 342; inequality in, 106, 111; inequality viewed in, 107, 116; inflation in, 301, 315; job insecurity in, 28–32; long-term unemployment in, *40*, 41, 71; manufacturing employment in, 173, 203; military spending in, 212; minimum wage in, 45; mortality in, 214, 230–32; multiple job holding in, 140; obesity in, 224; overemployment in, 122, 124–25, 137–38; participation rate in, 26, 94–95, 100, 102; physical pain in, 218–19; populism in, 179, 258, 264, 275, 280, 324, 325, 327; productivity in, 63, 65, 166–67; public sector employment in, 56, 64; quality of life perceptions in, 76–77; real earnings in, 61–62; retirees in, 62, 112; self-employment in, 62, 83, 103–4, 140; social fragmentation in, 329–30; underemployment in, 118–19, 126, 128, 129, 133, 136, 137–38, 144, 146, 206, 278, 310–12; unemployment in, 3–4, 6, 10–11, 21, 32–37, 41, 48, 49, 54–55, 84, 85, 130, 134, 137, 140–42, 144, 183–84, 209–10, 255, 273, 297–300, 310–12, 338; unemployment benefits in, 20, 34; unemployment measurement in, 20; unionization in, 113, 114; United States viewed in, 331; wage stagnation in, 3, 6, 35, 54–55, 56, 58, 61–62, 66, 68, 209, 307, 338, 339; work ethic in, 74; young people's living arrangements in, 39. *See also* Brexit

UK Independence Party (UKIP), 238, 275

UK Labor Force Survey (UKLFS), 124–25, 128

Ukraine, 254

United States: anti-intellectualism in, 286; austerity in, 329; consumer confidence in, 194–95, 210, 321; cyclicality in, 64, 96, 303; crime fears in, 257; deskilling in, 101–2; disability in, 95; drug and alcohol use in, 36, 214, 216–18, 220, *221*, 225, *229*, 230–31, 236; economic indicators in, 198; employment measurement in, 20, 118, 136; financial sector in, 84; Great Recession in, 3, 9, 23, 41, 78–79, 81, 100, 111–12, 129, 154, 168, 195–96, 199–201, 204; happiness and life satisfaction in, 28, 36, 73, 116, 215–16, 226, 333–34; housing market in, 84, 192, 193, 202, 208, 302, 345; immigration to, 24, 84, 93, 238–39, 241–44, 246–47, 250–52, 254, 258–62, 283; incarceration rates in, 102; income maintenance in, 183; inequality in, 105, 106, 108–12, 114, 116–17; inequality viewed in, 107, 116; inflation in, 71, 315; infrastructure in, 23, 339–40, 347; job insecurity in, 28–29; labor market concentration in, 125; long-term unemployment in, 40–42, 69–71; manufacturing employment in, 93, 173, 201, 214; mobility in, 39, 86–87, 116, 342; monetary policy in, 7, 67, 68–69, 83, 299, 313; mortality in, 229, 233, 236–37; multiple job holding in, 140; obesity in, 224; out of labor force cohort in, 26; overoptimistic forecasts in, 152, 154–55, 205; participation rate in, 25, 39, 94, 97, 100, 102, 104; physical pain in, 218–20; populism in, 7, 264, 279–80, 324, 325–26, 347; post–Great Recession expansion in, 83, 322; productivity in, 63, 65; protectionism in, 207, 317, 319; riots in, 270; self-employment in, 103–4, 140–41; social fragmentation in, 330–31; stock market crashes in, 3, 4, 79, 185, 212; suicide in, 7, 214, 225, 233; terrorism fears in, 249; underemployment in, 25, 32, 49, 54–55, 118–19, 126–30, 132, 134, 136–37, 141–42, 145, 231, 310; unemployment in, 4–5, 6, 18, *19*, 23, 43, 49, 84, 134, 141, 144, 145, 184, 195, 201, 214, 290, 297, 298, 305, 306; unionization in, 113–14; wage stagnation in, 6, 48, 51, 54–55, 58, 61–62, 71, 214, 301, 308; work-life balance in, 73; yield curve in, 208; young people's living arrangements in, 37, 39, 85

United States Conference of Mayors, 23

U.S. General Social Survey (GSS), 227, 330

United States–Mexico–Canada Trade Agreement (USMCA), 317

U.S. Steel, 290

Universal Basic Income (UBI), 343

universal credit, 34

University of Michigan, 194

unsecured debt, 74

U7 measure, 118, 119, 129, 136–37, 138, 143–44, 308, 310, *311*

vacation allowances, 54

Valletta, Robert G., 126, 128

van Baardwijk, Marjolein, 185

Vance, J. D., 21, 27

van der List, Catherine, 126, 128

Vandoros, Sotiris, 222

van Ours, Jan C., 90

Veblen, Thorstein, 335

Veliziotis, Michail, 128

Vermont, 231, 306, 342

Vespa, Jonathan, 38

Victor, David, 289

Vignolles, Benjamin, 58

Virginia, 289, 306

Visco, Ignazio, 120
Vlieghe, Gertjan, 310
vocational training, 73

Wadsworth, Jonathan, 256, 258
wage growth, 56, 71, 144, 214, 301; educational level linked to, 52; employment rate decoupled from, 49, 51, 55, 70; false alarms over, 307, 316; in Germany, 48, 57–58, 207; historical trends in, 49–50, 55; international, 57–60; labor market slack and, 6, 25, 84, 338; measurement of, 51–55; migration and, 84, 254–58, 306; outlook for, 65–70; productivity linked to, 64–65, 69, 84, 120, 121, 191, 302; underemployment and, 120–21, 124, 141–42, 145, 300, 312; in United Kingdom, 3, 6, 35, 54–55, 56, 58, 61–62, 66, 68, 209, 307, 338, 339. *See also* inflation
"wage ratchet," 28
Wales, 188, 272, 273, 275, 291
Wallop, Henry, 159
Walmart, 18
Wardle, Jane, 223
Wascher, Bill, 97
Washington State, 193
Watson, Mark W., 305
Webb, Beatrice, 182
Weidmann, Jens, 207
Weismann, Jens, 84
Weiss, Yoram, 252
Welch, Jack, 16
Wells, Claudia, 113
Wessel, David, 315
West Virginia, 224, 227, 231, 236, 243, 265, 289
Whirlpool, 319

White, Nicola, 342
Whittaker, Matthew, 276
Wilkins, Roger, 125
Willsher, Kim, 271
Winters, John V., 140
Wisconsin, 193, 326
Wolf, Martin, 160, 174
Wolfe, Richard, 334
Wolfers, Justin, 86
Wooden, Mark, 125
work-life balance, 71–77
World Bank, 205
World Database of Happiness, 116
World Economic Outlook (IMF), 120, 345
World War I, 328, 344
World War II, 5, 22
Worswick, G. D. N., 22
Wren-Lewis, Simon, 175–77, 214

Xi Jingping, 317
XpertHR, 308

Yagan, Danny, 96
Yamarone, Richard, 185–86
Yardeni, Edward, 208
Yellen, Janet, 165, 304
Yemen, 244
yield curve, 208

Zaninotto, Paola, 223
zero-hours contracts, 35, 104, 270
zero lower bound (ZLB), 160, 161
Ziblatt, Daniel, 347
Zimmermann, Klaus F., 57
Znojmo, Moravia, 189–90
Zuckerberg, Mark, 337
Zucman, Gabriel, 108, 109–10, 337
Zweimüller, Josef, 45